KU-004-660

HISTORY OF THE GERMAN NIGHT FIGHTER FORCE 1917–1945

GEBHARD ADERS

JANE'S PUBLISHING COMPANY
LONDON . SYDNEY

First published in 1978 by Motorbuch-Verlag, Stuttgart, as *Geschichte der deutschen Nachtjagd 1917–1945* © Motorbuch-Verlag, Stuttgart.
This English translation copyright © 1979 Jane's Publishing Company London-Sydney. All rights reserved.
First published in Great Britain in 1979 by Jane's Publishing Company,
Macdonald and Jane's Publishing Group Limited,
Paulton House, 8 Shepherdess Walk, London N1 7LW

ISBN 0 354 01247 9

Printed in Great Britain by
Fakenham Press Ltd.,
Fakenham, Norfolk.

HERTFORDSHIRE
COUNTY LIBRARY
940.544
9621119

4 JAN 1980

CONTENTS

Translator's Note

Originally published in West Germany in 1978, this edition, translated and edited by Alex Vanags-Baginskis assisted by Brendan Gallagher, includes various corrections and many additional details not available at the time.

1. The beginnings of night fighting in World War I

Night defence sorties by German fighters on the Western Front in 1916 – Long-range night fighting operations over enemy airfields in 1917 – Defensive successes against air raids behind the lines – Successful combined night fighting by Jasta 24 in 1918 – Two-seat ground support aircraft as night fighters – French night fighting actions

Though it is widely believed that the first night fighter force was formed by the Luftwaffe in 1940, the Central European powers and the Western Allies used aircraft both to repel night raids and to fly long-range intruder sorties already in World War I. In doing so they developed operational procedures which could have become definitive if they had not been forgotten within a few years of the Armistice.

In theory, the obvious method was to combat the night bombers and the aircraft which operated during the day in the same way: with fighters. However, there were many obstacles to their successful use. While the course of a daytime bomber could be closely followed and reported by air raid warning posts so that it was possible to repel it in good time with fighters, defence against night raids was much more difficult. The flightpath of the night bomber could not be followed exactly by visual observers or sound detectors, it could fly into cloud to escape the searchlights, and by changing course several times the night bomber was able to keep the defences guessing about the real target until the very last moment. There were only two possible means of defence: protection of the target by AA guns, or the use of fighter patrols across the flightpaths most frequently used by the enemy bombers. This was the method used for the first time in 1916 by German fighters against the increasingly more troublesome raids on their base airfields, support establishments and homeland.

To begin with they were completely unsuccessful, receiving neither radio reports of enemy attacks nor support from searchlights. The single-seat fighters also had other problems to contend with: as soon as they took off from their ill-lit stubble fields the pilots were almost totally occupied with keeping their inadequately in-strumented machines on course and, with hardly any navigational and directional aids, in trying to find the operational area. If, by skill and luck, they then arrived in the target area, there was still uncertainty about the height at which the enemy would attack. It is therefore not surprising that successful fighter pilots like Julius Buckler said that night fighting would be impossible in their single-seat aircraft. Either one did not see the enemy at all, or he went rushing past in the opposite direction. If the searchlights fastened onto an enemy aircraft, it was miles away and impossible to reach in the short time that it was in the light cone. This negative judgment, widespread among fighter pilots, was to have fateful consequences twenty years later.

The first night fighting victory[1] was achieved by an armed two-seat long-range reconnaissance aircraft, a C-type. At the beginning of 1917, when the German Supreme Army Command pulled back its forces in the Arras region, day and night bombers of both sides attempted to harass the opposing troops. On the German side the *Feldfliegerabteilungen* (Field Aviation Detachments) flew their sorties mostly against enemy aircraft, and during the night of 11 February 1917 *Lt* Peter and *Lt* Frowein flying a DFW C V of Fl.Abt. 12 succeeded in intercepting and shooting down two enemy bombers as they were coming in to land at Malzeville.

When, shortly after midnight on 6 April, raids on Douai airfield began, *Lt* Frankl (Pour le Mérite) of *Jasta 4* took off in an Albatros D III (W.Nr.2158/16) and shot down a British B.E.2b of 100 Sqn over Quiéry la Motte. This was the first true German night fighting kill, because the victories achieved by Frowein/Peters happened more by chance. After sundown on 7 April Frankl shot down a Nieuport 17 of 60 Sqn, and on the following night *Lt* Klein, also of *Jasta 4*, was victorious over another B.E.2b bomber at 0400 hrs south-east of Douai.

In the meantime, the German pilots had discovered that aircraft stood out very clearly against the sky on bright nights. Thus it became the custom from the spring 1917 on to have an aircraft circling low around the airfield as protection for the returning light and heavy bombers.

The summer of 1917 also brought the first defensive successes against night raids behind the lines. The honour of the first such victory belongs to a pilot of the Austrian Imperial and Royal Navy, *Linienschiffsleutnant* Gottfried Banfield. Since 1915 he had been flying successful daytime raids with seaplanes from Trieste and Pola, and had also been trying to intercept Italian aircraft and airships by night. But the Hansa-Brandenburg flying boats which he had been using up to this time were not fast enough to catch up with targets only briefly lit up by searchlights or moonlight. Banfield then tried an L 16 which had been converted to a single-seater, and in the autumn

2

of 1916 he received an aircraft specially built for him by the engineer Weichmann. This was the A 11, which soon became known in the services as the 'Blue Wonder'. On the evening of 31 May 1917 Banfield finally achieved the longed-for success: at 2230 hrs he intercepted and attacked an Italian seaplane near Miramar at 2,400 m (7,870 ft) altitude, came within 30 m (100 ft) and compelled it to make a forced landing in the estuary of the River Primero. For this deed Banfield was awarded the Maria-Theresa Order, which carried with it a hereditary peerage.

The first enemy bomber shot down over Germany had raided Frankfurt/Main during the evening hours of 8 August 1917. It fell victim to two single-seat fighters of *Kampfeinsitzerstaffel 2* (Home Defence squadron) near Saargemünd. It is possible that Home Defence single-seaters were also involved in the defensive successes against the air raid on Saarbrücken on the night of 25/26 October, during which a Handley Page bomber, among others, was forced down.

Until then, however, night interceptions had been improvised. Systematic co-operation between the fighters, the air raid reporting service, Flak and searchlights was not achieved until May 1918, during the closing phase of the last German offensive in Flanders, when the French and British air forces were attempting to interrupt German supplies and reinforcements. *Jasta 24*, deployed in the region of Noyon, used a combined night defence procedure: on light, clear nights Albatros D Va fighters would take off and circle singly at 2,500–3,000 m (8,200–9,840 ft) altitude over given searchlight positions; movement to other standby zones was strictly forbidden in order not to confuse the listening posts working with the searchlights. If aircraft were heard approaching from the enemy side, the AA machine guns would fire tracer in that direction and the searchlights would try to detect and light up the target. Then the fighter would set off to attack, warning the ground defenders by firing white star shells, the signal for the Flak to cease firing at once.

If the fighter was picked up by the searchlights or even shot at by its own Flak, it would identify itself by accelerating and then slowing down again. The first such sortie with four fighters on the night of 21/22 May 1918 failed because the Flak batteries, contrary to all agreement, continued to fire at a bomber picked up by the search-lights, so that the fighters never reached it. On the following night the system worked: *Leutnant* Thiede shot down three enemy aircraft, while other pilots of *Jasta 24* forced four bombers to jettison their bombs early. As will emerge, the 'combined night fighting' of 1941 did not differ tactically from this procedure.

Lt Thiede later became CO of *Jasta 38* in Macedonia, where he met Gerhard Fieseler, who had fitted two light machine guns into his aircraft in such a way that their barrels pointed forwards and

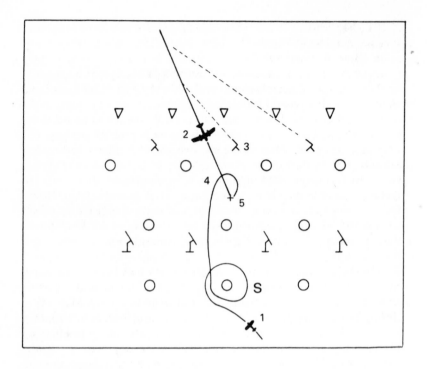

Illuminated night fighting in World War I

O	Searchlights
⅄	Heavy Flak
⅄	Light Flak
▽	Listening devices
1.	Fighter approaches standby zone S
2.	Enemy bomber
3.	Light Flak fires directional tracer towards the identified target
4.	Fighter turns in behind the bomber and
5.	Shoots it down.

upwards. Thiede enthusiastically adopted this arrangement, which allowed him to attack from below without being dazzled by the searchlights. Thus the *'Schräge Musik'* oblique-firing guns of World War II had their precursors over 20 years earlier.

The most successful night fighter squadron of 1918 must have been *Jasta 73* commanded by *Lt* Anders. In August and September it was based at St Remy le Petit and St Loup (Champagne) in the area controlled by the 1st Army. Between 20 August and 25 September *Jasta 73* shot down seven French Voisin V 10B2 bombers at night. The commander, *Lt* Gerhard Anders, achieved five night victories. The leader of *Jasta 74*, also based near St Loup, *Oblt* Theodor

Camman, also began flying night interception sorties and brought down a Voisin on 21 August.

The two-seat close-support aircraft took part in many more night interceptions than the single-seaters. The *Ko.Gen.Luft* (Commanding General Air) felt, quite rightly, that they were far more suited to this kind of operations than the single-seaters. It was not speed and climbing ability that was important when intercepting the slow bombers, but the presence of the second crew member, who could keep a lookout and at the same time attack the enemy with his machine gun. The armour protection of the close-support aircraft also proved to be very useful in combat with the well armed bombers.

Little is known of individual successes. It is however certain that *Schlachtstaffel 16* (close support squadron) attached to the 4th Army in Flanders carried out frequent night interception sorties. The crew made up of *Uffz* Muschen and *Uffz* Kratz is said to have excelled in combat against the British Handley Page bombers. Several night victories are also attributed to the *Marinesonderstaffel* (Masosta) commanded by Lt Majewski.

In response to these successes near the front lines, night fighters were also used experimentally in Germany in 1918, but without gathering much operational experience before the end of the war.

The British and French night fighting experiments should also be mentioned here. For a long time the Allies were convinced of the impracticability of night fighting, and the anti-aircraft artillery was left to combat the multi-engined German bombers single-handed. In June 1917 *Capitaine* Langevin, commander of a French fighter squadron near Dunkirk, decided to send out his Nieuports to try and intercept the German Gotha bombers which were appearing overhead practically every night. His main problem was the lack of a reliable means of establishing the altitude of the German bombers. This the anti-aircraft artillery were simply unable to tell him, their estimates varying between 200 m and 1,200 m (approx 660 to 3,940 ft). Langevin therefore had his fighters flying defensive patrols staggered in height 30 km (18.6 mls) east of Dunkirk and so discovered that the Gothas flew in stubbornly at 2,500 m (8,200 ft) altitude. Langevin then began to train his pilots in night flying, and achieved his first double success over Calais on 20 January 1918. At Langevin's instigation the French built up a regular night fighter group which was used operationally in three roles: long-range night intrusions with three-seaters over the bases of German bombers in Belgium, patrols with two-seaters between Calais and Dunkirk, and target defence with single-seaters and searchlight support over both towns. Some of Langevin's Span single-seaters even had searchlights in front of the propeller hub.

The British had also formed a night fighter unit, No 151 Sqn RAF, which was based at Fontaine-sur-Maye and managed to shoot down 21 German multi-engined bombers during the period June–September 1918.

Note
1 Specifically night fighting between aircraft. The first aerial night victory was achieved by FltSub-Lt R. A. J. Warneford in a Morane-Saulnier on 8 June 1915 when he attacked and shot down the German airship *LZ 37* at 0300 hrs over Gent.

2. Between the wars

Night fighter development and tactics neglected – Night interception experiments in France in 1934 – Night fighting in the Wehrmacht War Games after 1934 – Experiments and exercises in Germany after 1936 – Activation and disbanding of night fighter Staffeln in 1938–1939

After World War I there appeared in Germany a spate of publications about the air war, most of them personal memoirs rather than sober historical discussions. A detailed analysis of the use of German military aviation in World War I and its possible use in future conflicts was never written, probably as a result of the complete disarmament imposed on Germany. This is perhaps one of the reasons why night fighting techniques were completely forgotten, and why in the 1930s there arose the notion that only a very small number of pilots were suited for this kind of combat, making it impossible to set up whole night fighter formations. But logical evaluation of the available information from 1917–18 would have led to the conclusion that – given proper co-ordination of the air raid reporting service, searchlights, fighters and Flak – the bombers could be intercepted at a 'demarcation line' before the target as well as over it, or at least prevented from dropping their bombs at will. The specialised night fighter essential to the success of these tactics was seen as a well armed two-seater capable of flying blind, equipped with radio and with an endurance of several hours.

But while the whole of German military literature accepted the effectiveness of the night bomber, the use of night fighters was hardly mentioned. Defence against night raids was to be left to the Flak, a decision which, in view of the good results achieved during the last years of the war, was quite understandable. In any case, the performance of 8.8 cm Flak had so outstripped the modest achievements of the aircraft by the end of the war and in subsequent years that it was believed that improvements in anti-aircraft artillery effectiveness would match those in aircraft performance – a grave error, as it turned out later. In other countries too there was a low opinion of the practicability of night fighting. It is true that in Britain, Belgium and France a few fighter squadrons had been selected for night

7

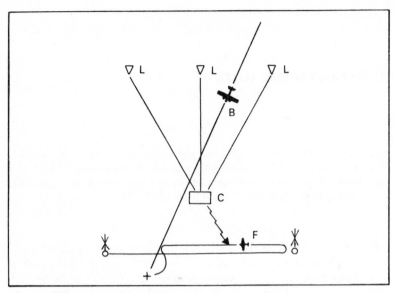

French night fighting experiments

L ▽ Listening posts
C   Central fighter command post
F   Fighter
     Light beacons
+   Successful interception

operations, but no moves were made towards any regular training of pilots or the evolution of special night-fighting procedures.

It was not until the beginning of the 1930s that certain air force officers began to think seriously about night fighting. In France *Capitaine* Idatte made a truly far-seeing proposal: a network of air observer posts equipped with listening equipment and special binoculars. They would detect the bombers and report on their estimated altitude, direction and speed to a central command post, where the flightpaths would be traced on to a glass panel with coloured pens or lights. A few kilometres behind the central command post the night fighters would fly patrol legs 10 km (6.2 mls) in length, also followed and reported by the air observer posts. Once the course of the bombers was clearly established, the central command post would send the fighters to intercept and attack. The type of engagement to be considered, the head-on attack, was abandoned because of the high closing speed, and it proved much more practicable to allow the bombers to fly over the patrolling fighters so that the latter could attack from behind. In 1936 the procedure was applied very successfully during the air exercises near Metz, when over 70 per cent of the interception attempts are said to have led to visual detection. Replace the visual and oral detection with ground radar, and one has the *Himmelbett* method which came into use seven years later!

Convincing though the Metz results were, all the documents on this procedure disappeared into the filing cabinets for three years. It was not until October 1939 that the French began to organise Idatte-style night-fighting zones around Paris and Lyons/St Etienne, and they were not yet fully operational by the beginning of the German offensive in May 1940.

The creators of the new Luftwaffe did not at first think about night fighting at all, however. During the build-up the Luftwaffe command emphasised offensive formations while largely ignoring the fighter units. Night fighting thus received only cursory attention in the first large-scale war games of the new Luftwaffe, held in November 1934, so that they gave only the barest indication of the problems associated with the simultaneous use of fighters and Flak. The deployment of long-range night fighters over enemy airfields seemed more important, and that task was passed over to the long-range reconnaissance units for want of any other suitably equipped formation.

Night fighting did not figure in the Wehrmacht's war games of 1935 and 1936, although it had already come to be recognised that France and Britain, with their night bomber formations, were strategically superior. The World War I fighter pilots' conviction that night operations were impossible with single-seaters had apparently made its way to higher quarters. Indicative of the prevailing attitude to the defensive warfare is Luftwaffe Service Regulation No 16 (*LDv 16*). Under the heading 'Command of aerial warfare' the problems of air defence are mentioned only in very general terms. Only Section 253 was devoted to night fighting: 'For operations at night, night fighting zones must be designed in order to prevent interference between the fighters and the Flak in their combat activities and to ensure support of the fighter pilots by searchlights. . . . Every unnecessary hindrance to the *offensive* forces caused by restrictive measures is to be avoided.'

But whether from personal recollection of night fighting in World War I or from the promptings of *LDv 16*, there were some higher officers who grew enthusiastic about night fighting and carried out exercises along these lines. The first of these took place within *Luftkreiskommando* II (air admin. area) near Berlin in May 1936, when the ability to co-operate of night fighters from II/JG 132 and a searchlight regiment was put to the test. The results were set down in a secret study prepared for the Air District school in November 1936. The *Ob.d.L.* (Commander in Chief of the Luftwaffe) ordered night-fighting experiments to be carried out with and without searchlights

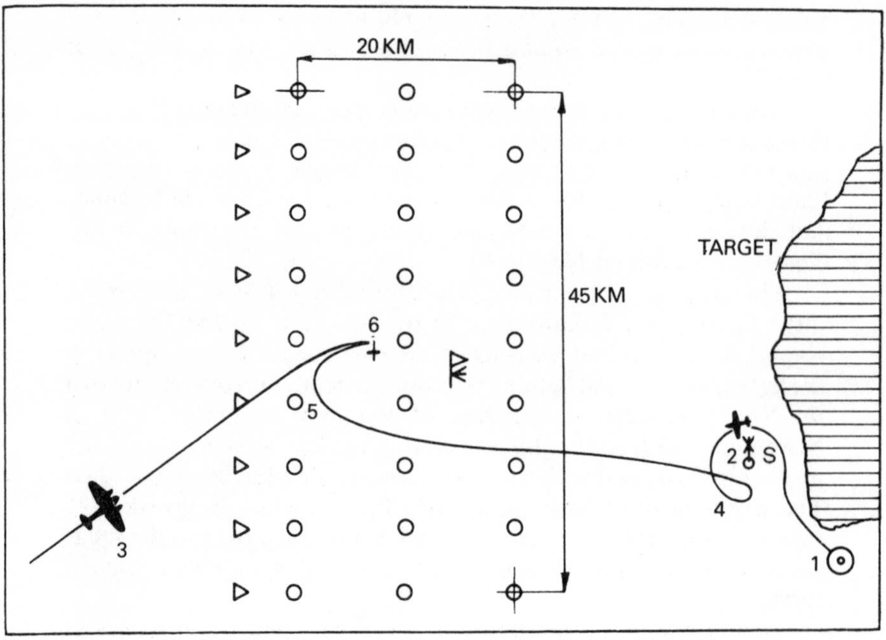

Night fighting experiments near Berlin 1937

- ⊙ Luftwaffe base
- S Standby zone near a light beacon
- Searchlight detachment command post
- ▷ Listening devices
- o Searchlights

1. Night fighter takes off
2. Circling in the standby zone
3. Approaching enemy bomber
4. Night fighter takes up position to fly into the searchlight zone
5. Turning in to attack
6. Successful interception and kill

in summer 1937. The former were to be carried out by II/JG 132 in the Berlin area, and He 111 bombers and Bf 109 fighters, recently delivered to the service, were expected to take part. The second type of operation was to be tested under the auspices of the CO of Luftwaffe instructional/training service. The results of these experiments were to be collated with those from night fighting exercises by a *Gruppe* of JG 134 *Horst Wessel* and I/JG 137; all reports were due in to the Supreme Command of the Luftwaffe by November 1937. The Air War Academy, which received the reports, published them in the form of a pamphlet which concluded that night fighting was possible both in the form of long-range operations over the enemy airfields and in the defence of specific objectives in the Reich territory. In the latter case the night fighting organisation would form defensive points and strengthen the Flak batteries – in other words, it was intended more or less as an adjunct of the Flak. Both night fighting methods, particularly the searchlight-supported target-defence arrangement, were dependent to a large extent on the weather, yet it was expected that a bomber caught and dazzled by searchlights would be easier to attack and destroy than a daylight raider. The pamphlet set out the following procedure in detail. A single-seater fighter (known as the *Überwachungsflugzeug* or surveillance aircraft) would take off from the base of the night-fighter *Staffel* and fly into the standby zone, situated over the objective or facing the enemy's probable line of approach. The illuminated zone, with its searchlights and listening posts, would be positioned between the enemy and the standby zone to avoid interference from the engine noise of the surveillance aircraft. Once in the standby zone, the surveillance aircraft would circle above the enemy's expected approach height and at the same time orientate itself by means of landmarks or light signals. If the searchlights began to search in a certain direction the surveillance aircraft would fly that way, gaining height at the same time. From a position outside the searchlit area the surveillance aircraft would then dive in to attack the enemy from the rear. Once in the searchlit area he would pull upwards (to avoid being dazzled) and attack the enemy from behind and below. The Flak would be forbidden to fire in the night fighting zones, and only allowed to join in on the orders of the night fighting district commander (CO of the searchlight regiment). This situation would arise only when the night fighter missed its target or failed to attack for some reason.

This procedure produced an almost ideal division between the night fighting and Flak zones. However, all those concerned were rightly sceptical about whether the illuminated zone was deep enough to permit successful interceptions. It was deep enough to allow the fighters to catch up with such slow aircraft as the Ju 52/3m or Do 23, but the He 111, for example, shot through it so quickly that even the Bf 109 had difficulty in getting into a firing position. Indeed, the faster fighters gave rise to a whole set of new problems: the Bf 109 needed a much larger standby zone than the He 51 or Ar 68, for one thing. It was also possible that the fighter would find itself on the side of the zone furthest away from the approaching enemy and would then have to fly at top speed towards the raiders, thus running the risk of overshooting. Before there could be a second attack, the enemy would have long since disappeared into the darkness. These problems could have been solved – by increasing the depth of the search-light zone or by guiding and controlling the operation by radio from the night fighting district command post (which had not been tried up to this time), for example – but the necessary effort did not seem justified to the Luftwaffe command. They also refrained from setting up full-time night fighter formations. However, some units were permitted to continue with these experiments. One such was 10./JG 132 *Richthofen* under *Hptm* Blumensaat, who was firmly convinced of the importance of night fighting. There were other experimental night fighter *Staffeln* in LG 2 (under *Oblt* Johannes Steinhoff) and II/JG 134 *Horst Wessel*. A night fighter detachment (*Kdo*) under *Lt* Boddem was also formed within II/JG 234 *Schlageter* in August 1938, only to be disbanded again a few days later.

During the Spanish Civil War three Ar 68s of the Condor Legion (5./J.88) flew a few night interception patrols over Castellon, but lack of success brought this experiment to an end.

By 1939 it appeared as if the RLM had finally been convinced of the significance of night fighting. On 1 February 10./JG 131 at Döberitz was officially activated as an experimental night fighter *Staffel*, followed by 10./JG 132 on 1 June. On 24 June this was followed by an order to form several other night fighter units: I/JG 20 near Berlin, I/JG 21 in East Prussia, 1. and 2./JG 70 and 71 at Aibling, 10./JG 72 at Mannheim, 11./JG 72 at Böblingen, and 11./LG 2 at Greifswald. But by 10 July all of these units, apart from 10./JG 2 and 11./LG 2, had been subordinated to the day fighter command, and after exchanging Ar 68s for Bf 109Ds they officially became day fighters on 16 August 1939.

3. Night fighting in World War II: Evolution and operations until the end of 1940

Twilight operations in the western areas of the Reich and in Norway – Activation of IV(N)/JG 2 – Night fighting experiments by I/ZG 1 at Aalborg – Activation of NJG 1 – Formation of additional night fighter Gruppen and the Night Fighter Division – Development of operational procedures – Illuminated night fighting – Radar development in Germany and abroad – Introduction of radar to night fighting – Development of dark night fighting – Strength, equipment and bases of the Luftwaffe night fighter Gruppen – Long-range night fighting operations over Britain

GENERAL OUTLINE OF EVENTS

1 September – 6 October 1939: Polish campaign. *9 April – 8 June 1940:* Occupation of Denmark and Norway. *10 May – 25 June:* Western campaign. *10/11 May:* First larger-scale RAF raid on residential areas. *16 August:* Beginning of the Battle of Britain. *August:* First RAF night raids on Berlin.

During the Polish campaign the German fighter and *Zerstörer* formations flew only daytime operations, and even before the end of the fighting some of them were withdrawn into the Western Air Defence Zone (LVZ) as protection for the industrial areas. The LVZ extended from Münster to Stuttgart, and the formations stationed there were directly subordinated to the *Ob.d.L.* (Commander-in-Chief of the Luftwaffe).

During that period the French and British had carried out day and night raids on the western areas of the Reich. At first they dropped only leaflets, but soon they were carrying deadlier payloads. Three more night fighter *Staffeln* were formed as support for the Flak batteries: 10.(N)/JG 26 at Bonn-Hangelar (from 1./LG 1, under *Oblt* Steinhoff), 10.(N)/ZG 26 in North Germany and 10.(N)/JG 53 at Heilbronn. These units were more like twilight squadrons, however, flying patrols in the late evening and early morning around Cologne and Stuttgart. But even then they were doomed to failure, lacking as they did any control or guidance from the ground and co-operation with the searchlights. In fact a Bf 110 of 10./ZG 26 piloted by *Fw* Zimmermann crashed in Holland on 3 October 1939 while pursuing a British bomber, and on 6 December *Uffz* Fuchs collided with a Wellington near Texel. As a result, the *Staffel* was deprived of its valuable Bf 110s and re-equipped with old Bf 109Ds.

The failure of these units and the non-appearance of stronger enemy formations probably lay behind a discussion between Göring and the Inspector of Fighters, who concluded that there was no need to expand the night fighter force. Their sole concession was the merger of the night fighting *Staffeln* 10./JG 26, 10./ZG 26 and 11./LG 2 as IV(N)/JG 2 under *Hptm* Blumensaat late in December 1939 (10./JG 53 was apparently disbanded). Detachments of this *Gruppe* were based in North-west Germany. In the following April and May it also had detachments at Aalborg in Denmark and Gardemoen in Norway, and in June at Vlissingen, Mönchengladbach and Cologne.

The *Gruppe* was equipped with Bf 109Ds from which the cockpit canopies had been removed to improve the general view and to prevent the pilots from being dazzled if caught in a searchlight beam. Little is known about their operations and successes, but there is evidence of at least three night kills: on 21 April at 0045 hrs near Wismar by *Ofw* Schmale, and on 25 April and 14 May near Hornum by *Ofw* Förster. It is also possible that the 'night-fighting victories' mentioned in the OKW reports of 30 May and 1, 3 and 6 June can also be attributed to this *Gruppe*. They may, however, have been pure propaganda, published with the intention of persuading the civilian population and the enemy of the existence of a phantom weapon. At the same time, photographs of 'He 113 night fighters' (actually He 100D-1s) preparing to take off at night appeared in the press and deceived many people in Germany and elsewhere.

In June the larger part of this *Gruppe* was deployed in the Rhineland and was flying night interception patrols with searchlight support, albeit following a senseless procedure that was destined to failure from the start. On cloudless nights, when the searchlights could operate with maximum effect, the commander of Searchlight Regiment 1 handed the whole defensive task to the Flak. The night fighters were allowed to operate only against bombers flying above cloud, and under such conditions they were seldom able to find and combat an opponent.[1]

K. O. Hoffmann's *History of the Luftwaffe Signals Service* contains a report about successful night fighting operations by I/ZG 76 and 4./JG 77 during the Norwegian campaign in April 1940. The *Zerstörer* and fighters of these units, alerted and directed by ground radar, are said to have shot down over a dozen of the RAF bombers which attacked Stavanger-Sola airfield on the dark nights of 23 and 25 April 1940. This detailed account has only one flaw, failing to agree with the official reports on dates and times. No aircraft were shot down at all on the night of 24 April. On 30 April two Bf 109s of 4./JG 77 took off at 1825 hrs – still in full daylight – and destroyed two Blenheim bombers, while the *Zerstörer* of I/ZG 76 achieved four victories in the last minutes of daylight between 2040 and 2100 hrs. These were therefore twilight operations rather than real night interceptions. It is however noteworthy that these victories came as a result of close co-operation with ground radar. The first true night interception took place on 30 April near Aalborg, where I/ZG 1 under *Hptm* Wolfgang Falck was based at that time. Immediately after the German occupation of Denmark, RAF bombers began to appear almost nightly to attack the hangars and dispersal areas with bombs and gunfire. Falck was firmly convinced that he could defend himself against these raids as long as his command post received ground radar reports of the incoming raids. He first tried to assess the night suitability of the Bf 110 with a few experienced pilots, discovering that aircraft stood out very well against the light northern sky at night and that, contrary to daytime practice, attacks should be carried out from below. Together with the radar control officer, Falck then worked out a procedure under which the night fighters would circle in specific 'standby zones' and then, after the enemy aircraft had been detected by radar, would be led to the target by dead-reckoning navigation over the R/T.

The first such operation was carried out without any preparation, however: during an attack in the last night hours of 30 April, Falck, *Oblt* Streib and *Fw* Thier jumped into their machines and chased after the westward-flying British aircraft without any radio contact with the ground radar station. All three crews encountered the enemy, and even if no British aircraft were shot down – the bombers dived into fog over the North Sea after the first bursts of fire – this action nevertheless proved that the enemy could be intercepted at night. Falck's report aroused interest in the RLM and things began to happen. A short time later he was able to put his point of view personally to Udet, Milch and Kesselring. Clearly, the Luftwaffe leadership had changed its attitude towards night fighting, prompted by the recognition of the fact that the Flak alone could not stop night raids. But with the beginning of the Western campaign on 10 May all night-fighting experiments stopped before Falck's theories could be put to the test. The *Gruppe* commanded by Falck also saw action in the West, originally under ZG 26 and finally as IV/ZG 26, according to the RLM Quartermaster-General's strength returns.[2]

The RAF responded to the Wehrmacht's new offensive with bombing raids on German towns. The first bombs fell during the night of 10/11 May on Mönchengladbach, and from 20 May attacks on residential areas in North-west Germany increased. The Flak was not in a position to fend off these raids, and the only flying formation tasked with defence against night raids, IV(N)/JG 2, was equally unsuccessful. These failures were embarrassing to both the political and military leadership, and the SD[3] was soon reporting the first jokes about Göring. Under pressure to find a way to stop the British attacks, somebody at the RLM remembered *Hptm* Falck and his report. On 22 June, a few days after the end of the Western campaign, Göring ordered Falck to transfer to Düsseldorf with his entire *Gruppe* (less 1.*Staffel*) and to form a night fighter *Geschwader*. Falck had not reckoned on such a response when he had made his report a few weeks previously, while his pilots resented being recalled just after the successful conclusion of the campaign and before the eagerly awaited offensive against Britain. While their comrades in the West would go on chalking up victories and collecting decorations, they would have to mess around 'trying to catch flies in a dark room'. Apart from that, they felt, they were far more likely to become casualties themselves than to find and shoot down enemy bombers at night. Nevertheless, the formation of NJG 1 went ahead. On 26 June Falck received his appointment as *Geschwader Kommodore*, the first time in the history of the Luftwaffe that a *Hauptmann* had been directly appointed to this position. On the same day IV(N)/JG 2 was put under his command as II *Gruppe* and, more significantly, the previous subordination of the night fighters to Searchlight Regiment 1 gave way to an equal partnership. Operationally, Falck's *Gruppe* remained subordinate to Luftflotte 2 (Kesselring).

Falck set about solving the problems associated with the new techniques with his own particular brand of energy. It was clear to him and the Luftwaffe command that the development of a completely new kind of defensive organisation – in which the air crews, the air reporting service, ground radar, searchlights and Flak would have to work very closely together – was beyond the abilities of a single *Geschwader* CO and that to co-operate all these elements a command post at divisional level would have to be created. The activation of the Night Fighter Division was ordered on 17 July, with *Oberst* Kammhuber named as commander; on 23 July the Divisional HQ was formed at Brussels and on 1 August a command post established at Zeist near Utrecht.

Throughout the year the new organisation grew steadily by process of 'cellular division' and transfers of *Zerstörer* formations. These developments are summarised as follows:

June: I/NJG 1 and II/NJG 1 (ex-IV/JG 2) formed.
      Zerstörerstaffel of KG 30 retrained as I/ZG 76 for night fighting.

July: *Z-Staffel* of KG 30 became 4./NJG 1 and, by the addition of more personnel and aircraft, was expanded to II/NJG 1 (two *Staffeln* with Ju 88C-0 and C-2 aircraft; one *Staffel* with Do 17Z-10); former II/NJG 1 became III/NJG 1 (with Bf 109).

7 September: II/NJG 1 became I/NJG 2 (long-range night fighter *Gruppe*); new II *Gruppe* formed from 3./NJG 1 and I/ZG 76 (except 1.*Staffel*, which became the new 3./NJG 1). III/NJG 1 re-equipped with Bf 110; one *Staffel* with Bf 109 remained as 10./NJG 1 until October, then disbanded.

October: V(Z)/LG 1 retrained for night fighting and became I/NJG 3.

November: 1./ZG 2 retrained for night fighting and became 4./NJG 2.

There was still no proper night fighting training school. The crews were retrained at blind-flying schools, mostly at Schleissheim, and received their final polish with the operational formations, which in 1941 began to form their own training *Staffeln*. Only those pilots and ground personnel most suited to this type of operation were chosen for transfer from *Zerstörer* formations to night fighting.

To return to the beginning of the story, before the Division started work, Falck had to see how he could manage on his own. Apart from his ideas, his *Geschwader*, the searchlight regiment and the goodwill of the command, he had nothing but a mountain of unsolved problems. His aircraft differed from the daytime fighters only in their overall black camouflage introduced in July 1940, and industry could give him neither exhaust flame dampers nor special radio equipment. Training guidelines for cadre crews and new recruits had to be painstakingly worked out from personal experience; there was no question of having his own school for pilots and radio operators. An especially difficult obstacle, and one typical of the time, was the chain of command. NJG 1 received its orders from Luftflotte 2, while the searchlight regiment came under *Luftgaukommando VI* (Air District HQ) at Münster; it was not until the formation of the Night Fighter Division that both came under one command.

The greatest problem of course lay in guiding the night fighters to the British bombers before they could reach their intended targets in the Rhineland-Westphalia industrial area. The single-engined fighters of Blumensaat's *Gruppe* had hitherto sought their targets very close to the towns of the lower Rhine, because this was where the searchlights were concentrated. But Falck realised that this area was not entirely suitable for night interceptions: industrial smoke and haze affected the intensity of the searchlights, the listening posts were affected by both the night fighters taking off to the west and by the

Flak firing away to the east. If the night fighters succeeded in engaging the enemy they immediately came into the fire zone of the Flak concentrated between Cologne and Duisburg and had to turn away. This meant that the Flak and night fighter zones would have to be clearly divided, and Falck quickly devised a temporary solution. As long as there was no ground radar to support the night fighters, he had Searchlight Regiment 1 and some of his night fighters transferred to the Westphalian zone, while searchlights and listening posts formed an 'illuminated belt' north-east of Münster. I/NJG 1, reinforced by a detachment from II/NJG 26, was based at Gütersloh. The night fighters flew into standby zones east of the searchlight ring, so that the listening posts could clearly hear the approaching bombers, unaffected by the engine noise of their own aircraft.

At this time there was still no ground control for the fighters. On hearing the code word *Fasan* (=enemy raid expected) the night fighters would take off into the standby zones east of the 'illuminated belt', and there lie in wait, often for hours. The flight logs of the pilots who took part reveal that sorties of three hours or more were not all that uncommon (three years later, pursuit night fighting with the Bf 110G-4 called for sorties of two hours at the most). When the sudden switching on of searchlights indicated the start of a raid, each night fighter pilot would go into action of his own accord. If he saw a target lit up by the searchlights, he would dive from his standby position above the estimated height of the enemy bomber and would fly at top speed into the searchlight zone. With only three minutes before the bomber disappeared into the darkness again, he had to fall behind the target, slow down in order not to overshoot, and attack from the side or rear. At this time some pilots were already trying the tactic, later to become universal, of attacking from below and behind. This was something quite different from daytime tactics and took a lot of getting used to. The pilots also needed an extraordinary feel for time and space, which no one acquired right away. Apart from the fact that the searchlights often 'hopped about' nervously without finding a target, there were many abortive operations, and it was a good two weeks before the crews of I/NJG 1 gained some practical experience. On 20 July *Oblt* Streib achieved the first kill of the 'illuminated' night fighting campaign, and on the following night Streib, Ehle, Wandam, Schramm and Pack together scored five more victories. However, the honour of the very first 'kill' by NJG 1 went to *Ofw* Förster of 8./JG 1, who destroyed a Whitley bomber near Heligoland on 9 July at 0250 hrs. According to OKW reports, six bombers had already been destroyed over Germany between 26 and 28 June, though the names of the successful pilots remain a mystery. II/NJG 1, which was activated at the end of July and equipped with the Ju 88C-2 and Do 17Z-10, tried, first from bases near Düsseldorf and then from Holland, to intercept RAF bombers flying in along the most commonly used routes, but without success.

The initial difficulties of I *Gruppe* and the failures of II/NJG 1 strengthened Falck's belief that night fighting was impossible without tight control from the ground and illumination of the target. At that time this was certainly so, and the result was the introduction of 'tied' or 'controlled' night fighting, in which the fighters were used in areas whose bounds were set by the range of the ground radar. Kammhuber, inspired by Falck's idea, was to develop controlled night fighting to a degree of perfection unimaginable in 1940. He did so at the expense of other methods, and when, three years later, new operational methods became necessary, the flying units, ground control personnel and the industry succeeded only partly in changing over to 'free' night fighting.

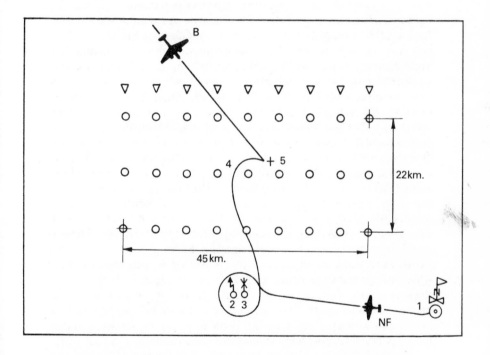

Illuminated night fighting – first phase: Standby zone behind the illuminated belt

The night fighter takes off (1) and flies to the standby zone (2) near the radio beacon ⚲ and light beacon ⚲. After the bomber (B) has been detected and acquired by the sound locators (▽) and searchlights (○) the night fighter (NF) flies into the illuminated belt (3), turns behind the bomber (4), attacks and shoots it down (5).

After their first losses in the illuminated belt near Münster, it became clear to the British what this 'magic' light strip, in which they were never fired on by the Flak, really meant, and they simply flew around it. As the Night Fighter Division had only one searchlight regiment under its command, it was compelled to dismantle the Münster light belt and send single searchlight batteries to the areas previously overflown by the British, in the vague hope that they would reappear. 'This 'running around after the bomb craters' brought no success at all, and the whole Luftwaffe started to make fun of the night fighters, calling them 'night watchmen' and worse. If the initial successes were to be repeated, the whole of North-west Germany would have to be protected by a continuous searchlight belt and night fighter zones. The energetic Kammhuber set about developing just such an organisation from scratch. Inside a year the Division had command of six Flak/searchlight regiments, each with three detachments. In the western approaches a continuous search-light belt extended from Jutland to the area of Liège; a second belt for the protection of Berlin stretched from Güstrow-Stendal to Gardelegen. The area covered by a searchlight detachment constituted a night fighting zone. The tactical night fighting zone leader was the commander of the searchlight detachment, which normally had its own command post at the airfield of the night fighter *Staffel* or *Gruppe*. The *Gruppe* CO had the right of veto in matters of flight safety only. The fundamental disadvantage of this procedure was that only one night fighter could be operated in each zone. As long as there was nothing more than single-aircraft incursions by the British, this defect was not too obvious. But it became fatal when the night fighter, irritated by the uncontrolled lighting up of searchlights, began an engagement from the wrong direction. Before he noticed his mistake, his opponent had dived into the protective darkness and was gone. It was this shortcoming that stimulated the further development of controlled night fighting. Furthermore, the search-lights were only effective in a maximum of 5/10th cloud cover, which happened only rarely in North-west Germany. If there was thick cloud the enemy bombers could fly into the Reich 'unlit' (ie unseen and unfought). Thus means had to be found and procedures evolved by which the night fighters could find their targets even under the very worst atmospheric conditions, and radar was the answer.

Frank Reuter published an excellent book in 1972 on the development and use of radar in Germany up to the end of World War II.[4] For that reason this field will only be covered as far as necessary here. In Germany the first usable radars were evolved as a result of a request by the Navy to its Experimental Signal Establishment (NVA) for a system which, from a given site or position, could detect and pinpoint a vehicle at a reasonably wide side angle and several thousand metres away by night and in fog, and determine its range for the purpose of an accurate torpedo attack. After experiments with acoustic and infra-red waves had led to no useful results, the NVA decided in 1933 to use electro-magnetic waves to determine the position of a target. In 1934 the NVA founded its own company, GEMA. By 1935 this establishment had produced a device working on the 50 cm wavelength. From it, by the outbreak of World War II, the 80 cm *Seetakt* radar had been developed for installation on larger warships. An experimental system working on the 1.8 m wavelength could track any incidental aircraft out to a distance of 28 km (17.4 mls). From this was developed the *Freya* ground radar, which, after a change to 2.4 m wavelength, could detect aerial targets up to 150 km (93 mls) away, depending on their altitude.

Within the Luftwaffe it was the Flak that first demanded radar which they needed to locate aircraft accurately even in hazy weather. The Lorenz company developed the FuMG 39L and the FuMG 40L, which both worked on the 53 cm wavelength and had a range of 10–51 km (6.2–31.7 mls). Though neither offered the required level of direction-finding accuracy, this was achieved by a short-range air raid warning radar developed by Telefunken under the cover name *Würzburg* (53.6 cm wavelength). Development was completed in April 1940, and *Würzburg* was used by the Flak instead of simply for air raid warning purposes. The first *Würzburg*-guided 'night kill' was made by a Flak battery near Essen-Flintrop in September 1940.

In 1936 the NVA started investigating the use of centimetric waves, but the results were so poor – due to the instability of the transmitters and receivers – that the experiments were suspended. In 1939, against the advice of some scientists, the powers that be decided to concentrate on experiments with longer waves, which apparently promised more success. The German research establishments and industry thus gave up the advantage over foreign countries which they had held hitherto. Britain started work on radar in 1935, and in 1939 the British early warning radars were operational on the 1.5 and 12 m wavelengths. Moreover, the British installations were much bigger and heavier than the German units. But the decisive difference lay in their tactical use: the British sites reported their sightings to the centre at Uxbridge, where all movements were displayed on maps, and since the radar also had IFF capability the enemy aircraft were immediately identified as such. In order to prevent enemy attacks in good time, the British planned to build up a network of GCI (ground controlled interception) stations which could direct their night fighters against the incoming German bombers. The AI (air interception) radar for fighters worked on the 1.5 m wavelength, and at the end of September 1939 the RAF already had 30 night fighters equipped with such systems. The USA had been working on radar already since 1922, but it was not until 1937 that the US Navy was able to install the first experimental aircraft-location radar on a warship. In the same year the US Army tried out the fire-control radar for anti-aircraft guns, though it was not until 1941 that large-scale production began.

Before the beginning of the Western campaign in May 1940 Germany had a chain of early warning *Freya* radars which was technically superior to Britain's Chain Home system. The installations were on Sylt, Heligoland, Wangenrooge, near Emden, Wilsum in the Emsland, near Kleve, Heinsburg, Stadtkyll, Trier, Landstuhl, and on the Kandel in the Black Forest. This meant that from the Danish to the Swiss frontiers the airspace was under surveillance to a depth of 120 km (74.5 mls). There was however no central command post at which all incoming flight reports could be evaluated and orders issued to the fighters and Flak. *Freya* data went to the Navy and the Luftwaffe; in the latter case the reports were received partly by the Luftflotten and partly by the *Luftgaukommandos*. The reports also naturally got to Berlin, but that was just the place where the individual night fighter formations were *not* led from.[5] This division of responsibilities was never completely overcome. Even when, in 1941, the Reich Air Defence was taken over by *Lw.Befh.Mitte* (Luftwaffe Commander Centre), Navy and Luftwaffe air reporting services remained separate, to which was added the ground radar reporting system of the night fighter force.

To return to the introduction of radar into night fighting, an experimental detachment of LN (Luftwaffe Signals) Regiment Köthen under *Lt* Hermann Diehl, based on the island of Wangenrooge and equipped with a *Freya* radar, made a name for itself by alerting the fighters in good time before an RAF raid on Wilhelmshaven on 18 December 1939. On that occasion more than half of the attacking force was shot down.

Diehl's detachment had started experiments on the guidance of fighters to aerial targets by day already a month before that date. The position of the target, located by a *Freya*, was reported to the fighter by radio. This method achieved little however, because the azimuth measurements were too imprecise and there were no height data at all. After a few experiments with radio beacons the AN circuit[6] was developed, resulting in much improved azimuth measurements, while the height finding task was taken over by a *Würzburg*; later came the *Freya-Fahrstuhl*, which also measured target altitude. The *AN-Freya* receiving aerial was divided into two parts which were switched over by an electric selector 75 times a second. On the cathode ray screen the target echoes appeared vertically, to the right and to the left, and in different sizes according to their bearing. The target was directly lined up when the double echo pointers were

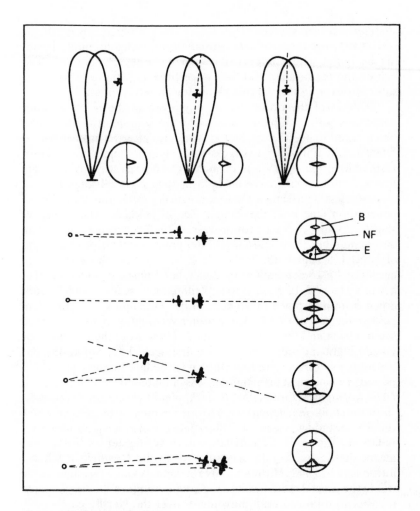

Freya AN direction finding

Top row, from the left: target at the extreme right hand edge of the radar transmit and receive lobes; target is just right of the centre; target is flying directly towards the device.

2nd row: Bomber B is in the centre ahead of the device, heading away; the night fighter NF is to the left and behind it; E is the permanent echo.

3rd row: Night fighter directly behind the bomber.

4th row: Heading away clockwise from 7 to 1; bomber in the centre ahead of the device, night fighter to the left of centre; large distance between the night fighter and bomber.

Bottom row: Heading away clockwise from 7 to 1; bomber in the centre ahead of the device, night fighter a little to the left directly behind the bomber.

symmetrical (see sketch). The fighter control officer observed the screen and gave the necessary corrections to the fighter pilot,[7] bringing the fighter echo pointers in line with the target echo pointers. The fighter and the target could then be as little as 50 m (164 ft) apart, sufficient even in the darkest nights for an interception.

Diehl tried the procedure by day, even in the worst weather conditions, with complete success. At the beginning of July 1940 Falck asked to see the method at work and afterwards encouraged Diehl in a memorandum to suggest it for night fighting. On 19 August Kammhuber received a report on AN but he was sceptical and said that his pilots would have no faith in such a complicated system. Nevertheless he assigned Diehl a practice zone in the main British penetration lane near the Zuider Zee in Holland. The Nunspeet station, 25 km (15.5 mls) south-west of Zwolle, became operational on 7 September 1940, and a week later practice operations with parts of II/NJG 1 began. *Lt* Becker of 4./NJG 1 flew the first 'sharp' operation on 18 September; on 2 October Nunspeet guided *Lt* Becker in a Do 17Z-10 *Kauz 2* to a Wellington bomber, which he shot down from a distance of 50 m (164 ft). Two hours later *Lt* Diehl guided the crew of *Uffz* Fick to another Wellington, but Fick opened fire too soon and the bomber escaped. These were the first ground-guided night interceptions and the first such 'kill'. Some 48 AN-controlled victories were reported up to the late summer of 1941, a period in which most night fighting was illuminated (*Henaja*, short for *Helle Nachtjagd*). Gradually 16 'dark' night fighting zones (*Dunaja*, short for *Dunkelnachtjagd*) were formed in the coastal area, in which the AN-method was also used. Slow delivery of *Freya* ground control radars and the method's high demands on the fighter control officers meant that it had to take second place to the *Himmelbett* scheme introduced in 1942. However, AN retained its value throughout the war in the coastal areas because the greater range of the *Freyas* made it easier to follow aircraft movements over the North Sea.

After many abortive illuminated night fighting operations Falck and, on his advice, Kammhuber concluded that the searchlights should immediately pick up the right target, that the night fighter should be guided to it, and that the fighter's run in to attack should be shorter. The first objective was however only possible with the help of ground radar. On 17 September 1940 Kammhuber ordered a *Freya* to be coupled with a searchlight (known as the '*Parasit*' installation) in the Arnhem area. *Parasit* was used for the first time on 26 September when an enemy aircraft was spotted immediately and lit up. Following this promising start the Division had another *Parasit* installation set up 10 km (6.2 mls) east of Zutphen; this unit achieved its first 'kill' on 1 October.

That month the searchlight detachments of the 'Kammhuber

Line' (the term was invented by the British) received the first *Würzburg-A* ground control radars. At the same time the Division introduced new operational principles for *Henaja* which did not turn out to be all that effective in practice. The fighter command post equipped with *Würzburg* (range about 30 km/18.6 mls) and situated ahead of the searchlight belt, received data on the incoming raid from the listening posts. The night fighter`was cruising in a standby zone now placed in the middle of the searchlight belt. The fighter control post, with the help of *Würzburg*, guided the night fighter towards the bomber and into the zone where the searchlights were expected to pick it up. But at this point both the bomber and the night fighter were in front of the listening posts, and the often inexperienced crews of the ring-type sound locators were overloaded by this 'noise salad'. The searchlights and *Würzburg* received the most contradictory data, and it often happened that the listening posts would identify the night fighter as the target. The command post would then have the fighters chasing themselves, believing that an enemy aircraft was very near.

The operational procedure outlined above had many critics. The commander of Searchlight Rgt 1, *Otl* Fischer, wanted *Würzburg* to guide a master searchlight, while some of the night fighter *Staffelkapitäne* and *Gruppen* COs protested about the fact that the fighters were guided directly at the enemy through the searchlight zone. But Kammhuber persisted with his guidelines, primarily because he believed that an unguided night fighter simply would not be able to find its target. On his own initiative Radusch returned with I/NJG 1 to the old method, standing by behind the searchlight zone and approaching for an attack within the illuminated area. With this method his *Gruppe* scored five kills during the night of 15/16 October, three of them being credited to Streib. On the other hand, II/NJG 1 under *Oblt* Ehle, which had been flying both dark and illuminated sorties in Zone 4 (Twente), had been unable to score any victories at all with the Kammhuber method.

In the autumn of 1940 Kammhuber instructed Radusch to fly experimental night interceptions around Berlin in which the bomber was to be picked up by a *Würzburg* and the fighter guided to it by dead reckoning. These experiments failed because of the inaccuracy of the navigational method. Kammhuber felt that this justified his method, and set up further zones in which the night fighters had to fly according to his guidelines. The criticism from the ranks that they could only be successful when both the enemy and the fighter were tracked by *Würzburg* was ignored at first. Nevertheless, up to the end of 1940 the night fighters were able to draw up a healthy balance: since its formation the new force had shot down 42 enemy aircraft against the Flak's 30 in the same period.

It would be appropriate here to include a few words about the

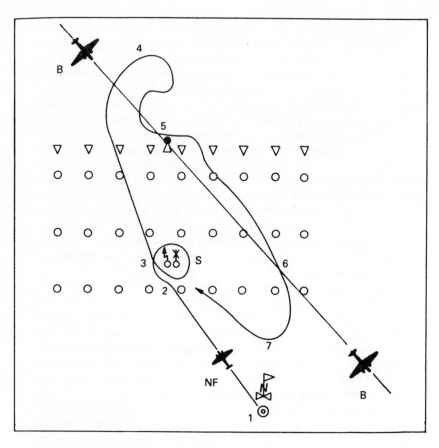

Illuminated night fighting – 2nd phase:
Standby zone in the illuminated belt, dark night fighting zone in front of it.

The night fighter takes off (1) to the standby zone (2) and, after acquisition of the bomber by *Würzburg* Ⓡ, sets off to attack the target in front of the illuminated zone (3).
Confusion over engine noise from the bomber and fighter results in abortive interceptions (4, 5), the bomber penetrates the illuminated zone (6) and the fighter returns to the standby zone (7).

men who achieved these successes: the pilots and the radio operators. Up to the middle of 1941 the majority of them came to the new force as various *Zerstörer* formations were transformed into night fighter units. They had mostly flown day fighters before the war and had gained combat experience in the previous campaigns. Like the newly trained crews who came to night fighting after spring 1941, they saw the Bf 110 as the ideal aircraft for the job: it was almost as fast as a single-engined fighter, was sufficiently manoeuvrable and very well armed, and was far superior to the Bf 109 in flight safety and endurance.

During the development phase up to the end of 1941, it was the new technology and secrecy surrounding night fighting that attracted the new blood (significantly, pictures of night fighters never appeared in the daily or technical papers, and propaganda reports on their operations were always couched in very general terms). Thereafter the desire to protect the civilian population began to predominate as the driving force behind the voluntary enlistments. The *Zerstörer* crews of KG 30, from which II/NJG 1 was formed, brought a different type of pilot to night fighting. He preferred the Ju 88, Do 17 and Do 217, dismissed by the former day *Zerstörer* types as 'lame birds' and 'unusable as fighters'. This kind of pilot valued the other qualities of these aircraft: more spacious cockpits, a third crew member to keep a lookout, the rather more powerful armament, good single-engined performance, automatic pilot and longer endurance. For these qualities he gladly sacrificed manoeuvrability, which was in any case not a significant factor in night fighting before the advent of the British long-range night fighters. These men did not feel comfortable in 'controlled' night fighting, and Kammhuber consciously directed them towards long-range night fighting/intruder tasks. From 1941 onwards this circle included former long-range reconnaissance, bomber and transport pilots, blind-flying instructors and former Lufthansa pilots, some of them men of quite advanced years. They never felt at home in the Bf 110 and hurried to join the Ju 88 units which were formed in greater numbers from the end of 1943. Highly experienced pilots from bomber and reconnaissance units were directed towards the 'Wild Boar' formations organised in summer 1943. Thanks to their great flying experience they usually had little trouble flying single-engined aircraft which were only marginally suitable for all-weather operations. Sometimes they even took pride in taking off on nights when all twin-engined night fighters stayed on the ground. When the 'Wild Boar' operations were curtailed in spring 1944, some of these pilots transferred to the Ju 88 units to fly aircraft that were closer to their hearts.

At the end of the year the Night Fighter Division had an establishment of 195 machines. With the exception of I/NJG 2 the *Gruppen* were equipped with the Bf 110C-2, C-4 and D-1, which did not differ in their equipment from the daytime *Zerstörer* except that the '*Dackelbauch*' ('Dachshund belly') ventral tanks had been removed from the Bf 110D-1. The outward sign of a night fighter – at least in the case of the Bf 110 – was all-over black camouflage. There were also a few oddities: I/NJG 2 flew Ju 88C-2s, which had been converted from Ju 88A-5 bombers and still had their dive brakes, useless in night fighting. Their armament was weaker than that of the Bf 110 –

3 × MG 17 and 1 × MG FF cannon as against 4 × MG 17 and 2 × MG FF of the Messerschmitt – but the Ju 88 could carry bombs, which was important for night intruder operations over Britain. The camouflage of NJG 2 was remarkably non-uniform. The aircraft were usually left in the standard daytime *Zerstörer* camouflage, with the black night camouflage mostly applied only to the upper surfaces and sometimes on the undersides of the wings; completely black aircraft were rare. Dornier also tried to join Messerschmitt and Junkers in the *Zerstörer* and night fighter business, and after the phasing out of the Do 17 bomber the company offered a long-range fighter version, the Do 17Z-7 *Kauz*. In essence, this was a modified Do 17Z-3. The glazed nose section was replaced with the Ju 88C-6 gun mounting, comprising 3 × MG 17 and 1 × MG FF covered by a streamlined metal fairing, with a powerful searchlight in the centre. Several operational sorties are known to have been flown with this modification, all of which were total failures: the night fighters gave themselves away too soon and came under heavy machine gun fire from the British bombers. Only nine Do 17Z-7s were completed before the production line changed over to the Do 17Z-10 *Kauz 2*. This version had a slimmer nose section carrying 4 × MG 17 and 2 × MG FF (later replaced by 1 × MG 151), and was fitted with the IR searchlight for the *Spanner* installation. However, the RLM felt that this version also had little future and halted production after only nine Do 17Z-10s.

The company tried again and built a night-fighter version of the Do 215, the B-5 or *Kauz 3*, which differed from the previous version only in that it had the lighter and more powerful DB 601 inline engines instead of the Bramo 323R radials. But the RLM did not want to know about this aircraft either and no more than half a dozen Do 215B-5 *Kauz 3*s ever reached operational units. The judgement of the RLM was at fault, as experience subsequently showed. The Do 215B-5 had better handling qualities than the contemporary Ju 88 and Bf 110, performed better than the Ju 88C-2 and, after changing over to 3 × MG FF and 3 × MG 17, was the best armed night fighter in 1941. It was not for nothing that the last serviceable Do 215B-5 should remain operational until spring 1944, while the Do 17Z-10 *Kauz 2* was serving only in the training role by the summer of 1942.

The strength and operational readiness of the night fighter units fell off rapidly in winter 1940. Their losses from flying accidents and enemy action were high and could not be made up completely by the factories. In November 67 per cent of the effective strength were ready for action; by December this figure had sunk to 59 per cent. The fact that 60 per cent of the Bf 110 production went to the night fighter force made little difference since total production had been cut back too drastically.

The crewing situation was even worse. On 4 January 1941 the 16 night fighter *Staffeln* had an average of only 3.7 crews ready for action, and it was already clear that, even during the early phase, there were not enough to go around. In order to protect the Reich territory even to halfway effectively with these limited forces, the Division was compelled constantly to shuttle around the *Gruppen* and individual *Staffeln* according to need. Thus in autumn 1940 I/NJG 1 was stationed in Gardelegen to protect Berlin. When the raids on Hamburg began the *Gruppe* transferred to Stade. Attacks on the Ruhr area were countered by detachments to Dortmund, Münster-Handorf, Düsseldorf, Cologne-Ostheim and Bonn-Hangelar. Meanwhile, there grew up along the 'Kammhuber Line' a chain of airfields suitable for night landings, some with concrete runways, impressive workshop/hangars and half-buried bomb shelters: Schleswig, Stade, Lüneburg, Wittmundthafen, Oldenburg, Vechta, Leeuwarden, Twente, Deelen, St Trond and Venlo. To mention one example, in developing the airfield at Venlo-Herongen on the German/Dutch border the Todt organisation[8] used over 18,000 workers simultaneously and on the German side over 1,180 hectares of land were taken in. The two take-off runways were 1,450 m (4,760 ft) long, and the third 1,200 m (3,940 ft) in length; 2,000 lamps were used for airfield lighting, and 48 km (29.8 mls) of roads led to workshops, command posts and accommodation. The new air base grew up in the incredibly short time between 1 October 1940 and 18 March 1941. It was to remain the home of I/NJG 1 until the evacuation of this unit on 5 September 1944.

Defensive night fighting, as described so far, took second place to attacking techniques in Kammhuber's estimation. 'If you want to render a wasp swarm harmless, it is better to destroy the nest along with the wasps than to wait until the swarm flies out and then chase each individual wasp', was Kammhuber's argument, which he expressed at every opportunity. In fact, the enemy was at his most vulnerable in the neighbourhood of his home base: at the dispersals, preparing for take-off, at take-off, coming in to land, landing and during the landing run.

As mentioned above, Kammhuber's division incorporated a unit which had already had experience in long-range *Zerstörer* raids, the *Z-Staffel* of KG 30. From this unit were derived II/NJG 2 and then I/NJG 2. The *Gruppe* was based at Gilze-Rijen, and was intended to be developed into a complete *Geschwader*. Then in December Kammhuber received Göring's personal permission to form a total of three long-range night fighter *Geschwader*. But Kammhuber had put the cart before the horse and he was thwarted at every turn; Hitler did not believe in the effectiveness of long-range night fighter/intruder operations, as up to this point there had been no noticeable decline in the number of RAF penetrations of the Reich airspace. At *Ob.d.L.*

headquarters they were annoyed that the commander of the night fighter division had taken upon himself to place so many units under his command, more even than in a *Fliegerkorps*. The Luftflotten and the *Fliegerkorps* in the occupied Western territories protested against having to share the prosecution of offensive against England with another command, which in their eyes would mean an intolerable dissipation of personnel and materials. The results of this criticism were catastrophic for Kammhuber: the expansion of long-range night fighting was refused and the force remained at the one *Gruppe*. This was removed from the tactical command of the night fighter division and placed under the control of Luftflotte 3. Finally, production of the Do 17Z-10 was stopped, and that of the Ju 88C series so cut back that the operational readiness of I/NJG 2 was seriously endangered. In November 1940 this unit had only 15 machines at its disposal, and at the end of January it was down to just seven aircraft. It was not until the end of January 1941 that the situation improved a little. Even so, in autumn 1941 the *Gruppe* never had more than 20 aircraft at its disposal. However, this relatively small force caused the RAF bomber crews no small amount of uneasiness and greatly disrupted night flights within the British Isles.

From autumn 1940 the radio monitoring service of Luftflotte 3 was able to determine from Bomber Command's radio tuning transmissions the number and location of the aircraft preparing to take off, and to report accordingly to the commander of I/NJG 2, *Hptm* Hülshoff. The first night fighter crews would then take off from Gilze-Rijen in order to be over the British take-off points on time. A little later the second wave would take off to catch the bombers along the most commonly used approach lanes over the North Sea.

It was difficult enough to catch the wasps as they flew out of the nest, but, as long as the fighters were neither guided from the ground nor equipped with airborne detection devices, even more luck was needed for the pursuit of individual wasps. The third method promised the most success. This technique called for the fighters to mix with the returning bombers, orbit over their bases, switch on navigation lights to cause confusion, and then to shoot down the unsuspecting enemy at point-blank range. The night fighters would then race low over the airfields and drop their 50 kg (110 lb) fragmentation bombs. The number of actual bombers shot down over England does not appear to have been especially high: according to British reports the long-range night fighters cost Bomber Command seven total losses and 20 badly damaged between 1 October 1940 and 31 March 1942.[9] However, the psychological effect on the bomber crews, who could no longer feel safe even in the dark over their own territory, was not insignificant. Many pilots crash-landed because they brought their aircraft down onto the runway at too high a speed, or did not dare risk going around a second time after an unsatisfactory first approach. Crashes were also caused by both bomb craters on the runway or forced landings on airfields which had switched off their landing lights at the approach of a night fighter. Finally, the British were compelled to put an end to night flying training in the counties most at risk: East Anglia, Lincolnshire and Yorkshire. Kammhuber was able to support these reports on the effect of long-range night fighting from prisoners' statements. But it was all in vain, and in autumn 1941 Hitler put a stop to long-range night fighter operations.

Notes

1 On 10 June 1940 *Lt* Lütje (later *Kdre* of NJG 6) reported combat with a Bristol Blenheim bomber. At that time he was flying a Bf 109D coded N + 3.

2 *Oberst a.D.* Falck and Radusch dispute the redesignation of this *Gruppe*.

3 *Sicherheitsdienst* = State Security Service.

4 Frank Reuter *Funkmess*. Opladen 1971.

5 The *Heimatflugmeldedienst* (Home Air Reporting Service), which also received *Freya* reports, did not do anything about them, for they knew nothing about the top-secret early warning radar. Besides, believing that it was impossible to establish aircraft movements more than 100 km (62 mls) beyond the horizon, the service decided that the reports just had to be false.

6 AN method: complementary keying of radiation diagrams forming an equisignal zone.

7 At first by W/T to the radio operator who then passed the information on to his pilot, later directly to the pilot.

8 Construction corps composed of various specialists and impressed labour.

9 To this should be added aircraft which did not belong to Bomber Command (such as Hurricane night fighters), and the successes scored by the night fighters during the inward and outward flights of the bombers over the sea.

4. Developments during the British individual and wave raids of 1941–1942

Intensification of British raids in spring 1941; first use of four-engined bombers – Organisational measures in night fighting: widening of the illuminated belt, changeover to larger zones, combination of the illuminated and dark night fighting zones – Introduction of combined night fighting over concentrated industrial areas – Experiments with single-engined fighters – New developments in radar – Effect of the Eastern campaign on the development of night fighting – Formation of XII Fliegerkorps; strength, operations and successes – German and British preparations for 1942; British large-scale raids – Night fighting in the Mediterranean area and the East.

GENERAL EVENTS OF THE WAR

March 1941: German *Afrika Korps* goes into action. *6 April – 1 June:* Balkan campaign. *22 June:* Beginning of Eastern campaign. *5 December:* Start of Soviet winter offensive.

When Göring dismissed the RAF attacks on the Reich in June 1940 as 'annoying pinpricks,' he was right: these raids were basically little more than an irritation. But in the winter of 1940–41 it became clear that the RAF was pursuing a long-term strategic aim of wearing down the population and causing loss of production through constantly repeated air raid warnings and, finally, the destruction of the German cities. The twin-engined Whitleys, Blenheims and Wellingtons had already proved no easy targets for the night fighters, and the four-engined Stirling, Halifax and Lancaster bombers which began to appear from spring 1941 onwards were truly formidable opponents.[1] Official German propaganda dismissed the four-engined bombers as 'tired crows'. That might have been true of the Stirling, but even this type reached high speeds in inclined flight, while the Halifax and Lancaster could easily put distance between themselves and the Bf 110C and D night fighters at altitudes of over 5,000 m (16,400 ft). When they went into a shallow dive to accelerate, the Bf 110 could only get closer if it was diving from a greater height.

Kammhuber, supported by intelligence reports, had correctly anticipated these developments and was demanding the expansion of the night fighter force, calling for the greatest possible application of men and materials. He hoped to destroy most of the bombers over the Western approaches of the Reich, in a widely spread out and well staggered defensive area of dark and illuminated night fighting zones. Any bombers which managed to break through were to be caught near the objective itself. Among the Luftwaffe leaders, Chief of Staff Jeschonnek in particular was torn by conflicting feelings towards the demands of the night fighting force: on the one hand he recognised that only night fighters could inflict destruction on the British formations; on the other hand he saw clearly that Germany was not strong enough to conduct a full range of defensive and offensive operations in the air. In 1941, despite all its deficiencies, the *Henaja* carried the main burden of the defensive battle. The illuminated belt stretched from the Danish border to Maubeuge, and an additional illuminated zone between Frankfurt and Mannheim was brought into operation in late autumn. Thanks to the increased supplies of ground control installations, and improvements in the evaluation of data, it was at last possible to perfect the *Henaja* procedure. Each searchlight site received up to three *Würzburg* radars. Positioned in the middle, at the front and at the rear edge of each searchlight position, these systems made it possible to detect and acquire the bombers and night fighters as they entered and left the zone. Only a few bombers were shot down as they left the zone because the RAF pilots would dive to accelerate before reaching the searchlight belt, flying through the hazardous zone at low altitude.

The disadvantages of this procedure were the limited range of *Würzburg*, the lack of any means of distinguishing between friendly and enemy aircraft (IFF), and imprecise evaluation of data on the *Würzburg* plotting tables. These negative aspects were clearly recognised in night fighter command circles, and together with the General of the Luftwaffe Signals Service (NVW), Gen Martini, Gen Kammhuber demanded the following: a ground control radar of greater range but with the same precision as *Würzburg*; substantially improved plotting tables; and reliable AI radars with a maximum range at least equal to the aircraft's altitude, minimum range of 200 m (656 ft), and IFF capability.

A possible contender for the ground control radar requirement was *Würzburg-Riese*, which did not however fulfil all the conditions, particularly the IFF capability,[2] but had been under development as a large early warning radar and could thus be put into production in summer 1941. It had a range of about 80 km (49.7 mls) and was as accurate as *Würzburg-D*.[3]

From the many types of *Würzburg* plotting table evolved by the operational units there was developed, through many intermediate forms, the *Seeburg* plotting table. Given a scale of 1:50,000, it could handle plots out to a radius of 36 km (22.4 mls). On the other side of the coin, the *Lichtenstein* AI radar had still not been cleared for series production.

After the delivery of *Würzburg-Riesen* in autumn 1941 Kammhuber was able to carry out wide-ranging changes in organisation. The width of the ten Western night fighting zones was increased from 40 to 90 km (24.8 to 55.9 mls). Each large zone was occupied by a searchlight regiment, whose three detachments each had the use of a radar and an evaluation post. The most notable thing about the new system was its provision for a *Dunaja* area 36 km (22.4 mls) in depth in front of the illuminated zone. It was also planned to introduce *Dunaja* areas behind the illuminated belt. Finally, it was hoped, in front of the *Henaja* zone there would be a radar installation with a

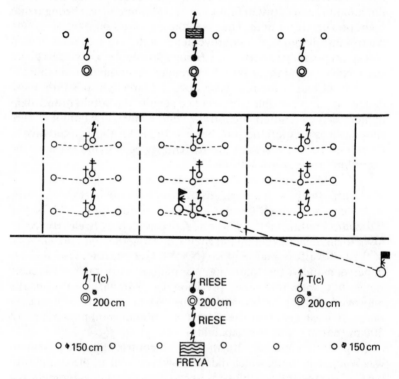

Large searchlight zone with dark night fighting zones

○ 150 cm diameter searchlights
◉ 200 cm diameter searchlights
⚲ Master searchlights
⚑ Searchlight detachment command post

⚑ Searchlight Regiment command post
⚲ *Würzburg-Riese*
⚲ *Würzburg-C*
▄ *Freya*

34

Freya for long-range early warning and a *Red Giant* (enemy aircraft tracking radar), plus a chain of six searchlights of 150 cm (59 in) diameter and three of 200 cm (78.7 in) diameter; controlled by *Würzburg*, these units would act as master searchlights.

A similar arrangement of radars and master searchlights was also to be set up behind the illuminated belt. This procedure, often erroneously referred to as *Himmelbett*, became operational in September 1941 but was so complicated that at first the number of enemy aircraft shot down in these areas decreased. Having overestimated the efficiency of this method and the maximum speed of the night fighters, Kammhuber then temporarily reduced the depth of the searchlight zone to 10 km (6.2 mls), with the result that the bombers could no longer be intercepted in the searchlight area. The performance advantage which the Bf 110C and D still had at the end of 1940 had disappeared nine months later. The latest four-engined RAF bombers pulled away from the Bf 110 at higher altitudes and the fighters' climbing speed was not enough to bring them within range of the bombers when their altitude was measured by *Würzburg-Riesen* 80 km (49.7 mls) in front of the night fighter standby zone. As it was, the bombers flew through the 10 km-wide illuminated zone in two minutes and in that space of time the Bf 110 could hardly get near the target, even if it descended to attack from a greater height. Kammhuber therefore had the illuminated zone widened to 20 km (12.4 mls) again, at least in the heavily raided areas west of the Ruhr. For this the searchlight batteries in the north and south had to give up some equipment.

The new large zones with the combined dark and illuminated night fighting arrangements began to work effectively only in the spring of 1942. Kammhuber could not have known that this would bring a new setback to XII *Fliegerkorps*: the *Gauleiters* of the areas most frequently raided by the RAF petitioned Hitler that the searchlights were a luxury to such a well equipped force, and that the light be much better used in support of the Flak in the rear areas. Thus after the first mass raids in March/April 1942 the searchlight batteries were gradually withdrawn from the illuminated belt on Hitler's orders. The dissolution of the Searchlight Division was ordered for 31 July 1942, leaving only a training and experimental regiment in the Venlo area.

The AN method was also improved at this time, so that each *Dunaja* station consisted of one detecting and one AN (=fighter guidance) *Freya* as well as two *Würzburg-Riesen* for bomber and fighter altitude measurements.

One more night fighting procedure was added in summer 1940: the combined night fighting method, *Konaja*. It was an answer to the introduction of the four-engined bombers, which could be attacked with only marginal success in the illuminated zone. These aircraft were however forced to approach their target at a fixed height (usually not over 5,500 m/18,040 ft), in a straight line and with no diversions. This is where Kammhuber saw his big chance of combating the raiders with searchlights, Flak and fighters at a time when, for a few moments, they were robbed of part of their advantages. The idea of using single-engined night fighters over certain targets was also being considered at that time. The Bf 109E was seen as being sufficiently equipped with blind-flying instruments to make its use in night fighting promising, and an experimental Bf 109 night fighter *Staffel* was formed at Cologne-Ostheim. Once they had proved themselves in action, it was hoped to work up the daytime fighter units as quickly available target-defence reserves. Though it was theoretically promising, there were many reasons why this experiment was doomed to failure: the pilots had no experience of blind flying, were often opposed to the method because they felt they were being pushed into something against their will, and often were not the most capable of men. On top of all that, they did not have any guidance methods of the kind enjoyed by the 'Wild Boar' night fighters; typical of these aids were the air situation reports from the *Tornado* direction-finders.[4] In 1941 the searchlight belts around the towns were not as wide as they came to be in 1943, and the British bomber did not attack in dense streams, so that the single-engined fighters could only spot and combat a small number of enemy machines during their short sorties.

At the end of August the *Vers.NJ-St.* changed to Bf 110s and became *Erg.Staffel*/NJG 1. In order to find the most suitable *Konaja* methods experiments took place around Berlin in May. The *NJ-Division* suggested dividing the area over the target into three sectors of 120°, each the province of a single night fighter. When an enemy aircraft entered a certain sector the night fighter would be guided to the illuminated target by radar; the Flak would be forbidden to fire in the active sector. This scheme eliminated the risk of a fighter being shot at by his own Flak, but if several enemy aircraft flew into a sector only one would be in danger of being attacked by night fighters, while the others would have been free to continue to the target.

The suggestion from *Lw.Befh.Mitte* was more practical. The whole defensive area was divided into seven zones: a circular zone of 12 km (7.5 mls) diameter was centred on the target, and around it were three sectors of 120°, each divided into two. The whole area was subdivided into 2.5 km (1.6 mls; later 1 km/0.6 mls) squares; the same divisions appeared on the 1:50,000-scale plotting map in the command post. Enemy penetrations reported by the *Flukos* (central observation posts) were drawn onto a special *Fluko* map in the command post. If the enemy aircraft reached a certain line (called the starting circle) the night fighters which were ready and waiting would take off to the standby zone of their sector. The minimum safety height there would be 5,500 m (18,040 ft), and guidance for the fighters consisted of one light and two radio beacons. Up to 20 Flak range finders would pick up the enemy and the friendly fighters, and pass on their readings to the command post. There, special projectors would throw points of light onto a glass plotting map, while on the reverse side of the map paths of the enemy bombers and night fighters were drawn in. The night fighter leader would then direct his aircraft towards selected targets. When the path of the night fighter reached a certain square on the map, the Flak commander would transmit cease-fire order to the batteries concerned. The chosen target would be subjected to harassing or effective fire until such time as the night fighter reported a sighting, whereon these batteries would be ordered to cease fire. After a successful interception the night fighter would return to its safety height and fly towards the standby zone.

After a few surprise successes in the summer – on 28 June the ADC of II/NJG 1, *Oblt* Eckhardt, shot down four bombers over Hamburg – the number of kills decreased again in the late autumn.[5] The main reason was (as in 1917) the fact that the Flak cease-fire orders came too late, or were not obeyed. It was no wonder therefore that the night fighter pilots preferred to turn away rather than be 'peppered' by their own Flak.[6] The *Lw.Befh.Mitte* thought however that he would be able to solve the problem in the future if the optical rangefinders and the plotting devices of the Flak, with their inherent inaccuracies and delays, could be replaced by ground radar. The theory had only to be proved in practice. As a result, the following *Konaja* zones were set up over several large towns: *Kiebitz* (Kiel), *Hummel* (Hamburg), *Roland* (Bremen), *Bär* (Berlin), *Drossel* (Düsseldorf-Duisburg-Essen), *Kolibri* (Cologne area) and *Dachs* (Wiesbaden-Frankfurt-Darmstadt-Mannheim). Even if, apart from the initial successes, there were no spectacular series of victories in these *Konaja* zones, this method still had its effect. The attacks on Hamburg, Berlin and the Ruhr decreased markedly and were not greatly stepped up again until 1943. For the same reasons, the *Konaja* occasionally operated in the *Languste* and *Hering* zones also proved its worth. At the end of the year a combined *Henaja-Dunaja* zone was set up west of *Dachs* and operated by II/NJG 3 based at Mainz-Finthen.

In spite of having fighter control officers on the instrument sites, Kammhuber insisted on keeping the whole night fighter organisation on a short leash. Reports from all sites and units were received in the divisional HQ at Zeist, where they were evaluated and marked on a large projection screen, similar to those used at the local plotting centres. For its part, the Division could intervene directly in the night fighter zones. The divisional command post itself was in a bombproof bunker but the amplifier station at Arnheim, where all the cables came together, was not. Thus a chance hit could have completely cut off the central leadership at a stroke! All *Dunaja* procedures had two basic drawbacks: first, even during the experimental phase the British were already interfering with R/T communications between the ground installations and the fighters;[7] second, interceptions guided by *Würzburg* and the plotting tables were affected by such big measurement and evaluation errors that the night fighters could only find their targets on very clear nights.

It was thus essential to find ways of reducing R/T communications to a minimum and of giving the night fighters their own eyes. In response to the first requirement the industry developed the FuG 135 *Uhu* (Owl) ground-based data-transmission device. Into this, the fighter control officer fed the course, height and range of the target, using information from the plotting table. One turn of a handle transmitted the figures to the fighter, where they appeared on a display screen. The course signal could even be switched in to the

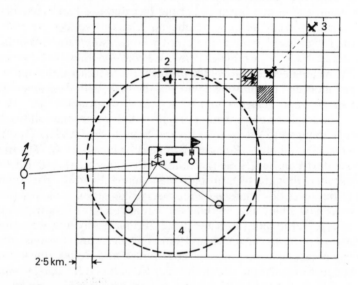

Schematic representation of combined night fighting

When the fighter sets off to attack (position 2), the Flak in the corresponding map square is ordered to cease fire.

Key:
- ⌧ Night fighter leader
- ⚑ Air defence command post
- ○ *Würzburg* radar
- T 4 cm rangefinder

1. Flak radio transmitter
2. Night fighter
3. Bomber
4. Standby zone

38

autopilot. In addition to the visual displays there was also *Papagei* (Parrot), a two-way communications system which encoded transmitted speech and could not be interfered with by the jamming devices then in use. But the hopes pinned on *Uhu* late in 1941 were to be disappointed. The transmitted signals did not have the precision of the *Seeburg* signals, the automatic transmission to the pilot often failed, and the pilots felt that an additional three visual display units would hinder the visual search for targets. However, as the *Uhu* was coupled with the very useful *Papagei*, XII *Fliegerkorps* went on demanding the combined system, even though half the available electronics (each *Uhu* had 45 relays) were not used. This did not escape the notice of the Technical Office, and so Kammhuber's request for 2,000 *Uhus* was cut to 400, and in 1944 production was stopped altogether.

Initially it was tried to give the night fighters eyes in the form of the *Spanner* ultra-red (now called infra-red or IR) systems. *Spanner I* consisted of an IR searchlight and a sight; *Spanner II* had only a sight with a wider acquisition angle. On the Do 17 the IR searchlight was mounted in the nose, while in the Bf 110 it was installed in a teardrop shaped container under the fuselage. The sight fitted in front of the pilot and protruded forwards through the armoured glass; in the Bf 110 it irksomely restricted the pilot's field of view. *Spanner I* worked satisfactorily once the aircraft's generators had been boosted so that they could supply a 1,000-watt bulb. *Spanner II*, which also worked passively in that it was supposed to show only the heat from the exhaust flames, proved unusable. At a distance, only when the target chanced to be in a position where its exhaust gases pointed directly at *Spanner* did the device register anything. But if the bomber's exhaust pipes ejected above the wings, and the fighter was beneath the target, nothing could be seen in the sight. Even when the aircraft were well positioned, *Spanner* could not distinguish between the exhaust flames and stars, and when the bombers used flame dampers there was again nothing to be seen. For these reasons *E-Stelle* Rechlin recommended that all further development should be stopped in favour of airborne radar. Nevertheless, experiments with IR devices continued right until the end of the war. It was only in long-range night fighting that *Spanner* proved useful, as the airborne radar could not pick up any target near the ground.

As already mentioned, Kammhuber had called for an airborne electronic locator in autumn 1940. Göring, who did not approve of the way night fighting development was going – he thought it too big, too expensive and too inflexibly led – rejected this demand as too far fetched (or, as he put it, 'a fighter cannot have things sprouting from its head'), and with that the matter was settled as far as he was concerned. Kammhuber received more sympathy from Martini and the Technical Office of the RLM, particularly since the industry had already come up with something useful. At the beginning of the war Telefunken was experimenting with a radio altimeter known by its factory code name *Lichtenstein B*, but the RLM declined it as too expensive. Telefunken then tried to find out if, by fitting the aerials horizontally, they could convert the altimeter into a system that would enable the bombers to keep in contact with each other at night. When Kammhuber issued his requirement for an airborne locator, the laboratory chief, Dr Ruge, and his assistant, Dr Muth, suggested the experimental *Lichtenstein B/C*. Although it was not expected to mass-produce this system in its experimental form, *Lichtenstein* was ordered into high-priority production in summer 1941. The first set was flight-tested at Rechlin, where the range and close-up resolution were found to be completely satisfactory at 3–4 km (1.8–2.5 mls) and 200 m (656 ft) respectively. The search angle of the beam was a mere 30°, however, so that a sharply turning target was easily lost. As yet, neither *Freya* nor *Würzburg* had any IFF capability. Nevertheless, with the help of the plotting table a night fighter could now be guided towards its target even on nights of only moderate visibility, before manoeuvring closer until visual contact was achieved.

The Rechlin test pilots gave the new radar a good report, but stressed one major disadvantage common to all airborne radars mass-produced by German industry during the war: high-drag of the aerials, which reduced the maximum speed of the Bf 110 by at least 40 km/h (24.8 mph). *Major* Helm, who led the experimental detachment at Rechlin and later the experimental centre for radar development at Werneuchen, then tried to find out if it was possible to retract the antennae into the fuselage or at least make them more streamlined. Impossible with the decimetric AI radar, this would have worked with the centimetric radar. But experiments in that line had been stopped once again in 1941 as a result of Hitler's order that no more new developments should be started during the war.

Following the *Lichtenstein* tests at Rechlin, *Major* Helm moved the experimental detachment (TVK) and a group of Telefunken engineers to II/NJG 1 at Leeuwarden. Initially the pilots struggled with all their might against what they saw as 'new-fangled rubbish'. Every criticism was levelled at the new radar: loss of speed, nose-heaviness, difficulties in trimming, overloading of the radio operator, the chances of receiving contradictory reports and instructions from the fighter command post and *Lichtenstein* operators, and so on. Only *Oblt* Ludwig Becker, who had already claimed the honour of the first *Dunaja* kill, flew a few operational sorties with *Lichtenstein*, and with his Do 215B-5 (coded G9 + OM) he achieved the first victory on 10 August. Between 12 August and 30 September 1941 Becker shot down five more bombers using *Lichtenstein* guidance. But then the first and only operational AI radar apparently became unserviceable, because the next *Lichtenstein* kills are not recorded until June 1942.

During the first *Lichtenstein* operations Becker developed a tactic which was later taken up by the whole night fighter force. He would fly towards the target at a height just below that shown by the radar. Then, on sighting the target, he would push over and accelerate to avoid being seen by the rear gunner of the bomber, match speeds and climb steadily to 50 m (164 ft) below the target. He would then pull up and open fire. Because the fighter had lost speed, the bomber had to fly through the stream of shells, and the fighter's gunsight was not needed at all.

A few more months passed before FuG 202 *Lichtenstein B/C* was really ready for service use. In November the Technical Office of the RLM agreed to the delivery of the first batch of 40 sets, and ordered that the requirements of XII *Fliegerkorps* were to be met by 1 April 1942. This unrealistic schedule was typical of the Technical Office, and a shortage of personnel at Telefunken and delivery bottlenecks at sub-contractors meant that all the deadlines were missed. At the end of 1941 Kammhuber hoped soon to be able to equip fourteen Bf 110s with the FuG 202. In January it was said that deliveries would be completed by the end of August 1942, the reason being that the re-equipment centre at Diepensee had a capacity of just six aircraft a week. In fact it was not until February 1942 that the first four sets were finally installed in aircraft belonging to II/NJG 1, and several more weeks passed before they were operational. After that, however, the *Gruppe* CO, *Staffel* commanders and leading crews fell over themselves in their eagerness to use the radar-equipped aircraft.

By this time the Night Fighter Division had grown into a very large and potentially unwieldy weapon. More than ever it needed a proper ground organisation to remain operationally effective. In the meantime, it had become clear to the Luftwaffe command that, without such an organisation, the Reich Air Defence could not attain maximum effectiveness. To this end the position of *Lw.Befh.Mitte* (Luftwaffe Commander Centre) was created. As a central command authority, this officer was responsible for the air defence of the Reich from 21 March 1941. The exceptions were *Luftgaukommandos* (district air commands) VI at Munich and XII/XIII at Wiesbaden, which remained subordinated to Luftflotte 3 (*Feldmarschall* Sperrle) in France, and East Prussia. *Generaloberst* Weise was appointed *Lw.Befh.Mitte*, and among his commands was the Night Fighter Division. In the course of centralising its command structure the *NJ-Division* also took over the leadership of the few day fighter units remaining in the Reich.

Structure of the Luftwaffe night fighter force in May 1942

Commanding General of XII *Fliegerkorps* and General of Night Fighters
GenLt Kammhuber
Command post: Zeist

1. Jagddivision	2. Jagddivision	3. Jagddivision
GenMaj Döring	*GenMaj* Schwabedissen	*Oberst* Junck
Command post : Deelen	Command post : Stade	Command post : Metz
Area : Holland, North Belgium, Ruhr	Area : North-West Germany, Berlin	Area : Northern France, Southern Belgium, South-west Germany
Flying units : NJG 1	Flying units : NJG 3	Flying units : II/NJG 2, III/NJG 4
Ground units : LN Rgt 201, 211	Ground units : LN Rgt 202, 212 and 222	Ground units : LN Rgt 203, 213

On 10 August the Night Fighter Division became XII *Flieger-korps*, which had command over a new Night Fighter Division under *GenMaj* von Döring with a command post at Oldenburg, two search-light divisions, Signals Regiments 201, 202 and 203, and the day fighter units which were still in the Reich. *GenLt* Kammhuber, as commanding general of XII *Fliegerkorps*, acted at the same time as General of Night Fighters, and was therefore responsible for the further development of this arm. He was also Inspector of all night fighter units and their ground organisations.

The spread of the war through the campaigns in the Balkans and North Africa had only minor effect on night fighting; only 1./NJG 3 was taken out of the Reich defence and moved to Benghazi.

On the other hand, the beginning of the Russian campaign mar-ked a significant stage in the development of the Reich Air Defence. Despite the fact that the effective power of the Luftwaffe was reduced by the removal of the fighters, *Zerstörer* and motorised Flak, the night fighters did not feel the effects of the Russian campaign until later; but then they did so with a vengeance. First of all, from August onwards the British intensified their night attacks on the Reich. The numbers of operations flown, aircraft used and bombs dropped increased noticeably, and targets east of Berlin were raided for the first time. At the same time, however, the number of experienced crews and aircraft assigned to night fighting decreased as a result of the re-establishment or formation of new *Zerstörer* units on the Eastern Front. Until June the crews of I/ZG 2 were still divided

Einsatzgliederung der Nachtjagdverbände

Anlage 8 zu
Lw.Befh.Mitte Nr. 330 /42 g.Kdos.(I)

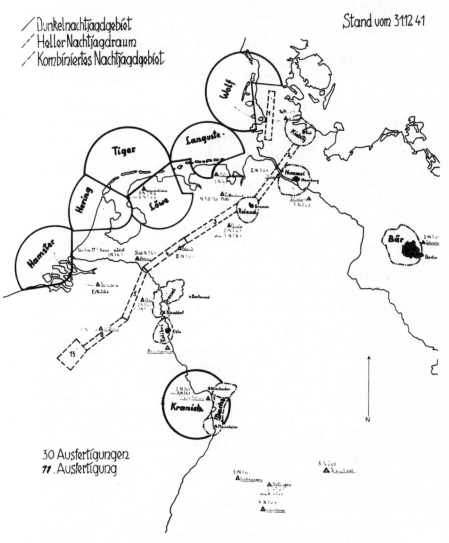

Dunkelnachtjagdgebiet
Heller Nachtjagdraum
Kombiniertes Nachtjagdgebiet

Stand vom 31.12.41

30 Ausfertigungen
11. Ausfertigung

Reproduction of an original wartime map showing the operational
deployment of the Luftwaffe night fighter formations on 31 December 1941.

between 1. and 4./NJG 2, II/ZG 26 was being retrained to become I and II/NJG 4, and II/ZG 76 was being similarly transformed into III/NJG 3. But II/NJG 3 had to be formed from the crews of two *Zerstörergänzungsstaffeln* (replacement units), and II/NJG 2 from contingents of NJG 1 and I/NJG 3. The recall to the Eastern Front in December 1941 of the first two *Gruppen* of NJG 4 (with the exception of 5.*Staffel*) as *Zerstörer* (ZG 26) was a heavy blow. This remaining *Staffel* formed the nucleus of the new II/NJG 4, which was gradually filled up with newly trained crews from the night fighter school at Schleissheim. From September 1941 onwards only two more complete formations were added to the night fighter force.[8] All other night fighter formations were made up by taking personnel from the existing *Geschwader* and topping them up with newly-trained crews.

From January 1941 to February 1942 the defensive night fighting force grew from four *Gruppen* and one *Staffel* to seven *Gruppen* and one *Staffel*, the establishment strength increasing from 195 to 367 operational aircraft (88 per cent). Effective strength only improved from 164 to 265 = 62 per cent, however, while the proportion of machines ready for action was even worse at 50 per cent.

The reasons for these disappointing figures which prevented the night fighters from achieving greater effectiveness were the collapse of Bf 110 production and the lack of other aircraft suitable for night fighting. In February 1941 123 Bf 110s left the line, but then production fell off steadily until in December only one aircraft was produced and in January 1942 none at all! It was not until March 1942 onwards that the rate topped 42. It is true that in June 1941 Göring had ordered *GenOberst* Milch to ensure a quadrupling of production for the Luftwaffe as soon as possible. But the Messerschmitt company had deceived itself and the RLM into believing that in the Me 210 they would be able to perfect an aircraft which would be superior to the Bf 110 in all respects, and had therefore concentrated all their efforts on this type. Unfortunately, the Me 210 was a complete failure. Its capricious flying characteristics meant that the Me 210 could only be flown by experienced pilots, and then only in daytime. Apart from that, the fuselage was too narrow to accommodate AI radar. It was not until late autumn 1941 – when it became clear that the Me 210 would never make a front-line aircraft, stocks of Bf 110s had been used up and the operational readiness of the night fighter and *Zerstörer* formations had fallen to a dangerous level – that Messerschmitt was requested to produce at least 42 Bf 110s a month. Even then it was four months before this target was reached.

Nor could the numbers be made up with other types. From the start it had been planned to produce only a few Do 17Z-10s and Do 215B-5s, and so there was no question of restarting their produc-

German Night Fighters—Spool 1

Flying a DFW C, *Lt* Peters and *Lt* Frohwein achieved the first German night fighting victory on 11 February 1917

Nowarra

Lt Frankl's Albatross D III

Nowarra

A flying boat night fighter: *Freiherr* von Banfield's famous A 11

Banfield

Bf 109C of IV(N)/JG 2
preparing for a night
sortie

An impostor. The He 113
'night fighters' were
actually He 100D-1s.
They never entered
Luftwaffe service but
their existence foxed
Allied intelligence
    Bundesarchiv

Part of IV(N)/JG 2
equipped with Bf
109Cs was deployed to
Trondheim and
Gardemoen in Norway
in May 1940
    (Bundesarchiv)

I/NJG 1 commissioning
ceremony at Düsseldorf.
Left to right: *Hptm* Falck,
Lt Wandam, *Oblt*
Radusch and *Lt* Frank
    Falck

The Bf 110Cs of NJG 1 initially flew in daytime *Zerstörer* camouflage. Shown here is the CO's aircraft coded G9 + GA

Falck

An adaptation of the Falck family crest, the Luftwaffe night fighter emblem came into being in August 1940

Falck

Bottom left: This variation of the night fighter emblem is displayed on *Ofw* Gildner's Bf 110

Creek

The famous German airwoman Elly Beinhorn in *Maj* Falck's Bf 110, which retained the 'Ladybird' emblem of 2./ZG 76 until 1941. Note the anti-dazzle curtains on the cabin windscreen

Falck

Top: Details for the modeller: wear and tear on the paintwork, fuselage frame numbers and white handgrips. Right and below: Before radar equipment was fitted the radio operator/gunner's station in the Bf 110 was very roomy   Autenrieth

Staff Engineer
Poppendiek with the
Spanner II infra-red
sighting device
                Hentze

Above: Do 217 dorsal
gun turret

Left: Do 217J cockpit
          Dornier

**Do 217J-2 in official
factory paint scheme
          Dornier**

The Do 217's
undercarriage failed all
too often
Zorner

Concentrated firepower
of the Do 217: four MG
151 cannon and four MG
17 machine guns
Dornier

A rare sight: Do 217J
night fighters in
formation. NJG 101,
April 1944
Heck

In 1943 most of the Do
217Ns were passed on to
II/NJG 4
Autenrieth

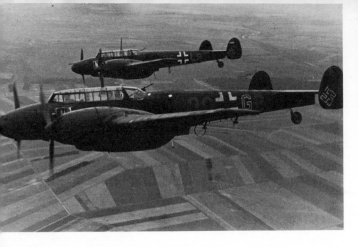

Above left: Bf 110C-4 of 7./NJG 4. 'LR', flown by *Ofw* Kollack, is seen here with 10 victory markings on its fin

Bundesarchiv

Above right: The former members of II/ZG 76 continued to decorate their aircraft with the 'shark's mouth' motif after joining the night fighter force as II/NJG 4—but their new shark had black teeth

Autenrieth

Left: Bf 110E, recognisable by the gun camera in the nose and the small apertures in the propeller spinners

Falck

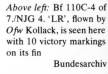

Bf 110E with elongated exhaust pipes.

(Falck)

Oblt **Kamp,**
Staffelkapitän of 7./NJG 4,
in a Bf 110F-2
Bundesarchiv

Right: The Bf 110F-4 was
recognisable by its new
propeller spinners, larger
oil coolers, muzzle
flash-suppressors and
exhaust flame-dampers
Bundesarchiv

Completely black Do
217J-2
Dornier

Above: The rarely used 2 × MK 108 oblique installation in a Bf 110G-4/U1   Nowarra·

Left: Schräge Musik from 2 × MG FF cannon in the Bf 110

Standard Equipment set *R22* (4 × MG 151) in a Do 217N   AMF Dübendorf

Bf 110G-4 of 9./NJG 3 on
a daylight operation in
summer 1943. This
particular aircraft still has
the small F-series
fin/rudder assembly
Bundesarchiv

Instrument panel (right)
and the rear MG 81Z
installation of the
Bf 110G-4

tion, while the output of the Ju 88 heavy fighter could not cover losses. Milch did not however think immediately of increasing Ju 88C production; in his opinion this aircraft was too expensive and costly for controlled night fighting. According to Milch, Kammhuber-style night fighting did not call for an aircraft with a rapid climb, high speed and long range, since if warned in time it would be awaiting the enemy at the right height and course. The Bf 110 or the Me 210 would fulfil this requirement exactly. As the Me 210 had failed, Milch reasoned the Bf 110 would have to be improved. It would then be able to serve for many more years as a standard night fighter, and Ju 88 output would only have to be stepped up to cover the losses of NJG 2.

Unconvinced, Kammhuber went on looking for a superior night fighter, and by autumn 1940 he had formulated his requirements for such a high performance aircraft: two engines, two seats (pilot and radio operator side by side), extensive glazing, and cannon armament carried in a tray under the fuselage and along the longitudinal axis of the aircraft to eliminate dazzle from the muzzle flashes. At that time there was a design on the drawing board that came near to this ideal: the He 219, which Heinkel had originally designed as a heavy fighter and reconnaissance aircraft. In 1941 Heinkel presented a modified design as a night fighter and in fact was given a development contract. However, this project had such a low priority that a prototype seemed unlikely to emerge within the next two years.

As a result, in 1941–42 the night fighter force had to make do with the Bf 110C-3, D-1, E-3 and E-4 versions, and the Ju 88C-2 and Ju 88C-4 which differed from the daytime *Zerstörer* only in that they had more radio equipment and black night camouflage. These aircraft left the factory with the standard day fighter equipment and had to be sent to the operational preparation centres at Werl and Gütersloh to be re-equipped for their role before they could be handed over to the units. NJG 2 also still had a few Do 17Z-10s and Do 215B-5s, the latter being seldom ready for action because of constant troubles with the engines.

As incursions by the RAF's four-engined bombers became more and more frequent, the night fighter units began to call for faster and better armed aircraft. The *Lw.Befh.Mitte* suggested a transitional solution, namely the fitting of DB 601N engines to the Bf 110 and the replacement of the now useless machine guns with 20 mm cannon. Apart from that the Bf 110 would be replaced by the Do 217J, which had made its first test flight at the end of 1941. Clearly miracles were expected from this powerful and well-armed machine. But when the first Do 217J-1 arrived at 4./NJG 1 in March 1942 the disappointment was general: its stalky undercarriage caused take-off and landing problems, it had insufficient reserve power and lacked manoeuvrability because of its high wing loading. As a result the Do 217J found few friends among the night fighter crews, and all hopes were pinned on the special night versions of the Bf 110 and Ju 88 which were on their way.

Correctly appreciating the weaknesses of illuminated night fighting in bad weather, *Lw.Befh.Mitte* had planned to move a quarter of the formations to the rear areas of the Reich to strengthen the *Konaja* in the autumn of 1942. In the event, this did not happen, as the prospects of success were even less than with the *Henaja*. As a result, most of the night fighters were in the Western approaches by the end of the year.

Base	Unit	Night fighting area	Gruppe CO
Schleswig	5./NJG 3	Illuminated zone 1 (HR1) *Wolf, Kiebitz*	
Stade	II/NJG 1	HR2	Ehle
Lüneburg	7./NJG 3	*Hummel*	
Wittmundhaven	5./NJG 2	*Languste*	Schoenert
Vechta	I/NJG 3	HR3, *Roland*	Knoetzsch
Leeuwarden	II/NJG 2	*Tiger, Löwe, Hering*	Lent
Deelen/Twente	*Stab*, III/NJG 1	HR4	Schön
Venlo/Hangelar	*Stab*, I/NJG 1	HR5, *Drossel, Kolibri, Hamster*	Streib
Gilze Rijen	E./NJG 2		
St Trond	1./NJG 1	HR6, 13	
Mainz-Finthen	II/NJG 3	*Kranich, Dachs*	Radusch
Werneuchen	3./NJG 3	*Bär*	

The night fighter training units were based in Southern Germany: Erg./NJG 1 at Echterdingen, III/NJG 3 at Nellingen, 8./NJG 3 at Ingolstadt and 4./NJG 4 at Laupheim.

A glance at the maps shows that once the British had broken through the dark and illuminated night fighting zones, they no longer had to fear attacks from night fighters in the greater part of Northwest and Central Germany. Many armaments centres such as Rostock, Hanover, Brunswick, Magdeburg, Kassel and Schweinfurt – to name but a few – were only protected by Flak at night.

During the summer months of 1942 with their short and light nights, *Henaja* was still the most successful operational method. From April to June the Luftwaffe in the area of *Lw.Befh.Mitte* destroyed 230 enemy aircraft, out of which the *Henaja* claimed 59, *Dunaja* 53 and *Konaja* 9. We must however take into account the fact that the successes in the dark zones were achieved with only one and a half *Staffeln* flying an average of three operational sorties per night, while the units of the illuminated night fighting force had to fly almost twice as many operations to achieve their successes.

On looking through the reports of aerial victories, combat reports and war diaries, it is noticeable that the same names appear repeatedly. For example, the first 50 victories by II/NJG I (from October 1940 to June 1941) were achieved by only sixteen pilots, of whom four could claim more than three successes each. Of course, this cannot be taken as proof that the majority of pilots were mentally and physically unsuitable for night fighting. The real cause appears to be more in the order of 'success breeds success'. The pilots who, thanks to their ability, courage, ambition[9] and luck, had managed to achieve the first kills, had several advantages over their less successful colleagues. The aces had their pick of the areas most commonly used by the enemy; *Staffelkapitäne*, *Gruppenkommandeure* and *Geschwader-kommodore* could, when it suited them, ignore the order not to fly into other night fighting zones and direct the lower-ranking pilots to wait at the radio beacons. Naturally, the successful pilots could also select the best radio operators and gunners for themselves, they were given the new aircraft first, and their mounts were specially modified for them in the operational workshops.

The result was that successful and experienced pilots could accumulate further experience which was denied to the newer crews. Of the 118 *Ritterkreuz* holders in the night fighter force, only 12 came to night fighting after July 1942, and of these nearly all had previously had extensive flying experience. The aces were therefore largely confined to the old guard, even though the night fighter force grew steadily in the last three years of the war and had an average of 90 new crews per month assigned to it from the training *Geschwader*. Regardless of the high victory figure of summer 1941 – amounting to the destruction of the equivalent of three complete RAF bomber wings – neither the leadership nor the crews were satisfied with themselves, for there was no sign of a let-up in the British raids. In fact the very opposite was the case. In 1940 the air reporting service had detected 17,498 aircraft, compared with nearly 10,000 more in 1941. On the German side, however, no one suspected how hard Bomber Command was being pressed by the Reich Air Defence. Losses on daytime operations were an unacceptable 10 per cent, and almost 7 per cent at night. And despite its highly exaggerated success reports Bomber Command was being criticised for wasting its forces on operations which were not particularly significant to the course of the war.[10] At the front there was still no indication of any impairment of the armaments industry, and on both the Eastern Front and in North Africa the German offensive continued. At this point it occurred to the British that the bombers might be better employed in disrupting supplies and in destroying Rommel's tanks. As a result

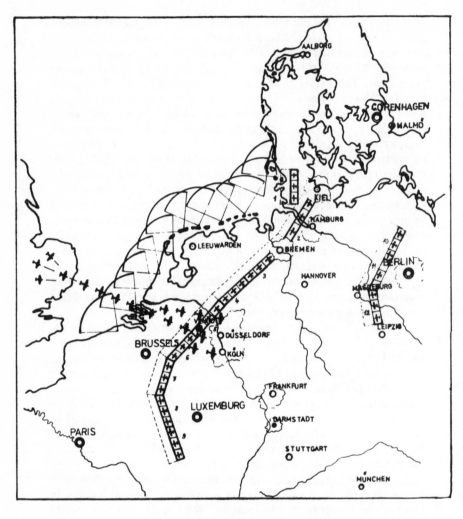

Schematic representation of a night fighting operation early in 1942

 Dark night fighting zone for *Freya-AN* operations
Illuminated night fighting zone with a forward dark night fighting zone
Combined night fighting zone

political pressure was brought to bear on the Bomber Command leadership in autumn 1941 to bomb other targets, and so the bombing raids on the Reich were temporarily cut back.

While the Luftwaffe knew nothing of these developments, the RAF for their part knew nothing of how serious a position the Reich

Air Defence, especially the night fighter force, was in. On the one hand, the widely scattered raids favoured defence by controlled night fighters. At the same time, XII *Fliegerkorps* was compelled by this very dispersion to spread the dark and illuminated night fighting zones far and wide. This over-extended the night fighter force and dissipated its strength. The northern part of the Schleswig-Holstein zone and Mecklenburg contained night fighter stations which were almost never approached by the enemy. The forces based there could therefore not be used to deepen the night fighting zones along the routes most used by the enemy.

By the end of 1941 both sides were at the limits of their capabilities. From October to the end of December 1941 the night fighters achieved only 52 victories, less than half the successes in the second quarter of the year. British losses fell to less than 4 per cent, partly as a result of a reduction in flying activity of the RAF, partly as a result of the bad weather, which hindered the night fighters and rendered the searchlights ineffective.[11] Thus only 700 illuminated night fighter sorties could be flown against the 1,065 reported RAF penetrations, and they achieved only 17 victories. The *Lw.Befh.Mitte* gave as a reason for this the fact that in the main newer crews were sent out. He also blamed the difficulties associated with the changeover to larger zones with *Würzburg-Riesen* radars which meant that only individual victories could be achieved with this complicated system. The same was true of the combined night fighting, which achieved only eight victories. The most promising method was the *Dunaja*, under which every ninth sortie resulted in a victory.

It is thus clear that the strengthening of the night fighter force, and the whole of the Reich Air Defence in general, was lagging behind the escalation of the bombing offensive against Germany. Germany *could* have built up a defensive Luftwaffe of such strength that air raids on the Reich territory would have been intolerably costly, but thus far the High Command had chosen not to do so. One possible reason is that the leadership was still labouring under the illusion that the Soviet Union would be brought to her knees in the near future and that the forces thus released could be used for the defence of the Reich.

Later in the war Bomber Command was pushed several times to the point where losses of personnel could only just be replaced, but that danger line was never crossed. The main reason for this could have been the offensive-mindedness of the Luftwaffe's leading personalities. Even in September 1945 the former *Lw.Befh.Mitte*, *GenOberst* Weise, was still saying that it would be impossible to conduct a purely defensive air war against equal or superior opponents over a long period. The fact that the British had reduced their offensive operations to a minimum during the Battle of Britain, and thus proved the opposite, had apparently never been fully absorbed by the German leadership.

In spring 1942 the prospects of the *Henaja* appeared to improve following the arrival of *Freya* radars and the improvement of co-ordination with the air raid warning system, while more favourable weather conditions were an additional bonus. From the point of view of the General of Night Fighters the situation was not unfavourable: the Bf 110F-4, Ju 88C-6 and Do 217J were soon to go into series production, air raid warning devices were being built at full speed, and the teething troubles with the *Lichtenstein* seemed to have been cured. The younger crews had gained in self-confidence, the older crews had gathered more experience, and the losses of the previous winter had – contrary to all expectations – remained within reason, and had been completely made up with new crews from the night fighter training school. Thus, in February the *Gruppen* had more flying personnel than aircraft at their disposal for the first time. If the British had stuck to their method of individual attacks, the night fighters could certainly have dealt Bomber Command some fatal blows in the summer of 1942.

Special mention should be made of the night fighter units which took part in Operation *Donnerkeil* (Thunderbolt), the breakthrough of the Brest naval force (comprising *Scharnhorst*, *Gneisenau* and *Prinz Eugen*) to Wilhelmshaven and Kiel between 11–13 February 1942.[12] This operation only had a chance of success if the airspace above the ships was secured day and night. The night fighters of II/NJG 2 and II/NJG 3 took over this task from nightfall to two hours past daybreak. The ships left Brest on 11 February at 2000 hrs without air support in order not to alert the British early warning system. It was not until the next morning between 0800 and 1100 hrs that 19 Ju 88s and Bf 110s began to guard the naval formation without seeking air combat with the British. The RAF did not begin its attacks until 1334 hrs. From 1730 hrs eight more night fighters which had taken off from Coxyde airfield in Belgium joined in the air fighting; the next wave of night fighters positioned themselves over the ships when they reached Ymuiden near Amsterdam. During the night the RAF attacks decreased in number, and even the German night fighters stayed away because of the bad weather conditions. It was not until 13 February that day and night fighters (the latter from II/NJG 3) once again secured the airspace around Wangerooge. The *Scharnhorst* entered Wilhelmshaven and the other ships, safely guarded by the Luftwaffe, sailed on to Kiel.

But though this setback was a blow to British prestige, the RAF had used the winter months profitably. Little troubled by the increasingly rare German bombing raids and freed from the attentions of long-range fighters, British industry was able to produce its heavy bombers and the RAF to carry out its training programme. Great emphasis was placed on the development of the VHF navigation devices to operational standard. On 14 February 1942 the British War Cabinet decided on an intensified bombing offensive, initially limited to six months. On 20 February Air Marshal Sir Arthur Harris was made Commander-in-Chief of Bomber Command. These two developments marked a fundamental change in the conduct of British air war. The German armament industry was now to be weakened by robbing the working population of their homes and by 'carpet bombing' of inner cities. This aim could only be achieved by massed attacks within a limited time. RAF pilots expressed the fear that Bomber Command would have to suffer losses as high as those recorded in daytime operations in the first years of the war. Up to this time many British bomber pilots had believed that the only reason they were not shot down by German night fighters was that they constantly changed their approach flight paths; in this they were to a degree correct. In the meantime, the British radio monitoring service had recognised the fundamental principle behind the German controlled night fighting. Armed with this information, Harris concluded that by flying many aircraft closely spaced so that they dropped their bombs within the shortest possible time, the German defences could be penetrated with a perfectly tolerable level of losses.

The first operation, based on this tactic and intended to destroy a town centre, was flown on 29 March 1942, when 191 bombers attacked Lübeck.[13] With a narrow front and in tight formation, the RAF force flew over Denmark. Touching the *Wolf* dark night fighting zone and illuminated zone No 1 only at their northernmost edges, they attacked the town in several waves for three hours. During this raid the night fighters and Flak destroyed 12 bombers (5 per cent). In the nights between 24 and 27 April Rostock suffered the same fate when a total of 468 bombers unloaded their deadly cargoes onto the historic town centre. The night fighter corps could get no more than eight fighters into contact with the enemy, and they shot down just 13 raiders (during the second attack they managed only two). The German military leadership reacted in a completely helpless manner: instead of doing something to strengthen their defences, they gathered together a few bomber units and ordered them to destroy historic English towns such as Exeter, Bath, Norwich, and Canterbury. Having carried out these 'Baedeker raids', named after a popular pre-war tourist guide book, the Luftwaffe once more withdrew from the British skies, redeploying the bombers to the Eastern Front. How deeply the attacks on Lübeck and Rostock had affected the political leadership of the Third Reich is evident from the fact that they were not reported in the papers until two days later, and then only in a few lines. To the people responsible for the Reich Air Defence these attacks were no more than a 'disturbance of their sleep'; the rude awakening was not to come until the next full moon.

Hitler's October 1941 order to stop long-range night fighter operations came as a complete surprise to the units concerned, who saw it as absolute nonsense. The crews had only just gathered the experience necessary for their difficult task, and had learned their hunting ground inside out. In summer their successes had climbed steeply, and at the time of the order they were the most successful night fighter *Gruppe* of all: 144 kills, 30 probables and 222 air combats whose outcome could not be seen. They had destroyed 52 aircraft on the ground, with another 58 probables, and they had attacked air bases and other targets, dropping 440 tons of bombs.[14]

General Kamhuber and the CO of I/NJG 2, *Hptm* Hülshoff, had expected much of the Do 217J in this area, mainly because of its greater depth of penetration, and the industry was working on a new fighting device that guaranteed wide ranging detection even at low altitude. But the order of October 1941 put an end to that, and the field of long-range night fighting over enemy territory was left open to the British. It was proposed at various times later that long-range night fighting should be taken up again, but it never came to more than a few individual raids which had no lasting effect on the enemy. Nevertheless, the 'old hands' found it hard to give up long-range night fighting operations. For example, *Ofw* Bussmann, who had been transferred to II/NJG 2, 'just flew quickly over there' on 7 November to shoot up a few airfields. On 30 June 1942 he single-handedly loaded his Ju 88 with bombs, left the *Hering* dark night fighting zone on his own initiative and attached himself to some returning British aircraft. He shot down one of the bombers over the North Sea and mingled with the homecoming aircraft over their airfield before spoiling their landing with his bombs.

Kammhuber then hoped to be able to use the experienced *Gruppe* in the *Dunaja*, but could not put his ideas into practice. Instead, the *Gruppe* was transferred to the Mediterranean war zone to replace the unsuccessful 1./NJG 3 (commanded by *Hptm* Peter). This unit had been ordered to Benghazi in May 1941. In all fairness it must be pointed out that the men of 1./NJG 3 never got around to any night fighting, constantly having to fly 'fire brigade' operations or ground support or reconnaissance tasks.

In November 1941 I/NJG 2 transferred to Catania. On 17 November 2.*Staffel* under *Hptm* Harmstorff flew to Benghazi with six Ju 88C-2s and C-4s, and at the end of the month 1./NJG 3 transferred back to Germany.

The former long-range night fighters suffered much the same fate as the relieved *Staffel*, being 'burned up' in all sorts of tasks. They flew long-range night fighter/intruder sorties over Malta and unguided night interceptions over North Africa, Sicily and Crete. Their aircraft had to circle at night for hours over convoy escorts, and there were submarine hunting, daytime operations and transport aircraft escort duties. The number of night kills was consequently small, and the losses that much higher. As a result of the constant demands and the difficulty of obtaining replacements (not a single Ju 88C was produced from May to October), by February 1942 the *Gruppe* had only ten aircraft at its disposal, of which no more than about six were ready for operations. In order to support the weakened *Gruppe* in their nocturnal 'convoy circling', selected crews of III/ZG 26 stepped in, some of them flying the Do 17Z-3s.

Up to this time it had been felt that there was no need to form a night fighter force to defend East Prussia and the Eastern Front. Although Soviet bombers repeatedly raided various targets in East Prussia, and even in the Berlin area, no defensive measures were taken initially because the authorities continued to insist that the Soviets had no long-range bomber arm. Fortunately, the training level of the Soviet bomber pilots was so low that they did hardly any damage. In addition to several bombers shot down by the Flak, documentary evidence also confirms a night kill by *Lt* Altendorf of 3./NJG 3 on 20 October 1941.

On the Eastern Front, the Luftwaffe had complete control of the air during the first few months of this campaign. However, as the resistance of the Red Army stiffened in winter 1941–42, so the Soviet Air Force also became more involved in the battles. Night after night hundreds of ground support aircraft, transporters and bombers flew into the German occupied area to raid base installations, set down or supply partisans and to attack airfields. But, just like the Home Defence Flak in Germany, the fixed local air defences did not manage to discourage the enemy from coming back again. Some fighters and *Zerstörer* then tried 'free' night fighting operations by moonlight. Various pilots from JG 54 around Leningrad were especially outstanding in these operations.[15] Even the He 111 crews of KG 53 attacked the unwieldy TB-3 bombers which circled their bases at night.

Notes

1 The first Stirling was shot down on 9/10 April by *Fw* Scherfling of 7./NJG 1, the first Manchester on 13 April 1941 by *Fw* Hohn of 3./NJG 2, and the first Halifax on 23/24 June 1941 by *Oblt* Eckhardt of NJG 1.

2 The lack of IFF capability meant that the ground radar often lost the fighters, which had to return to standby positions in order to be spotted and identified again. This also happened after each interception. This deficiency was not eliminated until the introduction of the airborne FuG 25a *Erstling* in 1942.

3 Not that *Würzburg-D* was very precise: given a target 80 km away, the accuracy of the elevation measurement could vary by as much as ± 250 m (820 ft).

4 VHF direction-finding installations guiding night fighters to the nearest airfield.

5 Comparative figures 1 October – 31 December 1941
   Dunaja: 235 operational sorties, 27 victories
   Henaja: 700 operational sorties, 17 victories
   Konaja: , 8 victories

6 On the other hand, co-operation with the Navy Flak could be described as almost ideal, and the night fighter crews were unanimous in their praise of the extraordinarily precise and disciplined shooting of the batteries of *Marine-Flak-Brigade I* in the *Kiebitz* area (around Kiel).

7 With German-speaking 'fighter control officers' already during 1941.

8 In December 1942 II/ZG 2 became I/NJG 5, and in early 1944 III/KG 3 became I/NJG 7.

9 One not to be underestimated encouragement was the award of higher than average decorations after only a few night victories.

10 According to British calculations, there was a fall-off in German arms production of 20 per cent; in reality it was less than 1 per cent. Of the 10,000 high-explosive and 5,900 incendiary bombs dropped between October and December 1941, almost half fell on open ground and a further 17 per cent on decoy installations.

11 *RAF penetrations   Night fighter victories*

	RAF penetrations	Night fighter victories
October	1,181	21
November	658	21
December	534	10

12 For these operations the night fighters were temporarily repainted in day colours and the Bf 110s took on a third crew member for the first time.

13 The *Gee* precision navigation method, similar in principle to the German *Knickebein*, was first used on 18 March 1942 during an attack on Essen.

14 The Luftwaffe officials regularly doubted these long-range victory reports, as the only witnesses were the pilots' own crew members.

15 *Hptm* Seiler 16 night victories, *Lt* Heyer 6, *Oblt* Fink 9, *Lt* Leykauf 8 (6 on 22.6.42), *Oblt* Dr Feise 2.

5. Battle against the bomber streams
   May 1942–July 1943

Reorganisation of XII Fliegerkorps *in three fighter divisions – The 1,000-bomber raids – Expansion of the night fighter barrier – Withdrawl of search-light divisions and intensified development of dark night fighting – Creation of the* Himmelbett *method – Kammhuber's demand for the expansion of controlled night fighting – Formation of new flying units – Partition of 2* Jagddivision *in February 1943 – Kammhuber's demand for strengthening of the night fighter force in May 1943 – Activation of JG 300 – Night fighter operations in East Prussia – Building up of a night fighter force in the East – Aircraft developments – Oblique weapons – The high frequency war – Stagnation of radar research in Germany – The Y-procedure,* Lichtenstein *and SN-2 wide-angle AI radar – British jamming measures – Successes of the German night fighting force – British air offensive on the Ruhr – New ways of achieving air superiority by night: Y-procedure, the 'Wild Boars' and pursuit night fighting – Fight against the Mosquitoes – Daytime operations by night fighters over the Reich – Night fighter operations in the Mediterranean area and on the Eastern Front.*

GENERAL EVENTS OF THE WAR

May 1942: German summer offensive in the East. *June:* Rommel reaches El Alamein. High point of U-boat successes in the Atlantic. *September:* German 6th Army enters Stalingrad. *November:* American and British forces land in Morocco and Algeria. Montgomery breaks through the German lines at El Alamein. German troops occupy Vichy France and Tunisia. The Red Army surrounds the 6th Army at Stalingrad. *February 1943:* The 6th Army capitulates. The *Afrika Korps* is surrounded in Tunisia and capitulates on 13 May. *10 July:* The Allies land in Sicily.

On 1 May 1942 XII *Fliegerkorps* was reorganised and the existing unwieldy Night Fighter Division was divided into three Fighter Divisions. But Kammhuber did not intend this to mean any diffusion of the chain of command. As before, the night fighter zone commanders received their operational orders direct from the *Korps* command post. Kammhuber was rightly of the opinion that a valid appreciation of the air situation could only be achieved when all the reports from the visual/sound observers and the radar sites came together in a central command post. Even if some individual devices failed or were interfered with, a unified air situation could still be established, the enemy's intentions recognised and main defence points organised.[1]

The formation of the new divisions thus happened more for organisational and administrational reasons. After the command posts were fully equipped with telecommunication installations, operations were also led from these locations.

At the same time as the *Korps* was being reorganised, the *Geschwader* were also being finally assigned to definite operational areas, putting an end to the frequent transfers. Frequent changes of operational area were even more detrimental to operational readiness and combat success in night fighting than in day fighting, obliging the pilots and fighter control officer to build up their hard-won operational support all over again.

The new divisional staffs had been in existence for exactly four weeks and were not yet completely operational when the catastrophic massed raid on Cologne took place. On the night of 30/31 May 1,042 bombers took off from Britain, of which over 900 reached the target over the city centre, picked out with flare markers, and every six seconds a bomber dropped its deadly load. The commander-in-chief of Bomber Command had brought together all his forces, even the training units, for this operation in order to demonstrate that a large-scale raid, closely concentrated in time, would inevitably result in increased destruction in the target area and fewer losses among the bombers. His calculations proved correct: he had reckoned on 50 losses but only 44 aircraft did not return to base. Of these, 37 were shot down by the Flak and night fighters, while a further seven damaged bombers broke up on the return flight.[2]

Though the night fighters had shot down more aircraft than ever before in this air battle, the score was of little importance in comparison with the numbers of the attackers. Instead, it clearly showed the limits of controlled night fighting. In this raid, which penetrated German airspace on a front barely 30 km (18.6 mls) wide, no more than eight night fighting zones were touched and only 25 night fighters were guided towards the enemy. The defenders' task was made more difficult by the fact that about 10 per cent of the night fighters which took off aborted due to technical defects or enemy defensive fire. It then took a long time before a replacement machine could be placed in the affected night fighting zone. After that night there were distinct feelings of dissatisfaction with the leadership among the night fighter pilots. After all, hundreds of pilots and radio operators had had to sit helplessly in their aircraft or in command posts and watch the catastrophe without being able to intervene. Many of these men wanted to know why it was not possible to form main defence points in the same way as against daytime attacks, and for the first time the subject of 'free' night fighting came up in mess-room discussions. However, the technical and control facilities needed for this method of operation were not yet available.

Understandably, Kammhuber feared that switching his reasonably well trained organisation to different tactics (which would at the same time have necessitated fundamental changes in equipment) would adversely affect the striking power of the night fighter force, and for him there was only one solution: the development of the existing system to the limits of its capabilities. He decided to extend the illuminated barrier as far as Jutland and the Swiss border to prevent the enemy from flying round it. A 200 km (124 mls) deep dark night fighting zone was to be set up in front of and behind the illuminated belt, and in it the bomber streams would be destroyed.

While the staffs were still working on their memoranda and preparing assessments of manpower and material needs, the RAF carried out its next massed raids. Essen was attacked with 800 bombers only 26 hours after Cologne; and the defences shot down 37 aircraft. On 25/26 June, the next full moon night, Bremen was the target of the third and (for the time being) last 1,000-bomber raid. A total of 52 aircraft of this formation were destroyed, a real success in view of the fact that the bomber stream had flown through significantly fewer night fighting zones than on previous massed raids.[3]

XII *Fliegerkorps* attributed the relatively high number of kills to the effectiveness of dark night fighting and the fact that many of the aircraft were equipped with AI radar. In so saying the *Korps* did itself a great disservice: it was concluded that the fighters could operate without support, so that the searchlight divisions were disbanded from 31 July and the Flak batteries redeployed to the belts around the towns. It has often been maintained that this was a blow from which the night fighter force took several months to recover. This is an overstatement. For one thing, the illuminated belts had long had closely spaced radar sites which helped to guide the night fighters to dark interceptions. In addition, not a few of the leading crews had looked on the searchlights as a doubtful location aid since the introduction of airborne radar, and they saw the changeover to purely dark night fighting as progress. After the withdrawal of the searchlights Kammhuber left the ground radars in their former places, even though their range would have allowed for wider deployment. One *Würzburg-Riese* ('Red Giant') at each station detected and acquired the enemy; the other ('Green Giant') took the bearings of the fighter, and both vectors were transmitted to the *Seeburg* plotting table. Acting on the information displayed on the tables, the fighter control officers would then guide the night fighters to the enemy. This procedure became known as the *Himmelbett* method.

Himmelbett had three basic disadvantages. For one thing, only one fighter could be controlled in each night fighting zone. Certainly, it was possible to send three aircraft from the control posts into one zone, for the *Himmelbett* zones overlapped each other by 50 per cent, but then the two outer zones would be unoccupied. Furthermore, if one fighter dropped out, it took some time before the replacement aircraft arrived on station. For a long time the *Korps* command resisted the suggestion from the flying crews that a second, unguided fighter should be allowed to circle the radio beacon in the night fighting zone, as they were afraid that the presence of two fighters would confuse the ground radar operators. The last disadvantage was that the fighter had to return to the radio beacon after each attack in order to be picked up by the 'Green Giant'. The fighters still did not have a system that would show them to be friendly (IFF), and this was the only way of identifying them.

The method was even more cumbersome when an inept ground radar crew lost the fighter during an interception and could not find it again amongst the multitude of target eihoes on their screens. The resulting chorus of 'Return to the little screw' (code for secondary radio beacon) was not eliminated until the introduction of the FuG 25a *Erstling* IFF.

On the whole, *Himmelbett* night fighting without AI radar was a matter of considerable luck. At longer ranges the difference between the altitude measurements of the two 'Giants' could be as much as 500 m (1,640 ft), while errors in reading the radar data and in their transmission could exaggerate the mistakes still more. Pilots often did not have a target in their field of vision at all, even when the red and green dots covered each other on the *Seeburg* table! Such abortive operations also happened in experienced *Himmelbett* zones.

Lichtenstein production was delayed by various setbacks and it was not until mid-1942 that the system reached the units in significant numbers. They were allocated according to a definite pattern: I and II/NJG 1 and II/NJG 2 received preferential treatment, while at first only the commanding personnel of NJG 3 were given the AI radar. The NJG 4 units stationed in the south fared even worse, and the training formations at first had to do completely without. However, once *Lichtenstein B/C* was available in large enough numbers the success rate increased so sharply that the night fighter crews soon got over the loss of searchlights.

These successes in the closely 'boxed' zones of the former illuminated belt prompted the night fighter command to reorganise other dark night fighting zones in a similar way and so to cover the whole approach to the Reich, the main 'bomber lanes' and the most important defensive areas with a dense network of *Himmelbett* positions. No gap would be left anywhere, and the enemy was to be ceaselessly attacked throughout his approach and return flight. However, even then the enemy could only be significantly weakened on deeper penetration flights into the Reich. Only a few fighters could be sent out against massed raids on targets near the coast, such as Hamburg and Bremen; even in attacks on the Ruhr hardly more than 20 aircraft would have been able to occupy the *Himmelbett* zones, always provided that no ground radar installation dropped out due to technical faults.

Seeking to realise his plans, Kammhuber demanded the delivery of 600 *Würzburg-Riesen* by September 1942[4] and the expansion of his flying units to eight night fighter *Geschwader* and 150,000 extra men. He also demanded the replacement of *Würzburg-Riesen* by the *Panorama* radar with a range of 150 km (93 mls), and that *Lichtenstein* be replaced by a wide-angle AI radar with greater acquisition range. However excessive these demands may have appeared at the time, they could have been met if the higher command had recognised in time the importance of the Reich Air Defence, and had made appropriate demands of the laboratories and factories. At the time, however, Kammhuber's demands seemed so utopian to Göring and Jeschonnek that they flatly refused. But Kammhuber and his operations officer, *Oberst* Hoffmann, were not so easily put off. If the Luftwaffe could do nothing about the lack of personnel in the command posts and on the radar sites, then the organisations of the Nazi Party, the SS, the SA, the Reich Youth Organisation and the Reich Labour Service would have to be brought in. In this way thousands of male and female Signals auxiliaries were gathered together under Luftwaffe command. By August 1942 the number of operational night fighting stations had grown to 96, with as many Luftwaffe Signals companies, while some 30,000 male and female Signals auxiliaries were serving with the night fighter force. In other words, each operational night fighter sortie required no fewer than 140 Signals personnel. In January 1943 the number of Luftwaffe Signals staff had grown to a strength of almost 40,000, of which 14,000 were female auxiliaries.

The flying formations also multiplied. At the end of 1942 there were five *Geschwader* with 15 *Gruppen* (of which some were of only *Staffel* strength); in June 1943 the strength had grown to six operational and one training *Geschwader*, with a total of 22 *Gruppen*, of which 18 were within the Reich.[5] NJG 2 was stationed mainly in the Mediterranean area, IV/NJG 5 was to transfer to the Eastern Front and IV/NJG 6 was under the command of *Lw.Befh.Südost* (Luftwaffe Commander South-east).

The last great organisational measure to be carried out at this time was the splitting of 2 *Jagddivision* in February 1943 into 2 and 4 *JDivisionen*. The defence zone of the new 2 *JDiv* covered North-west

Lower Saxony, Schleswig-Holstein and Denmark, while East Lower Saxony, Mecklenburg, Brandenburg, Saxony and Thuringia made up the area covered by 4 *JDiv*, commanded from Döberitz. In December 1942 the only flying unit at its disposal was the newly established II/NJG 5 (*Hptm* Schoenert), stationed at Parchim. In February the I, II and IV *Gruppen* also became operational, completing NJG 5; their bases were Stendal, Neuruppin and Döberitz.

One curious fact is worth noting in passing. Of the 28 airfields in the area covered by the four fighter divisions, most were not suitable for night landing. Thus the Ju 88s of IV/NJG 5 would take off from Döberitz, land at night at Staaken and transfer back to Döberitz by day.

Jafü Süd (Fighter Leader South), which later became the 5 *Jagddivision*, was also formed at this time. This formation was not under the command of the *Lw. Befh. Mitte*, but that of Luftflotte 3 in Paris! The *Jafü Süd* area contained the sections of NJG 4 stationed at Mainz-Finthen, as well as the operational units of the night fighter training school, which became NJG 101 after 23 March.

In May 1943 Kammhuber once again made a vain attempt to strengthen the night fighter organisation. This step was prompted by Germany's declaration of war on the USA, and the transfer of US Eighth Air Force to Britain, whence it first attacked targets in Western France on 17 August 1942. At the Casablanca Conference in January 1943 the Allies had established directives for the air war against Germany and had agreed that the USAAF would fly daytime raids and the RAF would continue with night raids. The American Boeing B-17s raided a German city for the first time on 27 January 1943, when the harbours of Wilhelmshaven were their target. This marked the opening of a new phase in the air war against Germany. Naturally the OKW could not have known that the USA would restrict itself to daytime raids, regardless of high losses, and it was assumed that the USAAF might begin night raids as well.

At first the Luftwaffe wanted to stop the American deployment by recommencing long-range night fighting, and in September 1942 I/NJG 2 was transferred back to Holland with orders to start long-range operations. But then this task was handed to the bomber formations of *Angriffsführer England*, *Oberst* Peltz, and I/NJG 2 moved back to Sicily between November 1942 and January 1943, even though Peltz did not have at his disposal a single aircraft which was suitable for long-range night fighting. Nothing could be done with the Ju 88 and Do 217 bombers; the re-equipping of KG 51 with Me 410s was not to take place until summer 1943 and, besides, Peltz considered the Me 410 unsuitable because of its short range. Instead, he wanted the He 219. So there was no more long-range night fighter activity over Britain, the nearest to this being the long-range pursuit of returning bombers over the North Sea by regular night fighter *Gruppen*.

The feared American contribution to the night raids, the abandonment of long-range night fighting, and the OKW's assessments of Allied air power, caused Kammhuber to present a memorandum in May 1943 outlining an enormous strengthening of the night fighter arm. He suggested forming a force on the lines of RAF Fighter Command and consisting of 3 *Jagdkorps*, each of 2 fighter divisions, each of 3 night fighter *Geschwader*, each of 4 night fighter *Gruppen*, each of 30 aircraft. This implied the creation of 18 *Geschwader* with a total of 2,160 aircraft at a time when the night fighter force consisted of about 500 operational machines.

On 21 May Kammhuber succeeded in obtaining Göring's unqualified agreement. Four days later Kammhuber reported to Hitler in the presence of Keitel and Göring.[6] Hitler did not even let Kammhuber finish speaking, declared the information about Allied air strength to be absolutely wrong and referred to his own experiences of German armament which in his opinion was far superior to the enemy's. According to Hitler, Kammhuber's suggestions would only be logical if the figures for Allied strength were correct. But since these were not accurate, a strengthening of the defences was not urgent. The defences were completely in order, and the victory figures of the night fighter force so high that they would not lose their deterrent effect. With that, Kammhuber's proposal was turned down. Göring and Keitel had sat there completely speechless, and had not dared to point out that the OKW data were in fact completely accurate.

Kammhuber then had to suffer Göring's criticism that he had put him in an impossible position with Hitler. The *Reichsmarschall* visibly lost control and finally shouted: 'You are a megalomaniac, you want to have the whole Luftwaffe, why don't you sit right down in my chair?' Ultimately the OKW report was withdrawn and replaced with one showing smaller figures.

On 26 May Forces Radio Calais[7] reported 'The *Wurzlsepp* has handed in a suggestion for strengthening the fighter defences and has been thrown out by Hitler as a megalomaniac.' After this, Kammhuber's star began to fall, and his decline became especially noticeable during the formation of the 'Wild Boar' night fighter force. At the beginning of 1943 *Major* Hajo Hermann, a former bomber pilot and then adviser to the Luftwaffe Command, had suggested the introduction of unguided single-engined night fighters in addition to the *Himmelbett* method. The suggestion was turned down at first, but on 8 April, when the British offensive against the Ruhr was reaching its peak, Hermann once more presented it to *Lw.Befh.Mitte*, who this time gave him permission to form an experimental detachment of four aircraft to test his tactics over Berlin. On 27 June Hermann presented his ideas to Göring on the Obersalzberg. He supported his idea by pointing out that in controlled night fighting only a limited number of fighters could be brought to bear on the enemy and that they could only be acceptably effective against scattered raiders. When used against raids that were tightly massed in time and space, they could achieve only a limited number of kills because the concentration of bombers over the target was not faced by a corresponding concentration of defending fighters. The simplest way to achieve that would be to allow unguided night fighters to fly in the light from the searchlights, over the searchlight and Flak zones of the Ruhr or other conurbations.

Hermann brought up several reasons why this tactic was likely to be successful. Since the disbandment of the searchlight divisions the bombers were being faced by a mass of searchlights around their targets, so that in the raids on the Ruhr up to 100 bombers were caught in the lights. There would therefore be enough time for several attacks on the bombers. When there was heavy cloud cover which could not be penetrated by the searchlights, it would be possible to illuminate the clouds with parachute flares so that the enemy bomber would show up like 'flies on a lighted ground-glass screen'.[8]

Compared with the Bf 109Es used two years previously by the single-engined experimental night fighter *Staffel* at Cologne, the Bf 109G-4 and FW 190A-4 carried much better instrumentation and could be used at night without much difficulty by pilots experienced in blind flying. Such pilots – blind-flying instructors, and former bomber and transport pilots being employed on flying duties for various staffs – were available in sufficient numbers in the Reich. In Hermann's opinion there was no need for great numbers of additional aircraft, as day fighters would do just as well. These aircraft would not even need to be transferred, for, thanks to the efficient early warning system and the high speed of the single-engined fighters, such a night fighter formation could always appear over the objective on time.

Hermann's criticism of the existing system was very much to the point. But what won the day for the new method was Göring's and Jeschonnek's vision of a large British bomber formation – already missing a few of its numbers, lost on the approach flight – being savaged by a hundred or more fighters over the target. The Flak would surely score additional hits, and the disintegrating formation would then meet its Waterloo on the return flight through the *Himmelbett* zones. That was the solution!

Hermann received permission to develop his experimental detachment further. After the first operation from Hangelar, when the unit shot down four four-engined bombers and reported 17 engagements on the night of 3/4 July, Hermann was ordered to form a complete *Geschwader*. Meanwhile, Kammhuber was left to cry in the wilderness.

In dealing with the build-up of the night fighter force mention should be made of the formation of units in the eastern part of the Reich and on the Eastern Front.

From summer 1941 onwards the Soviets had been raiding East Prussia in moonlit nights with twin and four-engined bombers. At first these attacks were carried out by handfuls of aircraft which dropped their bombs blindly without causing much damage. But, if only for propaganda reasons, aircraft of the Red Air Force simply could not be allowed to fly around unmolested over German territory. So in June 1942 a detachment of NJG 5 under *Oblt* Lechner was transferred to Dammgarten and Labiau, where, in co-operation with a rail-mounted ground radar station codenamed *Sumatra I*, it attempted to put a stop to the Soviet incursions. No precise details of their activities are known, and only two night kills, achieved by Lechner on 18 August, have been substantiated. The mobile radar station belonged to the *LN-Flugmeldeabteilung(E) z.b.V.*21 (Luftwaffe Signals Service Special Air Reporting Detachment, railway-mounted). Each of its companies had the use of a train consisting of a radar installation (one *Freya* and two *Würzburg* sets), an evaluation section, workrooms, generator wagon and accommodation wagons. Nine of these radar-equipped trains, coded *Sumatra*, *Java* and *Borneo I-III*, had entered service by summer 1943.[9]

On the Eastern Front the Soviet pilots were not at all deterred by the Flak or the improvised night fighting efforts of individual crews. Night after night light bombers and harassing aircraft would appear over German positions, supply lines and bases. Still more worrying was the use of Soviet aircraft to land partisans behind the German lines. The transfer of 2./NJG 3 under *Hptm* Böhmel to the Smolensk area during February–March 1942 gave only temporary relief because the unit had to return to the Reich Air Defence. When the calls for help could no longer be ignored, Kammhuber authorised Falck, his Operations Officer, to find a solution to the problem. Falck accordingly travelled along the whole Eastern Front in August 1942 before making his recommendations. He concluded that as the present supply of personnel and material was only just sufficient to maintain the operational readiness of the Reich Air Defence, a transfer of night fighter units to the Eastern Front was out of the question. Consequently, the local Luftwaffe formations would have to organise their own, either by retraining and re-equipping individual *Zerstörer Staffeln* or by giving special training to pilots who had already gained experience in air combat at night and then re-equipping their aircraft accordingly. It would also be possible to adapt slow but manoeuvrable aircraft for use against the Soviet night harassment aircraft, the obsolete U-2 (Po-2) biplanes. The most suitable German aircraft available in sufficient numbers would be the FW 58.

As a result of Falck's fact finding tour the Eastern Front Luftwaffe Command was ordered to begin 'auxiliary' night fighting operations in the Poltava area on 6 October. The successful crews from the various bomber, reconnaissance and *Zerstörer* units were ordered to Wiener Neustadt for night fighter training, and their aircraft were also adapted there; these often bizarre-looking machines will be dealt with later.

The training phase was completed by 10 November and the Luftwaffe High Command ordered the activation of five *NJ-Schwärmen* within Luftflotten 1 and 4 and *Luftwaffen-Kommandos Don* and *Ost*. In addition, 10. and 12./ZG 1 were also ordered to fly night fighting operations. However, the crews were hardly back at the front when the Soviet forces broke through the German lines near Stalingrad and Donets, and even Vyasma-bend had to be evacuated. Hardly any of the designated aircraft took part in night fighting operations: the auxiliary night fighters were used up in ground support operations and low-level attacks on Soviet supply columns and railways, and personnel of 2.*Schwarm* of Luftflotte 4 had to blow up their aircraft as Soviet tanks approached their airfield. The surviving aircraft were reassigned on 18 January 1943 to the railway *Jagdstaffeln* of the bomber *Geschwader* and the auxiliary night fighter force was disbanded only a few weeks after its creation. When the front stabilised once more in February the auxiliary night fighters reappeared in limited numbers, the three *NJ-Schwärme* of Luftflotte 1 and *LwKdos Don* and *Ost* together mustering six He 111s, one Ju 88C-6 and one Bf 110. The situation did not improve until April, when the Luftflotten had 28 aircraft operational. At the end of May the General of Night Fighters sent some experienced pilots to the east in order to help the auxiliary units to operate more effectively.

In spring 1943 the Eastern Front developed a broad westerly curve at Kursk and a concentration of strong Soviet forces pointed to a big offensive at this point. To pre-empt this, in June 1943 Hitler ordered a massive pincer operation (code-named *Zitadelle*) to straighten the front and surround the Soviet forces that had pushed to the west. These measures did not remain concealed from the Soviets, whose air force tried hard to disrupt the German preparations. At the start of the operation the German command had to reckon with massed

Soviet raids at night. But the *NNJ-Schwarm* of Luftflotte 6, with just three operational aircraft, was much too weak for this task and Kammhuber was therefore ordered on 26 June to transfer a regular night fighter *Gruppe* into this area. The only available formation was IV/NJG 5 under *Hptm* Prince zu Sayn-Wittgenstein, which had also already gained experience in fighting Soviet bombers, and in the last days of June this unit transferred to the airfields at Bryansk and Orel. *Himmelbett* units took over five of the nine available ground radar trains. When, at the end of July, the German offensive broke down, IV/NJG 5 was kept on in the east because of its extraordinary successes. Divided up into several *Schwärme*, it flew in the night fighter zones between Smolensk and Bryansk (Luftflotte 6 area) and near Poltava and Stalino (under Luftflotte 4). The command could not as yet do without the auxiliary night fighters, however, and Luftflotte 1 in the north and Luftflotte 4 in the south operated one *Schwarm* each; in addition there was 10.(N)/ZG1. Co-ordination of the flying formations and their control posts was taken over by the newly formed *Aussenstelle Ost des Gen.d.NJ* (External Command Post East of the General of Night Fighters); this centre was for some reason not made responsible for the auxiliary night fighters.

The successes of the night fighters could have been greater if the *Gruppen* had had anything like their full complement of aircraft. In the summer of 1942 their actual strength was 60 per cent of establishment, and of those only 65 per cent were operational.[10]

The consequences of the temporary drop in Bf 110 production were still significant. The stop-gap Do 217J did not reach the operational units in large numbers until the end of May, when the Bf 110 crisis had been solved and the type was once again available in sufficient numbers. The aces looked on the Do 217 as 'an absolute monster', and of the successful pilots only *Hptm* Schoenert, CO of 3./NJG 3, was able to get on with this type. Naturally enough, it was the newly trained or less successful crews who had to make do with the Do 217, for, apart from its extraordinarily powerful armament, the Do 217J-1 lacked everything required of a successful fighter. The factory had made things easy for itself by simply replacing the glazed nose with a unit housing fixed armament and by installing a 300 l (66 Imp gal) tank in the forward bomb bay. Everything else was left as in the standard Do 217E-2 bomber. Thus, this 'night fighter' carried a rubber dinghy and armour plating, bomb-release equipment and bomb-bay doors, dive brakes and dorsal and ventral gun positions – all completely useless in its new role. In fact, because of the heavy nose armament the J-1 weighed 0.75 tons (1,653 lb) more than the Do 217E-2 bomber! The installation of the FuG 202 AI radar pushed the weight up even more. The resulting excessive take-off weight – exacerbated by the lower efficiency of the engines due to the fitting of exhaust flame dampers and the drag created by the *Lichtenstein* antennae – made the Do 217J-2 into a real 'tired crow' which was of no use for night fighting. Maximum speed at optimum height was 430 km/h (267 mph) (E-2: 520 km/h or 323 mph); time to 5,000 m (16,405 ft) was 35 minutes, or seven minutes more than the bomber.

The operational units finally set about radically lightening the Do 217J themselves. They got rid of up to 2,000 kg (4,410 lb) of unnecessary ballast by removing the defensive guns, dinghy, sundry armour plating, bomb-release mechanism and dive brakes. Thus lightened, the Do 217J became competitive once more. The units naturally passed on their experiences with the Do 217J to their superiors, but at first the Dornier company took no notice and the Do 217N-1, which went into production at the end of December 1942, differed from the J-2 mainly in having DB 603 engines. It is of interest to note that a special night fighter version proposed by Dornier was suppressed by the RLM Technical Office. It is well known that Milch opposed all 'special versions' which might slow down output and increase production costs. In fact the Dornier Do 217 night fighter came into being simply because the bomber force could only absorb a limited number of Do 217s, resulting in a surplus. It was not until mid-1943 that Dornier produced the U1 conversion set, which among other things contained shaped wooden fairings to cover the empty dorsal and ventral gun positions, as well as a wooden cover to replace the bomb-bay doors. Shortly afterwards these sets began to be incorporated at the factory, resulting in the Do 217N-2, which took off some two tons lighter than the J-2. The weight-reduction programme, combined with more powerful engines and improved aerodynamics, gave the Do 217N-2 a maximum speed of more than 500 km/h (310.5 mph) at 6,000 m (19,685 ft), fast enough for night interceptions. However, constant problems with the DB 603 meant that Do 217N production never ran smoothly, and months after the programme was halted in September 1943 Dornier still had completed airframes standing around without engines. The same picture was repeated at the operational units. Lacking spare engines, and replacement parts, the mechanics were forced to 'cannibalise' a number of aircraft to keep at least a few Do 217Ns flying. But even these reserves dried up eventually, and by July 1943 all 14 Do 217Ns of II/NJG 3 were parked in the hangars and revetments with damaged engines, leaving the *Gruppe* to make do with just seven Bf 110s.

Thus the Do 217 remained a very rare bird, one possible reason why more Do 217Js and Ns were shot down by friendly night fighters than as other type. It has already been mentioned that *Hptm* Schoenert quite liked flying the Do 217, mainly because it was only in this aircraft that his 'invention,' the upward-flying *Schräge Musik* cannon installation, could be fitted without creating too much drag. A number of World War I pilots used fixed guns which fired obliquely upwards, and in 1938 the former *Leutnant* Thiede reminded the RLM of his experiences with such weapons, but without attracting any interest. The Japanese also informed the RLM of their experiments in the Pacific area with similar weapons, but again there was no response. *Oblt* Schoenert had the same experience when he suggested to Kammhuber in 1941 that he should build a vertically-firing machine gun into a Do 17. In Schoenert's opinion it would be easier for the average pilot to shoot effectively while flying horizontally past underneath the bomber than to use Becker's method, with its diving acceleration, pull-up, equalisation of speed and breakaway. Kammhuber turned down the method on the basis of reports from Lent and Streib. Nevertheless, in summer 1942 the weapon testing centre at Tarnewitz experimented with vertical weapons in a Do 17 and a Bf 110. When Schoenert was awarded the Knights Cross in July he once again petitioned Kammhuber, who this time approved the fitting of three Do 217Js with vertical armament. At least one of these aircraft went from Widtmundhaven to Tarnewitz for testing, where the night fighting adviser to the Technical Office, *Otl* von Lossberg, discovered that with vertical armament it was possible to score hits only if the night fighter and its target were on exactly the same course. He then experimented with various angles of installation, achieving the best results at between 65° and 70°, which also allowed a target that was turning at 8°/sec to be kept in the sights. On the basis of these results 2 *Jagddivision* ordered the re-armament at Diepensee of three Do 217s with four and six oblique-mounted MG 151 cannon. Field tests began early in 1943, carried out by Schoenert's old *Staffel*, 3./NJG 3. In the meantime, Schoenert had been made CO of the Bf 110-equipped II/NJG 5, to which he broulht his own 'special' Do 217. An armourer serving with this *Gruppe*, *Ofw* Mahle, had a closer look at the Do 217 and concluded that something similar could be done for the Bf 110. At that time the MG FF cannon of the Messerschmitts were being replaced by MG 151s and the MG FF mountings were piling up in the armament stores. Using whatever materials he could find, Mahle successfully built two of these weapons into the cabin of an Bf 110, and it was with this 'do-it-yourself' installation that Schoenert scored the first kill over Berlin in May 1943. Further victories followed quickly, and even the experimental Do 217s of 3./NJG 3 were so successful that from June 1943 onwards an official oblique-weapon Standard Equipment set, R22, was produced for the Do 217 and the Ju 88C-6. Similar equipment for the Bf 110 had still to be officially approved, but in the meantime the operational crews made do with various *ad hoc* variations on Mahle's theme and were no less successful.

67

As with the Do 217, progressive developments of the Bf 110 and Ju 88 were basically nothing more than emergency solutions. In summer 1942 the first true night fighter versions, the Bf 110F-4 and Ju 88C-6, reached the operational units. These definitive night fighters were however simply painted in black camouflage at the factory, fitted with exhaust flame dampers and left with space available for the installation of additional radio and radar equipment. Though the factory's preparations speeded up the process, the electronics still had to be installed at the forward operational preparation centres. The Bf 110F-4 was fitted with the new DB 601F of 1,350 hp, a rating which took the engine to its development limit. In addition, the first DB 601F production series proved to be thermically overloaded, tendi g to suffer from seized pistons and engine fires, and so could not be operated at the officially listed maximum boost of 1.3 atü.[11]

The first flame dampers had a catastrophic effect on the life of the engines: so much exhaust gas accumulated in the exhaust manifold that at the cylinder air-intake stroke the outlet valve could no longer get enough fresh fuel vapour to cool it down. The results were cracks in the valves after only about 20 hours of service use. For these reasons the crews preferred to fly with uncovered exhaust flames rather than risk engine failure.

The later *Eberspächer-FlaV* flame dampers had an air inlet at the front which ejected the remaining gases more quickly. A second air inlet in the rear half of the exhaust manifold produced complete combustion of the exhaust gases which then left the damper as weakly glowing bluish flames. The flame dampers also reduced the speed of the aircraft, however, as a result of drag created by their clumsy installation and the diminished jet propulsion effect compared to the open exhaust stubs. In fact, the improved performance of the DB 601F was completely cancelled out by the increased weight of the Bf 110F-4, which had to carry a third crew member as well as two MK 108 cannon in the ventral tray.

The General Staff of the Luftwaffe therefore demanded a much more powerful version of the Bf 110, and in response Messerschmitt offered a variant with DB 605 engines (of 37.7 l capacity) developing 1,475 hp; with the help of the DB 603 supercharger (the so-called 'Gustav-Lader') this could be briefly boosted to 1,800 hp. The company also suggested the use of the 200 kg (441 lb) heavier DB 628 engine, which would confer a useful combat performance up to 10,000 m (32,810 ft). While the choice of the DB 605 meant significant structural changes, the installation of the DB 628 would have meant a fundamental redesign of the complete airframe and wings, and so this proposal was abandoned. In any case, the DB 628 was then only in the initial test stages. The Bf 110G-4 with DB 605 engines went into production a few months after the Bf 110F-4 and reached the operational units in April 1943. The crew's joy was short lived, however: as with other higher-rated Daimler-Benz engines, the DB 605 turned out to be underdeveloped. The occurrence of fires due to piston and crankshaft failures reached alarming proportions, and by June most of the Bf 110G-4s were grounded, waiting for replacement engines. The complaints about engine fires did not cease until a year later.

Similarly, the Ju 88C-6 was no more than a retouching of its predecessor, the Ju 88C-2. Junkers had used the same formula as Messerschmitt: an increase in performance of the Jumo 211J engines to 1,420 hp, shutters over the exhaust pipes, and more extensive radio and radar equipment. Unlike the DB 601, however, the Jumo 211 was a more sound basic design and could take the increase in performance without losing reliability. But even this engine had reached its development limits.

Apart from a few initial problems of adaptation the operational crews enjoyed flying the Ju 88C-6.[12] All they wanted was de-icing for the wings and fuselage nose, which was soon incorporated on the production line. Forgiving handling characteristics and powerful armament could however not disguise the fact that its *Lichtenstein* aerials made the Ju 88C-6 far too slow. Whereas the specification gave the maximum speed as 550 km/h (341.5 mph), operational machines tried out at Rechlin reached only 470 km/h (292 mph) at 4,800 m (15,750 ft). In mid-1943 that was just about good enough to catch the Stirling, but the Lancaster and Halifax were faster than the Ju 88C-6 by at least 10 km/h (6.2 mph) at any altitude. That the Ju 88C-6 was nevertheless a successful aircraft was due to the fact that for safety reasons the British bombers often flew at well below maximum speed in their close formations.

Even though the pilots were generally satisfied with their aircraft, the more far-sighted among them, and especially the command of XII *Fliegerkorps*, were not. The *Korps* insisted firmly and repeatedly on the need for a really superior aircraft but in spring 1942 the industry had very little to offer in the way of projects and prototypes. Focke-Wulf had brought its FW 187 back into contention, but this twin-engined fighter could not be considered because its fuselage was too slender to accommodate AI radar. The Me 210 was dropped for the reasons already mentioned, and the Ar 240 also failed to make the grade because of its treacherous handling. The only really advanced project was the He 219.

Heinkel had received the development contract for this promising design in October 1941, and the plans laid before Kammhuber in January 1942 met with his unreserved approval. If Milch and the Technical Office had been able to make up their minds in favour of advancing this aircraft in time, the He 219 would have replaced all the other night fighter types in service by spring 1944. But Milch's attitude to this subject put an end to all these premature hopes. In June 1942 he declared his agreement to the replacement of the Bf 110 by the He 219 – but not before early 1945. The Luftwaffe operations staff objected most strongly to this decision and pointed out that the operational crews would, in the foreseeable future, be unable to carry out their tasks without high performance night fighters, but to no avail. The subject of night fighters was discussed at several conferences in the late summer and it is clear from the minutes that Milch attached more and more importance to war economic considerations: it was not quality that would be decisive in air warfare but numbers, and the necessary numbers could only be achieved with less expensive aircraft from the factories where such aircraft were already being built, ie Messerschmitt and Junkers. Once again, the Me 210 appeared as competition for the He 219; Junkers laid on a small series of Ju 88s with BMW 801 radials (the Ju 88R) and promised shortly to start producing a night fighter version of the Ju 188 bomber. Outsiders also had a say: *Otl* von Lossberg suggested using the surplus Jumo 211 engines, made available by the phasing-out of the He 111 programme, in combination with wooden airframes to produce *Zerstörer* or night fighters; such light-weight aircraft would be capable of respectable performance powered by an essentially obsolete engine. This idea was taken up and materialised as a development contract awarded to Focke-Wulf that led to the Ta 154. At the other end of the scale, the Fieseler company submitted a project for a rocket-propelled night fighter-interceptor which however was abandoned already in 1943.

Nevertheless, Heinkel received the contract to build 12 He 219V-series machines and between March and September 1943 to produce a total of 173 He 219A-0 series aircraft. The XII *Fliegerkorps* command saw in this a degree of surrender on the part of the RLM Technical Office and made concessions on their part: they remained firm in the decision regarding the final re-equipment of all formations with He 219s, but were satisfied with the Ju 88R for the time being and would accept the Me 410 if the He 219 did not materialise. That, however, only served to confirm the negative attitude held by Milch's office towards the He 219, which was now regarded as a development risk.

Ignoring these squabbles and adverse comments, Kammhuber held on to the He 219 and did everything possible officially and unofficially to promote its development. Among other things, he ensured that Heinkel was informed about the latest combat experiences to help improve the new design. The He 219 made its first flight in November 1942.

But Junkers did not let go either and tried to persuade Milch to make a decision in favour of a night-fighter version of the Ju 188. There exist photographs of two different fuselage mock-ups of this proposal which probably originated in late 1942/early 1943. One of these retained the fully glazed nose section of the Ju 188E, out of which projected the FuG 212 aerials and five MG 151s. The second mock-up featured a short 'tin nose' with AI radar aerials and two superimposed BK 3.7 cannon.

Ignoring the fact that manufacture of the Ju 188E required about 10 per cent more raw materials and that the type was clearly slower than the He 219V-1, Milch seemed inclined to favour the proposed Ju 188 night fighter, reasoning that the 188 was already being built as a bomber, had proved itself in action, and did not appear to need much development work. The final decision was to be taken after comparative flight tests in January 1943. For these Heinkel submitted a He 219 piloted by Streib, against which Junkers pitted a Ju 188 piloted by von Lossberg. The Junkers contender had been lightened and aerodynamically improved by removing the ETC wing bomb racks. The tests showed that the He 219 could climb faster, was distinctly superior to the Ju 188 in turns, and was faster at altitude. But Milch let himself be influenced by a spectacular low-level demonstration in which the Ju 188 recorded 440 km/hr (273 mph) to pull away from its competitor, which could only manage 410 km/hr (254.6 mph) at sea level; the BMW 801 was an unbeatable engine at low level.

And so we read in the minutes of a GL/C discussion dated 8 January 1943: '. . . for these reasons the He 219 would not be suitable to fulfil all the requirements. . . . From the quantity point of view, the 219 would not be in the position to cover the demands of the next two years. Therefore it is even more valuable that we already have alternative choices (Bf 110G and Ta 154) . . .' Imagine it, the Bf 110 as an alternative to the He 219! But that was not all. With malicious pleasure the RLM Technical Office then went into great detail in listing all the teething troubles of the He 219, from undercarriage failure, insufficient cockpit heating and a tendency for the cabin window to steam up, to troubles with the wing-mounted guns, whose ejected cartridge cases damaged the fin/rudder assembly. The enthusiastic reports of the crews who had test-flown the He 219 were deliberately overlooked. But official wheels have a way of turning, and finally Heinkel received a production order in January for 127 He 219V and O-series (experimental and pre-production) machines, with series production planned to start a year later. These aircraft were not night fighters, however, but *Kampfzerstörer* and long-range fighters for U-boat protection over the Bay of Biscay. A decision in favour of a night-fighter version was made only in March, mainly because of pressure for an antidote to the almost invulnerable Mosquito.

But the RLM's apathy towards a specialised night-fighter continued. If Kammhuber really wanted a heavy fighter the RLM felt he would have to be sutisfied with the Ju 88R. Thus, in slightly modified form as the Ju 88R-2, this aircraft was also delivered to the operational units, beginning in April 1943. There was no denying that the additional 400 hp developed by each BMW 801 radial (compared with the Jumo 211J inlines) was distinctly noticeable. Even today, pilots who flew the Ju 88R are still enthusiastic about its climbing performance, while forgetting that the 'R' also had some negative points. The origin fin/rudder assembly was too small for the more powerful engines, and stability in flight was not all it could have been.

On the other hand, the RLM had nothing against the Ta 154, which after all was also a specialised night fighter. Quite the opposite in fact: this project was given every possible promotion. For psychological reasons Göring believed it vital that Germany should have its own all-wooden high performance aircraft, and the unofficial designation 'Moskito' speaks for itself. While still only in the design stage, this new type was allocated higher priority and ordered in larger numbers than the far more advanced He 219 in 1942. And this despite the fact that already the initial calculations had shown the starting position to be anything but favourable: there was no experience in the construction and manufacture of high performance wooden aircraft; the specialist workers needed for series production were not available; and there was a bottleneck in supplies of impregnated laminated wood. Soon afterwards it became obvious that the Ta 154 would be heavier than the Bf 110, and that the planned Jumo 211 engines would not provide enough power. But the Technical Office of the RLM had no intention of dropping the project and recommended that it should be redesigned around the Jumo 213 then still on the test bench.

In June 1943 Kammhuber finally managed to have a few He 219A-0 pre-production aircraft allocated to the *Gruppenstab* of I/NJG 1 for operational trials instead of being flown by an *E-Staffel* at Rechlin. Like the Rechlin pilots, the operational crews gave the *Uhu* the highest marks, despite the fact that the aircraft was decidedly underpowered: designed for two DB 613 units (two coupled DB 603's) of 3,800 hp each, it had to make do with two DB 603 inlines developing only half as much. Nevertheless, the superior qualities of this night fighter were demonstrated on the night of 12 June when an He 219A-0 flown by the CO of I/NJG 1, *Maj* Streib, accounted for five of the 38 RAF bombers destroyed. (These were however the only victories achieved by Streib with the He 219.) That

72

the aircraft literally fell to pieces on landing[13] did not detract from its success in the air, although it did have negative effects. As a result of this mishap it was immediately decided that the He 219 should be stressed to fighter (H 5k) rather than *Zerstörer* (H 5) limits. This meant an additional 1,000 kg (2,205 lb) of weight, placing the He 219 below the Mosquito in the weight/power stakes.

In June 1943 most of the night fighter formations were still flying the Bf 110, including many obsolete Bf 110Cs, Ds and Es; a really superior night fighter was not expected before 1944. One can thus imagine Kammhuber's apprehension when he received intelligence reports that the Americans had supposedly carried out night training flights over Britain at 10,000 m (32,810 ft) altitude and speeds in the region of 500 km/hr (310.5 mph). His reaction was to order a speed-up in production of the Bf 110G-4/U7 (with GM-1 nitrous oxide injection), and an immediate start on specimen series of 10 He 219A and 10 Ta 154 fighters fitted with TK 11 exhaust-driven superchargers. Unfortunately, the Bf 110G-4/U7 showed all the signs of being an 'overcharged' design: it did reach an altitude of 12,000 m (39,370 ft) and had quite good rate of climb above the GM-1 injection height, but below 7,000 m (22,960 ft) level its climbing performance was markedly worse than that of the standard Bf 110G-4. Apart from that, the GM-1 tank altered the centre of gravity and made the aircraft unstable and decidedly difficult to fly at higher altitudes. Another drawback was the fact that it was impossible to go around again with flaps down after an abandoned approach. The centre of gravity was brought back within limits by removing the four nose machine guns, although the addition of an external weapon container would have made the flying characteristics extremely critical again. But, as no other high-altitude night fighter was available, the operational crews had to make do with another stopgap.

At first glance the list of aircraft used for 'improvised' night fighting on the Eastern Front suggests a scraping of the bottom of the barrel: next to some 'true' *Zerstörer* such as the Bf 110, Ju 88C and Do 17Z-10 there were the FW 58, He 111P, He 111H-3 and H-6, Do 17P, Ju 88D, Ju 88A-4 and Bf 109E. But this hotchpotch was not as crazy as it would seem. Some of these types had already been used in successful night interceptions and had won the confidence of their crews. Apart from that, fast fighters could not be used to combat the Soviet night harassment biplanes, and this naturally led to some 'remodelling' of bombers and reconnaissance aircraft. Thus, for instance, a He 111 would be fitted with a 'tin nose' accommodating up to four 20 mm MG FF cannon, plus four MG 17s in a ventral tray and two WB 81Z gun pods on the ETC bomb racks – in other words, a total of 16 fixed forward-firing automatic weapons. With such a hail of bullets one simply had to hit the target!

In the course of summer 1943 most of these improvised types such as the He 111, Do 17P and Ju 88D were apparently used up and replaced by true night fighters of the Bf 110 and Ju 88 series. Nevertheless, some Ju 88A-4s remained in operational service to hunt the slow Soviet night harassment aircraft. With their dive brakes out, the A-4s were able to slow down in level flight as well.

Unnoticed by the German command, the period 1942–43 also saw the Allies gain the upper hand in the electronic war. The reasons for this German loss of initiative are too complex to be explained in detail in this book. But broadly, it came about because neither Hitler nor Göring nor Milch understood anything about high-frequency technology and so did not recognise the decisive importance of radar and electronics in general until it was far too late. Apart from that, they were unable to sort out the complications arising from the competition between the Navy and the Luftwaffe, and within that, the quarrels about competence between the Technical Office of the RLM, the General Plenipotentiary of the Signals Service, Gen Fell-giebel, and the Chief of NVW, Gen Martini.

Furthermore, compared with the Allies, Germany had only a tenth as much research capacity in this still very new branch of science. Whatever research work was going on was dispersed among 100 small laboratories which for reasons of secrecy were not allowed to exchange their practical knowledge and experience. On the next level, a lack of experienced engineers and craftsmen prevented the industry from meeting the requirements of the fighting units, while the units themselves lacked knowledgeable and competent specialists capable of operating and maintaining electronic devices, and of training others. Until 1942 there were practically no useful service manuals for ground radars, the training and further education of serving soldiers suffered under the secrecy regulations, and there were no instructional courses at the signal-technical schools. Last but not least there was the long-lasting erroneous evaluation of the centimetric waveband and its usefulness for location and orientation purposes that led to the German inferiority in electronic technology.

In November 1942, only a few weeks before the discovery of the first British centimetric navigation radar in a shot-down bomber, the chief of Telefunken Laboratories, Dr Runge, said that very little would be achieved with centimetric waves, and that only at great cost. Thereupon the centimetric research laboratory was disbanded to concentrate all available technicians on further development of the 50 cm and 2.4 m wavebands, of which much was expected. This decision shows clearly that the research establishments and the

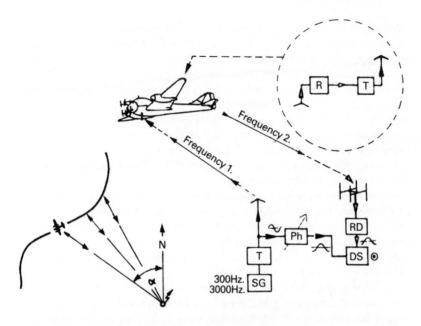

Simplified representation of 'Y' method of fighter guidance
(directional finding from the ground with range and angle
measurement)

SG Sound generator   R   Receiver
T   Transmitter   RD Ground receiver with D/F aerial
Ph Adjustable phase-slider   DS Visual display screen

industry had no idea of what the fighting units really required, a
conclusion which will also be supported by the recital of events as
they happened.

All ground radars delivered to front-line units in the period May
1942 – July 1943 were only developments of existing devices. This
does not mean that things were left as they were, however. After the
1,000-bomber raids of May–June 1942, Kammhuber, in accordance
with his ideas on night fighting methods, requested the replacement
of *Würzburg-Riesen* with all-round search radars offering 150 m
(93 mls) range, panoramic display and IFF capability. The combat
efficiency of the night fighters themselves was also to be improved by
an AI radar with a 90° forward search zone and a maximum range of
6–7 km (3.7–4.3 mls) down to low level and a minimum range of
50 m (164 ft) or better. A second airborne device would provide
accurate data for the fixed weapons and fire them automatically at the
right moment regardless of visual acquisition of the target. All these

75

devices were to have a range of alternative frequencies. Impressive as these requirements were, their realisation in Germany at that time was impossible. For one thing, only centimetric radar would have had the necessary performance, and hardly anything practical had been achieved in Germany in that field. During a discussion with Göring on 1 January 1943 Kammhuber therefore agreed that he would be satisfied with *Würzburg-Gigant* instead of the panoramic device, although this new ground radar was nothing more than *Würzburg-Riese* with improved range (72 km/44.7 mls) and IFF capability. At the same meeting Gen Martini expressed the view that the prospect for a wide-angle AI radar seemed 'hopeful'. Nothing was said about automatic fire control, probably because experiments with a modified *Lichtenstein* B/C had not yielded any useful results. A few *Gigant* specimen sets were delivered to front-line units[14] – but the system did not enter series production because developments in air warfare after August 1943 ruled out its use in controlled night fighting, which had anyway become meaningless.

To improve the effectiveness of the night fighters under the *Himmelbett* system of 1942 it was not enough simply to enlarge the night fighting zones, it was also necessary to introduce new methods that would enable several fighters to be used in one zone without leaving neighbouring zones uncovered. In May 1942 Gen Martini suggested the *Egon* method, originally intended for bomber guidance. This method was based on a *Freya* ground control radar with a *Gemse* IFF attachment that would send an impulse which would be received by an airborne *Erstling* device and retransmitted at a certain rhythm. This enabled the fighter control officer to distinguish his own fighters among the multitude of blips on the *Freya* display screen and guide them accordingly. However, since the *Erstling-Gemse* offensive navigation method had not yet been tried out in actual combat, the Luftwaffe command decided to adopt the Y-system, which had already proved itself as a bomber guidance method, for the night fighting role. In this case the fighter control officer gave instructions to the fighters via R/T. Using a special calibration sound sender, the ground transmitter then introduced a calibration sound into the FCO's speech which was heard as a faint whistling sound. This signal was received by the aircraft set, retransmitted and received by a special radio rangefinder on the ground which simultaneously was also receiving a signal from the calibration sound sender. The time lag between the ground transmission and airborne reception and vice versa gave the accurate range between the ground site and the aircraft, while the position of the aircraft could be determined by taking a bearing on its transmitter.

Using this system, each night fighting command centre could control one fighter via two *Würzburg-Riesen*, as before, and as many other night fighters as there were Y-guidance stations. In the extreme case it was even possible to forgo *Würzburg* guidance and leave both *Riesen*, in search/detection mode. Theoretically, it was even possible to terminate the Y-line to a fighter after it had been led to a contact and guide any number of other night fighters cruising in the standby zone one after another to the enemy. In practice, things were left to one fighter controlled by the *Würzburg* radars and two guided by the Y-system in each night fighting zone. The first Y-stations began to work experimentally in Holland in February, and by July they were operating in most night fighting zones within the area controlled by 1 and 2 *JDivisionen*. To begin with, the operational crews were most enthusiastic because the ground control centre could no longer lose the fighter on account of the automatic transmission of range data. Moreover, the new system also provided faultless IFF. Unfortunately it soon afterwards became obvious that the Y-method was even more inaccurate than *Seeburg* and that to ensure successful interception it was absolutely essential for the fighter to have an AI radar. The Y-method could also be jammed by enemy transmitters, while suitably equipped enemy long-range night fighters could home in on and shoot down German night fighters using *Erstling* sets.

The equipment of units with AI radar continued to cause headaches for the night fighter command, with the industry failing to achieve anywhere near the promised production figures. This situation was in part due to a lack of capacity on the part of the radio valve manufacturers. Even in August 1943 about 80 per cent of all AI radars delivered to the Werl and Gütersloh operational preparation centres were still defective, so that technicians were overloaded with repair work. A large proportion of the new *Lichtenstein* AI radars were in such a condition that they had to be sent back to the manufacturer. As a result, first choice of equipment went to the units operating over Holland (I/NJG 1 and II/NJG 2), the area most used by the RAF for night penetrations. Thanks to the careful maintenance by their ground engineers, both *Gruppen* in fact had an above-average operational availability record with *Lichtenstein*. For a time a service test detachment from *E-Stelle* Werneuchen was stationed with II/NJG 2, and that helped too. By September 1942 both *Gruppen* were probably fully equipped with *Lichtenstein B/C* AI radars, but the situation was much bleaker elsewhere. Thus, for instance, even in March 1943 the night fighter units stationed in Southern Germany, including *NJ-Schule 1*, did not have a single aircraft equipped with AI radar. This meant that radio operators trained in the latter unit had no idea about the most important night interception device when they joined an operational formation.[15] Of the night fighters flown by operational formations, only about 80 per cent would have been equipped with the FuG 202 *Lichtenstein B/C* by July 1943.

A redesigned AI radar, the FuG 212 *Lichtenstein C-1*, was produced by Telefunken in spring 1943. Experiments had been going on with this installation since the summer of 1942 and it was intended as a replacement for *Lichtenstein B/C*. The aerial arrangement, frequency, range and detection angle were identical with those of the *B/C*, but the set itself was substantially lighter. Flight tests with a Do 17Z-10 and two Ju 88s equipped with the new radar had been completed by May 1943. But the report prepared by *E-Stelle* Werneuchen was not all that enthusiastic, the most criticised feature being the retention of the triple visual display arrangement, which was difficult to interpret. Even worse was the fact that, due to the remote-control installation of its aerial selector switch, the FuG 212 could only be fitted to the few operational Ju 88 and Do 217 night fighters, and not to the Bf 110. However, despite these defects and various other unsolved manufacturing problems, large-scale production began in mid-1943, with the result that production fell way below expectations and scarcely any of the *Lichtenstein C-1*s which reached the operational preparation centres were fit for installation in operational aircraft.

Gen Martini's statement of January 1943 that the development of wide-angle AI radar looked promising could have been based, at that time, only on a few early experiments with surface ship detection devices which had a search angle of more than 90° but no altitude capability. Experiments carried out by Telefunken with *Lichtenstein B/C-S*, which had supplementary aerials fitted on the outer wings of the carrier aircraft, did not yield any useful results. Nevertheless, the FuG 220 *Lichtenstein SN-2* wide-angle AI radar was evolved from a surface ship detection device. In spring 1943 *E-Stelle* Werneuchen had carried out comparative trials with the FuG 200 *Hohentwiel* (Lorenz) and FuG 213 (Telefunken), which featured two different aerial arrangements: wire aerials parallel to the wings of the carrier aircraft, and the 'Stag antler' group (dipoles with supports) on the outer wings. Its large wavelength (3.3 m) made this device unsuitable for surface ship detection, but it was found quite promising when used against flying targets. Because of this, and the system's wide search angle of 120° *E-Stelle* Werneuchen recommended the FuG 213 for development into a night fighter AI radar and work began at once. Telefunken built in an elevation-finder switch and produced the first set, designated *Lichtenstein SN-1*, in May 1943. This system had wing-mounted aerials and proved to have a very poor minimum range of 1,200 m (3,937 ft). This was overcome by using a FuG 212, resulting in a rather heavy and unwieldy installation. A transitional model, this was then developed into the *SN-2*, which underwent service trials in a Ju 88C-6 in June. The reports were absolutely damning, the only characteristic to win any praise being the well arranged twin visual display. The *E-Stelle* did not mince its words when it came to the negative points: an insufficient minimum range of 750 m (2,450 ft), malfunctioning of the FuG 212 wide-angle aerial (only one instead of the usual group of four), and reduction of flying speed and manoeuvrability to such an extent that the aircraft with this installation had to be described as unsuitable for operational service. The search angle too was rather disappointing, being hardly more than that of the FuG 212, and the radio/radar operator had to find target elevation and azimuth by means of two hand switches. And finally, Werneuchen pointed out that the long-wave *SN-2* could be affected by VHF harmonic wave vibrations and that aircraft equipped with this device could interfere with each other if flying less than 50 km (31 mls) apart.

As a result, this version of the new AI radar was declared unsuitable for operational use, and XII *Fliegerkorps* requested a modified variant with fuselage nose aerials, improved minimum range (or a simplified and more reliable supplementary aerial) and an automatic selector switch for elevation and azimuth direction-finding. Though a fuselage nose aerial suitable for installation in a Bf 110 (coded C9 + DK) was delivered by Telefunken late in June 1943, the company's technicians were still struggling to make it operationally usable by the end of August.

In the meantime, the increasing activity of British long-range night fighters, which from early spring 1943 began to accompany bomber formations or to ambush German aircraft near their bases, made a tail-warning device a matter of some urgency. Telefunken offered the *Lichtenstein B/C-R* and the FFO, the FuG 216 *Neptun R*. Both devices had four rod aerials fitted vertically under the wings, but the better visual display of the *Neptun* made it more suitable for procurement.

To begin with, British interference with the radio and ground control radars of the Reich Air Defence was directed only against ground-to-air radio communications, which they attempted to neutralise by means of jamming transmitters. From September 1942 the British began to jam the *Freya* ground control along the Channel coast, gradually extending this interference to cover the whole of Western Europe and North-west Germany, so that the Luftwaffe command assumed the RAF was using airborne transmitters. In March 1943 the British even succeeded in occasionally neutralising all the *Freya* sets in Southern Germany. On the German side, attempts were made to provide the *Freyas* with alternative frequencies and to develop a passive emission detector. This homing device, the *Freya-Halbe*, responded to aircraft carrying *Freya* jamming transmitters. Trials with operational crews at Werneuchen gave satisfactory results, but hardly was the *Freya-Halbe* aircraft back at its unit when the allegedly useless device was removed again. As far as is known, only crews from IV/NJG 5 made systematic flights from Lorient with *Freya-Halbe*-equipped night fighters in spring 1943.

Meanwhile, the electronic war was really getting into its stride. In March and April came the first reports of British jamming from *Würzburg* crews stationed in Western France, none of whom could explain the cause. Such interference had been expected for some time: a *Würzburg* had been captured by a British Commando unit on the Channel coast in February 1942, and additional *Würzburgs* had fallen into British hands in North Africa. By comparing the serial numbers and examining the undamaged high-frequency parts, the British analysts had had no difficulty in determining that the system was being built in large numbers and worked on only one frequency.

A crushing blow to the German night defences was delivered by the crew of a Ju 88R-1 of 10./NJG 3 (coded D5 + EV) when they deserted to the British on the 9 May 1943. Equipped with the FuG 212, this aircraft revealed that *Würzburg* and *Lichtenstein* worked on the same frequency, so that one single means of jamming could neutralise the Luftwaffe air reporting service, Flak control and AI radars.

German engineers had already recognised how best to jam radar during the first *Würzburg* trials at Rechlin in spring 1940, namely by releasing tinfoil strips cut to half the wavelength of the radar. Even so, the research establishments and industry did not bother about defences against this source of interference but busied themselves exclusively in finding countermeasures against the jamming transmitters. In 1942 the possibility that the enemy could be jammed by tinfoil strips (known as *Düppel* in Germany) was raised again, but once again without much practical result. In fact the British had discovered this method of jamming some time earlier and had originally intended to use it, under the designation *Window*, during the 1,000-bomber raid on Cologne on 30 May 1942, but then it was decided to delay the operational debut of *Window* until the British radars had been made immune to similar jamming by the Germans.

The last large-scale experiment with *Düppel* in Germany took place in March 1943, when it was demonstrated how *Würzburg* could be completely neutralised. Following this startling experiment, Gen Martini insisted that the most urgent task of the industry was to ensure that all ground radars were made *Düppel*-proof. But then Göring refused to play along. Fearing that the enemy would get to know about the vulnerability of German radars, he ordered the strictest military secrecy about all radar devices, and then extended this order to cover research as well. This effectively stopped all the work then in progress on finding some protection against tinfoil jamming.

It should have been obvious to the technically educated senior officers that sooner or later the scientists on the other side would also discover this means of interference, and that it would then only be a question of time when the RAF decided to use it. The fact that during the first half of 1943 the British had at times been quite successful in jamming most of the German systems and ground radars and possessed a serviceable centimetric radar, the H2S, is sufficient evidence today that the Germans had lost the lead in the high-frequency field which they had enjoyed in 1940. At the time, however, this was realised by very few people. The concentration of efforts under the State Research Council and the appointment of a Deputy in charge of all high-frequency research in November 1942 came too late to make up for this, while the leading experts themselves reached some wrong conclusions that were to have dire consequences later on. Thus, for instance, the fact that the H2S (known in German circles as the *Rotterdam-Gerät* after its place of discovery) proved to be first-rate for air-to-ground purposes was taken as proof that centimetric radar would be completely unsuitable for ground-to-air or air-to-air use. Instead of considering the true implications of H2S, the scientists began to look around for something else. The increasing jamming of ground radars attracted attention to the research work being carried out on airborne infra-red. Seeking a second iron in the fire as an insurance against the neutralisation of *Lichtenstein*, AEG developed *Spanner* III, which combined the wide-angle optics of *Spanner* II with the 1,000-W IR searchlight of *Spanner* I. Nothing is known about its operational use by night fighters of the Reich Air Defence, but this device is supposed to have proved itself in action on the Eastern Front.

In June 1943 Staff Engineer Poppendiek of *E-Stelle* Werneuchen proposed a new kind of night-fighting method based on *Spanner*. Although it did not succeed in being adopted, it is nevertheless of some interest to this story. Poppendiek knew about Becker's attack tactics and the experiments with oblique armament, and his proposal combined both, with some improvements. Poppendiek's proposed night fighter was a Do 217 armed with 6–8 vertically mounted MG 151 cannon and equipped with the *Lichtenstein* AI radar and an additional upwards-looking IR searchlight. The pilot would detect the enemy aircraft with his *Lichtenstein*, descend and approach the enemy again from 300 m (984 ft) below. At this stage the IR searchlight would acquire the target and show it on a special projection sight. With this sight the pilot would not have to crane his neck as he had to with the standard fighter reflector sight fitted under the cabin

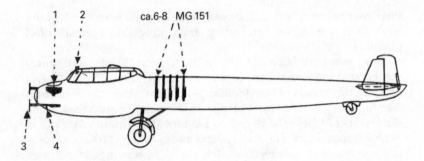

Staff Eng Poppendiek's proposed night fighter

1. *Spanner* IR searchlight
2. *Spanner* sight
3. *Lichtenstein* AI radar
4. Forward-firing guns

roof in accordance with Schoenert's proposed method of firing oblique weapons. The advantages of Poppendiek's idea were that it was not necessary to pull up under the enemy aircraft to fire before bunting away downwards, as in Becker's attack, and that the pilot could aim more easily and fire from a greater distance without worrying about debris from the victim hitting his own aircraft.

The introduction of bomber streams by the RAF was followed by a slight increase in losses, a brief reduction after the withdrawal of the searchlights in August, and then another increase as *Lichtenstein* was introduced and co-operation between ground control sites improved. On 10 September 1942 XII *Fliegerkorps* reported its 1,000th victory, comprising 648 bombers destroyed in dark night fighting, 200 in illuminated night fighting, 141 shot down by long-range night fighters, and 11 that had crashed after being blinded by searchlights. By mid-July 1943 the number of enemy bombers shot down by Luftwaffe night fighters may well have reached 1,700. This high figure is also indicated by another statistic: in 1942 65 per cent of all interceptions resulted in kills; in 1943 this had risen to 76 per cent. In fact the German night victory tally may well have been much higher: according to official British sources, in the period June–August 1942 the RAF reported the loss of 482 bombers, of which 129 were probably shot down by night fighters and 142 by Flak, and 211 crashed due to unknown causes. Consequently, some of the probables and combat encounters reported by the German night fighters could retrospectively be credited as actual victories because the damaged bombers crashed unobserved on their way back to base.

Examined on its own, the German night fighter victory tally was imposing enough, and the high command was suitably impressed. For the British, however, these figures meant only that their losses had increased from 4.7 to 5.6 per cent.[16] True enough, these losses were bitter, but they were not insupportable. Only if their losses had exceeded 10 per cent would the British have been forced to abandon their night raids.

The evidence suggests that, however hard they tried, the German night fighters would have been restricted by the nature of the system to a maximum kill ratio of six per cent. Only once did the British lose as many as nine per cent of a force over German territory – during the raid on Pilsen in occupied Czechoslovakia on the night of 17 May 1943 – but that was hardly surprising considering the very long flight to and from the target. During shallower penetrations – over the Ruhr, for instance – it was simply impossible to achieve higher kill ratios. One also has to take into consideration other factors: technical faults leading to the loss of coverage from ground radars, or electronic interference blinding whole night-fighting zones and letting the bomber stream pass through unmolested. And when all is said and done, success depended ultimately on the individual pilot and his radio/radar operator, their teamwork, and co-operation between the aircrew and ground control. When all these factors could be described as 'excellent' – and when the aircraft itself was good, all systems aboard the fighter were working the way they should, the weather was good, and there were enough enemy aircraft in the area – some crews achieved exceptional success. Up to six victories were achieved in a single night several times by the same pilots and their crews.[17] But such scores remained very much the exception, even for the aces, because too many factors had to coincide to make them possible.

Victories could also be achieved only if there were enemy aircraft in the air. During the summer of 1942 the RAF bomber streams tended to cross the North Sea coast between the Zuider Zee and the Schelde estuary, thus loading NJG 1 and NJG 2 fairly equally. As time went by this led to considerable wear and tear on these *Staffeln*, but the *Himmelbett* system did not allow even short-term transfers of other crews from less endangered parts of German territory to create concentrations of defensive effort in Holland. In fact the opposite was the case: as there was a danger that the British would unexpectedly fly in far to the north or south, a number of *Staffeln* had to be deployed there as well, many of them not flying a single combat sortie for weeks on end. Or the RAF would fly widely dispersed spoof raids resulting in scores of German night fighters taking off, cruising around in vain in their standby areas and landing again without coming into contact with the enemy. How much precious fuel was wasted like this it is impossible even to guess.

How much the successes of a single *Gruppe* depended on

weather, the number of enemy sorties and enemy interference with ground radar installations is shown by the War Diary of II/NJG 1 based at St Trond. Thus, out of a total of 64 operational sorties flown during September and October 1942, every 10th resulted in a victory. Only two night fighters were lost and 10 had to return early due to technical problems. But then began a fruitless period:

30 Nov 1942: Seven Bf 110 airborne without success.

3 Dec 1942: 15 Bf 110 airborne to intercept six penetrations, without success.

7 Dec 1942: Six Bf 110 airborne, all *Freya* radars out of action; one victory.

21 Dec 1942: Five Bf 110 airborne, *Freya* interfered with; no successes.

4–15 Jan 1943: Various minor operational sorties, without success.

16 Jan 1943: Six Bf 110 airborne, without success.

15 Feb 1943: Major raid on Cologne, 20 ingoing and 13 outgoing enemy flights. Five contacts, two victories.

27 Feb 1943: Major raid on Cologne. Eight Bf 110 airborne, without success.

28 Feb 1943: Eight Bf 110 directed to two outgoing enemy aircraft, without success.

2 Mar 1943: Four Bf 110 directed to five ingoing and 39 outgoing flights, without success.

5 Mar 1943: Two Bf 110 and one Do 217 airborne, without success.

On the night of 6 March 1943 the RAF began its offensive against the Rhine-Westphalia industrial area with an attack on Essen, and during the following four months RAF bombers raided nearly every town between Hamm and Aachen. This offensive cost the British 572 bombers, but that represented on average only 4.7 per cent of the total sorties flown.

At this stage the bomber streams tended to fly almost directly into the airspace over the Schelde estuary, meaning that under the existing system only the night fighters of I/NJG 1 could be set against them. As a result, the *Gruppe* came under such physical and mental strain that in May *Fliegerkorps* had to transfer leading night fighter crews from all over Germany to reinforce I/NJG 1. Drastic as it was, this measure had its effect: when their losses began to mount along their usual penetration routes, the British started to swing around to the north or south again and thus to come into the operating zones of less heavily loaded night fighter formations.

This offensive was broken off in June after the RAF had suffered its highest losses to date – or, to put it another way, after the German night fighter force had achieved its greatest successes – but not before the bombers had burned out the centres of every large town between Aachen and Hamburg. Nevertheless, on the German side it was believed that the RAF had taken a beating and would suffer even heavier losses in the near future. All the signs seemed to point that way: apart from the successes of the night fighters, it was hoped that the introduction of the Y-method (combining monitoring of RAF signals traffic, radar interception and electronic interference) would at long last make it possible to use so many night fighters that the air would be practically thick with them. In addition, the *SN-2* AI radar, then still under development, would surely make the night fighters even more effective. It was at this stage also that it was proposed to get some high-speed night fighters equipped with the *SN-2* to fly along with the RAF bomber stream and search out targets on their own.

Behind the main night defence belt the unguided single-engined night fighters would then also make it hot for the RAF. And so a certain – and justified – optimism began to spread: 'Just let Tommy come again! A few more weeks and he will wonder what hit him!' That must have been the mood in those days.

The first step towards the introduction of 'free' night fighting was taken in spring 1943 by the night fighting adviser to the RLM Technical Office, *Otl* von Lossberg, in a report to his chief, *GenMaj* Vorwald. He and Lossberg then presented this proposal to Gen Kammhuber. The idea was to introduce selected crews with fast aircraft such as the He 219 into the bomber stream and let them operate on their own within that airspace, carrying out 'free chases', detecting, intercepting and attacking the enemy bombers during their approach, over the target and on the way out. This method depended on the availability of a wide-ranging AI radar and a 'running commentary' from the *Korps* command post to keep the night fighters informed of the progress of the bomber stream. But Gen Kammhuber was not convinced. In fact, he considered the chances of operating this way as remote from the start. Without ground control, he believed, the night fighters would not be able to find the enemy; without IFF (then still not available) they would shoot each other down; over the target they would come under fire from their own Flak batteries; and finally they would be unable to find landing places in unfamiliar areas. He ramained unconvinced by Lossberg's presentation on the expected performance of the *SN-2* (with which the night-fighter pilot could find his target completely independently), the practicability of a pilot correcting his course in response to a running commentary from the ground, and the fact that the enemy bombers were without exception four-engined, which would preclude any shooting encounters between German night fighters. Kammhuber persisted in his opinion, although he did agree later to

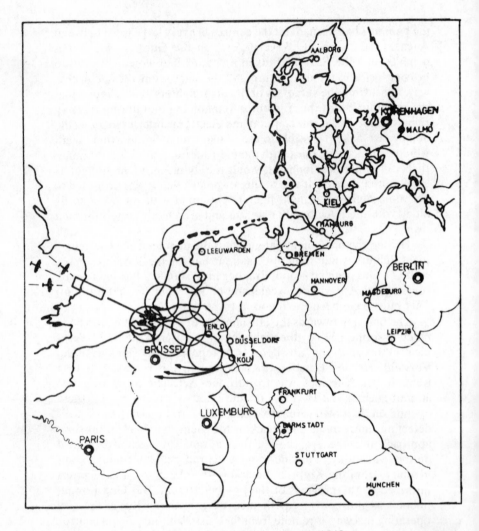

The climax of *Himmelbett* night fighting in summer 1943

This sketch shows clearly that an RAF raid on Cologne had to penetrate only a few *Himmelbett* zones and the 'combined night fighting' area (*Konaja*).

accept 'pursuit' night fighting – provided he was given a way of keeping the fighter formations 'on the leash'.

While the possibilities of free night fighting were still being discussed at a higher level, some night-fighter aces had already flown such sorties off their own bat by leaving the *Himmelbett* zones and finding their own way into the enemy bomber stream. Eventually von

Lossberg got to know about these 'freelance' activities, which led him to hope that he would get a certain amount of backing from the operational crews during any future arguments with Kammhuber.

While there was thus some hope that it would soon be possible to cause such losses to the RAF heavy bomber formations that they would be forced to give up their raids, for the time being the German air defences were completely unable to do anything about the extremely high and fast-flying Mosquitoes. True enough, the Mosquitoes could not start any large conflagrations with their limited bomb loads, but they were nevertheless decidedly irksome. They caused air-raid warnings all along their flightpath, forcing civilians to leave their homes and places of work, leading to loss of production; and induced Flak batteries to fire countless rounds into the sky and night fighters to chase in vain behind them, practically burning out their engines. A successful interception was very rare, and the Mosquitoes shot down by *Maj* Lent on 20 April 1943 and *Oblt* Linke during the following night were more of a fluke than anything else. Even more dangerous than these nuisance bombers were the Pathfinder Mosquitoes, which, equipped with precision navigational instruments, marked the targets for the following heavy bombers. If the Luftwaffe had had a night fighter capable of shooting down some of these Pathfinders in good time, more than a few German towns would have been spared at least some of their suffering.

After some fruitless attempts it soon became evident that the acceleration and maximum speed of the available twin-engined night fighters were just not good enough for this task, and the command formed a few special 'Mosquito hunter' detachments equipped with Fw 190s and operating under the *Himmelbett* system. Thus, on 15 July 1943, two such FW 190s were attached to II/NJG 1 and stationed at Hangelar; these single-seaters operated in the area coded *Kolibri* (Cologne) in defence of the hydrogenation plant at Wesseling.

The British also produced Mosquito night fighter versions which developed into extremely dangerous opponents for the Luftwaffe night fighters. The Mosquito night fighters were first encountered by II/NJG 1 on 12 March 1943, when 12 aircraft of this type shot up their base in a low-level raid. To begin with, attempts were made to keep these uninvited guests away by mounting standing patrols with Bf 110 night fighters. But this soon proved to be not only unsuitable but downright dangerous because the Mosquitoes were equipped with an AI radar that could also detect targets near ground level. The standing patrols were therefore abandoned and the task passed on to the light Flak batteries, which did not prevent two Do 217s being shot down by Mosquitoes late in May and in July. The Do 217 was particularly vulnerable to such attacks by marauding long-range night fighters. The cabin glazing would regularly steam up during the approach, obliging the pilot to open one of his side windows and fly a few circuits until the glazing was clear again. Such an aircraft, cruising slowly around its base and possibly with its navigation lights on, was an ideal target for any long-range intruder. Most of these sudden attacks resulted in panic landings that ended with fractured undercarriages and badly shaken crews.

The use of night fighters by day in the Reich Air Defence forms a tragic chapter in this story. The first USAAF daytime raid on a German town took place on 27 January 1943, when a formation of Boeing B-17 heavy bombers attacked Wilhelmshaven. They met very little opposition, since at that time only parts of JG 1 were allocated to the defence of the North Sea coastline. In the erroneous belief that the heavily armed night fighters would be a welcome reinforcement of the day defences, it was decided to pit a few 'alarm pairs' (*Rotten*) from NJG 1 against the next American daytime raid. They did not have to wait long: the B-17s came again on 4 February, and eight Bf 110 night fighters of IV/NJG 1, led by *Hptm* Jabs, threw themselves against 60 Flying Fortresses advancing in a typically tight formation, covering each other with their heavy machine guns. From the very start this first daytime operation was a disaster for the night fighters, and a portent of things to come. Although they managed to shoot down three B-17s they themselves lost two Bf 110s, and the other aircraft were so badly damaged that they were out of action for some time. Though the aircraft could still be replaced easily enough, much more damaging was the loss of precious AI radars and highly qualified night-fighter crews. Granted, some of the more experienced night-fighter pilots were *Zerstörer* veterans well versed in the daytime fighter tactics of attacks in sections of two or four to increase the firepower and to cover each other. But they had long since forgotten these techniques and tried to attack just as they did at night – alone. That was nothing short of suicide against heavy American bombers in daytime. The first serious blow fell on 26 February 1943, when Ludwig Becker, *Staffelkapitän* of 12./NJG 1, was killed while attacking an American formation. The loss of this great night fighting tactician in a senseless operation caused deep bitterness among the crews, and a new word, *verheizen* ('burned up'), made the rounds. Nevertheless, the Luftwaffe command did not withdraw the order, but only diluted it so that henceforward no leading night fighter crews were allowed to fly operationally by day. As a result, the alert sections of the various NJG had to fly daytime interceptions until the end of January 1944, simply because the Reich Air Defence could not muster enough day fighters and because the available machines were too lightly armed to combat the extremely damage-proof American heavy bombers.

The successes of the night fighters on the Eastern Front, in Romania and the Mediterranean area cannot in any way be compared with those achieved by units of the Reich Air Defence. This has nothing to do with the lower qualifications of the crews. Rather these units were too weak and too thin on the ground, and had no compact net of air reporting and ground control centres to support them. Even the occasional major defensive effort gave only a temporary boost to their achievements. The enemy soon recognised areas with night fighter concentrations and simply avoided them, attacking elsewhere.

The NJG 2 units deployed in the Mediterranean area were also hampered by a lack of *Lichtenstein* AI radars, withheld by the Luftwaffe command on the grounds that in the event of a forced landing they might fall into enemy hands. As a result, the crews of I/NJG 2 had to fly half blind. Guided by only a few ground radar sites, they drove themselves and their aircraft to the very limits of their capabilities. There was no peace in daytime either, with the night fighters having to fly their share of day interceptions, low-level attacks, and convoy escort sorties. The occasional night interceptions flown by III/ZG 26 did not give much breathing space to the regular night crews either. Nevertheless, the *Gruppe* was quite successful in June and July 1942; in June alone its crews shot down 25 enemy aircraft in free close-range night fighting. Four night fighter pilots serving in North Africa were decorated with the German Cross in Gold.

Early in August I/NJG 2 was moved back to Sicily, presumably because, following the recent victories of the German *Afrika Korps*, the powers-that-be expected an early end to that campaign and wanted to have the *Gruppe* on hand for the coming invasion of Malta. One *Staffel* that had lost all but one of its aircraft in a British Commando raid had to be pulled out of action for re-equipment and rest in any case. But the situation changed rapidly: by 10 August I/NJG 2 was back under *Lw.Befh.Mitte* command again because it was planned to restart long-range night fighting operations, and only a small detachment remained at Iraklion in Crete. As we now know, the intended long-range night fighting never materialised, and after the British had forced Rommel's army to retreat in November and the air situation in North Africa became more and more precarious, the complete *Geschwader* was moved bit by bit back into the Mediterranean area, and *Kdo Iraklion* was also used operationally over North Africa.

In October Gen Kammhuber ordered the activation of an External Post South (*Aussenstelle Süd*) of the General of Night Fighters and authorised his operations officer, *Oberst* Hoffmann, to form a *Himmelbett* night fighting organisation in Southern Italy, Sicily and Tunis. Accordingly, three ground control sites were established in

Tunis, one each on the islands of Pantelleria and Lampedusa to guide the night fighters intercepting aircraft supplying Malta, and one each in Sicily and Sardinia. The most successful fighter control officers from the Reich Air Defence were ordered to Tunis, but by that time nothing could have staved off the approaching defeat. The Allied air forces and navies had an almost complete stranglehold on supplies to the remaining troops of the *Afrika Korps* in the Tunis bridgehead. The available night fighters did their utmost to keep the air space over Tunis and Bizerta free, and not without some success, but the Allied bombers found plenty of targets in areas not protected by German night fighters. Apart from that, NJG 2 again had to split up its forces just like before, taking over some convoy escort tasks and flying long-range night intruder sorties over the enemy airfields and the supply port of Bone in Algeria using Ju 88A-4 bombers.

On 11 May 1943 the Anglo-American forces broke through the last defensive positions of Army Group Africa and the final desperate struggle began. The night fighters had managed to pull out to Sicily in good time, while the Fi 156 Storchs of *Gruppenstab* were flying out ground radar specialists from the Tunis bridgehead until literally the last hour.

In June the Allies took the islands of Pantelleria and Lampedusa, and on 10 July invaded Sicily. After these developments NJG 2 moved to Pontecorvo and Aquino in Central Italy. During June and July the night fighters managed to shoot down only three enemy bombers near the Messina Straits, the area covered by the sole operational ground control site. The badly battered *Geschwader* was then transferred to Parchim and Neubrandenburg for rest and re-equipment.

Although the Allies had now broken into 'Fortress Europe' and the general military situation was beginning to look unfavourable, the threat to Germany posed by the enemy air forces was considered the greater danger and it was decided not to deploy any German night fighter units in the Mediterranean area for the time being. Instead, the Italians were given a small number of Bf 110 and *Lichtenstein*-equipped Do 217 night fighters with which to form their own units. The first Italian crews were instructed on the Do 217 at Venlo, and the formation of Italian units had begun in 1942. The first fully trained crews left the Luftwaffe night fighter training school at Schleissheim in August of that year.

Night fighting on the Eastern Front was affected by the peculiar conditions of that theatre and presented quite a different picture. In summer 1942 there were only a few fighter and bomber crews who felt confident enough to take off and face up to the Soviet bombers on moonlit nights. Among the earliest recorded night interceptions are the successes achieved by *Lt* Leykauf of JG 54, who shot down six Soviet aircraft during the night of 23 June, and *Uffz* Döring of 9./KG 55, who in his He 111 pursued and fought down three large TB-3 bomber-transports near Stalingrad.

The newly activated auxiliary night fighting sections (*BehNJ-Schwärme*), which still had not managed to get into their stride during the winter of 1942–43, had to face up to overwhelming odds in the early summer of 1943. However, by this time the training they had received from experienced Reich Air Defence crews began to pay dividends. Thus, during April–June 1943 the few available night fighters shot down more than 30 Soviet bombers in the Orel-Bryansk area alone. Among the more successful pilots were *Hptm* Schneeweis of NNJSchw Lfl 6 with 17 victories and *Ofw* Heiner of NNJSchw Lfl 4 with 11. But while these were remarkable personal achievements, the Soviet losses did not even amount to one per cent of the aircraft used. The picture began to change only after the arrival of IV/NJG 5 in the Orel area. In July 1943 alone this *Gruppe* achieved 49 confirmed victories. It was at that time that Prince zu Sayn-Wittgenstein established a new record by shooting down seven aircraft during the 24 hours of the night of 25 July.[18] Size for size, even more successful was 10./ZG 1, which shot down 28 Soviet aircraft in June while flying 'illuminated' sorties over the Kertch peninsula. Most of these victories were achieved by *Ofw* Kociok. The German Flak also began to profit from these night fighter successes. Until then the Soviet bombers had not seemed to be particularly worried by German Flak and searchlights; now the aircraft had only to be lit up by one searchlight and the Soviet pilot would hurriedly drop his bombs and turn back.

These local successes were all interceptions of Soviet medium bombers. Combating the Polikarpov R-5 and U-2 (Po-2) night harassment aircraft was quite a different story. These biplanes were extremely difficult to intercept because they tended to fly very low and slow and were also highly manoeuvrable. The ground radar sites were very hard put to detect them at all, or – because of ground echoes – would give the night fighter pilots bearings that varied by 180° so that they were forced to fly dangerously low, practically skimming the ground, to make out the enemy aircraft against the lighter sky (the AI radar was also useless so close to the ground). To add to the difficulties, the night fighter had to fly with its engines throttled right back to avoid overshooting the target. To slow down a Ju 88 and Do 217, as used by 12./NJG 5, to about 200 km/hr (124 mph) it was necessary to lower the flaps and sometimes even the undercarriage. At this low speed the controls of the Ju 88 were decidedly sloppy, while the Do 217, with its higher wing loading, could hardly be held on course. And when the fighter finally reached a firing position, victory was still far from assured: standard HE ammunition simply went straight through the fabric-covered target, only taking effect if it hit the small engine or the pilot. The aircraft best able to intercept and combat these 'highway crawlers' was without doubt the FW 58 proposed by Falck. For a while some of these aircraft were temporarily allocated to various auxiliary night-fighting sections, but inexplicably they disappeared again after the catastrophe of the winter of 1942–43. It took some time before somebody started to pay attention to the loud requests for similar aircraft from the Eastern Front night fighter units.

Night defence of the South-eastern sector was the responsibility of *Befehlsstelle Südost*, established in June 1943 by *Otl* Falck. The next step was the formation of a new night fighter unit, IV/NJG 6, the main task of which was the protection of the Romanian oil fields. Though this new formation moved to Zilistea and Pipera in July, everything remained quiet on this sector until the end of August.

Notes

1 The *Korps* command post was a bombproof bunker. But all telephone communication lines to it came together in the completely unprotected amplifying station at Arnheim. A chance hit would have left the night fighters shorn of central operational control. This situation never particularly worried the *Korps* and it first became obvious to the RLM only in November 1942. The command post bunkers of the Fighter Division were not yet operational in July 1943.

2 Added to this were 116 damaged bombers, of which 12 had to be written off as total losses.

3 During this raid II/NJG 2 alone achieved 16 victories. At that time it had several Bf 110s equipped with the FuG 202 AI radar.

4 Production at that time totalled 30 *Würzburg-Riesen* per month.

5 The following formation dates are known:
May 1942: NJG 4 with III *Gruppe* of 1., 4. and 8./NJG 1; *September:* I/NJG 5 from II/ZG 2; *1 October:* II/NJG 2 became IV/NJG 1; III/NJG 2 became II/NJG 2; *October:* I/NJG 4 from parts of I/NJG 3 and III/NJG 4; *November:* IV/NJG 3 from parts of III/NJG 2; *December:* II and IV/NJG 5; *1 Jan 1943:* IV/NJG 4; *April:* III/NJG 5; *May:* IV/NJG 6; *July:* III/NJG 2 (from V/NJG 6?)

6 Not on 24 June, as stated by Cajus Bekker in *Luftwaffe War Diaries*.

7 British psychological warfare station broadcasting a mixture of popular music, news and propaganda.

8 A bomber unit, III/KG 3, had been withdrawn from operations by Whitsun to begin retraining as 'illuminators' at Münster-Handorf. Under Hermann's method, this *Gruppe* was to light up the operational zone by using parachute flares in heavy cloud.

9 Lechner's *Kommando* succeeded only temporarily in stopping the Soviet raids. In the winter of 1941–42 the Soviets came back in straggling formations of 30 or more aircraft, and the precise timing of their arrival was almost uncanny. But this rigid method of attack also allowed the defenders to prepare themselves. This went on until January 1943, when Lechner's *Kommando* was relieved by 10. and 12./NJG 5, the nucleus of the future IV *Gruppe* under *Hptm* Prince zu Sayn-Wittgenstein. Wittgenstein and his formation were so successful in the time they were stationed in the Insterburg area that the Soviets stopped their raids completely, freeing the *Gruppe* for duties in Western France.

10	Establishment		Actual strength	Available for operations
9 Sept 1941	254		263 (!)	174
2 Feb 1942	367		265	159
30 June 1942	406		255	167
1 Aug 1942	465		322	214
10 Dec 1942	548		375	282
10 Feb 1943	653		477	330

11 Equal to approx. 19 lb/sq.in boost. The fact that in the engine manual take-off and emergency power were listed as 'temporarily prohibited' speaks for itself.

12 At the beginning of 1943 the Ju 88C-6 was used by NJG 2, IV/NJG 3 and IV/NJG 5.

13 During the approach the cabin glazing misted over in Streib's He 219A and he flew towards the airfield too fast and with restricted vision. When Streib finally saw the airfield illuminations and lowered the flaps the servo-motors were suddenly short-circuited and the flaps sprang back into the retracted position. As a result, Streib had to land too fast and at too high a sink rate.

14 Sited mainly in Jutland to detect British courier aircraft flying to Sweden.

15 According to a report by *Jafü Süd*, III/NJG 101 (former III/*NJ-Schule 1*) and the two *Staffeln* of IV/NJG 5 based at Lechfeld finally received a few FuG 202 radar sets only late in March 1943.

16 These percentages indicate losses over Germany or German-occupied territories. On average about 10 per cent of the total bomber force would turn back early as a result of technical defects.

17 For instance, *Hptm* Geiger, *Hptm* Frank and *Hptm* Prince zu Sayn-Wittgenstein each scored six victories in one night several times.

18 Wittgenstein brought two Ju 88C-6 night fighters with him to the Eastern Front, coded C9 +AE and C9 + DE. He used the latter ('Dora-Emil') on nights when there were many Soviet aircraft about and when it was advantageous after attack to return to the radio beacon as quickly as possible to search for the next victim. The specially modified 'Dora-Emil' – the ventral gun position and all armour protection were removed and the skin was highly polished – was capable of achieving a good 40 km/h (25 mph) more than the standard version.

6. Free night fighting, July 1943 – May 1944

The July raids on Hamburg and their effect – Origin and development of the 'Wild Boar' and 'Tame Boar' night fighting methods – Organisation and deployment of night fighter units in late summer 1943 – Disadvantages of the 'sit-on' crew system at JG 300 – The crisis of confidence in September – October 1943 – Departure of Kammhuber and reorganisation of the Reich Air Defence in October 1943 – Additional organisational measures until May 1944 – Night fighting in the East – Attempts to counter jamming of ground radars – New AI radars (SN-2, Neptun, Naxos and Flensburg) – Improvement of fighter guidance and control methods – Aircraft production – Developments and new aircraft – Types of night fighters – Operations, successes and losses by the Reich Air Defence and on the Eastern Front.

GENERAL MILITARY EVENTS

5 July 1943: Start of the German offensive at Kursk. *15 July:* Offensive halted; Soviet counter offensive. *10 July:* Allied landing in Sicily. *25 July:* Fall of Mussolini. *5 August:* Orel captured by the Red Army. *13 August:* Air raid on Vienna-Neustadt. *September 1943 to January 1944:* Loss of Ukraine and the Kuban bridgehead; Red Army reaches the former Polish borders. *3 September:* Allied landing in Calabria; Foggia becomes base for Allied air raids into Southern Germany. *October:* Loss of Greek islands; British landing on Piraeus; increased U-boat losses in the Atlantic. *November:* Battle of Monte Cassino. *December:* Loss of battleship *Scharnhorst*. *January 1944:* Allied landings at Anzio and Nettuno. *March/April:* Red Army advances into Galitsia and Romania. *May:* Evacuation of Crimea.

The night of 25 July 1943 put paid to all the German command's hopes for a change for the better in the air war over Germany. That night 791 RAF bombers raided Hamburg and the German night fighters and Flak managed to shoot down only 1.5 per cent of the attackers. This raid did not really come as a surprise to the German defences, since the short summer nights meant that the RAF could not risk any deeper penetrations over Germany. In any case, since the equipment of its Pathfinder aircraft with the H2S navigation radar, RAF Bomber Command had preferred new moon nights or bad weather over Central Europe for its major efforts. Just before the

Hamburg raid the conditions were ideal for the RAF, with thick rainclouds covering most of Central Europe while the British Isles enjoyed perfect flying weather. Correctly evaluating the enemy's intentions XII *Fliegerkorps* transferred leading night fighter crews from all *Geschwader* to Northern Germany. They did not have to wait long. On the morning of 24 July the German radio monitoring service reported heavy British radio tuning traffic – a certain indication of a coming major raid. At 2300 hrs that night the early-warning radars detected the enemy bombers gaining height and followed their course to the German Bight. But as soon as the enemy formation came within acquisition range of the *Würzburg-Riesen* ground radars outside the Elbe estuary it disappeared from the display screens behind a curtain of other echoes. For the first time, the RAF was using *Window*, dropping 92 million tinfoil strips cut to exactly half the *Würzburg*, *Würzburg-Riese* and *Lichtenstein* wavelength. With one blow all German fire-control and air reporting systems were rendered useless, while the remaining *Freya* ground radars were jammed by transmitters. The whole *Himmelbett* night fighting system was disrupted and it was impossible either to direct the night fighters or fire radar-predicted Flak barrages. In this seemingly hopeless situation 2 *JDivision* had no choice but to give permission to all night fighters in its sector to search for the bomber stream in the Hamburg area on their own. But the night fighters were also blind, and only a few exceptional radio/radar operators recognised that the target blips from aircraft moved slower than the interference. Fighting under these conditions, the interceptors managed to shoot down only nine bombers, while the Flak batteries destroyed another three for the expenditure of 50,000 rounds of ammunition.

These raids on Hamburg had a shock effect on the German command. If the British were going to raid one large German town after another in this way, the end of the Reich was in prospect. This was a real emergency and extraordinary measures were called for. From 25 July onwards the highest echelons were buzzing with activity, trying to find new technology and tactics that would allow the night fighters to regain their effectiveness. An order issued by Milch to the Plenipotentiary for high-frequency research, State Counsellor Plendl, on 27 July was specific. Listed as most urgent were requirements for measures to overcome the jamming of *Würzburg* and *Lichtenstein*; the development and production of new, interference-resistant radars; and a speed-up in deliveries of ground and airborne installations for the Y-control system. These instructions owed much to the thinking of Kammhuber, who was determined to retain the highly advanced *Himmelbett* system. However, jamming-proof ground radars would be needed even if *Himmelbett* were abandoned, since such systems were absolutely essential to the effective functioning of the air reporting service, the means by which a basic picture of each air battle was built up.

But as no new electronic developments could be expected for some weeks to come, the night fighters had to search for the bomber streams as best as they could on their own, and then either fly interceptions within the streams or attack the raiders over the target. Both methods were still quite possible under the circumstances: although the *Window* clouds hid individual aircraft from the ground radars, they also clearly indicated the course of the bomber stream to the air reporting service. It was thus necessary 'only' to direct enough night fighters towards it and, what with the close staggering of the RAF bombers, they were bound to find a choice of targets. Just before and above the target the bombers were relatively defenceless, having had to fly a straight course through the searchlight belts. Initial attempts to fly such 'unguided' night fighting sorties over the target had already been made by *Maj* Hermann, and a few night fighters from 2 *J Division* also had shot down bombers over the target during the first Hamburg raid. Now it was only a matter of making the best possible use of this method, and developing it.

Although Gen Kammhuber regarded 'unguided' target defence night fighting – officially code-named *Wilde Sau* (Wild Boar) – as an emergency solution only, he did not oppose the arguments in its favour and even ordered night fighters from his own *Korps* to fly interceptions in this way. The really amazing thing about this method was that initially it was quite successful. To be sure, the organisational conditions were highly favourable: whenever a major raid was expected, the *Korps* informed all units of their respective forming-up areas, and the altitude at which the individual *Staffeln* had to circle the radio beacons in left-hand turns. While the night fighters flew into their standby zones they could listen in to a running commentary on the air situation broadcast on VHF and short- and longwave bands. This means of guidance was developed specifically for the new night fighting method. The *Korps* command post was the nerve centre where the reports from its own and the general air reporting services were received, filtered and then projected on a large situation map. In this way the running commentators could give the fighters continuously updated information on the

– *weather,* including the position of thunderstorm fronts, best ways of crossing mountain ranges, weather deterioration near airfields, and so on
– *position, course and altitude of the enemy*
– *direction* of the enemy's approach to the target
– *skymarker and bomb drops.*

96

These *Korps* reports were augmented by running commentary reports from divisional command posts, broadcast on different frequencies. Orders to the night fighter pilots were accompanied by a course set a certain angle away from the approaching enemy formation. This had to be held strictly so that the air reporting service, thus informed of the approach of its own night fighters, would not be confused. The main reason for this was to make it less difficult for the air reporting service and searchlight units to detect and follow the enemy formation. The night fighters were to turn into the enemy aircraft and attack them only directly over the target, since only then were conditions at their best for successful interception. The so-called 'boundary night fighting', interception over the outer searchlight belt or earlier, was not considered very promising. This was also the greatest drawback of the whole 'Wild Boar' method: it could not be used to weaken the enemy either during his approach flight or to force him away from the target. That the enemy was thus virtually free to cause area conflagrations was accepted in the knowledge that the bombers would then stand out particularly clearly against the blazing background. In return, it was hoped that this method might cause the RAF such losses that it would be forced to abandon the air offensive for some weeks to rest and re-equip its shattered formations.

Hermann's own idea of the 'Wild Boar' method was much simpler. The fighters, on account of their maximum endurance of about 85 mins, would take off into the standby zones only when the course of the enemy formation pointed towards a definite area. The superior speed of the single-engined fighters of JG 300, based at Bonn, Rheine and Hangelar, would then ensure that they would arrive over their objective in good time, be it in North-western or Central Germany. Naturally, the pilots of JG 300 also listened in to the *Korps* and divisional running commentaries and were thus fully informed about the air situation. Hermann was however striving for more independence from these sources and began setting up special 'Wild Boar' command posts at Air District headquarters which received their information from the general air reporting service. Because of his distrust of acoustically transmitted orders, which were prone to distortion, Hermann laid on additional optical signals. When the enemy's objective had been determined with some certainty the Flak batteries would fire previously agreed light signals to indicate the areas in which the night fighters were to form up. On the way there their guidance was taken over by flashing searchlights. In the following months almost the whole Reich territory was covered by various optical orientation aids: special illuminated lanes were laid on between some larger towns, Cologne and Münster, for example; night fighter standby zones were marked by a so-called 'hour glass' (three searchlights whose beams crossed at 7,000 m/22,960 ft altitude); at certain places, mainly near prohibited Flak zones, light AA guns would continuously fire light signals vertically into the sky; special direction searchlights would indicate the nearest airfields equipped for night landings, and so on.

Good as it was, this optical guidance system also had its drawbacks. The Flak and searchlight batteries were subordinated to the Air Districts, which received their information from the general air reporting service. Unfortunately this service had hardly any ground radars at its disposal on the Reich territory, and consequently its reporting net still had too large a mesh. For this reason it could sometimes happen that the single-engined night fighters were directed towards a diversionary raid. Apart from that, the 'Wild Boar' fighters also confused matters by not reporting their flight paths to the ground radar service of XII *Fliegerkorps* and the general air reporting service. As a result these night fighters appeared on air situation maps as high-speed bomber formations which were then fired on by the Flak, if not chased by their own night fighters. These errors were usually cleared up very quickly when the pilots of the single-engined aircraft fired their fighter recognition flares. Such unexpected appearances by previously unreported formations did however waste valuable defensive time.

Thus it came about that, although everybody spoke with respect of the reckless courage of the JG 300 pilots, the 'Wild Boars' were often bitterly criticised by headquarter staffs and air reporting centres.

If, as Hermann intended, such a defence was to be put up against concentrated major bombing raids, operational methods and conditions had to be greatly improved. For one thing, the term 'concentrated major defensive effort', borrowed from the ground troops, by no means fitted this new air warfare method. While a concentrated major defensive effort was intended to prevent the enemy from breaking into the defender's positions, the 'Wild Boars' caused losses to the enemy only after he had already broken in. It was thus vital to know of the actual target much earlier than hitherto, in order to be able to attack the enemy at the outer edge of the objective and try to intercept and shoot down the so-called 'Master of Ceremonies' aircraft.[1] To improve the fighting conditions near the object a large number of searchlights had to be positioned in a wide circle around the towns, just as in the 'illuminated night fighting' of 1941–42. In clear weather the searchlights could single out individual bombers. When the sky was overcast they could light up the cloudbase to produce a kind of 'ground glass screen' effect against which the silhouettes of the bombers stood out clearly. Such lit-up cloud layers were given the macabre designation 'shroud'. This brightening up of operational zones was constantly improved during the winter of 1943–44, especially around Berlin, where the searchlights were augmented by countless 'light boxes'. But in August 1943 the news of the special requirements of the 'Wild Boar' fighters had still not penetrated everywhere, which explains why the searchlights were withdrawn from the Hamburg–Kiel area on 17 August and transferred to Southern Germany, to be returned again following energetic protests on the part of Kammhuber and Hermann.

During August and early September the British operated mostly in single bomber streams and it was not particularly difficult to make out their flight path and the target in good time. But on 17 August the night fighters had fallen for a diversionary raid on Berlin when the real target was Peenemünde.

The final major problem affecting the 'Wild Boars' was co-operation with the Flak. As mentioned before, the first attempts to use night fighters and Flak together had been made already in 1941. Officially, these *Konaja* (combined night fighting) zones and their specially equipped command posts were still in existence, although the high losses of night fighters meant that this method had practically been given up after summer 1942. However, as each night fighter was controlled separately from the ground, it was more foolproof than the system prevailing in August 1943 under which whole flocks of 'uncontrolled' night fighters would plunge into the enemy formations through an even more formidable Flak umbrella. It was believed that a solution could be found by fixing a maximum altitude for Flak fire. Thus, when an enemy bomber formation was reported and the local Flak commander was informed of the staggering in height of the enemy bombers and of the arrival of his own night fighters, he would order, for example: 'Permission to fire on all targets below 2,000 m [6,560 ft] altitude, permission to fire on all targets recognised as enemy aircraft, and not engaged in combat with night fighters, up to 4,000 m [13,120 ft] altitude.' It was believed that these arrangements did enough to ensure the safety of the night fighters. In practice, however, the picture was quite different. For instance, a Flak crew spots several enemy bombers lit up by searchlights, all of them at an altitude of over 4,000 m; there is no sign of any night fighters, or they are far away, attacking other bombers. The Flak predictor is providing a stream of exact values, so are the enemy bombers to be permitted to fly past as if they were on parade? In such circumstances, the Flak crews could hardly be blamed for joining in. But then, when a night fighter suddenly appeared from the darkness, he had little chance of avoiding the barrage of shells. It would also have been too much to expect the Flak to stop firing immediately a fighter turned in to attack a bomber already under AA fire below the 'safety' altitude. The new men of night fighting, von Lossberg and Hermann, were

Organisation of the Luftwaffe night fighter force in August 1943

(less formations and units in the East)

Luftwaffe Commander Centre
GenOberst Weise
Commander post: Berlin-Wannsee

Commander of XII Fliegerkorps (also General of Night Fighters)
Gen.der Flieger Kammhuber
Command post: Zeist

1. Jagddivision
GenMaj von Döring
Command post: Deelen
Flying units:
I–IV/NJG 1

2. Jagddivision
GenLt Schwabedissen
Command post: Stade
Flying units:
I–IV/NJG 3
NJKdo 190

3. Jagddivision
(subordinated only for
night fighter operations)
GenMaj Junck
Command post: Metz
Flying units:
II/NJG 4

4. Jagddivision
GenMaj Huth
Command post: Döberitz
Flying units:
I, III/NJG 4
I, II/NJG 2
I,II,III/NJG 5

5. Jagddivision
Oberst von Bülow
Command post:
Schleissheim
Flying units:
I/NJG 6
Operational sections
(Schwärme) of NJG 101
(tactically subordinated
to I/NJG 6)

Directly subordinated to *Lw.Befh.Mitte*:
JG 300 at Berlin/Hangelar

100

both former bomber pilots who had had some experience of flying through AA barrages and considered it unlikely that Flak could hit a hard-turning night fighter. But while this might apply to single-engined fighters, the slower and larger twins were frequently damaged by shell fragments. Nobody could accuse these crews of cowardice, but they were men who knew their own value and that of their hard-to-replace aircraft and electronic equipment, and who also knew how far they could go in combat. For these reasons it was understandable that they would break off their attacks when flying into Flak fire. As things were, Kammhuber had to repeat again and again his orders to the night fighters to open fire at 200 m (656 ft) or less.

Despite all these drawbacks, 'Wild Boar' was the only promising method early in August 1943. In principle, this also applied to another method developed by *Oberst* von Lossberg which soon received the code name *Zahme Sau* (Tame Boar). Lossberg's idea was to use the Y-control system to 'sluice' a few night fighters – preferably equipped with the *SN-2* (then still under test) – into the bomber stream. Once there, these machines would constantly transmit direction-finding signals and attract other night fighters. On 29 April 1943 von Lossberg flew Milch to a conference with Göring and put his ideas to his important passenger during the flight. Next day von Lossberg reported his proposal to Göring, who promptly replied: 'Well, Lossberg, get going then!'

On 31 August there began a series of hard negotiations with Kammhuber and Weise, both of whom feared total chaos as a result of introducing two unguided night fighting methods. However, von Lossberg had the necessary backing in the person of *Oberst* von Brauchitsch, Göring's ADC. Every objection from the generals was countered by a quiet reminder that the method was being introduced 'On *Reichsmarschall*'s orders'.

These discussions of the new methods resulted in none too clearly expressed orders by Göring dated 1 August 1943:

1. With immediate effect the Commanding General of XII *Fliegerkorps* is empowered to adopt the pursuit night fighting method proposed by *Oberst* von Lossberg within his *Korps*.
2. The night fighting controlled by him up to now remains unchanged.
3. All units not required for controlled night fighting are available for pursuit night fighting.
4. In co-operation with XII *Fliegerkorps*, the General of Bombers will commence long-range night fighting over Britain.

From these vague guidelines Kammhuber then evolved usable operational instructions:

1. In night fighting zones penetrated by the enemy the *Himmelbett* zones were to remain manned, if possible with double or triple crews, during both the inward and outward passage of the bomber stream.
2. Fighters from neighbouring areas not penetrated by the bomber stream were to be directed to the enemy by the 'Tame Boar' method, flying with the enemy and then going over to the attack by the 'Wild Boar' method at the target.
3. Fighters from unpenetrated divisions were to be directed immediately to the target area to attack by the 'Wild Boar' method.
4. The reverse procedure was to be used during the return flight of the bombers. All fighters engaged in 'Wild' and 'Tame Boar' operations were to fly along with the enemy until their available fuel was exhausted. The pursuit was to be continued to the British coast by the *Lange Kerle* (Tall Fellows) method.

How much the bomber crews actually carried out this long-range night fighting over Britain is not known. It is highly probable that their operations petered out after only a few raids by weak forces against some airfields.

The first pursuit night-fighting operation under von Lossberg's command was carried out by 2./NJG 3 to everybody's satisfaction in the first week of August.[2] Other units also tried out the new method, but the first real test had to wait until the RAF raid on Nürnberg on the night of 28 August. The tally achieved on that occasion – 12 victories – was not particularly convincing because the new method still had some very special problems from both the technical and operational points of view. Von Lossberg and Günthner had imagined that it would be possible by means of the Y-control system to infiltrate one night fighter after another from radio beacons into the bomber stream. They were also under the impression that the fighters would be informed of the dimensions of the bomber stream, but that was not the case. The running commentary gave only the position of the bomber spearhead and its stagger in height. Even when the fighter was correctly positioned in the stream and his radio operator was accurately following the course by dead reckoning, the pilot still had no idea whether he was alongside, above or below the bomber stream. Apart from that, his *Lichtenstein B/C* or *C-1* AI radar was also probably being jammed by *Window* so that he had to rely solely on his own eyes. When the proposals were made, both von Lossberg and Günthner had based their plans on the assumption that

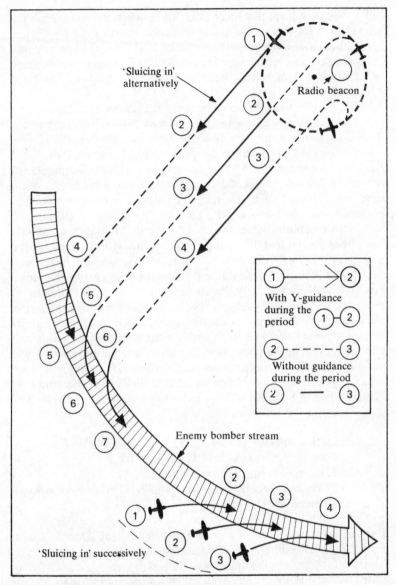

Zahme Sau (Tame Boar) infiltration into the bomber stream

within a short time the night fighters would have the *SN-2*, an ultra-long-range AI radar that would show the radio/radar operator the whole extent of the bomber formation in elevation and azimuth, and that these systems would be fitted to high-performance night fighters such as the He 219. Unfortunately the night fighter force was still a long way from this ideal state. Even when the first *SN-2* had been cleared for service use that autumn, the situation did not change overnight. Their range was disappointing and the night fighter could easily lose the enemy bomber formation if the running commentary reporter gave him wrong bearings based on false or distorted information.

Despite all these defects the night fighter force achieved 250 victories in August, a new record. Of these, over 200 went to the 'free' night fighters and only 48 to the *Himmelbett* force; the pattern was changing. In its operational report the headquarters staff of XII *Fliegerkorps* expressed fears that it would probably not be possible to repeat this kind of success in the near future because the enemy could split the defences with diversionary raids – and yet apparently nothing was done to counter this danger. The ground organisation – in fact the complete organisation of the Reich Air Defence – should have been fundamentally changed in keeping with the new tactics. Thus, for instance, the *Korps* command post should have been situated in the middle of Germany; all establishments of the Reich Air Defence – particularly the air reporting and the instrument air reporting services – should have been combined into one organisation and subordinated under the divisions; and the night-fighter formations should have been deployed in a different pattern, reinforced and increased in number. But for some reason everything was initially left as it was, despite some indications that the night fighting organisation should have been extended to Western France and East Prussia. On 15 October 1943 the Luftwaffe Commander Centre had at his disposal the following:

2 *JDiv* with NJG 3 securing the northern flank of Germany
1 *JDiv* in the west with NJG 1 and NJG 2
4 *JDiv* in Central Germany with NJG 5
5 *JDiv* in Southern Germany with NJG 6 and operational sections of NJG 101.

But the chain of command was anything but logical. Thus 3 *JDiv* in France was subordinated under *Luftflotte* 3 (HQ Paris) but with its neighbouring units came under XII *Fliegerkorps*, while the *Luftgaue* (Air Districts) in the 5 *JDiv* area which were responsible for the air reporting service in that area still remained outside the control of Luftwaffe C-in-C Centre. Strangely split also was the subordination of V/NJG 5, activated at Insterburg/East Prussia in August 1943. In service matters it came under NJG 5 and 4 *JDiv*, operationally it was directly under the *Korps*, and from September onwards it was commanded by *Jafü Ostpreussen*, who was subordinated to 4 *JDiv*.

A glance at the chart showing the deployment of Luftwaffe night

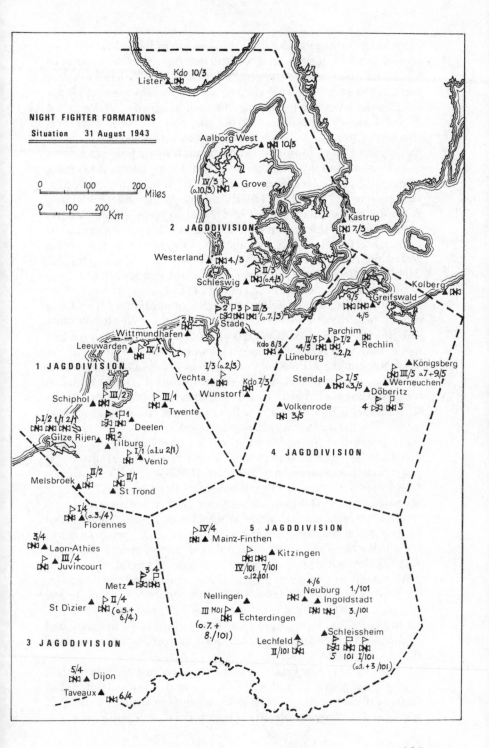

NIGHT FIGHTER FORMATIONS

Situation   31 August 1943

Lister ▲Kdo 10/3

Aalborg West ▲ 10/3

IV/3 ▲ Grove
(o.10./3)

Kastrup 7/3

2 JAGDDIVISION

Westerland ▲4./3

II/3
Schleswig ▲(o.4./5)

Greifswald
9/5
4/5

Kolberg

2   3 III/3
Stade (o.7./3)

Wittmundhafen ▲

2/3

Leeuwarden ▲IV/1

Parchim
II/5   I/2
Lüneburg o4/5   o.2./2   Rechlin

Kdo 8/3

1 JAGDDIVISION

I/3 (o.2/3)

Königsberg

III/5 o.7+9/5
Werneuchen

Vechta
Wunstorf   Kdo 7/3   Stendal   I/5
o.3./5   Döberitz

Schiphol ▲III/2

III/1

4   5
Volkenrode

Twente   3/5

I/2 1/1 2/1   1 1
Deelen
Gilze Rijen   2
Tilburg
I/1 (o.1.u 2/1)
Venlo

4 JAGDDIVISION

II/2   II/1

Melsbroek   ▲ St Trond

I/4
(o.3./4)
Florennes

IV/4
Mainz-Finthen

5 JAGDDIVISION

Kitzingen

3/4
Laon-Athies

III/4
Juvincourt

IV/101   7/101
o.12./101

4./6
Neuburg   1./101
Nellingen   Ingoldstadt

3 4

Metz

III MOI
Echterdingen
(o.7. +
8./101)

3./101

II/4
St Dizier   (o.5.+
6/4)

Lechfeld
II/101

Schleissheim

5 101 I/101
(o.1.+3 /101)

3 JAGDDIVISION

5/4
Dijon

Taveaux ▲ 6/4

fighter units in August 1943 and the strength of individual divisions reveals clearly that everything was still determined by the concept of 'tied' night fighting. 2 *JDiv* appears with an establishment of 160 night fighters and an actual strength of 122, of which about 60 per cent would have been available for operations. But of these the aircraft flown by 10./NJG 3 could not take part because that unit was specialising in co-operation with *Wassermann* early warning radars in the interception of Mosquito courier aircraft flying between Britain and Sweden and was therefore bound to its bases at Aalborg (Denmark) and Lister (South Norway). In these fruitless efforts it was assisted by 10./JG 11, latterly the *NJ-Kommando FW 190*. 1 *JDivision* had an establishment of 277 and an actual strength of 109 night fighters. Among its units NJG 2 had only I *Gruppe* more or less fit for operational service; the other two *Gruppen* were again being rested and replenished. For this reason it was decided not to use this exhausted *Geschwader* in *Himmelbett* night fighting. 3 *JDiv* was weaker still, with an establishment of 121, and actual strength of 60, with only about 36 night fighters available for operations. NJG 4 was of no practical value for 'Wild Boar' operations in the Berlin area. The Bf 110s of this *Geschwader*, based in Burgundy, were out of fuel by the time they reached the capital, and the Do 217s were just too slow. Nor could 5 *JDiv* be of much help in the defence of Northern Germany, having only one combat-worthy unit, I/NJG 6; II/NJG 6 was just being formed with inexperienced crews, and the operational sections (*Schwärme*) of NJG 101 did not have much combat value either. Finally, 4 *JDiv*, which was supposed to defend Berlin, had a paper strength of 200 night fighters but in actual fact disposed of only 63. In other words, only about 40 aircraft were available for operations at any given time. The old IV *Gruppe* of NJG 5 had been transferred to the Eastern Front (being redesignated I/NJG 100 on 8 August), a new IV *Gruppe* was activated early in September and did not have a single aircraft, while V/NJG 5 was marking time in East Prussia which had been left in peace by Soviet aircraft since May.

For the time being nothing could be done to improve this situation. Against a total loss of 61 twin-engined night fighters in August (plus aircraft written off or grounded due to wear and tear) could be set only 59 new aircraft received from the operational preparation centres[3], while the 40 pilots killed in action had been replaced by just 28 newly trained crews from NJG 101. Nearly twice as many had commenced their training in March, but they would not start reaching the units until December 1943.

The original 'Wild Boars', JG 300, were also not much more than a drop in the ocean. Certainly, the experienced old sweats detailed to this unit could be retrained on single-seat fighters within two or three weeks at *Jagdfliegerschule* 101 (Fighter Training School) at Alten-burg, but there was a dire shortage of aircraft at the operational *Gruppen*. If the cadre *Gruppe*, I/JG 300 – the only one intended to have a full complement of its own aircraft – had difficulties in keeping its Bf 109s operational because only a few ground crews knew anything about the type, the situation was catastrophic at II/JG 300 (Rheine) and III/JG 300 (Oldenburg), where Hermann's 'sitter-on' plan had boomeranged. After the first operations the 'host' formations, III/JG 11 and II/JG 1, simply refused to play the game, and for very good reasons. If the daredevil pilots of JG 300 came back at all, they landed their borrowed aircraft peppered with Flak splinters, or crashed their shot-up machines on the airfield. From then on, the day crews let them have only second-class materiel or simply declared their aircraft unserviceable. Consequently the day and night crews began to drift apart noticeably, and their relationship was further worsened by various personal frictions. Before long the day crews made it known that they considered the 'Wild Boars' simply incapable of handling a fighter aircraft in a sensible way, while the solo night fighter pilots sometimes posed as the 'real saviours of the Reich in direst need' and made capital of their direct subordination to the Luftwaffe Commander Centre.

The successes of August had once again generated optimism in high places about future developments in air warfare, but that did not last long. As Kammhuber had foreseen, in September the RAF began to adjust its tactics to the German defensive methods. Bomber Command preferred to operate in bad weather, which made 'Wild Boar' operations more difficult or even impossible; they concealed their intentions by making diversionary and feint raids with sky and ground markers; and they introduced new electronic countermeasures. As a result, the German success rate began to sink again and the losses, particularly among the single-engined night fighters, continued to rise. Coming so soon after a period of progress, this development had repercussions in the highest places and Göring's confidence in the night fighter force began to wane. As usual in such situations heads had to roll, and Kammhuber was the first to be hit by Göring's edict. On 15 September he had to relinquish his post as Commanding General of XII *Fliegerkorps* to *GenMaj* 'Beppo' Schmid, although he remained General of Night Fighters, at least for the time being. Göring was already looking around for a successor and offered the post to von Lossberg, who turned it down. This loss of confidence in the 'established' night fighter force manifested itself again on 26 September, when Göring ordered the activation of two additional single-seat night fighter units. The future JG 301 was to be deployed in Bavaria, and JG 302 in Brandenburg. These *Geschwader* were each to receive enough aircraft for one cadre *Gruppe* though it was expected to equip the other *Gruppen* later. Göring's attitude was expressed quite clearly in the wording of his order: 'As the creator of this new weapon *Oberstlt* Hermann will remain in operational command. He will be directly subordinated under the Luftwaffe Commander Centre by means of an appropriate new headquarters (30 *JDivison*). JG 300, 301, 302 and the Illuminator *Gruppe* (III/KG 3) are in every respect directly subordinated under *Oberstlt* Hermann.' As if to make this change in attitude even more obvious, the Weapons General (*Waffengeneral*) responsible for this new formation was not the General of Night Fighters but the General of Fighters.

The crisis of confidence did not end there. The next move came after the complete failure of the defences to protect Kassel during an RAF raid on 3 October. This fiasco resulted in a complete reorganisation of the Reich Air Defence. An involuntary catalyst in this reaction was the general air-raid reporting service, the neglected stepchild of the Reich Air Defence. As long as Kammhuber was in charge of night fighting he had steadfastly opposed the incorporation of the air-raid reporting service, despite repeated arguments that only by consolidation of the ground radar organisation and the air-raid reporting service would it be possible to provide a comprehensive picture of the air situation. This of course would also have created a real jumble of secondary organisations, such as the *Hauptflukos* (Main Central Air Observation Posts), *Fernflukos* (Long-range Central Observation Posts), *Raumführer* (Air Defence Zone Commanders), *Jafü* (Fighter Leaders) and 'Wild Boar' command posts, the co-ordination and subordination of which was not clearly defined. Besides, such an amalgamation would have led to intolerable expenditure of personnel and material. By 1943 the whole air-raid reporting organisation had become hopelessly involved. The RLM and the OKL had lost track of its complexities, while the immediately concerned Reich Air Defence command posts were ensnared more and more in the chaos of overlapping responsibilities, or did not know how best to make full use of the highly technical air signals organisation.

During the RAF raid on Kassel everything seemed to go wrong for the Luftwaffe from the very beginning. The series of mishaps began when the air districts and therefore the Flak were not informed in time about the course of the German night fighters. As a result, the the aircraft of I/NJG 1, which had formed up near the *Ida* radio beacon (near Münstereifel), came under heavy fire from Flak batteries around Bonn immediately after they had received an order to proceed in a north-easterly direction. One night fighter received a direct hit that blew off one of its engines; others, including the aircraft flown by von Lossberg, were severely damaged. Then there were hitches when it came to passing on information about the air situation

Ju 88C-6 with FuG 212 AI radar.

(Schliephake)

Ju 88C-6 frontal battery. *Left:* 1 × MG FF cannon and 3 × MG 17 machine guns; *right:* 2 × MG FF in the ventral tray.

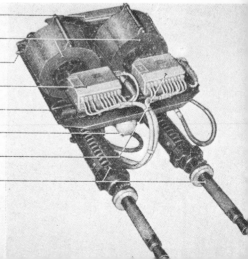

Above and below: Ju 188R mock-up with
5 × MG 151 cannon in the nose   Heise

Ju 88G V-1. Note the experimental radar
aerial arrangement   Nowarra

Above: He 219A-0

Left: MG 151 installation
in the He 219A-0 wing
Schliephake

The Ar 240 proved
unsuitable as a night
fighter
Bundesarchiv

The FuG *Lichtenstein S*
ASV radar was developed
into FuG 220 SN-2 via
the SN-1
      Bundesarchiv

The initial *Lichtenstein*
AI radar installation, with
wing-mounted aerials and
FuG 212 located in the
nose to overcome
problems with
close-range acquisition
      Heise

Wing-mounted aerials of
the *Freya-Halbe* homing
radar
      Bundesarchiv

Staffel commanders in the II/NJG 4 command post follow the course of the bombers, **drawn in by a** ghostly hand on the illustrated ground-glass situation map. *From left to right:* Unknown, *Oblt* Kamp, *Lt* Flandrich. (Bundesarchiv)

From mid-1943 onwards the twin-engined night fighters were painted in grey camouflage

Fladrich

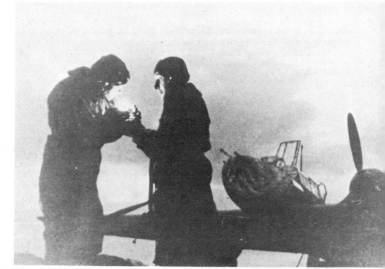

A last cigarette before take-off, and then it's off on a 'Wild Boar' chase over the Reich. II/NJG 5 at Jouvincourt

Fladrich

Unlike their twin-engined
counterparts, the
single-engined night
fighters remained in very
dark camouflage. *Left and
below:* Bf 109G of
I/JG 300 at Hangelar,
1943

Döring, Stamp

Fw 190 of *NJ-Kdo 190* at
Aalborg, Denmark, 1943

Bundesarchiv

The fighter control ship
Togo in the German
Bight, late 1943. She was
equiped with a
Dreh-Freya at the bow,
two Y-lenses amidships
and a *Würzburg-Riese* on
the after deck
Drüppel

Bf 109G-6/R6 fighters
of I/JG 302 on
detachment at Malmi,
near Helsinki, in
March 1944. Note the
flame-dampers over
the exhaust pipes.
(Helsinki War
Archives)

between the divisions and air districts. Hardly had the enemy formation reached the area controlled by 4 *JDiv* than it was lost by ground radar. Nevertheless, the running commentators reported the bombers flying towards the East, and the night fighters gathered near Magdeburg. At this stage the air-raid reporting service saw through the enemy's trick. Its warning report reached the Luftwaffe Commander Centre, but he could not prevail upon XII *Fliegerkorps* and only managed to order the single-engined fighters directly to Kassel. Of the twin-engined night fighter pilots, only the CO of II/NJG 3 had noticed the wheeling movement of the enemy bomber stream and followed the formation. His radio operator, *Fw* Kümmritz, shouted himself hoarse trying to call up the other *Gruppe* aircraft, but in vain. The heavy night fighters began to line up only after the first 'Christmas tree' markers had gone down over Kassel. The next complication was created by the Kassel Flak batteries. Ordered to limit their fire to below 4,000 m, they sent shells to all altitudes, forcing the fighters to detour around the fiery umbrella and search for their targets outside the searchlight zone. That despite these difficult conditions the heavy night fighters still managed to shoot down 19 bombers and the single-engined fighters another five is nothing short of astonishing. But that was not the end of the run of bad luck. The next misfortune followed on the night of 8 October. That night the RAF raided both Bremen and Hanover, and the command wavered for a long time trying to decide which of these two objectives should have defensive priority. In the event, 40 twin-engined and 35 single-engined night fighters (bad weather meant that no more could take off) chased hither and thither, sharing a meagre total of 10 victories.

On that day, 8 October, *Generalluftzeugmeister* Milch called a conference to establish the reasons for the declining success rate. Taken as a whole, the minutes of this meeting testify to the German sense of helplessness in those weeks. The search for causes and remedies ranged over the whole air defence organisation, resulting in a long list of negative findings: faulty co-ordination of the various means of air-raid reporting, combined with inadequate quantities of electronic and other equipment; breakdowns during the transmission of orders; and communications difficulties and misunderstandings between the various command posts and headquarters. All this led Milch to express fears that simultaneous raids on Berlin and Munich would cause the air defences to break down completely. The minutes also make it obvious that Milch was trying to lay the blame on Kammhuber and the divisional commanders: 'I am not attacking anybody individually, nor any command headquarters; I would only like to say that the system is not in order. It is all the same to me whose fault it is. . . . I would like to stress once more that I am fighting against the system. It is wrong.'

A few days later the existing system gave way to what was believed to be a better one. The final stimulus for this change was the American daytime raid on Schweinfurt, which failed to result in the number of kills expected by Göring. According to the *Reichsmarschall*, apart from the alleged 'lurking' of the fighters, the failure of the Luftwaffe was closely connected with the clumsiness of XII *Fliegerkorps* and its divisions, and this called for fundamental changes. Soon after Schweinfurt the *Korps* was disbanded, redesignated I *Jagdkorps*, and its authority limited to three *Jagddivisionen*. At the same time all divisional commanders were relieved of their posts, and Kammhuber had to stand down as General of Night Fighters.

Subordinated under the new I *JKorps* were:

1 *JDiv* (former 4 *JDiv*), CO *Oberst* Lützow. Its area of command was extended eastwards to West Prussia and Lausitz. Subordinated were the *Jafü* East Prussia and *Jafü* Silesia (intended to become 9 and 10 *JDiv*).

The former 1 *JDiv* was redesignated 2 *JDiv*, CO *Oberst* Grabmann.

The former 3 *JDiv* was redesignated 4 *JDiv* and was removed from the Luftwaffe Commander Centre area of command to come under II *Korps* (Luftflotte 3).

5 *JDiv* was activated in Western France but, like the *Jafü* Southern France (intended to become 6 *JDiv*), had no night fighter units. On the other hand it received a most welcome gift in the form of the newly installed ground radar sites in the area, to be used for day fighter control. The former 5 *JDiv* was now 7 *JDiv*, CO *GenMaj* Huth, and was directly subordinated to Luftwaffe Commander Centre. It was intended to come under the new III *JKorps*, to be formed later under the command of *GenLt* Schwabedissen. This division was subordinated to *Jafü* Ostmark (Eastern frontier district of Germany), intended to become 8 *JDiv*, CO *Oberst* Handrick.[4]

30 *JDiv* also remained directly subordinated to Luftwaffe Command Centre.

All that these measures meant for the Reich Air Defence was a multiplication of higher staffs and headquarters; not one new operational unit came into being. Even more unfortunate, there were now no fewer than four completely independent higher commands in Central Europe, all drawing up their own tactical air situations: the two *Jagdkorps* and 7 and 30 *JDiv*. This reorganisation of the Reich Air Defences had its positive sides, however. Thus, for instance, the command structure had been tightened up by combining both day and night fighter command staffs in the divisional command posts, and Air Districts VII (Munich) and XII/XIII (Wiesbaden) with their air-raid reporting services, formerly under Luftflotte 3, now came under Luftwaffe Commander Centre. But these advantages did not outweigh the problems created by the decentralised night-fighter command structure. Göring's abrupt decision to combine the posts of General of Night Fighters and General of Day Fighters – vigorously resisted by Gen Galland – was no solution at all: it was impossible for one authority to look after both day and night fighters. But Göring would not have it, and despite repeated demands by Galland for the separation of these two headquarters he remained responsible for the night fighters until he was relieved of his command early in 1945.

This change in the Reich Air Defence organisation might perhaps have had a positive effect if many more flying and ground personnel had been trained months before, and aircraft production increased to such an extent that several new *Gruppen* could have been made available late that autumn. But there was a constant shortage of aircraft, trained pilots and jamming-proof ground and airborne radars, while the air-raid reporting service had still not been reorganised. The Luftwaffe began to feel these defects in growing measure from November onwards.

On the night of 19 November the RAF opened its 'Battle of Berlin', and the subsequent series of heavy raids on the capital did not cease until February 1944. Although RAF losses frequently reached the nine per cent mark during these raids, Bomber Command in the meantime had grown so strong that it could even afford to carry out several dual raids on Berlin and another objective in Southern Germany, just as Milch had feared. In general, each RAF penetration was now accompanied by a number of harassing and diversionary raids against which the defences could rarely deploy any night fighters. As a result, average British losses sank to only two per cent while night fighter losses climbed to three per cent. The German losses were caused by enemy defensive fire, technical defects, Flak and, most of all, bad weather. Thanks to their radar navigation aids the RAF bombers could fly in even the worst weather conditions and then return home to land on brightly lit airfields. The picture was quite different in Germany: fog would frequently ground the night fighters, and if they did manage to take off the pilots had to find their way through low clouds and were slowed by icing during the climb. Hardest hit of all by this winter weather were the single-seat fighters, for which Hermann had laid down unbelievably harsh take-off conditions. This led to a number of crashes, sometimes with fatal results. Many night fighters were also lost after operational sorties because for various reasons their pilots were unable to find a landing place in

111

time. In most cases the cause was fuel shortage, but aircraft also crashed because of overloaded or jammed home base D/F frequencies. In addition, there was the increasing threat of enemy long-range night fighters, which forced the base airfields to keep their lighting to the minimum, both in extent and duration.

For the Reich Air Defence in general, and the night fighter force in particular, the 'drought' that had started in October would not end until March 1944 at the earliest. Only then would enough personnel, materiel and more jamming-proof electronics be available. Until then the command had to do the best it could with improvised organisational measures. Typical of these was the shuttling around of units, starting in November 1943 and becoming more frequent as time went on. Galland advocated a concentration of forces in one area for both day and night fighting so that it would be possible to face any major enemy penetration with overwhelming force. But he could not prevail upon Göring and Milch, who with some justification distrusted the inadequate fighter control system and preferred a dispersal of defensive formations 'for mass psychological reasons' – to demonstrate that the fighters were still active everywhere.

Such transfers also took place within the other divisions. Which division controlled any given night fighter *Gruppe* – its tactical or its service superior – depended entirely on communication links. For instance, the *Gruppe* of NJG 6 based at Mainz-Finthen was often controlled by 3 *JDiv* and not by 7 *JDiv*, its tactical superior, because communications with Schleissheim were totally inadequate. The various changes that were ordered between October 1943 and the eve of the invasion are listed here:

October: Activation of II/JG 301, formed of 10./JG 4 at Seyring for the defence of 'Ostmark'; CO *Hptm* Resseguir.

7 November: Formation of a night reconnaissance *Staffel* attached to I *JKorps*, based on experience of operational units with running commentary aircraft. This unit was to keep in contact with the enemy bomber stream, release sky markers for its own night fighters, pass on all observations as a running commentary to the command, interfere with or attack the enemy Master Bomber ('Master of Ceremonies') aircraft, and report on its own air defences (the performance of the night fighters and Flak, and the effect of artificial fog and decoy installations). In the event this *Korpsstaffel* was never formed; instead seven day and night observer *Staffeln* were activated and distributed among the seven *JDivisionen*. The aircraft used by these *Staffeln* were to be equipped with the latest electronics, and each crew was made up of an experienced night fighter pilot and a Flak officer.

29 November: A plan to equip each night fighter *Geschwader* with only one aircraft type and to use at the most two night fighting methods was considered and dropped again:

NJG 1: He 219; *Himmelbett* and 'Tame Boar'

NJG 2: Ju 88R; 'Tame Boar'

NJG 3: Bf 110; *Himmelbett*

NJG 5: Ju 88; *Himmelbett* and 'Tame Boar'

November: Completion of several new bases at Steenwijk, Volkel and Hilversum in Holland.

December: All of the less frequently penetrated dark night fighting zones, to be known henceforth as *Jagen*, were disbanded and NJG *Gruppen* COs became *Jagen* commanders.

7 *JDiv* area equipped for the *Egon* and Y-control systems. The night fighter control ship *Togo* entered service in the German Bight. To close the gap in the *Ostmark* area 10 crews of II/ZG 1 were retrained for night fighting at Wels. To speed up the training of new night fighter crews a second training unit, NJG 102, was activated on 15 December. Its nucleus formed III and IV/NJG 101. Originally intended to form at Jüterbog and Brieg, NJG 102 was established at Kitzingen' and Echterdingen. A number of seasoned *Zerstörer* and bomber pilots, as well as flying instructors, were posted to this new training *Geschwader*.

January 1944: I *Korps* planned the establishment of an *E-Kdo* under Maj Wittgenstein but this did not materialise. Instead, NJGr 10 was formed on 1 January 1944 (CO *Hptm* Schoenert), and tactically subordinated to 1 JDiv. This new *Gruppe* was to co-operate with the Werneuchen, Rechlin and Tarnewitz centres on the testing of new aircraft, systems, weapons and techniques. 1./NJGr 10 (CO *Hptm* Friedrich Karl Müller) with single-seat fighters formed from personnel drawn from I/JG 300; 2./NJGr 10 (CO *Hptm* Lüdtke) received the He 219 and Ta 154; 3./NJGr 10 (CO *Hptm* Tham) equipped with the Bf 110 and Ju 88. This new formation was based at Werneuchen and Eberswalde.

On 18 January *Gen Oberst* Stumpff relieved *GenMaj* Weise as Commanding General Luftwaffe Commander Centre; this command headquarters was renamed Luftflotte Reich on 31 January. Shortage of trained new personnel forced operational availability down to a new low level. Each *Gruppe* was ordered to disband one *Staffel*; the materiel and personnel thus released were distributed among the other *Gruppen*. Average strength until July: *Stab* four aircraft, two *Staffeln* with 12 aircraft each. III/KG 3 transferred as an Illuminator *Gruppe* to Reich Air Defence and redesignated I (Bel.)/KG 7; the provisional Illuminator *Gruppen* were disbanded. The new *Bel.Gruppe* flew the Ju 88A-4 and Ju 88C-6 and in May became the first unit to be completely equipped with the Ju 88G-1. Parts of

I/JG 300 were assigned to II/NJG 1 for Mosquito interception by the *Himmelbett* method.

February: 30 *JDiv* subordinated operationally to I *JKorps*. II/NJG 101 transferred to Parndorf in the *Jafü Ostmark* area. 28 February saw the long-overdue amalgamation of the instrument and general air-raid reporting services, subordinated to I *JKorps*.

March: New operational boundaries between 3 and 7 *JDiv*; the northern sector of 7 *JDiv* became *Jafü Mittelrhein* (Fighter Leader Central Rhine) and was attached to 3 *JDiv*, while 7 *JDiv* was subordinated to I *JKorps*. I/NJG 6 transferred from Mainz-Finthen to Illesheim to remain in 7 *JDiv* area; replaced at Finthen by III/NJG 5. 30 *JDiv* disbanded on 16 March and the badly mauled single-seater *Gruppen* were subordinated to the divisions; an exception was 1./JG 302, which was transferred to Helsinki. *Otl* Hermann was appointed CO of 1 *JDiv*. From this time on the 'sitter-on "Wild Boar" ' *Gruppen* were effectively equipped with their own aircraft; until March II/JG 302 had neither its own equipment nor a 'host' formation. I *JKorps* command post transferred to Brunswick-Querum. KG 51 based in France began long-range night intruder operations with the Me 410 over Britain.

April: Air raids on Central Germany began to taper off significantly. Instead, the Allies concentrated on targets in West and South-west Germany, but most of all in France. For this reason Luftflotte 3 requested the subordination of 3 *JDiv* but was unsuccessful in the face of tenacious opposition from Luftflotte Reich. Instead, Luftflotte Reich transferred other formations westward: II/NJG 1 to St Dizier, III/NJG 1 to Laon-Athies and I/NJG 5 to St Dizier, all within the command authority of IX *Korps*. The complete NJG 5 left the Berlin area and East Prussia and was transferred mainly westwards during April and May. II/NJG 5 came to Hagenau before going to Hungary. The gap left in East Prussia was filled by both *Gruppen* of NJG 102. The night-fighter force in France received limited reinforcement with I and II/KG 51 and I/SKG 10, which could in an emergency be impressed for 'Wild Boar' operations. The *Zerstörergruppe* of KG 40, equipped with the Ju 88C-6 and Ju 88R-2, was based at Nantes and was engaged in long-range day and night fighter operations against British anti-submarine aircraft. In April this unit was redesignated 9./ZG 1 and redeployed to Lorient.

May: More night-fighter units were transferred to the Reich periphery: III/NJG 5 to Laon-Athies, IV/NJG 5 to Mainz-Finthen. One detachment of the latter unit operated from Stubendorf in Upper Silesia against aircraft flying supplies to the Polish partisans; V/NJG 5 was redesignated II/NJG 5 and dispersed at Gütersloh, Twente, Chateaudun and Hagenau airfields. II/NJG 6 was given the

Organisation of the night fighter force in April 1944
(less night fighter formations and units in the East)

Luftflotte Reich
GenOberst Stumpff
Command Post: Berlin-Wannsee

I. Jagdkorps
Gen Lt Schmid
Command Post: Driebergen

directly subordinated
to Luftflotte Reich

Luftflotte 3
GenFM Sperrle
Command Post: Paris

II. Jagdkorps
GenMaj Junck
Command Post:
Chantilly

4. Jagddivision
Oberst Vieck
Command Post:
St Pol-Brias

Units:
Stab I, II,
III/NJG 4

1. Jagddivision
Oberst Lützow
Command Post:
Döberitz

Units:
Stab, I, II, IV/NJG 5
I/NJG 2, NJGr 10,
LBeoSt 1, 1./Beh.BelSt
Stab, I, II/JG 300
III/JG 301

Jafü Ostpreussen

V/NJG 5

2. Jagddivision
GenMaj Ibel
Command Post:
Stade

Units:
II/NJG 2,
Stab, I, IV/NJG 3,
LBeoSt 2,
III/JG 302

*Sector commander
Denmark*
10./NJG 3
NJKdo 190

3. Jagddivision
Oberst Grabmann
Command Post:
Deelen

Units:
Stab, I–IV/NJG 1,
Stab, III/NJG 2,
Ekdo 410,
I/(Bel) KG 7
LBeoSt 3
Stab, I, II/JG 300

*Sector commander
Central Rhine*
II, III/NJG 3,
III/NJG 5,
I/NJG 6,
2./Beh.BelSt
III/JG 300

7. Jagddivision
GenMaj Huth
Command Post:
Schleissheim

Units:
Stab, II/NJG 6
Stab I/NJG 101,
Stab II/NJG 102,
Stab, I/JG 301,
LBeoSt 7

Jafü Ostmark

II/NJG 101,
II/JG 301

task of flying free night interceptions from Ghedi near Brescia to protect the Appenine roads between Rome and Florence against night raids. Another unit earmarked for transfer to the outer borders of the Reich (Wiener-Neustadt), I/NJG 6, remained where it was because of bad airfield conditions in the planned operational area.

The *Jafü Ungarn* (Hungary) was subordinated to Luftflotte Reich. Within its command area were III/NJG 6, II/NJG 100 and the Hungarian night fighter squadron 5/1, equipped with the Me 210. Transfer of night fighter units to II *Korps* area was rejected for fear of a resumption of bombing raids against the Reich territory.

Deployment of the night fighter formations in March 1944

1	Stab/NJG 1 Bönninghardt	31	14./NJG 5 Powunden
1a	I/NJG 1 Venlo	32	15./NJG 5 Powunden
1b	II/NJG 1 St Trond	33	Stab/NJG 6 Schleissheim
2	III/NJG 1 Athies-Laon	34	I/NJG 6 Mainz-Finthen
3	10./NJG 1 Quakenbrück	35	II/NJG 6 Schleissheim
4	IV/NJG 1 Leeuwarden	39	I/NJG 7 Münster-Handorf
5	Stab/NJG 2 Deelen	40	3./NJG 7 Hopsten
6	I/NJG 2 Kassel	41	NJGr 10 Werneuchen
7	II/NJG 2 Deelen	46	4./NJG 100 Laksberg (Estonia)
8	III/NJG 2 Twente	47	Stab, I/NJG 101 Ingolstadt
9	Stab/NJG 3 Stade	48	II/NJG 101 Parndorf
10	I/NJG 3 Vechta	49	Stab, I/NJG 102 Kitzingen
11	II/NJG 3 Schleswig	50	II/NJG 102 Echterdingen
12	III/NJG 3 Stade	51	1./NJG 200 Tartu (Estonia)
13	IV/NJG 3 Aalborg, Westerland	52	4./NJG 200 Neuburg
14	2./NJG 3 Wittmundhafen	54	Stab/JG 300 Krefeld
15	6./NJG 3 Werneuchen	55	I/JG 300 Bonn-Hangelar
16	7./NJG 3 Nordholz	56	II/JG 300 Rheine
17	8./NJG 3 Lüneburg	57	III/JG 300 Wiesbaden
18	10.DNR E Grove	58	Stab/JG 301 Schleissheim
19	Stab/NJG 4 Florennes	59a	1./JG 301 Neubiberg
20	I/NJG 4 Florennes	59b	2./JG 301 Leipheim
21	2./NJG 4 Athies-Laon	59c	3./JG 301 Zerbst
22	II/NJG 4 St Dizier	61	III/JG 301 Zerbst
23	III/NJG 4 Juvincourt	63	Stab/JG 302 Döberitz
23a	5./NJG 4 Dijon	64	I/JG 302 Brandis, Jüterbog
23b	6./NJG 4 Tavaux	65	II/JG 302 Ludwigslust
24	Stab/NJG 5 Döberitz	66	III/JG 302 Oldenburg
25	I/NJG 5 Stendal	67	LBeoSt 1 Neuruppin
26	II/NJG 5 Parchim	68	LBeoSt 2 Stade
27	III/NJG 5 Königsberg/Neumark	69	LBeoSt 3 Venlo
28	IV/NJG 5 Erfurt	70	LBeoSt 7 Echterdingen
29	9./NJG 5 Brandis	71	BehBelSt 1 Rhein-Main
30	V/NJG 5 Insterburg	72	BehBelSt 2 Celle

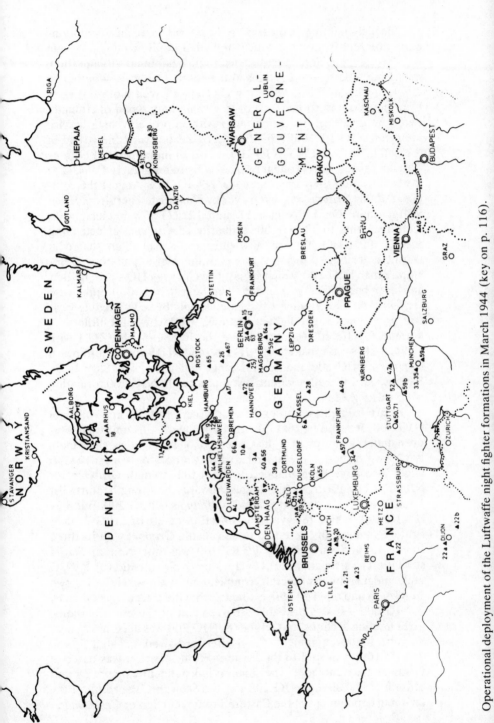

Operational deployment of the Luftwaffe night fighter formations in March 1944 (key on p. 116).

The night fighting on the Eastern Front was based on assumptions quite different from those which applied in the Reich territory, and the development of its aircraft, electronic equipment, organisation, strength, tactics and operations also went its own way. Whether to differentiate the Eastern Front night fighters even more distinctly from the Western formations, or to give an impression of strength, two new night fighter *Geschwader* with improbably high service numbers, NJG 100 and NJG 200, were created with one stroke of the pen in August 1943. NJG 100, of which initially only I *Gruppe* actually existed, was brought into being by redesignating IV/NJG 5; it was allocated the formation code W7 +. On 8 August the command of this *Gruppe* was taken over by *Hptm* Schoenert from *Hptm* Wittgenstein. On 17 August 11. and 12./ZG 1 were detailed as reinforcements to I/NJG 100, primarily as a means of activating 3./NJG 100. NJG 200 was also officially activated on that day. During its existence this unit was even more of a 'phantom' *Geschwader* than NJG 100, which at least had *Gruppen* HQ staffs; neither unit ever had a *Geschwaderstab*. The largest NJG 200 units were *Staffeln*. The *Geschwader* was created simply by redesignating various provisional night fighter sections: NNJSchw of Luftflotte 1 became 1./NJG 200 (equipped with the Ju 88C-6), 10./ZG 1 with eight Bf 110s was renamed 4./NJG 200, and NNJSchw of Luftflotte 6 became 7./NJG 200 and flew a strange collection of Ju 88A-4s, Ju 88C-6s and FW 190s totalling just four aircraft. NJG 200 formation code was 6V +.

Apart from these strength returns very little is known about NJG 200. It could be that, like its forerunners, this unit was never even under the auspices of the General of Night Fighters, since there is not a word about NJG 200 in his activity report for August 1943. It might also have been planned to form full-strength *Gruppen* for NJG 200, because from mid-August onwards the strength returns list 1.*Staffel* as I/NJG 200 and 5. and 7.*Staffeln* as II/NJG 200. But only II/NJG 200, which received an allocation of 20 Bf 110G-2 night fighters, numerically deserved to be called a *Gruppe*; with its three Ju 88C-6s and one Bf 110 I/NJG 200 was not even of *Staffel* strength. The strength returns of late August also mention an 8./NJG 200; judging by its aircraft complement – three He 111s, two Ju 88A-4s and one FW 190, evidently from the aircraft passed on by 7./NJG 200 – it was probably a descendant of the old provisional night fighting sections. In October 8./NJG 200 was at Neuburg near Danube for re-equipment. Soon afterwards, redesignated 3. and 4./NJG 100, it moved to the Eastern Front, where it was based at Orsha and Baranovicze. The smallest independently operating unit of both NJG 100 and NJG 200 was the *Schwarm*, the result of the far-flung deployment of the Eastern Front night fighter *Geschwader*.

Each of these *Schwärme* was practically a small *Staffel*, and had full disciplinary powers. Each NJG 100 *Schwarm* operated with its own rail-portable *Himmelbett* station, while NJG 200 was presumably confined to illuminated night fighting.

In summer 1943 all Eastern Front night fighter *Schwärme* were still operating near the front lines. Their operational bases changed frequently, depending on the intensity of Soviet air activity, or had to be moved westwards because of Soviet advances. Tactically, they were employed by Luftflotten 1, 4 and 6. In August a night fighter 'barrier' between Bryansk and Smolensk was being patrolled by *Gruppenstab*, 1. and 3./NJG 100; further north were two *Himmelbett* zones around Vitebsk and Nevel, all in the area controlled by Luftflotte 6. Operating in the southern sector of the front under Luftflotte 4 were *Schwärme* from 2./NJG 100 based at Stalino and Poltava. The gap between the northernmost and southernmost *Schwärm* was 1,000 km (621 mls) in a straight line. The operational areas of NJG 200 were even more widely spaced out. Thus, during bright summer nights 1./NJG 200 would fly moonlight interceptions along the Baltic coast while 5./NJG 200 was operating mainly in the Crimean area; nothing is known about the bases and activities of 4., 7. and 8./NJG 200.

During the autumn of 1943 Allied air incursions into the Danube and Carpathian areas increased in frequency. These aircraft attacked the Romanian oil fields, mined the Danube and flew in supplies to the partisans in the whole of Eastern Europe. When this trend became evident, sections of 3./NJG 100 were transferred back to Galitsia (based at Radom, Bielce and Biala Podlaska). IV/NJG 6, until then the only unit combating these Allied forays, was reinforced by 3./NJG 100, and its three Ju 88C-6s and two Bf 110s. At this time the Romanians formed their own night fighter squadron, equipping it with four Bf 110C-1s and E-4s.

In winter 1943/44 the Soviets achieved significant successes in the Northern sector and the Ukraine, and the front stabilised again only in March 1944. At this point in time the deployment of Luftwaffe night fighter units on the Eastern Front was more or less as follows:

Lfl 1 tactical area and the newly set up Fighter Sector Tallinn-Helsinki:

NJ-Kdo JG 302 at Helsinki

1./NJG 200 at Jékabpils (Latvia)

4./NJG 100 at Riga, Tallinn-Ulemiste and Helsinki-Malmi.

All these units were guided from the night fighter control ship *Togo* stationed off Tallinn from 15 February.

Lfl 6 tactical area:

Stab, 1. and 3./NJG 100 at Orsha, Bobruisk, Pinsk and Radom; 8./NJG 200

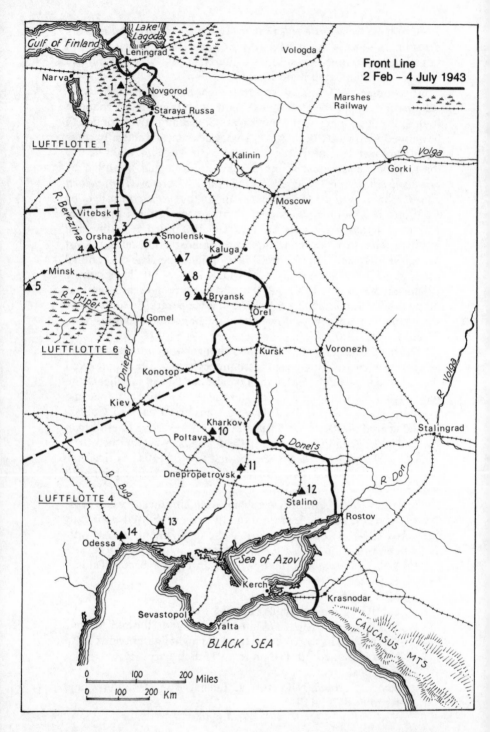

Front Line
2 Feb – 4 July 1943

Marshes
Railway

LUFTFLOTTE 1

LUFTFLOTTE 6

LUFTFLOTTE 4

Gulf of Finland
Lake Lagoda
Leningrad
Narva
Novgorod
Staraya Russa
Vologda
Kalinin
Gorki
R. Volga
R. Berezina
Vitebsk
Orsha
Smolensk
Moscow
Minsk
R. Pripet
Kaluga
Bryansk
Orel
Gomel
Kursk
Voronezh
R. Volga
Konotop
Kiev
R. Dnieper
Kharkov
Poltava
Stalingrad
R. Donets
Dnepropetrovsk
R. Bug
Stalino
R. Don
Rostov
Odessa
Sea of Azov
Kerch
Krasnodar
Sevastopol
Yalta
BLACK SEA
CAUCASUS MTS

1
2
3
4
5
6
7
8
9
10
11
12
13
14

0   100   200 Miles
0   100   200 Km

Lfl 4 tactical area:

5./NJG 200 (reduced from II/NJG 200) at Nikolaiev. This *Gruppe* had apparently suffered terrible losses, having only four Bf 110s and one Ju 88C-6 on hand by this time.

Lw Kdo Südost (South-Eastern) tactical area:

IV/NJG 6 and 2./NJG 200 deployed at Bucharest, Focsani, Buzau, Otopeni (all in Romania) and Telish (Bulgaria). In April, these units were reinforced by the transfer of 1./NJG 200 to Bulgaria. In May 5./NJG 200 was disbanded after the loss of Crimea.

This deployment remained largely unchanged until the start of the Soviet offensive against Army Group Centre on 23 June 1944. 1./NJG 200 was however disbanded on 27 January and redesignated 5./NJG 100, followed by the new 6./NJG 100 (also in the South-Eastern area) which came into being on 7 May, formed from 4./NJG 200 which until then had been based at Neuburg/Danube.

The night air war over the Reich territory, which had begun in 1940 with the most primitive of technical aids, had by 1943 turned into a battle between the electronics scientists in which the British had obviously gained a decisive advantage. Thanks to its H2S navigation radar the RAF could fly into Germany in any weather conditions, and with the help of *Window* late in July the British had managed temporarily to completely disrupt the German air-raid reporting service, Flak and night fighters, or at least to limit their effectiveness. Within the next few months, however, the German researchers managed to make up lost ground, and by spring 1944 it even seemed that Germany had again achieved the lead in this race. Unfortunately a typically German insistence on perfecting everything again led to a dissipation of effort that resulted in a delayed start to series production, a reduction in the number of units completed, and finally, in February 1944, a complete halt to research and development work.

Airfields used by night fighters on the Eastern Front July–September 1943

1. Siverskaya	6. Smolensk	11. Dniepropetrovsk
2. Dno	7. Shatalovka	12. Stalino
3. Orsha	8. Sestchinskaya	13. Nikolaiev
4. Bobruisk	9. Bryansk	14. Odessa
5. Baranowicze	10. Poltava	

This map shows clearly how strongly the night fighting operations in the East depended on the railway lines.

German high-frequency work was determined by three requirements:

1) A solution to the jamming of existing radars to permit controlled night fighting to begin again as soon as possible.
2) The development of ground and airborne radars that would permit wide-zone fighter guidance and simultaneously allow the night fighters to hunt enemy aircraft as independently as possible, detect them at great distance, and follow them even at low level.
3) The development of control/guidance and airborne systems that would effectively turn the night fighter into a remotely controlled weapon. The pilot would have only to take off and land; the rest – detection of the bomber stream and individual enemy aircraft, and their destruction – would be controlled from the ground.

A counter to enemy electronic jamming was naturally the most pressing need late in July 1943. Within three days of the first Hamburg raid Dr Schulze of *E-Stelle* Werneuchen had developed an anti-jamming aid, *Würzlaus*, for the *Würzburg* and *Würzburg-Riese* ground control radars. This appliance used the Doppler effect, enabling the operator to differentiate between the slowly fluttering *Window* strips and the faster aircraft on his display screen. *Würzlaus* was highly praised, but it also had some drawbacks: it reduced the range of the *Würzburg* radars, was extremely complicated to use in service, and worked satisfactorily only if there was no wind at higher altitudes. If the *Window* strips were blown along at more than 40 km/h (25 mph) they again showed up like real aircraft. This led to the development of *Nürnberg*, which made use of propeller modulations to produce different echoes for aircraft and decoys on the display screen. *Nürnberg* was easier to use in service but did not fulfil all the requirements. However, it became evident that controlled night fighting using the *Himmelbett* method would no longer be possible, and for that reason the system was abandoned in late autumn 1943. For all that, the anti-*Window* effort had been successful enough to make it possible to realise the full potential of the Y-control system. All the Luftwaffe officers in Hitler's entourage, absolute laymen that they were, had tried to reassure him by ascertaining that the Y-method would not be affected by the tinfoil strips, without however mentioning that *Würzburg* was still needed to detect and acquire the enemy aircraft in the first place. The *Freya* ground radar could also overcome jamming, but likewise not without a sometimes significant loss of performance.

The *Lichtenstein B/C* and *C-1* airborne radars were similarly modified, making it possible to change frequencies (the so-called *Streuwellen* or 'dispersal wavebands'), but again at the cost of some reduction in performance. Development of the *Wismar* anti-jamming appliance was slowed down in anticipation of the appearance of the interference-secure *Lichtenstein SN-2* AI radar. This promising system had however been delayed when Telefunken ran into difficulties in its attempts to evolve a standard set with fuselage nose aerials that would fit all night fighter types (the FuG 220b). It was only in September 1943 that the first Bf 110G-4 fitted with the nose aerial array was test-flown (C9 + DK of NJG 5).

Because of these initial difficulties Telefunken had to continue producing *Lichtenstein B/C* (for the Bf 110) and *C-1* (Ju 88 and Do 217). In August, after much hard work, the technicians succeeded in installing the remote-control device for the aerial selector switch in a Bf 110, allowing the company finally to discontinue *B/C* production. But there were also other problems. The need to deploy manpower and facilities on the ṛroduction of a technically out-of-date radar like the *Lichtenstein C-1* while making all the preparations for *SN-2* production had stretched Telefunken beyond its limits. Possibly for that reason, 80 per cent of the *C-1*s delivered in August had first to be overhauled at the Gütersloh operational preparation centre before they could be declared serviceable. Similarly, only nine satisfactory *Lichtenstein SN-2s* could be delivered in September. On the whole, the output of AI radars was so low that, two years after the first night 'kill' with a *Lichtenstein*, only 83 per cent of the actual strength (or 49 per cent of the establishment) of the night fighter force was equipped with the *B/C* or *C-1*.[5] In fact, the AI radar situation in September 1943 was so catastrophic that installation of the *Spanner* infra-red detection system was once again considered. But even these could not be made available in sufficient numbers: only nine *Spanner IIa* sets were delivered to the night fighter force that month – the rest went to the Army tank destroyer units on the Eastern Front – and there was no chance of starting large-scale series production before October or November. During these months Telefunken actually surpassed its *Lichtenstein* production target, although hardly any of the completed *SN-2* sets were usable. Of the total of 300 *SN-2*s manufactured by early November, only 49 had been fitted to night fighters, of which only 12 were serviceable. It was not until early 1944 that Telefunken finally managed to master *SN-2* production; the company also established several radar installation centres which doubled as training schools for maintenance crews and airborne operators. From then on things began to move quickly: the 200th *SN-2* was delivered to the night fighter force in early spring, followed by the 1,000th set in May. By that time the close-range definition had been improved to such an extent that the separate

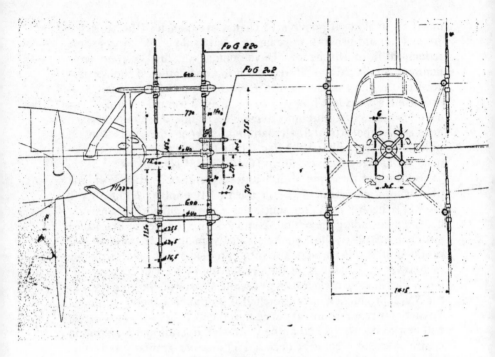

FuG 220 and FuG 202 aerial arrangement on Bf 110 C9 + EN (reproduction of an original drawing).

aerial for the *B/C* or *C-1* – the so-called 'Wide-angle aerial' which took over between 1,000 and 300 m (3,280–984 ft) – could be deleted. This meant that the radio/radar operator now had to observe only three instead of five display screens, much simplifying his task. The deletion of this aerial also improved the aerodynamics of the aircraft. Production of the older *Lichtenstein* sets continued until mid-1944 because they could still be used in the East and South, where there was no *Window* interference. The few night fighters of the Italian, Hungarian and Romanian air forces were also fitted with *Lichtenstein B/C* or *C-1* radars.

Enthusiastic as the pilots and radio/radar operators were about the *SN-2* – they occasionally reported acquiring up to six targets – the expectation that this new wide-angle AI radar would show the bomber stream as a three-dimensional image on the display screen proved to be unfounded. Despite the running commentary, 'swimming with the bomber stream' still remained a matter of luck, especially under bad weather conditions.

In addition to the *SN-2* there were another two AI radars in advanced development in Germany during the summer of 1943. The first of these, known as *Wendelstein*, was developed by Naval Construction Counsellor Prof Dr Scherzer and was originally intended as an ASV radar. In 1942 this system was fitted to a Do 217 and Scherzer carried out a series of trials over the Mediterranean. The set, working on the same frequency as the *Freya* early-warning radar, proved to have a range of 80 km (49.7 mls) and good wide-angle acquisition sideways and backwards, and could also detect flying targets. Initially its minimum range, reportedly 20 km (12.4 mls), made *Wendelstein* completely unsuitable for night fighters, but this was progressively improved by Scherzer until it had reached an acceptable 300 m (984 ft). In April 1943 *E-Stelle* Werneuchen described this radar as a promising development and arranged for a set to be installed in a Do 217 of 5./NJG 5 at Dijon. These tests were discontinued in August, the main problems being excessive wear and tear on the valves, the possibility of interference between *Wendelstein* and *Freya* (curiously enough, no such fears were ever expressed about *Lichtenstein* and *Würzburg*, which shared the same frequency), and misgivings about the ability of a naval man to oversee the introduction of a new radar into the Luftwaffe.

More successful were the trials with the FuG 217 *Neptun-J*, evolved from the FuG 216 tail-warning radar. As some versions of *Neptun* had proved suitable as radio altimeters and in the ASV role, Milch's staff experts were hopeful that it might be possible to develop a low-altitude AI radar by combining the aerial of one system with the processing equipment of another. Though this was not to be, *Neptun* had several other advantages over the *SN-2*: it was capable of approximately the same performance but weighed only half as much, was easier to maintain, and could display all three parameters (range, azimuth and elevation) in turn on the same screen. All this made *Neptun-J* seem highly suitable for single-engined fighters, and in autumn 1943, at the instigation of *Jafü Otl* Gordon Gollob, five FW 190s of the French-based JG 2 were fitted with *Neptun-J*. This gave the Luftwaffe the world's first all-weather fighter. Thanks to the streamlined rod aerials these aircraft were little slower than the 'pure' day fighters, and so were reasonably successful in action. However, by December this use of *Neptun* near the Channel coast was looking too risky to Galland and Martini, who feared an untimely discovery of the system by the British during their daytime operations. They therefore recommended further *Neptun* tests over the Reich territory, especially since *Maj* Hermann was also demanding the system for his 'Mosquito hunters'. Early in 1944 35 FW 190 and Bf 109 fighters were equipped with the *Neptun-J* and underwent operational trials (mainly with NJGr 10). These pilots were not exactly enthusiastic about the new radar. True enough, detecting and following a target were no longer a problem, but difficulties began to appear during the final approach to a firing position. After staring into the display screen for long periods the pilot had lost practically all his night vision, so that on lifting his head and searching for the bomber in the darkness he could see nothing. Nevertheless, development was pushed ahead so as to have a second iron in the fire in case the *SN-2* did not prove itself or was jammed by the enemy.

From late autumn 1943 onwards quite a few victories were also achieved with the passive homing devices, the FuG 227 *Flensburg-Halbe* and the FuG 350Z *Naxos Z*. *Flensburg-Halbe*, also known as *ASV-Halbe*, had been under test since September 1942. It detected the emissions from British tail-warning radars up to a range of 100 km (62 mls), and occasionally even up to 200 km (124 mls). From this distance the night fighter radio/radar operator could guide his pilot to the enemy bomber with deadly accuracy as long as its tail-warning radar remained switched on. In such situations even the hardest evasive manoeuvres by the bomber could not shake off the night fighter. Though the FuG 221a *Rosendaal-Halbe* homer also reacted to the emissions from British tail-warning radars, this device was only used in small numbers because its centrally positioned aerial precluded the use of the *SN-2* (*Flensburg* had low-drag wing aerials).

Oddly enough, despite this record of operational success only 250 *Flensburg* sets were built individually by various small engineering firms because the powers-that-be did not want to 'burden' the big companies with its production! The FuG 350Z *Naxos Z* variants fared much better: a total of some 1,500 sets were completed and fitted mainly to the Ju 88 night fighters. This radar could detect the emissions from the H2S navigation radar (German covername *Rotterdam*) up to a range of 50 km (31 mls). After the FuG 350 had really proved itself in a few air observer aircraft late in 1943 Hermann demanded priority for these sets and for *Neptun*, with which his fighters could intercept the RAF Pathfinders. A few Bf 109G-6/N and a FW 190 were then fitted with *Naxos* and underwent operational trials with NJGr 10. But the detection of a Pathfinder among scores of other aircraft proved too difficult for the pilots of these single-seaters and it was decided not to equip a larger number of single-engined fighters. Instead, *Naxos* was used only in air observer aircraft and later delivered to regular night fighter units, equipping several Ju 88 *Gruppen*.

The Luftwaffe radio/radar operator had to look after a staggering number of electronic devices in a fully equipped night fighter in 1944. There was the *SN-2* with the wide-angle *C-1* appliance (total of five display screens), the double display screens of the *Flensburg*, and one screen for the *Naxos*. Used for radio communications by R/T and W/T on long wave and VHF bands were the FuG 10P, FuG 29 and FuG 16ZY. Then there were the tail-warning radar (*B/C-kurz*, *SN-2R* or *Neptun-R*), the FuG 101 radio altimeter, the FuBl 2 blind landing/navigation set and the FuG 25a IFF set. But that was not all: the operator was also expected to keep a lookout either to help detect the bombers or warn his pilot of an approaching enemy night fighter. In that event he also had to act as an air gunner.

The FuG 25a IFF responded only to ground radars; a solution to the problem of air-to-air identification, so urgently needed for pursuit night fighting, eluded the Germans until the end of the war. This lack of reliable identification was circumvented by instructions permitting attacks only on four-engined aircraft. Later on the night fighters were issued with special identification searchlights with which they could give intermittent Morse-type signals.

At least as important as a counter to enemy jamming of ground radars was the improvement of long-range fighter control. This was achieved by the introduction of the *Jagdschloss* panoramic radar, which was delivered from April 1944 onwards and had a range of 120 km (74.5 mls), and the *Egon* system, which could be used to guide and control fighters up to a maximum range of 200 km (124 mls), much further away than with the Y-system. Using *Egon*, only about 70 *Freya-Gemse* ground radars were needed to cover the whole Reich territory.

It was also obvious that if the night fighters were to be controlled more effectively and accurately, the air situation would have to be analysed even more quickly. Promising experiments to this end were carried out already early in 1944, with television transmissions going from the fighter control centres to their neighbouring posts, and automatic transmission of data from the ground radar sites to the large air situation tables in the divisional command posts. But by that time German industry had been affected by enemy bombing to such an extent that it was unable to produce such devices quickly and in quantity, and in February 1944 all such improvements in command post technology were crossed off the development list.

Milch also deleted most of the other new developments that would have led to an extensive automation of night fighting operations. It is true that this was never expressly demanded, but when one takes into consideration all the airborne and ground control electronics that were under development and accorded the highest priority by Kammhuber until late autumn 1943 (remembering also Kammhuber's mistrust of the 'free' night fighting), one must conclude that the leading personalities of the Reich Air Defence regarded the remotely controlled night fighter as the ideal, even after Kammhuber's fall from grace.

Such largely automated operational sorties would have taken place more or less as follows. After take-off the fighter would fly automatically by means of a homer towards a given radio beacon, where it would fly a standby pattern. After the division had detected an enemy bomber stream or an individual target the fighter would receive its orders, with its course determined by the data-transmission installation on the ground. Alternatively, it would seek its target by the *Licht* (Light) method. This involved the use of high-powered ground radars that would 'light up' the enemy target, the resulting reflections being received by the *X-Halbe* homer carried by the fighter. The attack would then be taken over by an automatic blind-firing device (several types of which were under development or under test), with the subsequent return flight home being taken over by another homing device.

As mentioned above, *GFM* Milch cancelled all high-frequency projects in February 1944, the only exception being those that had made good progress and could be realised within a reasonably short time. Of the AI radars only the *SN-2* was in large-scale production until mid-1944. *Neptun* was being tested, and work was in progress on the development of the wide-angle FuG 228 *Lichtenstein SN-3* and the centimetric FuG 240 *Berlin N1a*; both types were expected to be ready for series production in August 1944.

Compared with the electronics industry, the German aircraft manufacturers performed very poorly indeed during the period August 1943 to April 1944. Disregarding Göring's loud exhortations uttered from August 1943 onwards, to concentrate all efforts on strengthening the Reich Air Defence, the German aircraft industry practically stagnated and the output was even lower than in 1942:

	Bf 110G		Ju 88C-6		Do 217N		He 219	
	Plan	Actual	Plan	Actual	Plan	Actual	Plan	Actual
1943 July	100	47	NA	43[1]	NA	28	6	1
August	100	28	NA	73	NA	20	7	–
October	115	124	NA	87	NA	–	9	7
December	140	88	NA	76	NA	–	10	–
1944 January	145	85	NA	30	NA	–	11	11
February	150	4[2]	NA	89	NA	–	12	5

NA = Not available. [1] The July-December 1943 figures also include the Ju 88C-6 day *Zerstörer*. [2] During the so-called 'Big Week' offensive USAAF bombers destroyed the complete Bf 110 night fighter manufacturing facilities; many completed airframes were also wrecked.

But enemy bombing was only one side of the story. For the real cause of this performance shortfall we have to look at the aero-engine manufacturers, which, largely because of raw material shortages, did not succeed in producing more powerful engines with longer service lives. By mid-1943 the basic BMW 801, DB 605 and DB 603, and the Jumo 213 engines had reached their development limits. But even with these powerplants it was still months before their service lives were satisfactory, while in the case of the DB 605 there were still frequent engine fires in August and September, resulting in a number of Bf 110 crashes. The large-capacity DB 603 ran into so many difficulties that it was accepted only conditionally by the RLM, which cleared it for use in just one aircraft type, the Do 217M (and its Do 217N night fighter variant), and even that was nearing the end of its production run. But there were simply not enough engines even for the relatively few aircraft of this series, so that completed but engineless airframes were standing about on the factory premises for weeks on end, and there was practically no hope of getting hold of any replacement engines or spare parts for operational aircraft. In September 1943 XII *Fliegerkorps* had to report: 'Supply of Do 217N has come to a complete standstill and consequently this aircraft can now hardly be considered as an operational type. . . . The operational availability of the existing aircraft is extremely low because of the lack of DB 603 engines. A large number of these machines are parked without much hope of receiving the necessary replacement engines. . . .' For this reason production of the Do 217N was terminated in that month.

The DB 603 was also intended for the He 219 and Me 410, but when production of this powerplant finally got under way the Me 410 had priority and the He 219 could only have a few engines surplus to the production programme.

The BMW 801 was fitted mainly to the FW 190 and all other types just had to wait. This had a catastrophic effect on the Ju 88, production of which had to keep going with the Ju 88C-6/Jumo 211 despite the fact that this underpowered version was considered only 'conditionally suitable for operations' in August 1943. Only a few examples of the Ju 88R-2 with the BMW 801 radials, so urgently needed in service, were completed now and again; in August 1943 the total reached just two aircraft, and there were not many more during the following months.

Because of the constant problems with the more powerful DB engines the aircraft industry and the RLM Technical Office laid great hopes on the Jumo 213 and Jumo 222, but the Jumo 213 did not reach series production before early 1944, while the Jumo 222 did not advance beyond tests. As a result, several new aircraft types designed around this engine – including several He 219 variants – could never be built.

Only a few pre-production examples of the promising new He 219 were available to the service in 1943; only 11 had been completed, and most of these were used up in tests at Rechlin. Series production only began early in 1944, and then initially at a rather modest monthly rate of 13 aircraft, a figure that was never to be much improved on.

The reluctance of the day fighter formations to lend their aircraft to the 'Wild Boars' is explained by the drop in Bf 109 production figures at that time: from 704 aircraft in July to only 350 in December 1943. The slump in aircraft production meant that in the autumn of 1943 the night fighter units took only a fraction of their establishment into battle, in the course of which their operational strength declined even further.

Obviously, the multiplication of *Staffel* figures did nothing to increase the number of available operational aircraft. This table shows how actual strength was declining at this time:

		Strength	
	Establishment	Actual	Operational
9 August 1943	831	577	376
26 August 1943	966	627	421
7 February 1944	966	557	350

These figures cover all twin-engined night fighters, including those on the Eastern Front, but not the single-engined *Wilde Sau* formations and the training *Geschwader*. In the area controlled by I *Jagdkorps* the number of operational fighters sank from 304 on 8 October to an average of 220 in January 1944 and reached an all-time low of 179 aircraft on 1 February 1944. For reasons already described the fighters of 30 *JDivision* made little difference to the number of the night-fighter force.

At least as detrimental as the low production rate was the fact that, apart from a handful of He 219s and Ju 88G-1s, no really new types reached the manufacturing stage until May 1944. The paradox in all this was that Milch hung on to the proven Bf 110 and Ju 88 because he feared that switching over to a completely new type or a fundamentally new development would affect the 'high' production figures.

Of course a few advanced types were in the development stage: the Tank Ta 154V-1 had first flown on 7 July 1943 after eleven months of development, and the third Ta 154 prototype – already equipped with an air interception radar – had made its first flight on 25 November. As far as speed was concerned the Ta 154 was convincing, but when flown by *EKdo Ta 154* the new aircraft revealed so many defects that the whole pre-production series had to be sent back to the works. Most noticeable of all was the fact that the aircraft had been conceived at a time when the *Himmelbett* tactics held sway and at its present stage of development was not really suitable for pursuit night fighting. The most serious criticism concerned the limited fuel tankage and resulting lack of range; further, only the pilot had a reasonably good view. During firing trials pieces of the fuselage skin became loose, and later in production there were problems with the adhesive, which proved damaging to the plywood. Although 250 Ta 154As were ordered by the RLM in November 1943, by early 1944 there was still no sign of a start to series production. Milch favoured a Ju 88-class night fighter, hence the Ju 188 night fighter modification, or the Ju 388, which was scheduled to be in series production from late autumn 1944. He supported this line of reasoning by pointing to the production capacity at Junkers and the ability of these types to accommodate without much difficulty the three-man crew ideally needed for pursuit night fighting. Milch also used this final point as an argument against the He 219 by quoting a few pilots who allegedly were dissatisfied with the He 219 because of its two-man back-to-back seating arrangement. Prof Heinkel countered this with a three-man cabin for the He 219.

Also under consideration was the Do 335, the prototype of which had first flown in the autumn of 1943. But under RLM plans the Do 335 was to be built primarily as a fighter, then as a bomber and only then, using whatever remained from the production run, as a night fighter.

By and large, until March/April 1944 there were not enough proven types available, still less new machines of higher performance. A decisive breakthrough was achieved only by the *Jägerstab* (Fighter Staff), founded by *Reichsminister* Speer in February 1944, which mobilised all reserves. From then on the production figures began to climb rapidly, though manufacture of the Bf 110 was later cut back in favour of the more efficient Ju 88G-1:

	Ju 88C/G	Bf 110G-4	Bf 109	FW 190
March	77	67	660	320
April	163	190	719	346
May	229	179	1,017	431
June	285	116	1,206	607

Concentrating on fighter output, the RLM drastically limited the production of other types that used up particularly large quantities of material, such as the Me 323, various flying boats, the He 111, Ju 88 bombers and several transport and communications aircraft.

The first three Ju 88G-1 night fighters were delivered to the service in January, effectively as substitutes for the Ju 188R, which had failed to materialise. Thanks to some ruthless pressure from the *Jägerstab* the changeover to the G-1 – which used many standard

Ju 88 components – was almost problem-free. In February the production lines delivered 27 Ju 88 'Gustavs', followed by 50 in March.

Let us now look at the technical aspects of German night fighters in some detail.

The basic Bf 110G-4, used operationally from April 1943, carried a standard armament of 4 × MG 17 in the upper and 2 × MG 151/20 in the lower nose; the defensive armament comprised one twin-barrel MG 81Z in the rear cockpit. As time went by this standard built-in armament was augmented by a multitude of *Rüstsätze* (Standard Equipment) and *Umrüstsätze* (Conversion) sets designed to make the aircraft better suited for the operational purpose of the time. The performance could be increased by fitting the GM-1 nitrous oxide injection system to the engine, while the range could be improved by supplementary built-in or external fuel and lubricant tanks. Above all, there was a wide choice of armament variations, including ventral weapon trays with MG 151 or MK 108 cannon, possible replacement of the nose MG 17s with MG 151s or MK 108s, and oblique-mounted (*Schräge Musik*) MG FF or, less often, MK 108 cannon. But it is almost impossible to identify these aircraft from external features on photographs taken during the period 1943–45 because, in addition to the factory-installed equipment, they were often fitted with extras at the various front-line workshops. These modifications, based on operational experience, were carried out quite officially, often resulting in significant alterations. For instance, the older versions were adapted as far as possible to the latest standard; the Bf 110F-4 and G-2 were retrofitted with the broad rudders of the G-4, and so on. Naturally, operational experience was also evaluated by the manufacturers and incorporated on the production lines, though by that time these changes were often already out of date and had been superseded by new modifications.

Individual night fighter aces often had their own ideas and knew how to get their new aircraft 'tailored' at the front-line workshops to fit their special requirements. Thus, for instance, the brand-new Bf 110G-4 flown by *Hptm* Johnen that landed in Switzerland on 28 April 1944 does not fit any of the standard descriptions: it had a fixed armament of only 2 MG 151s, fairings over the muzzle apertures of the upper 4 × MG 17s, 2 × MG FF/M oblique guns, no defensive armament, no GM-1 installation, and 2 × 300-l supplementary fuel tanks on underwing racks. Its electronic equipment comprised FuG 8, FuG 10, FuG 16, FuG 25a, FuG 202 and FuG 220.

The following example shows how an instruction on certain modifications led to a completely new Standard Equipment set (*Rüst-*

satz). From 22 May 1944 under Modification T 106 all Bf 110 night fighters leaving the production lines or arriving for repairs in the front-line workshops were to be re-equipped as follows: removal of GM-1 installation (no longer needed because the interception of high-flying bombers, particularly the Mosquito, was to be taken over by the single-engined fighters and the He 219); MG 17s in the upper nose replaced by 2 × MG 151 cannon with muzzle flash suppressors; the MG 151s in the lower nose replaced by 2 × MK 108 cannon; installation of 2 × MG FF/M as oblique weapons and 1 × MG 81Z in the rear cockpit as standard. In this case, *Rüstsatz M 1* (ventral weapon tray with 2 × MG 151s) was not intended to be fitted. This particular modification was built in series by Messerschmitt as the Bf 110G-4/R6.

In addition to these externally apparent changes, continuous interior modifications resulted from operational experience: alterations to the seats, layout of the instruments and operating switches, improvements to the gunsights, installation of windscreen washers, modernisation of radio equipment, and so on. None of these changes added anything to the performance or made the Bf 110 faster, but they certainly improved its fighting value. Flown by an experienced pilot the Bf 110 remained a deadly weapon right until the end of the war, as proved by the long list of confirmed victories credited to the most successful German night fighter pilot, Wolfgang Schnaufer. The uninterrupted series of successes achieved with the Bf 110 persuaded Milch in May 1944 to consider the continuation of Bf 110 production – originally intended to phase out in 1945 – as soon as the DB 605D engines of 2,000 hp take-off power became available. Another factor that influenced the decision to retain the obsolescent Bf 110 and Ju 88C-6 in production was that early in 1944, contrary to expectations, the British bombers were not flying noticeably faster or higher than in 1943. True enough, they were fitted with more powerful engines but hardly used them to advantage. In fact quite the opposite was the case: the bombers now flew slower than before – at about 360–370 km/h (223.5–230 mph), because they were keeping closer to each other in a stream, while also flying continuous defensive manoeuvres. Under these conditions higher speed would have led to many more collisions. The new engines also conserved more fuel while the distances involved in raids became longer and longer. Since the fuel tankage could hardly be increased at the expense of the bomb load, the bomber formations simply could not afford to fly as fast as they were capable.

In 1944, however, the Ju 88 began to bear more and more of the night fighting burden. In June 1943 only NJG 2 and IV/NJG 5 had the Ju 88C-6; by August Ju 88 night fighters also equipped I,II and III/NJG 3, and NJG 100. After the start of the Ju 88G-1 production the above-mentioned units were progressively re-equipped with this type. In addition, until July 1944 the Ju 88G-1 was also supplied to IV/NJG 3, II and III/NJG 6 and I/NJG 7. Apart from that, individual Ju 88G-1s were on the strength of almost every other unit, mostly flown by formation leaders.

The Ju 88C-6 remained in production until about April 1944. The Ju 88R-2, with BMW 801 radial engines, was built in parallel but only in small numbers. It was intended as a 'Mosquito hunter' but was not particularly successful in that role. Personally, I know of only one Mosquito kill with this version, on the night of 13 December 1943. The Ju 88R-2 performed far better with the Air Zone Observer sections (*Luftraumbeobachterstaffeln*). The strongest points of the Ju 88C-6 were its superior endurance and an armament comprising 3 × MG FF cannon and 3 × MG 17 machine guns in the nose. Also, for 'Tame Boar' operations side-by-side seating for the pilot and radio operator proved far better than the tandem arrangement of the Bf 110. On the other hand, the Ju 88C-6 was slightly slower than the Bf 110G-4; fully equipped, it could just about reach 470 km/h at 4,800 m (292 mph at 15,750 ft) altitude, although a longer burst of fire from all fixed weapons would briefly reduce this by some 30 km/h (16.8 mph).

However, the Ju 88G-1, which became operational in April 1944, was clearly superior to its forebears, clocking 540 km/h at 6,000 m altitude (335 mph at 19,685 ft) without flame dampers. The Ju 88G-1 was developed late in 1943 to prove that it was possible to evolve the Ju 88C into a more powerful aircraft if it proved impossible to build the Ju 188J or the Ju 188R.[6] The Ju 88V-58, an aircraft similar to the C-5, served as the prototype, fitted with Ju 188 vertical tail surfaces and narrow, low-drag cockpit glazing. The fixed forward armament was reduced to 2 × MG 151s and the ventral weapons tray enlarged to accommodate 4 × MG 151 cannon. The Rechlin experts were impressed by the performance and handling and, after Junkers had assured the *Jägerstab* that it was possible to effect a change-over in production because the jigs were already in hand, series manufacture and deliveries began in April 1944. The nose guns were subsequently removed following complaints by pilots of temporary blinding caused by their muzzle flashes. Another important change was that beginning with the G-1 series the radio/radar operator was seated next to the pilot and the flight engineer doubled as air gunner. Although the Ju 88G-1 had weaker fixed forward armament than the Bf 110, it did not matter so much because the pilots preferred to use their oblique guns anyway. On the Ju 88G-1 these comprised 2 × MG 151s. Even if the Ju 88G-1 was not exactly armed to the teeth, it proved itself outstanding in action. It was 50 km/h (31 mph) faster than the Bf 110G-4 because its large fuselage tanks made external tanks unnecessary, it had a better rate of climb and flew well with one engine out. In fact, the operational crews were so satisfied with this version that the originally planned developments, the Ju 88G-2 to G-5, were cancelled, although a few Ju 88G-4s were completed.

Compared to the Bf 110 and Ju 88 the Do 217 night fighter steadily declined in importance, although as far as armament and endurance were concerned it was far superior to the first two types. There were several reasons for this: the short production run, which ended in the autumn of 1943, a lack of power, and modest performance. By and by the Do 217Ns were concentrated in NJG 4, which, as the most south-westerly formation, had the longest flightpaths for 'Wild Boar' operations over Central Germany. The OKL temporarily allocated a substantial number of Do 217s to NJG 100, being convinced that its endurance made it particularly suitable for use with the 'railway-*Himmelbett*' night fighting system. Unfortunately the Do 217s undercarriage disagreed with the rough Russian airfields and began to buckle on touchdown. When this was compounded by difficulties in obtaining spare parts for the engines, the Do 217Ns were withdrawn and passed on to NJG 4 or night fighter training schools, which also used up the remaining Do 217Js.

Although the Do 217N was powered by the same engines as the He 219, its higher weight and poorer aerodynamics resulted in much lower performance. The Dornier night fighters achieved their last successes in August and October 1943 in, of all things, daytime operations against USAAF B-17 bombers, when their fixed fuselage armament of 4 × MG 151/20 cannon and 4 × MG 17 machine guns had a chance to demonstrate its hard-hitting power in frontal attacks. Their oblique armament – 4 × MG 151 cannon – was also the heaviest carried by any German night fighter.

Until spring 1944 various *Gruppen* of NJG 1 used a Do 215B-5, the same one in which *Oblt* Becker had achieved the first *Lichtenstein* victory.

A few He 219A-0s – actually modified He 219V-series aircraft – were operational with NJG 1 in May 1943. By June series production of 200 aircraft per month should have long since started, but nothing happened because no engines were available. The first ten DB 603s were finally delivered by Daimler Benz to Heinkel in July, allowing one He 219A to be completed that month and the next delivered to Venlo in September. At that time there was still a certain amount of confusion about a start to series production because the Technical Office of the RLM could not decide which factory to use. A look at the situation at that time shows why: at Rostock preparations were in hand for series production of the Ju 88G-1, the He 219A's main competitor; the Heinkel plant at Vienna-Schwechat was due to change over to production of the Do 335; and Mielec was fully occupied with the production of He 177 components. Then there were MK 108 delivery bottlenecks which led to renewed consideration of the possibility of getting away with a fixed fuselage armament of 4 × MG 151s. Finally Heinkel took matters in his own hands, instructing his design bureau to agree to every modification suggested by the Technical Office, resulting in a multitude of proposals for specific versions:

He 219A-1 day *Zerstörer* and night fighter
He 219A-2 pure night fighter
HE 219A-5 night fighter with 3-man cabin, more powerful engines and extended range
He 219A-6 } lighter unarmoured high-altitude night fighters
He 219A-7 } with reduced armament
He 219B-series night fighters with Jumo 222 engines
He 219C-series high-speed bombers and heavy fighter-bombers.

In the event, this over-zealousness on Heinkel's part led to an unexpected reaction: the Technical Office began to express doubts about the quality of Heinkel's designers – the troubled He 177 was still very fresh in their memory – and the production capacity of Heinkel plants. Problems with He 219 cabin heating during the winter of 1943–44, and remarks by some pilots criticising the seating arrangements, were fresh grist to Milch's mill.

In the event, only eleven He 219A-0 series machines were built in 1943, and that at the enormous cost of 90,000 man-hours per aircraft. It was all very well for Heinkel to put an estimate before the Technical Office experts stating that from the 800th aircraft it would need only 10,000 man-hours and less, but what counted with Milch was that by the end of 1943 a Ju 88C-6 needed only 30,000 man-hours to complete, and the Ju 88G-1 probably not much more.

By early June 1944 a total of 20 He 219s were operational with I/NJG 1, and a few more aircraft had been delivered to II *Gruppe* and NJGr 10. In the latter case, they were all prototypes which spent more time under test on the ground than flying. As for equipment, the aircraft serving with I/NJG 1 were He 219A-2s, but were designated A-0 because deliveries of the pre-production series had not yet been completed. Compared with the A-0 series, the He 219A-2 differed externally only in having rearwards-sloping flat cabin glazing (without the dorsal machine gun), which was also retrofitted to all pre-production aircraft. As completed, the He 219As carried a standard armament of 4 × MG 151/20 cannon in two vertically staggered ventral trays (*Rüstsatz M 1*). Due to delivery problems with the 30 mm MK 103 cannon only a few of the Standard Equipment M 2

(*Rüstsatz M 2*) with 2 × MK 103 and *M 3* sets with 4 × MK 103 were available. However, so that the pilots would not have to go short of heavier armament the works offered Standard Equipment sets with two and four 30 mm MK 108 cannon. The MK 108 was much lighter than the MK 103 but had much poorer ballistic characteristics.[7] Some aircraft also featured an oblique armament of 2 × Mk 108, though this was removed by most pilots. When intercepting the ponderous heavy bombers the pilot had difficulty in achieving matching speeds in time and preferred to attack with the forward-firing guns while pulling up underneath the enemy.

Though the He 219 is recognised by all as the most efficient German night fighter, its performance was not as extraordinary as is often claimed. In fact, the type never achieved even the values given in its manual. For instance, with almost full fuel tanks and full armament the He 219 could not get above 8000 m (26,250 ft) altitude, and passed the 10,000 m (32,810 ft) mark only at an equipped weight of about 10 tons – in other words, with almost empty tanks and nearly all ammunition used up. And then it hung in the sky like a 'ripe plum,' as the pilots used to say, and would stall at 5 m/sec (16.4 ft/sec) from a normal blind flying turn. Level performance was also less than it appeared: the He 219 could only reach its 'paper' maximum speed of 605 km/h (376 mph) if no night fighting equipment was fitted. With *Lichtenstein* and engine flame dampers the maximum was a good 45 km/h (28 mph) less at 6,200 m (20,340 ft) altitude and fell to about 500 km/h at 8,200 m (310.5 mph at 26,900 ft) – much too slow to catch a Mosquito flying at full power. Until June 1944 only two Mosquitoes are known to have been shot down by He 219s (*see* Appendix 15). A comparison of these official and actual values suggests how much lower the performance of the other operational German aircraft types must have been. Incidentally, the He 219A was also the only German night fighter that could still climb on one engine, and even go round again for another landing attempt.

The future 'Mosquito hunter' on which Milch had set such high hopes, the Ta 154 Moskito, was still a long time coming. Extensive material and static stress tests had indicated a need for additional strengthening. The all-up weight climbed after each new calculation and the third prototype, first flown in November 1943, had to be fitted with Jumo 213 engines before it would achieve the required speeds. Equipped with *Lichtenstein* and flame dampers, the Ta 154V-3 reached 620 km/h (385 mph), making it by far the fastest German night interceptor. In December the first prototypes were delivered to *EKdo Ta 154*, and then to NJGr 10, which took delivery of several other V-series aircraft. But all these aircraft suffered from so many teething troubles that they were seldom airborne.

The single-engined night fighting force had its own problems. At the beginning it was flying the same types as the day units – the Bf 109G-5 and G-6 and the FW 190A-5 – then the *Gruppenstab* sections and one *Gruppe* each of JG 300 and 302 received their own aircraft. The *Stab* aircraft were without exception FW 190s, while the *Gruppen* equipment comprised Bf 109G-6/U4 with 2 × MK 108 cannon in underwing gondolas. In addition, there were a few Bf 109G-5s for Mosquito hunting. These aircraft were powered by DB 605AS engines with DB 603 'Gustav' superchargers and featured the GM-1 installation. The armament consisted of one cannon firing through the propeller boss and 2 × MG 131s above the engine. The FW 190 fighters flown as 'Mosquito hunters' under the *Himmelbett* system by JG 300 from Hangelar in late summer were purpose-built variants of the A-5 series, specially lightened and highly polished by the ground crews. From the late autumn onwards the cadre aircraft of the single-engined night fighter force were modified at the front-line workshops to meet specific operational requirements. These modifications included a flashing identification light under the port wing, heated armoured glass panels, protective fabric blinds at the cockpit side panels which could be pulled up by the pilot when he flew into a searchlight cone, ultra-violet illumination of the instrument panel, and anti-glare screens over the exhaust stub slots. The radio equipment comprised the FuG 16ZY, FuG 25a IFF set and a long-wave running commentary receiver. In the spring of 1944 the Bf 109s received the Erla clear-view cabin glazing (today wrongly described as the 'Galland hood') and the Galland armour plate behind the pilot's back. The 'Mosquito hunters' were also supposed to have fully faired main undercarriage wheel wells and a retractable tailwheel, and the aircraft were to be sprayed with a special high-gloss insulating lacquer.

The Bf 109 was better liked by the pilots than the FW 190. Apart from its better high-altitude performance it was the very weakness of its undercarriage that made the Bf 109 more suitable for night operations, simply shearing off in a hard landing. In a similar situation the FW 190 had a tendency to noseover onto its tail and than nothing could help the pilot, seated as he was under a canopy that projected above the fuselage.

Until March 1944 the specially modified Bf 109 and FW 190 night fighters equipped with the FuG 217 *Neptun* and FuG 350Z *Naxos Z* were used only by NJGr 10; afterwards some aircraft with *Neptun* were flown by 6./JG 300, the so-called *Kommando Plöger*.

In conclusion mention should be made of some of the 'lone wolves' used by the night fighter units. In September 1943 a few Me 410s were in service with the 3 *JDivision*, and also possibly with NJG 1. These machines were intended to bridge the gap until the arrival of the He 219 and were used with the latter for night interceptions. From about March 1944 Venlo was the base of *EKdo 410*. Intended as a 'Mosquito hunter' unit, *EKdo 410* is believed to have had no success in this role. Curiously, the Me 410 could not compete in the climb with the Bf 110, being held back by its unfavourable power/weight ratio. The Mosquito hunt was then still being conducted by means of the *Himmelbett* system: the interceptors took off only after the long-range radar had acquired the approaching enemy aircraft, and by the time the Me 410s were at operating altitude the high-speed bombers had long since flown through the *Himmelbett* zone. The Me 410 was more successful on long-range night fighter/intruder operations over Britain, in which role it was flown by I and II/KG 51 from early 1944 onwards. The Me 410 was also used on 'Wild Boar' sorties over France, together with FW 190F-3s of SKG 10.

Probably the strangest German night fighter type of all belonged to NJG 100 late in 1943: a Ju 87D-5 acquired by *Hptm* Schoenert to hunt the Soviet 'runway crawlers', the slow Po-2 biplane night harassment aircraft. Schoenert wanted his aircraft fitted with oblique armament, but it is not known if it was ever used operationally. In any case, Schoenert, who was transferred to Werneuchen late in December, did not fly it again, but 'his' Ju 87D-5 appeared on strength returns for some time afterwards.

Meanwhile, the FW 189, a make-shift 1942 night fighter, was reborn. At Werneuchen an aircraft of this type had been equipped with the wide-angle FuG 212, and an oblique-firing MG 151 was fitted at Tarnewitz. Thus modified, the FW 189 was sent back to the Eastern Front, where the pilots practically fell over themselves to fly it operationally. Two more similarly converted FW 189s followed in May.

On the other side of the coin, the Ju 88P-2 was a failure as a night fighter. Originally built as a 'tank buster' and armed with 2 × 37 mm cannon in a ventral tray, at least one night fighter derivative of this type was tested by NJGr 10 but rejected because of its low speed and clumsiness.

The few He 111H-20s equipped with *Lichtenstein SN-2* were certainly no night fighters. Used for training and instruction, they were however considered as contact aircraft for pursuit night fighting. These machines had been modified for night-fighter training at the Lufthansa workshops at Werneuchen in December 1943.

On the nights between 25 and 30 July the RAF had completely neutralised the night fighters a e Flak, but had not defeated them. It was only a question of time where the Reich Air Defence, with changed tactics and technology, would once again contest control of the airspace over the Reich territory with the RAF. Admittedly, the Hamburg raids cost some 41,000 victims among the civilian population, but the night fighter force was able to prevent similar catastrophes until February 1945 by changing over within three weeks to unguided night fighting, a method that had been under consideration for some time. During the first raid on Hamburg the RAF lost only 12 bombers (equal to 1.5 per cent of the total[8]); on 28 July, when the night fighters flew their first 'illuminated objective-defence night interception', aided by a running commentary, the RAF lost 17 bombers; on 30 July the tally reached 27 bombers. This ratio of 3.4 per cent was of course still too low but signified a visible improvement on the defensive effort of only five nights before. The only completely preserved report from XII *Fliegerkorps* covers August 1943, and shows clearly how successfully the night fighting force had changed over to the new method. Until the end of July the night fighters had achieved 2,062 confirmed victories on all fronts, and August added another 230 enemy aircraft shot down by twin-engined night fighters. This figure was well above that achieved by the single-engined 'Wild Boars': JG 300 probably achieved no more than 50 kills[9] that month. The night-fighter crews were loudly enthusiastic about this revolution, not least because it went a long way towards satisfying their thirst for action, revenge, ambition and craving for decorations, and the cases of multiple victories in one night began to increase. Thus, for instance, out of the 230 confirmed victories in August, 102 were achieved by 31 crews. And it was not only the 'old hands' (the 25–30-year-old pilots) who started adding victory markings to their fins; quite a few new crews also proved exceptionally successful. The champion marksman of August 1943 was *Lt* Hager of II/NJG 1 with 11 kills, followed by *Hptm* Wohlers (I/NJG 6) and *Hptm* Frank (I/NJG 1) with seven each, *Lt* Baake and *Lt* Grimm with six, and *Maj* Radusch, *Maj* Ehle, *Hptm* Strüning, *Hptm* Geiger and *Oblt* Schnaufer with five each. No less than three crews – led by *Maj* Wohlers, *Lt* Musset and *Lt* Ehrhardt – also achieved four victories in one night. All together 47 new crews scored their first victories in August. Among the experts, 18 pilots ended the month with more than 22 victories each. This list was headed by *Maj* Lent with a total of 69, followed by *Hptm* Prince zu Sayn-Wittgenstein with 64, while the most successful NCO pilot was *Ofw* Kollak with 30 victories (No 10 on the list).

The proportion of 48 *Himmelbett* victories to 200 achieved in uncontrolled night fighting shows how far that method – loudly praised only a few weeks earlier – had been superseded. In fact, *Himmelbett* was by this time suitable only for the interception of individual bombers that had become separated from the main stream during the return flight. In areas of strong *Window* jamming the *Himmelbett* crews were in a hopeless situation from the start, as shown by the total lack of success of 4 *J Division*. However, after the

Wendelstein ASV and AI radar aerials on a Ju 88   Bundesarchiv

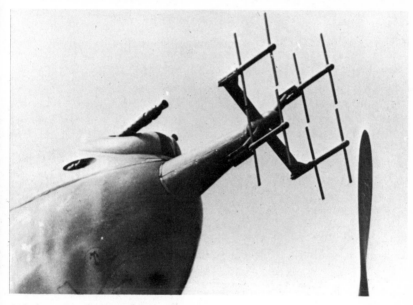

Lichtenstein C-1 wide-angle AI radar aerials   Hentz

Do 17Z-10 fitted with oblique armament and aerials for the *Lichtenstein B-0* gun-firing set
Malchow

FW 190A-5 flown by *Oblt* Krause of 1./NJGr 10. Note the FuG 217 *Neptun* rod aerials in front and behind the pilot's cockpit
Krause

Bf 109G-6 with an experimental *Naxos* installation

Hentz

Ju 88G-1s of air observer *Staffeln* were equipped with *Naxos*, *Flensburg* and *Neptun R*.

Hentz

Bf 110G contact aircraft of *Stab*/NJG 4 equipped with FuG 227 *Flensburg*

Creek

Bf 110E retrofitted to spring 1944
standard with FuG 220b and
FuG 212 wide-angle AI
radars   Messerschmitt

Right: The Soviets did not use tinfoil
jamming over East Prussia, allowing Bf
110F-4s of 14./NJG 5 to keep their FuG
212 sets until April 1944   Boy

Below: Ju 88C-6 test aircraft for FuG 351
Korfu   Trenkle

Antennenverkleidung

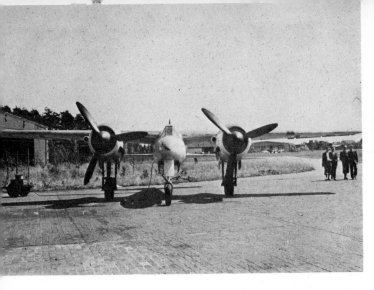

Ta 154. Head-on view
reveals the slim fuselage
cross-section of this
interceptor

Nowarra

Ta 154V-2

Nowarra

Ta 154V-3 undergoing
static tests

Creek

Bf 110G-4 of 6./NJG 6 in
virtually standard day
Zerstörer camouflage and
with the small F-series
fin/rudder assembly.
March, 1944

Below: Bf 110G-4 of
IV/NJG 3. The fuselage
sides were sprayed in
RLM 76 without any
patches

Briegleb

The Luftwaffe Reich operations room. *Left:* the Ia (Operations Officer) of Night Fighters, *Oberst* Falck. The white telephone in front of him was a direct line to Göring. *Right: GenMaj* Nielsen, Chief of Staff

Falck

The route of the bomber stream begins to emerge. *Oberst* Falck has I *JKorps* on the line

Falck

The relative positions of the bomber stream and the night fighters are continuously plotted by dead reckoning

Falck

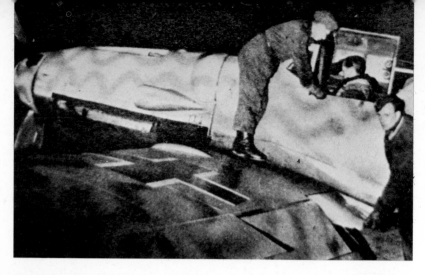

An unusually camouflaged Bf 109G-6 of JG 300   Signal

Hunter becomes the hunted. An RAF Beaufighter suddenly appears from behind a night fighter during a 'Wild Boar' operation over a burning German town.   (März)

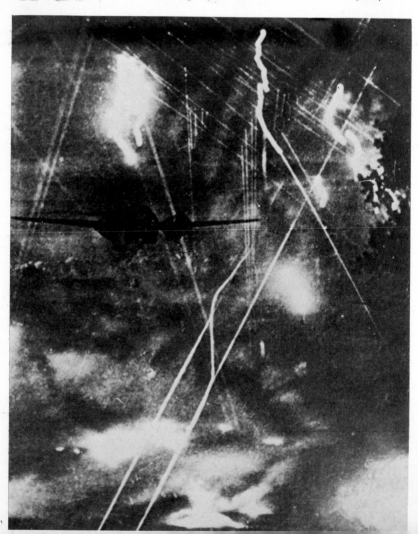

Above: Bf 110G-4 flown by *Oblt* Briegleb of IV/NJG 3. Note the windscreen washers, nose-over protection and armour plating on the pilot's seat   Briegleb

Right: Standard Equipment set *R4*: 4 × MG 151 with muzzle flash-suppressors replaced the MK 108s. 5./NJG 5, summer 1944

Boy

Bf 110G-4 with the seldom-used *Rüstsatz M1* (2 × MG 151) under the fuselagé   Thiele

Right: Ju 88R-2 with
more streamlined FuG
220 SN-2 aerial supports
Zenker

Below: I/NJG 7 was
the first unit to receive
the Ju 88G-1.
Illustration shows
D9 + NL of 3./NJG7.
(Widtfeldt)

Ju 88G-1 instrument
panel.
(Briegleb)

Bf 110G-4 with an experimental MK 103 installation

Bundesarchiv

Ju 88P during operational trials with movable MK 103 cannon in the ventral tray. This type proved too unwieldy as a night fighter. Note the organ pipes under the fuselage as a means of identification for friendly Flak

Hentz

The Do 217N-2 had disappeared from operational units by 1944. This aircraft is 3C + IP of 6./NJG 4

AMF Dübendorf

Three night fighters in flight. The Do 217 looked ungainly even in the air
Autenrieth

Three night fighters in flight.
Above: The Do 217 looked ungainly even in the air.

(Autenrieth)

Centre: Bf 110G-4 displaying the split black/grey undersurface colouring used briefly at the beginning of 1944.
(Bärwolf)
Bottom: Ju 88G-6. This view clearly shows the long-span Ju 188 tailplane.
(Weise)

He 219A-2 of *Hptm*
Modrow (2./NJG 1)
Habicht

He 219A-5 ventral
gondola with MG 151s
fitted in staggered pairs

He 219A-6 high-altitude
interceptor with reduced
armament in the ventral
gondola
Danish Air Force

Highly polished white Bf 109G-10 'Mosquito hunter' of 1./NJGr 10. *Oblt* Krause is in the centre

Krause

Right: The Me 410 was not successful as a Mosquito hunter. The cover of the remotely controlled MG 131 installation has been removed for inspection

Bundesarchiv

Bottom: Muzzle-flash suppressors for the MG 131s of Bf 109 night fighters were tested at the Luftwaffe Weapons Test Centre at Tarnewitz

Bundesarchiv

first *Würzburg-Riesen* GCI radars had been fitted with the *Würz-Laus* anti-*Window* screening device, the Y-control system began to offer improved prospects of success. The first victory was achieved by *Oblt* Schnaufer on the night of 11 August. But it was essential that the Y-stations worked faultlessly; if not, there was no point in attempting 'Tame Boar' interception because without Y-control it was impossible to achieve satisfactory infiltration into the bomber stream.

Although the initial trials had confirmed *Oberst* von Lossberg's idea of pursuit night fighting, these had taken place without any *Window* jamming. The reality was quite different. Attempts were made several times simply to direct the contact aircraft into the *Window* clouds, but then the radio operator could see nothing but jamming on his radarscopes and the running commentary was too vague to give him the exact position of the bombers. For the time being then only the 'Wild Boars' remained as an active means of defence, intercepting the bombers in the general area of the assumed target. The difficulty lay of course in recognising the objective in good time. As before, the RAF bombers penetrated German airspace on the narrowest possible front and were staggered in great depth, with Mosquitoes swarming ahead and alongside the main bomber stream, dropping decoy markers or carrying out diversionary raids. And as if that was not enough, the Central Observation Post reports on these secondary formations came in at extended intervals and greatly confused the whole picture. However, as a rule the British would give the German defences a chance: they tended to formate over areas with the lightest Flak defences, lingering like this for some time about 50 kms (31 mls) from the target before starting their attack in a tightly staggered stream. This final forming-up revealed their intentions and gave the night fighters about 30 min in which to formate in front of the assumed target. But then again, the forming-up and initial point did not always reliably indicate the actual target, a good example being the RAF raid during the night of 18 August. This action also impressively supported Kammhuber's demand for a central fighter control. On this night the *JKorps* identified a main bomber formation flying in the direction of Mecklenburg and assumed that the target was Stettin. The night fighters were ordered to the Great Müritz lake, which was believed to be an RAF landmark.

A decoy on Berlin by eight Mosquitoes was recognised for what it was, but not by the Luftwaffe Commander Centre and *Luftgau* Berlin, which assumed the Mosquitoes to be the vanguard of the main force and alerted JG 300. On receiving their orders, the 'Wild Boars' hurried towards Berlin from their bases at Hangelar, Rheine and Oldenburg without notifying the other *Luftgaue* and *Divisionen*. As a result these formations received scores of new reports about aircraft flying towards the capital. On the air situation maps at the 4 *JDivision* command centre at Döberitz there suddenly appeared an enemy formation cruising west of Berlin, and night fighters were called up to combat it. Thus began a crazy escalation of erroneous judgements and decisions. As about 100 night fighters were turning and banking above the capital a number of nervous Flak batteries opened fire, thereby persuading everybody on the ground and in the air that the enemy *must* be there. The constant panicky reports from 4 *JDivision* began to make the *JKorps* nervous too, and finally it ordered all of its remaining night fighters towards the steadily more furious fireworks at Berlin. That shooting is infectious is a well-known fact, and by then most of the Berlin Flak batteries were past bothering about recognition flares or orders to cease fire.

The confusion came to an end only when the RAF bombers raided Peenemünde, but by that time it was too late for co-ordinated defence measures. A few twin-engined fighters still had enough fuel in their tanks to intercept the last waves of the raiders and follow them as they retreated, but most of the single-engined night fighters and those of NJG 4 were forced to land in the Berlin area. The moonlit night was ideal for pursuing the enemy and 31 bombers went down over Mecklenburg. Another six were shot down by *Himmelbett*-controlled night fighters over Schleswig-Holstein, and the Flak and single-engined 'Wild Boars' accounted for four more, including a Mosquito shot down by *Fw* Hakenjoos of JG 300.

The RAF lost more bombers on the return flight than while flying towards the targets even though, relieved of their bomb loads, the aircraft could fly considerably faster and the running commentary had been discontinued because it was impossible to mark the dispersed bombers on the air situation maps. The reason for this higher loss rate was largely the behaviour of the crews, who, after fulfilling their task, 'dropped their guard' and sometimes even became downright careless. Among the bombers shot down on the way out were aircraft damaged during the raid and trying to limp back home with smoking engines and stationary propellers. But attacking such 'stragglers' could sometimes result in some very unpleasant surprises, as happened o the night of 18 August, when five Bf 110s of IV/NJG 1 led b *Oblt* Schnaufer closed in on what they assumed to be a group of slowly flying bombers over the Dutch coast. Within a few minutes three Bf 110s were going down in flames: the 'bombers' turned out to be Beaufighters led by the British night fighter ace WgCdr Braham. His aircraft were equipped with the *Serrate* homing device, which responded to the impulses emitted by the German *Lichtenstein B/C* AI radars. Total losses recorded by XII *Fliegerkorps* that night amounted to 12 night fighters, nine of which had been shot down in combat with bombers or night fighters.

German night fighter losses increased steeply in August, with aircraft falling victim about equally to aerial combat, Flak, technical faults and fuel shortage. To begin with, the British night fighter units, limited by the combat range of the Beaufighter, made themselves noticeable only in the *Himmelbett* area. The Mosquitoes began to intervene more frequently in October, and from then on no airfield in Central Germany was safe from the *Indianer* (Red Indians, cover name for long-range night intruders).

However, the rapidly increasing losses still had no effect on the morale of the night fighters. The dead came largely from among the relatively inexperienced and therefore lesser-known crews, while the highly decorated *Experten* seemed to lead charmed lives. Only the *Fliegerkorps*, which had an overall view of the situation, was worried about the unfavourable 2:1 ratio between the enemy's losses and its own up to 18 August. For one thing, the night fighter force still had not achieved a single convincing defensive victory. During the RAF raids on Hamburg (night of 2/3 August) and Peenemünde the bombers were intercepted only on their way back; during the raids on Mannheim (night of 9/10 August) and Nuremberg (night of 10/11 August) the night fighters had shot down only six and ten bombers respectively. Most of the successes were achieved during the last week of August, with the defensive battle for Berlin on the night of 24 August serving as a prelude. Several bombers were caught by NJG 1 on their way in over Holland and Lower Saxony, and on his way to the assumed target *Hptm* Geiger encountered the bomber formation and shot down a Lancaster near Cloppenburg. Most of the crews of NJG 1, 3, 4 and 5, reinforced by a few leading crews from NJG 2 and the single-engined JG 300, flung themselves at the enemy west of the capital. Within 30 minutes they had shot down 30 four-engined bombers, and with three kills to his credit *Oblt* F. K. Müller of *Stab*/JG 300 was the most successful night fighter that night. The return flight cost the RAF several aircraft, and at least eight bombers are known to have gone down over the North Sea. The total RAF losses amounted to 57 bombers, or 9.1 per cent of the 727 aircraft operational that night. The German units lost only three Bf 110s (two in action, one crashed due to fuel shortage), with several temporarily out of action as a result of mechanical faults or combat damage. According to statements made afterwards by captured airmen, the RAF was no longer expecting such a defensive effort, and the sheer weight of the fighter attacks came as a shock to those RAF aircrew who were lucky to get back home. The point was taken, and the RAF command changed the target to Nuremberg three nights later. During this raid the German defences succeeded for the first time in infiltrating night fighters into the enemy bomber stream. Operating as 'Tame Boars', crews from NJG 4 and NJG 6 shot down

12 RAF bombers while the night fighters of NJG 1, 3, 5 and 101 formed up in good time near Nuremberg and struck into the bombers while they were still forming up 50 km west of the town. That night the RAF lost 48 bombers to night fighter crews of XII *Fliegerkorps*, against only one Do 217 shot down in error by another German night fighter. The victories were shared by 37 crews, the most successful pilots, with three kills each, being *Hptm* Frank (I/NJG 1), Lt Hager (II/NJG 1) and *Hptm* Wohlers (I/NJG 6).

Next time the RAF settled on a target nearer home: Mönchen-gladbach. But here too things did not go entirely their way, and 20 crews from NJG 1, 3 and 4 shot down a total of 25 bombers. Once again, *Hptm* Frank had the most success, with three victories; he flew the only serviceable He 219A-0 of I *Gruppe*.

During the night of 1 September the RAF again raided Berlin, and again the night fighters were on time. The 'Tame Boars' were successful seven times over Lower Saxony and another 40 RAF aircraft were shot down over Berlin, including 14 by single-engined night fighters and Flak. As in previous raids, these figures meant a loss ratio of 9.1 per cent.

Once the precedent had been established the Luftwaffe command did not want to lose night fighter support on daylight operations, particularly because it was in August that the USAAF began to make its first deep penetration raids into Germany. And so the highly specialised night fighter units were drawn into round-the-clock operations that were to cost them many experienced crews.

On 17 August the Americans attacked the Messerschmitt plant at Regensburg and the ball-bearing factories at Schweinfurt. Parts of NJG 1 were ordered to intercept the Regensburg raid and four crews of II *Gruppe* achieved a victory each and two probables. One of these was claimed by *Hptm* Rupprecht, who had followed the departing American B-17 formation all the way to the Brenner Pass. During the Schweinfurt raid the Do 217s of EJG 101 demonstrated their devastating firepower by destroying three Flying Fortresses; another B-17 fell victim to *Fw* Becker's crew from I/NJG 6.

These successes were of course achieved against isolated American bombers, a fact whose significance was not appreciated by the high command. What counted was the number of kills and that these were achieved without loss, and from this the Luftwaffe command drew the conclusion that the heavily armed night fighters could be used further in daytime. They were however prudent enough to detail day *Zerstörer*, mainly Bf 110G-2 but also some Me 210s, to protect night fighter formations on such operations.

But though all these Luftwaffe counterblows during the second week in August came as a surprise to the Allies, they failed to act as a deterrent. The nights when the RAF had to suffer losses in the region of nine per cent were too few to decisively weaken its fighting power; in fact these losses did not even have a real attrition effect. Meanwhile, thousands of new bomber crews were being trained in Britain and Canada, and the production of four-engined bombers continued at full speed and well-nigh undisturbed by German air raids. The Americans too had harnessed their enormous industrial potential and were sending their Flying Fortresses to destroy the German armament industry.

At best, the Luftwaffe could only harass the enemy during his approach flight; there could be no question of any weakening of his offensive power. Only once during the entire war did the Luftwaffe manage to achieve a real defensive success against a major day or night raid;[10] as a rule most of the bombers always reached the target area and devastated it, killing countless people in the process. And when the night fighters and Flak managed to achieve the destruction of a larger number of enemy aircraft the Luftwaffe could never be sure that Air Marshal Harris would grant his physically and mentally tired crews a longer rest. As if working to some formula quite unfathomable to the Germans, the RAF might raid the same target again the following night, or change to a different objective, or stay at home. And then there were double and diversionary attacks, deception manoeuvres and unexpected changes of course, all of which made the task of the defences more difficult – as did unreported or undetected movements by their own formations.

All this did not really concern most night fighter crews, however. They saw only their own successes and were convinced that the enemy could not stand such losses much longer. They had no idea of the enormous Anglo-American industrial potential, nor of the difficulties besetting the German armament industry. They still believed their own propaganda claims about their own strength, and did not go short of anything needed to keep them fit for night operations. The Reich Air Defence had also achieved a success in that the RAF did not raid Berlin again in September. Cities like Ludwigshafen, Mannheim, Hanover and Munich were now the targets of smaller harassing raids, mainly by Mosquitoes. Combating these small-scale raids was very difficult, and some *Gruppen* did not achieve a single success for days on end.

On 22 September the RAF target was Hanover. To begin with, the *JKorps* thought the bombers were going to Hanover, before deciding that the real target was Berlin. As a result, night fighters appeared over Hanover only when the bombs were already falling. The *Flg Korps* reported 19 bombers shot down, of which at least five were claimed by pilots of I/JG 300 (one by the *Gruppenadju*, three by *Oblt* Plewa of 2.*Staffel*, and one by *Fw* Döring). On the night of 27/28 September the RAF again succeeded in deceiving the defences. The raid was detected early, and near Trier 3 *J Division* infiltrated three Me 410s, two He 219s and one Ju 88 into the bomber stream, though these aircraft did not manage a single victory. At 2210 hrs one of the contact aircraft reported cascade skymarkers going down over Mannheim, cancelled the warning five minutes later and reported that the enemy was still flying eastwards. In fact, the main bomber force flew over Mannheim, only to form up outside the city. Ignoring reports from the local night fighting zone controller of loud aircraft sounds east of Mannheim, the *J Korps* assumed a raid on Nuremberg and ordered all night fighters to that area. Their 'confirmation' came at 2230 hrs in the form of aircraft sounds west of Nuremberg (made by its own night fighters) and skymarkers dropped by a handful of Mosquitoes. Five minutes later bombs from more than 600 RAF bombers hit Mannheim.

To be on the safe side most of the night fighters of 1 and 3 *J Divisionen* had ignored the order to form up near Nuremberg. They managed to intercept the last raiding waves at Mannheim and shot down 30 bombers. 7 *JDiv* came too late.

Such continuous operations wore out the night fighter force too. On 20 September the *JKorps* reported 390 operational night fighters; a week later the total was only 308. A day later the total had risen to 319, of which 207 took off to repel an RAF raid on Hanover. They managed to shoot down 32 bombers for only five losses, but among the dead was a Knights Cross bearer *Hptm* Frank, whose He 219 collided with a Bf 110. October began with two failures. On the night of the 3rd an RAF bomber formation which had flown in over Switzerland was able to raid Munich almost unhindered. The 193 available night fighters took off too late and managed to intercept the force only as it withdrew, shooting down three bombers over the Continent. That 22 night fighters had followed the RAF bombers all the way to their bases and shot down several aircraft did not count in the eyes of the Luftwaffe command. Hitler condemned this action bitterly, asserting that it could have no useful psychological effect on the population, and none of the victories were recognised. The defence of Kassel failed on the following night, as described below, and a night later, despite bad weather, the RAF raided Mannheim.

In these two actions the twin-engined night fighters shot down a total of 21 bombers for nine losses. One of these was the aircraft flown by *Hptm* Siegmund, CO of III/NJG 3, who was fatally hit by Flak over Kassel.

Hanover was the target for RAF bombers twice more in October, and on the night of the 23rd it was intended to 'plough up' Kassel once again. To make sure of success the RAF had devised a new trick. The bombers came in the usual way over the Schelde estuary, covered by strong *Window* jamming. The bomber stream carried on towards Bonn and then swung south. The *JKorps* assumed a raid on Frankfurt/Main and ordered the night fighters that way. As usual, all running-commentary channels were jammed by the enemy, until suddenly the voice of a fighter control officer came through giving a clearly understandable running commentary about the run-up of the main bomber force to Frankfurt. But this fighter control officer was speaking from Britain! This was the first time that the RAF had used the *Corona* procedure, whereby a bogus running commentator gave misleading reports and orders to the night fighters.

The night fighter crews were greatly confused: they thought they could detect the English accent, but the voice of the genuine German speaker was not always clearly distinguishable either. Which was the real one, the voice that ordered them to Frankfurt or the one that had ordered them to change course for Kassel?

In the meantime, however, an infiltrated running-commentary aircraft equipped with *Naxos* had noticed that the bombers had turned north-east when south of Bonn, and immediately notified the *JKorps* and divisions accordingly. The reports of this air observer had the necessary impact and, assisted by strong tailwinds, 180 night fighters hurried to Kassel and shot down 39 bombers. Another three were destroyed by the single-seaters and Flak, while German losses totalled just six. This made up for the failure of 4 October, but also remained the only defensive success in October. During the whole of this month the *JKorps* shot down only 121 bombers while losing 37 of its own aircraft. This victory tally did not include successes scored by NJG 4 and the 'Wild Boar' *Gruppen*, but with the arrival of autumn the single-engined night fighters began increasingly to suffer from the bad weather conditions.

Otl Hermann, who was determined to justify the high hopes placed in him, now insisted on some very exacting minima: take-off with the cloudbase down to 75 m (246 ft) and visibility down to 2.5 km (8,200 ft); landing, cloudbase 150 m (490 ft) and airfield illuminations visible from a distance of 2.5 km (8,200 ft). In short, the 'Wild Boars' had to take off when 'even the birds had to walk'. To begin with, this meant a rapid increase in aircraft losses because many pilots simply baled out if they could not find an airfield or the aircraft had become uncontrollable because of icing. Then more and more pilots fell victim to these more demanding operating conditions because many of them lacked the all-weather experience of Hermann or *Hptm* F. K. Müller, who became the most successful fighter pilot of 30 *JDivision* with 23 confirmed victories. But some of the experienced pilots too were killed that winter, many of them *Staffel-kapitäne*. What Kammhuber had feared already in July had now proved itself: *Wilde Sau* was cheap in material but cost a lot of blood.

The night fighters were again used on day operations, on 14 and

18 October, but by this time the bomber formations were escorted by Thunderbolts and against them the unwieldy night fighters had little chance. It was more luck than anything else when a Bf 110 rear gunner of II/NJG 1 shot down a P-47 with his machine gun.

The month of November was a new low point: in 728 operational flights the night fighters of I *Korps* shot down only 82 bombers. German losses amounted to 24 aircraft and crews, among them the CO of II/NJG 1, *Maj* Ehle. Admittedly, the bad autumn weather forced the British to reduce the frequency and strength of their raids, but their jamming reached new peaks of effectiveness. The running commentary could no longer be clearly understood on any wavelength or frequency, and everywhere one heard noisy roars, whistling, bells or quotations from Hitler's speeches. The many contradictory or missing Central Observation Post reports and *Window* jamming also complicated the work of the divisional operational stations. In such cases the crews in the air were completely helpless, even on clear nights when the visibility was better. In his earphones the pilot would hear noisy interference and occasional scraps of contradictory reports and orders. Over a wide area he could see winking searchlights, Flak bursts, flares, skymarkers, burning decoy installations and bomb explosions all over the place. How could he still make out the actual target of the raid?

So it was during the night of 17 November. Only a few leading crews took off, orbited the radio beacons and, because the situation in the air was completely confused, waited in vain for orders. As a result, the British were able to unload their bombs on Mannheim almost unmolested. But this night was also notable for a rare type of kill: after the fixed forward guns had jammed in *Maj* Lent's Bf 110 he positioned the aircraft so skilfully that his radio operator, *Lt* Kubisch, was able to shoot down a Lancaster with his rear gun.

On 19 November the RAF began the so-called 'Battle of Berlin'. Air Marshal Harris had set himself the objective of destroying the capital 'from one end to another,' even if it cost him 400–500 bombers. It was intended in the course of this battle to 'bleed white' the Reich Air Defence, to destroy numerous other large towns in addition to Berlin, and to force the Reich to capitulate by 30 April 1944.

Indeed, the RAF had grown into such a terrible striking force that from 19 November onwards it could carry out two or more raids with several hundred bombers in the same night on targets far apart from each other. What Milch had feared in October had now come true.

On the opening night the main RAF force divided into two, 325 four-engined bombers raiding Mannheim while 444 aircraft reached Berlin almost unnoticed. Other aircraft bombed coastal defence installations and Flak positions. The Luftwaffe could put up only 120 fighters, which battled almost exclusively against the Mannheim raid and managed to shoot down 25 bombers, while only nine were lost from the Berlin force.

On 22 November the British came to Berlin again and lost 29 bombers. The city was still burning when the air raid sirens sounded again on the 23rd. The next raid followed on 26 November. Just as on the night of 19 November, the RAF tried to make a double raid on Berlin and Stuttgart to confuse and weaken the Reich Air Defence, sparing no effort to make this deception a success. The German long-range radar and *Naxburg* each detected a formation of Mosquitoes or heavy bombers flying in from the Somme estuary towards Frankfurt. A weak formation of minelaying aircraft flying in the direction of Heligoland was recognised as such and ignored. I *JKorps* took Frankfurt for the main objective and ordered up the 70 leading night fighter crews who could take off in the prevailing bad weather. A few 'Christmas trees' went down over this city, but the bombers flew on south-east. On the German side it was assumed that the British were going to repeat the Mannheim trick and raid Frankfurt from the east, and the fighters were held back near that city. At Frankfurt a formation of Mosquitoes left the main force and sped on towards the Ruhr area. The Mosquitoes were left to continue on their way because they would have outdistanced the fighters anyway. But no ground station noticed that the bomber force divided east of Frankfurt: about 400 aircraft flew over Thuringia to raid Berlin and only about 50 bombers carried on to Nuremberg, where they unexpectedly dropped marker bombs.

The night fighters of 2, 3 and 7 *JDiv* began to search for this bomber formation, which raided Stuttgart after overflying Kitzingen. Many of the night fighters were already short of fuel and had to land, while those which still remained in the air managed to shoot down only six bombers.

In the meantime, near panic had broken out in the Luftwaffe Commander Centre operational HQ because an air observation post at Gera had reported several hundred bombers moving in a north-easterly direction. The bad weather had grounded the night fighters of NJG 5 in the Berlin area, but now they were ordered up regardless of losses, as were the single-seaters of JG 302. But too much valuable time had been lost already: before the night fighters had even reached their operational altitude the first bomber wave had already dropped its bombs. Only the following waves were attacked by the fighters, which managed to shoot down seven per cent of the Berlin raiders. On this night the RAF lost 42 bombers, including 14 that reached their home bases fit only for the scrap heap.

Compared with the previous month, the success ratio of the night fighters improved markedly in December. At the end of the month, I *JKorps* reported 128 certain victories for 28 losses. In the area controlled by 7 *Division* crews of NJG 6 shot down 10 bombers for only two losses. On the other hand, the operational sections of training *Geschwader* had not achieved a single victory since October, additional proof of how necessary experience had become. Also alarming was the low degree of serviceability: compared with November's average of 258 aircraft, only 247 were available for operations in December.

Despite this, the signs were encouraging. The improved success rate was due to the increasing availability of *SN-2*, *Naxos* and *Flensburg*, the spread of Y- and *Egon* stations and the more intense training of night fighter crews in infiltration methods. Apart from that, the running-commentary aircraft (code name *Salvator*) of the air observer *Staffeln* reduced the effectiveness of diversionary raids.

Jamming of radio telephone communications was countered by a fairly primitive but at first really effective means. The *Anne-Marie* Forces radio station broadcast music to indicate the areas under attack: dance music meant Berlin, shanties Hamburg, carnival songs Cologne-Düsseldorf, public house songs Munich, and so on.

In December it was mostly dance music as the assault on Berlin continued. Secondary raids concentrated on Frankfurt, Mannheim and Ludwigshafen, while the Ruhr area was attacked by RAF Mosquitoes. Against these aircraft there were still no effective means of defence; not even the specially modified FW 190s of I/JG 300 stationed at Hangelar and Venlo could report any successes.

The raid on Berlin during the night of 3 December cost the RAF 30 aircraft. The Luftwaffe had strengthened the defences around Berlin even more. In addition to III/NJG 2, stationed at Neuruppin since summer, I/NJG 4 was also transferred from France to Brandis. Playing a decisive role in this success was the night fighter control ship *Togo* in the German Bight, which was instrumental in the early infiltration of night fighters into the bomber stream. Although the night fighters did manage to largely break up the raid, they could not prevent more than 1,800 tons of bombs falling on the city.

Nevertheless the RAF losses were so high that for the time being only Mosquitoes were sent to Berlin, the heavy bombers being kept back until 16 December, when a thick blanket of fog covered all north-western Germany and Holland. A total of 418 bombers set course for Berlin, along with some Mosquitoes that raided Kassel and Hanover. Apart from this diversion the British also tried to block the German fighter control system with every possible means at their disposal: the *Korps* short-wave communications were jammed with recordings of Hitler's speeches, *Korps* alternative radio frequencies were blotted out by bagpipes, and *Anne-Marie* by a continuous signal. Despite all this interference the Y-control system succeeded in infiltrating 28 leading crews into the bomber stream near Bremen and Osnabrück. 1 *JDiv* sent a few fighters to Hanover, while 30 night fighters, mainly from NJG 5, gathered together near Berlin for a 'Wild Boar' action. These fighters achieved 18 confirmed kills, four of them – including a 'Master Bomber' – by *Oblt* Schnaufer. Another seven RAF bombers were accounted for by Flak and single-seat fighters of 30 *JDiv*, and no fewer than 29 of the returned bombers were so badly damaged that they had to be written off. The Luftwaffe lost at least three Bf 110s which could not find a landing place in the fog. The 'Battle of Berlin' was beginning to cost the RAF dearly.

As it seemed obvious that most of the night fighters had been concentrated around the capital, the RAF tried another tack on 20 December: a raid on Frankfurt/Main, a target that in the past had seemed reasonably safe. But here too the RAF ran into heavy fire and lost 41 bombers. The highest individual scorer was *Maj* Herget of I/NJG 4 with four victories. The lesson was clear: even these relatively short bombing trips were no longer walkovers, and one might as well stick to Berlin.

The next raid was on Christmas Eve when 1,300 tons of bombs fell on the capital. Except for NJG 6, grounded by fog, the whole night fighter force took off to intercept and managed to destroy 11 bombers for six losses. On 29 December the RAF tried another double raid and this time the German defences were also forced to operate in unfavourable weather. A total of 600 bombers battered Berlin almost unhindered, while most of the leading 66 night fighter crews concentrated on the RAF formation raiding Leipzig. It is interesting to compare the kill and loss figures for this and the previous raid:

I JKorps	24 December	29 December
Total night fighters operational	166	66 ('experts' only)
Victories	11	11 (from a total of 20)
Losses	6	3

In the new year the battle of attrition continued unabated. Both opponents were nearing a state of complete exhaustion, but the RAF could replace its aircraft and aircrews far more easily than the Luftwaffe. It could determine the time and target of every raid and, thanks to its 5:1 numerical superiority, could divide the German defensive effort.

Britain had also achieved an indisputable lead in the high-frequency field and there was always some delay before the Luftwaffe could counter a new kind of British electronic interference. The RAF navigational methods had become so precise that the bombers could fly under any weather conditions. When the British were transmitting the bogus running commentary it was believed in Germany that the speakers were sitting in aircraft. The Luftwaffe therefore used young women for this task, only for the RAF to respond in kind. The Luftwaffe introduced new cover names, but these confused the RAF only for a brief period and led to a change of tactics. Instead of transmitting situation reports, the German-speaking RAF operators in Britain requested the night fighters to 'count down for tuning in'. To this the Luftwaffe replied with keying telegraphy despite the fact that the younger aircrew radio operators were not very conversant with it. Within a short time the British were jamming this too. Known as *Drumstick*, their method consisted of transmitting completely senseless morse code signals that mixed with the German signals to create an incoherent noise. To begin with, the running commentaries transmitted by German air observer aircraft remained undisturbed. These messages were received by radio operators in the aircraft of *Geschwader* or *Gruppen* COs and retransmitted to the aircraft of the formation. With this command system the Luftwaffe was not yet as helpless as it is frequently described in British publications. For one thing, the *SN-2* was still not being jammed, and the RAF bombers were still giving away their positions by keeping their H2S and tail-warning radars permanently switched on.

During the night of 3 January another 'fat dog' (raid) was flying in towards Berlin. The night fighter command ship *Togo* again directed in several night fighters over the German Bight before the bomber formation could avoid interception by dropping *Window*. Six four-engined RAF bombers went down on the way in, and another 22 were shot down in the Berlin area. The new CO of NJG 2, *Major* Prince Sayn-Wittgenstein, achieved six victories, all four-engined bombers. Like others before him, he had previously scored six in one operation, but at that time they had all been mainly twin-engined bombers.

On the following night the RAF lost another 28 bombers, equal to nine per cent of the force operational over Berlin. But the sacrifices of the German night fighters were no less severe: during these two nights I *JKorps* lost 22 out of 295 operational night fighters and the number of available aircraft sank to 227.

The unmolested RAF attack on Stettin during the night of 6 January showed once more how much the Reich Air Defence depended on technology. The ground stations managed to track a strong bomber stream to the Mecklenburg area, where it divided. Quite by chance, several ground radars and control links north of Berlin failed at this stage, so that neither the *Jagdkorps* nor the Luftwaffe Commander Centre were informed about the actual target of this raid. All that the situation maps showed in both command posts were a few enemy aircraft making a diversionary attack on Berlin, and as there was a lot of 'windowing' going on, it was naturally assumed that Berlin would be once more the principal target.

With Göring's consent, the Ia (Operations Officer) of Night Fighters of the Luftwaffe Commander Centre, *Oberst* Falck, ordered 7 *JDivision* to assemble its fighters near Berlin. The RAF raid on Stettin was recognised only after the night fighters had noticed widespread conflagrations in the area. As a result, only the last wave of the raiders and bombers already returning home could be intercepted. The successes were correspondingly meagre, and only 11 bombers were shot down. Naturally, a scapegoat for this fiasco had to be found and the blame was put on *Oberst* Falck's shoulders.

During the night of 11 January the single-engined 'Wild Boars' managed to destroy a few bombers over Brunswick. On 15 January the town was raided again. This time the bombers tried to get away spread out wide apart in a south-westerly direction, and thus presented welcome targets to the night fighters. I *JKorps* claimed at least 39 bombers, and two more were shot down by NJG 6 of 7 *JDivision*.

During the next raid, on 21 January, the RAF attempted to minimise its losses by all kinds of feints and diversions. Reports of bombing came from Düsseldorf, Hanover and Kiel, followed soon afterwards by Brunswick and Magdeburg, while the main force, almost 700 bombers strong, aimed for Berlin. This time I *JKorps* could send up only 98 leading crews, a puny force which nevertheless managed to shoot down 33 of the 35 bombers destroyed. On the following night the RAF smashed Magdeburg. Although no fewer than 169 night fighters were in the air they scored only 35 victories, additional proof that in this kind of aerial war individual ability counted more than numbers. During this action the night fighter force lost only four crews, but two of the pilots were irreplaceable: Maj Prince Sayn-Wittgenstein, who was shot down by a long-range RAF night fighter after his fifth kill that night, and *Hptm* Meurer, CO of I/NJG 1, whose He 219 was accidently rammed by a Bf 110 after his second victory that night. Next day it was reported by the media that Prince Sayn-Wittgenstein had been rammed by a long-range night fighter but had managed to land his damaged aircraft safely. His death in action was officially admitted only on 26 January.

Berlin remained the main RAF target on the last three nights of January. On each of these nights some 1,700 tons of bombs rained down on the capital, and it was obvious that Air Marshal Harris was going for a knock-out blow.

According to its own statements, during these raids the RAF lost 114 aircraft against the Luftwaffe's 16 night fighters.[11] This meant that a total of 71 twin-engined night fighters had been lost since 18 August. In January the night fighters also flew their last operations against US day bombers. The single-engined fighters of I/JG 300 had been used to intercept a raid on Emden in December, but had arrived on the scene too late. In January I/JG 300 flew day interceptions with varying results in the Emden, Bremen and Kiel areas. Near Bremen, the CO *Hptm* Stamp, and *Lt* Döring together shot down a B-17 but all seven Bf 109s used on this operation were damaged and had to crash-land. In the Kiel area 10 Bf 109s of I/JG 300 shot down 10 bombers, while on 30 January 18 fighters went empty-handed and lost six of their number.

The twin-engined night fighter force also shed some blood in such senseless interceptions. Thus on 29 January NJG 6 shot down four B-17s but lost six aircraft and their crews; the twin-engined night fighters were easy prey for the Lightnings and Thunderbolts. But next day it was even worse: the night fighter force lost so many twin-engined aircraft to US escort fighters that from then on it was authorised to fly day interceptions only against unescorted US bomber formations. On the other hand, the single-engined night fighters took over more and more of the day fighter role, although their pilots had never been trained in close-formation flying or attacks in pairs.

In February the *Gruppen* of JG 300 and JG 302 were subordinated to I *Korps* but brought along so few serviceable aircraft that they could hardly be regarded as reinforcements. Quite the opposite in fact: the daily average of fighters available for operations sank to 223 aircraft, less than the total in December 1942. To compound this, the month began with a series of unsuccessful operations that simply wore out aircraft for hardly any returns. In eight nights the *Korps* ordered up more than 200 fighters, mainly for Mosquito interceptions, and all for the sake of only one reported probable.

Meanwhile, RAF Bomber Command had been gathering its strength for the heaviest blow yet at Berlin on the night of 15 February. A force of 891 heavy bombers took off on this raid, and 809 dropped 2,642 tons of bombs on the capital in 39 minutes; a diversionary attack was aimed at Frankfurt/Oder. The destruction in the sorely tried city was enormous. Against it the 43 RAF bombers shot down paled into insignificance – even more so considering the fact that the night fighter force also lost at least 11 aircraft.

On 20 February the Allies began what they called 'The Big Week,' an aerial offensive during which they dropped some 19,000 tons of bombs on numerous German towns ranging from Brunswick to Leipzig and Augsburg. Even Posen and Graz were bombed. At the end of it the Americans had lost 224 bombers, the British 157. The most costly operation for the RAF was on the night of 20 February. A force of 816 heavy bombers and 25 Mosquitoes took off from Britain and after flying in over Holland set course directly for Berlin. As usual on such occasions, minelaying aircraft appeared outside the German North Sea ports. Unsuccessful attempts were also made to bomb the bases at Venlo, Leeuwarden, Gilze Rijen and Deelen to hinder the take-off of the night fighters. Mosquito raids on Aachen and Dresden left the night fighters unimpressed. In general it was believed that Berlin was once again the main target, not least because the Mosquitoes appeared there too. Moreover, the course of the bombers was followed by an air observer aircraft from Terschelling Island onwards. The first night fighters were infiltrated into the bomber stream near Bremen, while the single-seat night fighters gathered near Berlin. All in all, I *JKorps* ordered up 294 fighters which succeeded in shooting down 74 bombers. Total RAF losses amounted to 78 aircraft, against 17 German night fighters lost.

At the end of 'The Big Week' the RAF sent in two raids of 400 bombers each over France to South-west Germany, but here too the air observers proved their worth and did not let the formations get away. They called in night fighters from all over Germany to destroy at least 46 bombers, five of them falling to *Hptm* Schnaufer and his crew.

During the following weeks it seemed that the RAF had given up its Berlin raids and selected South-west Germany as the main target area. On these raids the British bombers were faced mainly by parts of NJG 4 and 6 and could make their return flights over Switzerland. And not only that: the RAF even made intrusions infringing the neutrality of that country. The Luftwaffe countered these developments by transferring II and III/NJG 1 as well as I, II and III/NJG 5 to France. The first large-scale RAF raid in March was intended for Augsburg, but the air situation on the 15th was once again completely confused. The bombers formed up several times over Eastern France, and then came *Fluko* reports indicating raids developing in the direction of Liège, Aachen, Düsseldorf, Frankfurt and Stuttgart. The weather added its share of problems, with spring storms and snow showers keeping most of the night fighters on the ground. I *J Korps* let only 93 leading crews take off, while NJG 6 sent its fighters in the direction of Radio Beacon 4, whence they chased from one target to another. This toing and froing cost I *Gruppe* seven aircraft, which crashed after running out of fuel. Most of the victories – totalling at least 33 – were achieved only during the return flight of the bombers. Among the night fighter losses were *Ofw* Treynogga of II/NJG 6, who was forced to land at Zürich, and the CO od I/NJG 6, *Major* Wohlers, who crashed into the Schwabischer Alb.

Frankfurt was the target for the 18 March raid, which cost the RAF just 22 bombers while the Luftwaffe lost eight fighters. The morale of the still relatively new NJG 6 was especially affected by the losses of the last few weeks, particularly when their aircraft were shot down by Mosquitoes. Several aircrews who had been suddenly fired on in the air started a rumour that the British long-range night

fighters were fitted with oblique weapons just like their own, a story
that had no basis in fact. The result was that some pilots – after being
warned by their radio operators, who could hear the radar impulses
from a Mosquito in their FuG 16 sets as a constant ticking noise – did

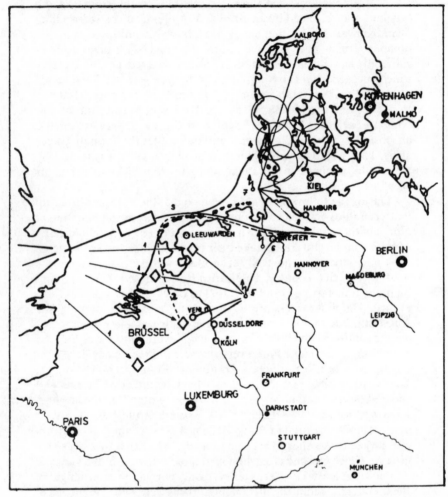

Course of the raid on Leipzig during the night of 19/20 February 1944

1. Mosquito raids on night fighter bases
2. Route of German air observer aircraft
3. Separation of RAF bomber stream
4. *Himmelbett* zones of combat the northerly bomber stream
5. Collection point of 3 *JDivision* night fighters
6. Infiltration into the bomber stream
7. Collection point of 2 *JDivision* night fighters
8. Infiltration into the bomber stream

not dare to make a steep diving turn, fearing that it would bring them directly in front of the enemy guns. They felt safer flying a full circle, and were then caught doing just that.

On 22 March it looked like another raid on Berlin, but at Osnabrück the RAF formation swung directly southwards, towards Frankfurt. The British thus managed to confuse the night fighters, but lost

1, 2. Collection points of 1 *JDivision* night fighters and their infiltration into the bomber stream
3.   Turning point of the bomber stream
4.   Mosquito diversionary raid on Berlin
5.   Route of single-engined night fighters to a
6.   Collecting area south of Berlin
7.   Operations of single-engined night fighters over Leipzig

44 bombers just the same. The six victories claimed by NJG 6 were all 'booked' by *Oblt* Martin Becker – a 'rising star' among night fighter pilots who had achieved his first confirmed kill on 23 September 1943.

The following night saw the last raid on Berlin, which turned into a disaster for the RAF. The night fighters of I *JKorps* reported 80 kills for 14 losses, another RAF bomber was shot down by NJG 6, and the Flak also reported successes. As was usual in the case of such high losses the British statements admitted less than the German claims, saying that 73 bombers had been lost.

Two days later the RAF took its revenge during a raid on Essen. Everything indicated an intrusion into Central Germany, and the night fighters chased all over the place but managed to shoot down only eight bombers while losing 20 of their own.

Then came the night of 31 March, with a full moon shining in the cloudless sky. It had been a long time since the RAF had attempted a raid under such weather conditions. More than 246 night fighters took off to intercept this raid, and the first were infiltrated into the bomber stream near the radio beacon *Ida* south of Bonn. Near Frankfurt/Main they were joined by aircraft from 1 and 7 *Divisionen*, and next morning the wrecks of 97 bombers lay scattered on the ground from Eifel to Nuremberg. The raid had been completely broken up; in many cases the horrified crews had dropped their bombs before reaching the target area. In fact only a few bombers had attacked Nuremberg itself and the damage was relatively insignificant. That night *Oblt* Martin Becker excelled himself, establishing a new record with seven confirmed kills. That night was also the absolute zenith of the German night fighter effort. Air Marshal Harris' aim of bombing Germany into capitulation by April had not been achieved. Certainly, Berlin had been badly battered but it was not completely destroyed and still had considerable importance as an industrial city. The death blow to Berlin was delivered only by the USAAF day bombers.

The price paid by the RAF was high indeed: since 18 November 1943 it had lost 1,047 aircraft, with another 1,682 seriously damaged. But the fight went on, and even the successes of the last few weeks could no longer change the course of the air war in Germany's favour, so great was the superiority of the two Western Allies. Nevertheless, both the RAF and USAAF needed a break, and during the next two months the raids on Germany dropped off significantly in scale and frequency. The raids on Cologne and Düsseldorf on 22 and 23 April again brought the RAF a 'bloody nose': 33 bombers were shot down on the first operation, and 37 on the second. April also saw an increase in low-level attacks on the Dutch airfields that cost the lives of quite a few German night fighter pilots who happened to be engaged in test or transfer flights. But their heavy machines were by no means defenceless victims when flown by an experienced pilot. For instance *Hptm* Jabs, CO of NJG 1, shot down two Spitfires on 29 April with his Bf 110G-4.

In those weeks the RAF raided various targets in Northern France, where it ran into some unexpected opposition from KG 51 and SKG 10, flying 'Wild Boar' operations in the area. On 20 April they were joined by III/NJG 1, which had been transferred to Laon. Night fighting over France also turned out to be surprisingly costly for the Luftwaffe, however. Contrary to their usual practice the bombers arrived only on moonlit nights and accompanied by an exceptionally strong escort of Mosquitoes, which let the German night fighters get hardly a shot in.

Late in April the RAF made several raids on targets in South-west Germany, and the course of the defensive operations that they provoked is typical of that period. The night fighter formations regularly succeeded in infiltrating into the bomber stream at a very westerly-situated radio beacon and soon afterwards the first enemy aircraft began to explode in the sky. Then the RAF would start jamming the running commentary and Y-control system and the night fighters lost contact with the bombers. As it was not possible to determine the target before the start of the actual raid, the next bombers shot down came from the second departing wave. Another factor was that following such raids on South-west Germany the RAF bombers regularly made their getaway by infringing the neutrality of Switzerland. This went on until the night of 28 April, when the night fighters made a determined effort to follow at all costs, and *Hptm* Friedrich, CO of I/NJG 6, and *Oblt* Kraft of II/NJG 5 each shot down a Lancaster over Switzerland. Among the other pursuers over Swiss territory was *Oblt* Johnen, *Staffelkapitän* of 5./NJG 5, who had already destroyed a Lancaster with a few bursts from his *Schräge Musik* guns that night. During the wild chase the port DB 605 of his aircraft started losing oil, the coolant temperature shot up rapidly, and Johnen had to switch of the offending engine. When he tried to return home with a feathered propeller his aircraft flew into the cone of light from several searchlights which so blinded Johnen that he completely lost his bearings. When he fired a distress flare the search-lights were momentarily switched off, but then he was unmistakably directed towards a lit-up airfield, where he landed his Bf 110G-4 (coded C9+EN) at 0215 hrs. It was Dübendorf, near Zürich, and unwittingly Johnen had thereby caused a conflict that almost grew into a military incident between Germany and Switzerland. When the Swiss military attaché in Berlin, Major B., reported the forced land-ing to the RLM it created a near panic. The Bf 110 was equipped with the *SN-2* radar and armed with oblique weapons, both until then unknown to the enemy. Apart from that, Johnen's radio operator, *Lt* Kamprath, was also the Signals Officer of II/NJG 5 and had received the latest radio codes that very night – and, contrary to all regulations, taken this secret material with him on operations. Finally, the rear gunner, *Ofw* Mahle, was the man who had developed *Schräge Musik* for series production. And now this highly secret material, and these important people, were in Switzerland, that playground of enemy agents!

When Hitler was informed next morning of what had happened there was no doubt in his mind: it was treason. The enemy had to be prevented at all costs from getting to know about the landing and its implications. Hitler contacted Himmler, who passed the task to the Chief of RSHA (Main State Security Office), Kaltenbrunner, who in turn authorised Skorzeny, Mussolini's liberator, to seize the aircraft by a surprise attack. By Saturday 29 April Skorzeny had gathered a special unit at Memmingen and was preparing to strike the following Monday morning.

According to Skorzeny's plan, fighter-bombers would fly in first to subdue the Dübendorf AA defences, followed by transport aircraft from KG 200 carrying a paratroop commando that would either take the Bf 110 with them or blow it up. But by the time Skorzeny reported his unit ready for action the operation had already been called off. In the meantime, the Chief of Foreign Intelligence of the SS(SD), *SS-Oberführer* Schellenberg, had pulled all kinds of strings to prevent this *coup de main*. For one thing, he was on good personal terms with the Chief of the Swiss Intelligence service, *Oberst-Brigadier* Masson, carefully cultivating this relationship in the hope of obtaining important information about Allied plans, particularly those for the forthcoming invasion. At this point Schellenberg made the following proposal: he would send one of his agents, *SS-Hauptsturmführer* E. (who had already done some business for the SS in Switzerland before), to Masson to offer the supply of or licence-manufacturing rights to the Bf 109 fighter in exchange for the return of the Bf 110 and its crew. In Schellenberg's view the whole business could be sorted out without much ado and without involving the Foreign Office or the embassies. The role of the official go-between would be played by the Swiss military attaché.

Before his departure Major B. was called to see Göring, who expressed the hope that B. would surely find a mutually satisfying solution, for otherwise he would be forced to destroy the Bf 110 at Dübendorf by bombing; a Luftwaffe formation was already standing by. This arm-twisting had the required effect on B., who, together with E., arrived at Berne on 3 May to meet Masson. E. immediately informed the Swiss representatives of his demands: absolute secrecy and return of the aircraft. In return, Germany offered to sell

12 Bf 109G-6 fighters and grant licence-manufacturing rights to the Bf 109 and certain weapons. E. could then satisfy himself that nothing had happened to the night fighter and that the radar devices had been removed and stored in a secret bunker under the strictest security. Of course the fact that the Swiss had already thoroughly examined, photographed, drawn and prepared detailed reports on everything was kept from the Germans. But then matters started to go slightly awry. The German military attaché heard through the grapevine that a Luftwaffe officer had examined the aircraft, only for a check at the RLM to reveal that no such officer had travelled to Switzerland. With its right hand not knowing what the left was doing, the RLM immediately suspected agents at work, another good reason to retrieve the Bf 110 at all costs. The rumours began to spread further, and the completely unsuspecting German Ambassador was suddenly called before the Swiss Federal President and had to listen to some strongly worded complaints. The whole affair was then referred to the Federal Council, who at first were not inclined to play along. The telephone wires between the secret services in Berlin and Berne were getting red hot until finally – and after still more setbacks – Germany agreed to sell Switzerland 12 Bf 109G-6 fighters at 500,000 gold Swiss francs each; in return, the Swiss would blow up the German night fighter and all its equipment in front of German eyewitnesses.

On 18 May the Operations Officer of NJG 6, *Hptm* Brandt, arrived in Dübendorf to check that the aircraft had not been tampered with before destruction. Brandt noticed at once that the *SN-2* had been removed and replaced and refused to sign the protocol, which contained the word 'intact'. However, thanks to the persuasive powers of E. the text of the protocol was altered, Brandt was finally induced to sign it, and the Bf 110 went up in flames at 2200 hrs the same night. The promised Bf 109 fighters arrived the very next day, E. received a cheque for six million Swiss francs – on 21 May he handed it over to Göring, who nonchalantly put it in his breast pocket and everybody was satisfied.

But the German part of the deal was not quite what it seemed either. The engines of all twelve Bf 109Gs were almost complete write-offs, and the final act of this drama was played out six years after the end of the war when Daimler-Benz and Messerschmitt had to pay compensation for their 'oversight'.

The interned airmen were returned to Germany, including the crew of *Ofw* Treynogga, who had landed on 16 March, and that of a Do 217N-2 of 6./NJG 4 which had landed at Berne on 2 May. No great fuss was made about these machines because they were equipped only with the FuG 212 radar.

In the meantime, word about Skorzeny's plan had gone around

the night fighter force and a few hotheads of II/NJG 4 were seriously considering the possibility of taking matters into their own hands and destroying the Do 217s at Basle from the air. In the event, both aircraft were taken over by the Swiss Air Force and remained in service until after the war. *Ofw* Treynogga was killed on 6 June, when his *Staffel* was operating from Ghedi in Northern Italy.

In May there were hardly any major raids, but smaller attacks hit a number of towns in Western Germany and Austria, and the Mosquitoes were whirring around unhindered almost every night. The RAF and USAAF limited themselves to the bombing of communications centres in occupied Western Europe and the Western Rhineland area. The only exception was the night of 3 May, when during an RAF raid on the railway installations at Mailly-le-Camp the night fighters shot down 42 bombers, but they had no further chance to demonstrate their high skills at that time. During the last few weeks the British jamming of German ground-to-air radio traffic had been so intense that the night fighters were again forced to change their tactics: the *Staffeln* and even entire *Gruppen* were now controlled from the air, and the individual fighters of the illuminated night fighting days were replaced by formations. The night fighters had even started to adopt the day fighter tactic of attacking in pairs.

The figures on the air warfare balance sheet for the period December 1943 to April 1944 were impressive: the night fighters of I *JKorps*, 7 *Division* and 30 *Division* had flown over 7,000 sorties over German territory, during which they had shot down 1,100 bombers and deprived the RAF of over 7,000 trained aircrew. But even these high figures amounted to only 5.1 per cent of the 21,600 RAF bomber sorties over the Reich territory during this period. The loss rate had to be twice as high if the RAF was to be deterred from continuing its aerial offensive. While the above excludes the victories achieved by NJG 4, since no reliable records are available, this formation's contribution could not have been more than 150, a figure that would have had little effect on the overall balance.

The seriousness with which the RAF regarded the Luftwaffe night fighter threat was indicated at this time by a steady increase in daytime raids on airfields in West and South-west Germany. As soon as this tactic became evident, the night fighters would disappear from their regular bases on most days and hide away at well camouflaged 'snake in the grass' fields, from which they would return at the end of the day.

In May several airfields were hit so severely that the *Korps* transferred whole *Gruppen* deeper into Germany. The night fighter force was getting a foretaste of what it had to expect when, after the codeword 'Threatening Danger West,' it would be transferred to France to resist the invasion.

Relatively little is known about the operations, successes and losses of the night fighters on other fronts. Long-range night fighter/intruder activities over Britain were revived for a short while in February 1944 when a *Staffel* of II/KG 51 under *Major* Puttfarken began flying such operations with Me 410s. Puttfarken achieved five kills before he was shot down near Canterbury on 23 April. Occasional successful interceptions of returning bombers were also achieved during 'Wild Boar' operations by II and III/KG 51 and SKG 10 with FW 190 fighter-bombers.

After the withdrawal of I/NJG2 from Italy some Italian night fighter squadrons were formed with Bf 110s and some Do 217Js equipped with the FuG 202 and FuG 212. After the Italian capitulation in September 1943 a few Italian night fighter crews went over to the Allies and the rest were disbanded by the Germans. It was not until May 1944 that another Luftwaffe night fighter formation appeared in Italy. II/NJG 6 was deployed at Ghedi, near Brescia, but night interceptions without ground control proved almost impossible from the outset and in the course of numerous sorties on moonlit nights along the Rome–Florence highway this unit managed to shoot down only six bombers.

Except for the period July–August 1943 hardly anything detailed is known about the successes of the night fighters on the Eastern Front. During the Kursk offensive IV/NJG 5 shot down 49 enemy aircraft, and another Soviet aircraft was destroyed on the ground. In the following months this *Gruppe* achieved 41 confirmed kills and 17 probables, and there were another 28 inconclusive combats which may well have resulted in additional victories. Most of the victims were twin-engined Il-4 (DB-3F) bombers, but the tally also included some four-engined Pe-8 (TB-7) and single-engined Po-2 (U-2) light night harassment bombers known to the Germans as 'sewing machines'. These victories were achieved by 14 pilots, of whom the most successful was *Hptm* Wittgenstein with nine, followed by *Hauptleute* von Meien, Lechner, Schoenert, Bonow, *Oblt* Pützkuhl and *Fw* Düding.

Then came the autumn nights, during which the Soviets did not fly at all. Nevertheless, the night fighters were always in their *Himmelbett* zones, ready for action. The Eastern Front night fighters had no choice but to wait in this way because, unlike their Western allies, the Soviets never gave away an impending operation hours beforehand by detailed tuning of radio sets or switching on of electronic devices.

The rail-portable *Freya* and *Würzburg* sets remained the only search and ground control radars on the Eastern Front because the Soviets never used any electronic devices that could be detected by a ground position indicator. As a result, there was a great disparity between the number of operational flights and shot down enemy aircraft, a fact that served the Inspector of Night Fighters several times as grounds for criticism. His alleged observations that 'the Eastern Front night fighters would be better employed digging anti-tank ditches' was also anything but helpful and only strengthened the view among fighting troops that the gentlemen in Berlin had no idea of the true conditions in the Soviet Union and the needs of the units. Examples of such ignorance were not in fact hard to find. Thus, for instance, NJG 100 was allocated the completely unsuitable Do 217 night fighter, while deliveries of the FW 189 to combat the Soviet biplane night harassment aircraft were continually refused.

Night fighting in the East was a waiting game for which quite a large proportion of the officers serving there were particularly well suited. In no other units were there so many former factory, test and Lufthansa pilots who, partly because of their advanced years, were no longer daredevils but made up for it with invaluable experience, flying skill and perseverance. Nevertheless, there were some stars among them with quite respectable victory scores, the most successful being Gustav Francsis with 56 confirmed kills.

The night fighting methods used in the East remained the same until the end of the war: *Himmelbett* for NJG 100, and illuminated night fighting for NJG 200. When in February 1944 the Soviet bombers began to break through more frequently north of the Courland night fighting zone over the Baltic area to raid Helsinki or Riga, the control ship *Togo* was deployed to the Gulf of Bothnia. With her support aircrews of 4./NJG 100 and 1./NJG 200 managed to score numerous victories, particularly on the night of 23 March 1944, when the night fighters and Flak destroyed 23 Soviet I1-4 (DB-3F) bombers near Tallinn. The most successful pilot that night was *Hptm* Bellinghausen with four kills.

NJG 200's sections fought under the most unfavourable conditions: their aircraft had no AI radar; all they had to rely on for operational control were the general air reporting or Flak air reporting services; and, to cap it all, their activities near the front line were limited to between 2300 and 2400 hrs because the rest of the time the Flak had permission to fire at anything that happened to be flying. To extend the interception time without endangering themselves some crews attached organ pipes to their aircraft which emitted morse-type tones in a predetermined rhythm, making it known to everyone over a radius of 5 km (3.1 mls) that they were friendly. The NJG 200 sections (*Schwärme*) stationed in the north – 1.*Staffel* under *Oblt*

Jank at Dno and Siverskaya, for example – enjoyed far better hunting conditions than the units in the southern sector of the Eastern Front. For one thing, the nights were never really dark over Courland, which helped considerably. *Oblt* Jank himself achieved nine kills in the course of illuminated night fighting, his score including a four-engined Soviet courier aircraft that was on its way to Leningrad with several generals aboard. From its remains German Intelligence recovered an intact Soviet cypher machine.

Night fighting in the southern sector was the responsibility of 2./NJG 200, which flew long-range night interceptions over the Crimea from Nikolaiev and achieved its 30th kill in May 1944. Air defence of the valuable oilfields in Romania was in the hands of IV/NJG 6, although to begin with this unit had little to do because these targets were attacked mainly by US day bombers. Night intrusions from the east and south began to increase only in May 1944 and then grew in intensity so rapidly that it was decided to form II/NJG 100 to operate over the south-eastern sector.

Notes

1 Aircraft with selected crews cruising above the bomber formation and directing the sky and ground markers.

2 The technical aspects of the method were handled by *Oberstabsingenieur* Günthner.

3 In the case of the Bf 110s the figures were 79 losses and write-offs against only 22 new arrivals.

4 In the event, 8 *JDiv* was the only one of these major formations to be activated. 8, 9 and 10 *JDiv* were to come under the command area of III *JKorps*.

5 A total of 302 Bf 110s, 70 Ju 88s, 88 Do 217s and 2 He 219s.

6 Three prototypes of the Ju 188R are supposed to have been built and flown, although it has not been possible to confirm this.

7 A full listing of *R-Sätze* is not attempted here because for some reason their numbers changed with each new He 219 version. Thus, for instance *R1* on the He 219A-0 series indicated 4 × MK 108 in a ventral tray, on the A-2 a drop tank, on the A-5 2 × MK 108s, and on the A-7 2 × MG 151s + 2 × MK 103s in a ventral tray and 2 × MK 108s the wing roots. Likewise, *R4* on the He 219A-5 indicated widened cabin glazing for the third crew member, and on the A-7 the reduction of ventral tray armament to 2 × MG 151.

8 Including six shot down by night fighters.

9 On 31 August *Maj* Hermann reported that since 12 July a total of 75–80 victories had been achieved by 55 pilots, including seven by Hermann himself and nine by *Hptm* Müller.

10 Nuremberg, 30 March 1944.

11 One of whom was *Ofw* Vinke, Oakleaves to Knights Cross (11./NJG 1, 54 confirmed victories).

7. The hunters become the hunted

The effect of the invasion on air warfare – Organisation of the Reich Air Defence from June 1944 until the end of hostilities – Development of new radars – Progressive developments of the Ju 88, Bf 110 and He 219 – New night fighter projects; turbojet-powered night fighters – Falling success rate, rising losses – Operation 'Gisela' – The end of night fighting in the Reich Air Defence area – Night fighting on the Eastern Front

GENERAL MILITARY EVENTS

6 June–August: Invasion by Western Allies; major Soviet offensive on the central sector of the Eastern Front; Rome occupied by the Allies: Collapse of the Romanian front; capture of Paris. *September:* Finland signs a special peace treaty with the USSR; Army Group North surrounded in Courland (Latvia). *November:* The Soviets and the Western Allies reach the German borders. *16 December:* German offensive in the Ardennes. *12 January 1945:* Major Soviet offensive on the Vistula Front. *February:* Loss of the western area of the Rhineland; Soviet forces capture Budapest. *March:* The Western Allies cross the Rhine at Remagen and Wesel; the Red Army reaches the Oder. *April:* Capture of Vienna; Soviet and American troops meet at the River Elbe. *2 May:* Capitulation of Berlin. *9 May:* Total capitulation of the German armed forces.

The inevitable decline of the German night fighter force started just three months after its greatest successes. Apart from everything else, D-Day also marked the beginning of near-total Allied aerial superiority; as Britain and the USA used more and more aircraft, so German resistance declined by day and night.

The number of operational sorties flown by the night fighters fell steadily from June to December. The success rate suffered equally, reaching its lowest point in December, when only 0.7 per cent of the attacking bombers were shot down. By this stage, as Gen Galland has admitted, the night fighter force had become insignificant, but not because the night fighter units had been decimated or because their command structure had collapsed. Quite the opposite in fact: in December 1944 the Luftwaffe night fighter force was numerically stronger than ever, and its aircraft included the most modern and powerfully armed types which could intercept and shoot down any enemy bomber except the Mosquito. Why, then, did the night fighters lose their effectiveness? In general terms, the overall superiority of the Western Allies from 6 June until the end of the war permitted only occasional successes; as a weapon the night fighter force had been blunted.

This was primarily due to the overwhelming Allied use of jamming, against which every German countermeasure proved useless after only a few days. The British lead in this field, which had shrunk measurably following the introduction by the Luftwaffe of the *SN-2*, *Flensburg* and *Naxos*, lengthened again at a stroke on 13 July 1944 when a Ju 88G-1 of 7./NJG 2 piloted by *Obgfr* Mäckle and equipped with these three systems landed at Woodbridge. Mäckle had lost his way following a sortie against minelaying Stirling bombers. After finding their compass out of action, the inexperienced crew had taken bearings on a radio beacon which seemed to them to be in the east but was in fact in England. This successful deception made the RAF a free gift of the most important German electronic systems, along with their operational methods and frequencies. The first results did not take long to materialise: only a few days later the RAF bombers began switching on their tail-warning and H2S radars for such brief intervals that the German night fighters could not take any bearings, making an interception by this means impossible.

During the summer months of 1944 the RAF made only limited use of *Window* against the *SN-2*, but the bombers were flying in at such low altitudes that the effectiveness of the *SN-2* was greatly reduced anyway. However, the *SN-2* jamming soon grew in intensity and from September onwards this AI radar was practically useless.

The loss of the early warning stations in the west following the rapid Anglo-American advances, and the total jamming of the German ground and AI radars and R/T communications, forced the German night fighter force to react to every major night raid like a badly battered boxer swinging desperately in the hope of scoring a lucky hit on his opponent. At about the same time the night fighter force also became unable to make use of its numerical strength because of the increasing shortage of aviation fuel. The Romanian oilfields were lost in August, and in the same month the USAAF started to knock out one German synthetic oil refinery after another. By the end of 1944 only a few leading crews could still fly operationally, while the majority of crews sat around doing nothing for weeks on end.

On the other hand, during this period operational availability reached a level believed impossible only a few short months before, because for the first time the ground crews had an opportunity to look after their aircraft properly. Even the mounting losses caused by

Allied strafing attacks could be quickly made good because until the end of 1944 both the aircraft and component part industries could report ever-increasing production figures. Only during the last four months of the war, when the general collapse began to make itself felt, did aircraft production fall off and with it the strength of the night fighter units. Despite this, the nucleus of the force achieved such successes in February and March 1945 that British air superiority by night perhaps could have been endangered if the latest German developments in the aircraft and high frequency sectors could have become operational in time.

It is clear that the Luftwaffe command had not foreseen the sudden collapse of its day and night fighter forces. For one thing, until D-Day it held the view that the Luftwaffe could prevent an Allied landing in France. In fact from May 1944 onwards, on the assumption that RAF Bomber Command would not restart its costly deep-penetration raids over Germany in the near future, the Luftwaffe command had moved its night fighter formations (except parts of JG 302) from Central Germany to the periphery of the Reich Air Defence area: the west, Northern Italy, Austria and Hungary. There remained in Germany only parts of NJG 1 and NJG 3, stationed in the north, and the replenished *Staffeln* of single-engined night fighter *Gruppen*. With its units thus deployed, the Luftwaffe command believed that it could counter any raid, from whatever direction, by means of timely interception and subsequent concentrated attacks by single-engined night fighters near the target.

In the case of an Allied landing – which would of course be preceded by aerial bombardment of the landing area – the Luftwaffe command intended to use the bulk of the night fighter units deployed in the west to attack and destroy the enemy bomber and transport formations. This operation was to take place at dawn, the aircraft attacking with bombs and gunfire as heavy fighter-bombers.

The actual course of events on D-Day and subsequent developments upset all these arrangements. Perfect British electronic jamming effectively concealed the actual course of the invasion forces until the start of the landing; the few operational sorties flown by night fighters were completely unsuccessful, yielding a mere four kills; and the perfectly worked out countermeasures for 'Threatening Danger West' only started coming into effect after long delays. In the meantime, German losses, particularly of day fighters, reached undreamed-of levels, the morale of the troops sank, and the staffs were at a complete loss as to what to do.

As it happened, the planned transfer of the bulk of night fighter units to France never took place. Only the first two *Gruppen* of NJG 2, III/NJG 3, II/NJG 5 and I/JG 301 were ordered to Chateaudun, Coulommiers and Epinoy. The last-mentioned unit, reinforced by crews from the disbanded 9./ZG 1, took over the air cover of V-weapon sites and even managed to achieve some successes.

While the day-fighter arm collapsed as a result of its terrible losses, the British jamming largely contributed to a reduction in the night fighters' success rate, which sank from 4.5 per cent to 2.9 per cent in June.

Just as in the early days of 1940, the Luftwaffe command tried to achieve success by constantly transferring units to the presumed areas of maximum enemy effort, but that tactic did not work this time. The 'castling' of I/NJG 6 is typical:

6 June: Transferred from Hailfingen to Deelen. Subordinated to 3 *JDivision*.

15 June: Transferred back into Germany to Kitzingen (7 *JDiv*); ground crews remained at Deelen. Ordered at 2400 hrs to continue transferring to Neubiberg.

16 June: Following operations over the Ruhr area I/NJG 6 landed at Deelen, II/NJG 6 at Venlo.

17 June: 10 crews of I/NJG 6 remained at Deelen, remainder returned to Neubiberg. All ground crews of I *Gruppe* moved to Neubiberg.

18 June: Flying crews of I/NJG 6 transferred to Mainz-Finthen.

19 June: I/NJG 6 transferred to Deelen, II/NJG 6 to Venlo.

20 June: Both *Gruppen* pulled out of Holland and stationed at Neubiberg and Echterdingen.

This constant movement served only to lower the morale of the *Gruppe*. During an inspection by the commanding General of I *Jagdkorps*, *GenMaj* Schmidt, this poor showing resulted in his unconcealed displeasure. As usual, the faults in the system were not seen, and the CO of the *Gruppe* was made the scapegoat: *Hptm* Hadeball was transferred to *Stab*/NJGr 10 and *Hptm* Friedrich took over I/NJG 6 with orders to 'get it in full swing again'.

Unmoved by the impossibility of letting all available fighters take off on operations, the Luftwaffe command ordered an expansion of the night fighter force. For the time being, the existing formations were brought up to strength. In November a 3rd *Staffel* was once again formed in each *Gruppe*, and even completely new units came into being during the last nine months of the war. In retrospect, the evolution of the German night fighter force in this period is reminiscent of a star that expands explosively just before its sudden extinction.

These developments in the organisation of the Luftwaffe night fighter force can be summarised as follows:

June: I/KG 7 redesignated I/NJG 7 and subordinated to I *Jagdkorps*; the illumination tasks dropped. *Jafü Ostmark* became 8 *JDiv* on 15 June; subordinated were III/NJG 6, II/NJG 101 and the Hungarian night fighter squadron 5/1. New formations in this area: *Stab* and II/NJG 100 from 2./NJG 200 and 1. and 4./NJG 200. 5./NJG 200 withdrawn from operations and intended to become the nucleus of the new III/NJG 100. Planned to equip the new formation exclusively with Do 217N-2 night fighters. II/NJG 6 recalled from Italy and transferred to Echterdingen; from then on there were no German night fighter units on the Italian Front. 12./KG 51 served as nucleus for the newly formed 4.(Erg.)/NJG 7; eventually operational from Brieg/Upper Silesia.

July: Formation of the independent *NJ-Staffel Finnland*, directly subordinated to Luftflotte 5. Unit code: B4+; equipment: Ju 88G-1, Bf 110G-4 and He 219. Disbandment of all Air Observer flights (*LBeoStaffeln*); instead each *Gruppe* formed a Lead Section (*Führungsschwarm*). All night fighter formations temporarily subordinated to Luftflotte 3 for defence against invasion recalled to Reich Air Defence control. NJG 2 deployed at Cologne, Kassel and Langendiebach; NJG 1 temporarily spread out among various Westphalian airfields. NJG 5 extensively fragmented by this redeployment: I *Gruppe* at Parchim, II at Hagenau (subordinated under NJG 6), III at Lübeck-Blankensee, and IV at Powunden (East Prussia). Strength of the German night fighter force on 27 July 1944: establishment 1,059 aircraft; actual 849; available for operations 614.

August: II/NJG 5 transferred to Stendal on 29 August. After the Romanian collapse IV/NJG 6 moved to Leipheim. As a result of the Soviet breakthrough on the Central Front I/NJG 100 sections (*Schwärme*) were based in East Prussia, Western Poland (then *Wartheland*), Warsaw area and Upper Silesia. II/NJG 100 deployed further south, in Hungary and Northern Serbia. Air defence of East Prussia reinforced by operational parts of NJG 102. On 10 August 1./NJGr 10, 6. and 10./JG 300 became target defence (*Objektschutz*) and Mosquito *Jadkommandos* deployed at Werneuchen, Jüterbog, Rheine, Oldenburg, Hangelar and Darmstadt. On 28 August 6./JG 300 reformed as 1./NJG 11 at Lippstadt, and from parts of 1./NJGr 10 – 2./NJG 11 at Hangelar. The rest of 1./NJGr 10 remained at Hangelar and Darmstadt-Biblis. Equipment: FW 190A-8, Bf 109G-6 and Bf 109G-14. 7 *JDiv* evacuated its command bunker *Minotaurus* at Schleissheim and withdrew to Pfaffenhofen/Ilm.

September: NJG 1 evacuated its airfields in Holland and transferred to Münster-Handorf, Dortmund, Düsseldorf and Fritzlar; several dispersal fields occupied by operational sections (*Kdos*). I/NJG 7 moved from Handorf to Kastrup and Varlöse in Denmark. Formation of III/NJG 100 halted and available personnel used to bring 2./NJG 100 up to strength. Strength of the night fighter force on 17 September 1944: establishment 1,086 aircraft; actual 959; available for operations 792.

October: 3 *JDiv* transferred its command post from Deelen to the Duisburg area and then, after it was knocked out by a bomb hit, to Wiedenbrück. Due to increased bombing raids by British and Soviet formations East Prussia was declared Main Defence Effort area and strengthened by the addition of I and III/NJG 5. Hungarian night fighter squadron 5/1 withdrawn from 8 *JDiv* (and therefore Reich Air Defence) and subordinated to Luftflotte 4. A second Hungarian *Gruppe* with Ju 88G-1s was in the process of forming. II/NJG 100 subordinated to NJG 6 at Novy Dvor.

November: I *Jagdkorps* established a command post at Treuenbritzen. NJG 2, strongly reinforced, was supposed to recommence long-range night fighter/intruder operations. However, as IV/NJG 3 seemed better suited for that purpose than III/NJG 2, both units exchanged designations but remained on their present airfields. Former illuminator *Gruppe* I/NJG 7 joined NJG 2 as IV *Gruppe*. III/KG 2 retraining for night fighter role at Mengen and Neubiberg as future V/NJG 2; it was planned to equip it with Do 335 early in 1945. The rest of 1./NJGr 10 became 3./NJG 11. I/NJG 11 was dispersed once more: *Stab* at Biblis, 1. *Staffel* at Fassberg, 2. at Biblis and 3. at Hangelar (with an operational *Kdo* at Twente). Late summer saw frequent transfers of 'Mosquito hunters': 10./JG 300 (25 aircraft) became II/NJG 11 (4. to 6. *Staffeln*) stationed at Jüterbog, Köthen, and possibly also at Biblis. Twente in Holland again temporarily used as base for parts of NJG 1 and NJG 2; bulk of NJG 2 transferred to East Frisian airfields at Brokzetel, Wittmundhafen, Jever, Bookhorn, Varel and Marx. *NJ-Staffel Finnland* transferred to Norway and redesignated *NJ-Staffel Norwegen* on 27 November.

All *Gruppen* again formed their third *Staffeln*, resulting in an increase in the established strength of the night fighter force to 1,101 aircraft. At this stage all formations were fully equipped – there were even some aircraft surplus to establishment – and on 17 November the Luftflotte Reich disposed of 1,170 night fighters, of which 905 were available for operations.

December: All night fighter *Geschwader* formed training and *Stabs-staffeln* (Staff Flights). The strength of the night fighter force reached its highest peak: establishment 1,319 aircraft; actual 1,355; available for operations 982.

January 1945: I/NJG 11 reduced to its 2.*Staffel*; soon afterwards unit redesignated 1./NJG 11. Former 1. and 3./NJG 11 became 7. and 8./NJG 11 of the new III/NJG 11; 9./NJG 11 formed from newly trained personnel from *Erg.Gruppe* Ludwigslust. New 1./NJG 11 transferred to Southern Germany (based at Echterdingen and elsewhere). On 28 January formation of 10./NJG 11 with Me 262 jet fighters from *Kdo Welter* at Burg bei Madgeburg. III/NJG 6 transferred from the area controlled by 8 *JDiv* to 7 *JDiv*. *Jafü Ostpreussen* and *Jafü Schlesien* subordinated to Luftflotte 6.

Deployment of the night fighter formations in November 1944
  Key to map on p.173

1	Stab/NJG 1 Paderborn	31	II/NJG 5 Stubendorf
2	I/NJG 1 Münster	32	III/NJG 5 Lübeck
3	2./NJG 1 Niedermendig	33	Kdo III/NJG 5 Lüneburg
4	II/NJG 1 Düsseldorf	34	IV/NJG 5 Powunden
5	Kdo II/NJG 1 Paderborn	35	10./NJG 5 Praust
6	III/NJG 1 Fritzlar	36	Stab/NJG 6 Schleissheim
7	Kdo III/NJG 1 Giessen	37	I/NJG 6 Gross Sachsenheim
8	IV/NJG 1 Dortmund	38	II/NJG 6 Schwäbisch Hall
9	Kdo IV/NJG 1 Störmede	39	III/NJG 6 Steinamanger
10	Stab/NJG 2 Köln	40	IV/NJG 6 Schwäbisch Hall
11	I/NJG 2 Kassel	41	NJGr 10 Werneuchen
12	II/NJG 2 Köln	41a	1./NJGr 10 Bonn
13	III/NJG 2 Gütersloh	42	3./NJGr 10 Jüterbog
14	IV/NJG 2 Grove	43	10./JG 300 Jüterbog
15	Stab/NJG 3 Stade	44	Stab, 2./NJG 11 Darmstadt
16	I/NJG 3 Schleswig	45	1./NJG 11 Fassberg
17	Kdo I/NJG 3 Nordholz	46	3./NJG 11 Bonn
18	II/NJG 3 Grove	47	Kdo 3./NJG 11 Twente
19	III/NJG 3 Westerland	48	I/NJG 100 Prowehren
20	Kdo III/NJG 3 Haderslev	49	1./NJG 100 Hohensalza
21	IV/NJG 3 Marx	50	2./NJG 100 Breslau-Udetfeld
22	Kdo IV/NJG 3 Wittmundhafen	51	II/NJG 100 Malacki
23	Kdo IV/Varel	52	4./NJG 100 Powunden
24	Stab/NJG 4 Rhein-Main	53	Schwarm 4./NJG 100 Gross Schiemanen
25	I/NJG 4 Langendiebach	54	I/NJG 101 Ingolstadt
26	Kdo I/NJG 4 Darmstadt	55	II/NJG 101 Parndorf
27	II/NJG 4 Mainz	56	3./NJG 101 Finow
28	III/NJG 4 Ebelsbach	57	III/NJG 101 Kitzingen
29	IV/NJG 4 Rhein-Main	58	I/NJG 102 Oels
30	Stab/NJG 5 Jesau	59	II/NJG 102 Schönfeld
30a	I/NJG 5 Jesau	60	III/NJG 102 Stubendorf

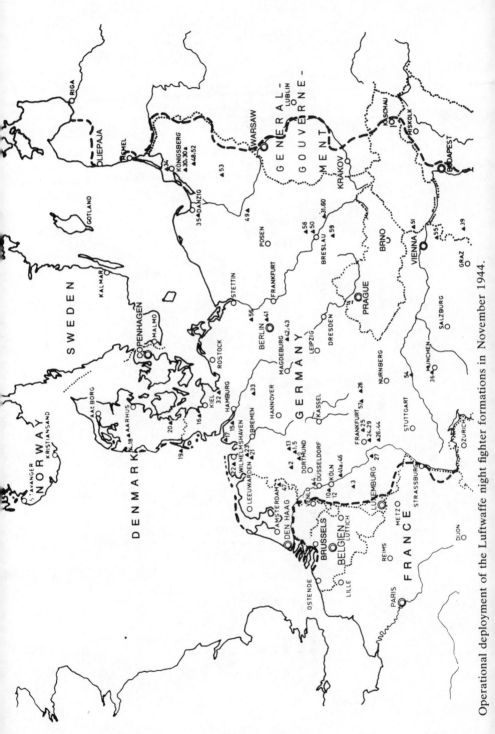

Operational deployment of the Luftwaffe night fighter formations in November 1944.

Organisation of the German night fighter force in November 1944

Luftflotte Reich
GenOberst Stumpff
Command Post: Berlin-Wannsee

I. Jagdkorps
GenLt Schmid
Command Post: Treuenbritzen

1. Jagddivision
GenLt Heinrath
Command Post:
Döberitz
NJGr 10
3./NJG 11
Jafü Ostpreussen East
Prussia:
Oberst Nordmann
Insterburg
Stab, I., IV/NJG 5
I/NJG 100
III/NJG 102
Jafü Schlesien Silesia:
Oberst Witt
Cosel
II/NJG 5
I, II/NJG 102

2. Jagddivision
GenMajor Ibel
Command Post:
Stade
Stab,
I–IV/NJG 3
I/NJG 5
1./NJG 11

(Section CO)
Absch.führer
Dänemark: Denmark
Oberst Vieck
Grove
IV/NJG 2
Kdo III/NJG 3

3. Jagddivision
Oberst Grabmann
Command Post:
Wiedenbrück
Stab,
I–IV/NJG 1
Stab,
I, II/NJG 2
1./NJGr 10
2./NJG 11

Jafü Mittelrhein:
(Central Rhine):
Oberst Trübenbach
Darmstadt
I – III/NJG 4

7. Jagddivision
GenMajor Huth
Command Post:
Pfaffenhofen
Stab,
I, II, IV/NJG 6
Stab,
I/NJG 101

8. Jagddivision
Oberst Handrick
Command Post:
Wien-Kobenzl
Stab,
III/NJG 6
II/NJG 100
(less 4. Staffel)
II/NJG 101

Tag- und *NJ-Jafü*
Ungarn (Day and
Night Fighter Leader
Hungary): Budapest
4./NJG 100
Hungarian NJ Sq 5/1

February: The collapse began to show. I *Jagdkorps* disbanded on 17 February, its tasks taken over by the newly formed IX *Flieger-korps(J)* under *GenMaj* Peltz. 1 *JDiv* transferred to Ribbeck; *Oberst* Hermann gave up his command to *Oberst* Wittmer; 2 *JDiv* also got a new CO, *Oberst* Rödel. *Jafü Ostpreussen, Schlesien* and *Ungarn* disbanded; operational boundaries of 1 and 8 *JDiv* extended to the Eastern Front. IV/NJG 2 and II/NJG 3 withdrawn from the night fighter force and disbanded, and their personnel used to reinforce NSGr 4 and NSGr 30.

March: Following the crossing of the Rhine at Remagen by the Americans the rest of the Reich began to split into northern and southern parts. NJG 4 evacuated its airfields in the Rhein-Main area and withdrew to Northern Germany; II/NJG 2 withdrew to Southern Germany. On 28 March 7. and 9./NJG 11 were forced to evacuate Hangelar; their next operational base was Bad Lippspringe. The day before orders went out to disband 17 night fighter *Gruppen* (total of 51 *Staffeln*). Of the remainder, I/NJG 100 and NJGr 10 were absorbed by NJG 5, *NJ-Staffel Norwegen* became 4./NJG 3, the Hungarian squadron 5/1 was disbanded, and the re-equipment and re-training of V/NJG 2 discontinued.

The night fighter force then consisted of 37 *Staffeln*, with *Gruppe* strength amounting at the most to two *Staffeln*. Some of the remaining *Gruppen*, amounting to only one *Staffel* each, nevertheless retained their impressive-sounding *Gruppe* designations. *Staffel* establishment was fixed at 16 aircraft and 26 aircrews; all surplus aircrews transferred either to paratroop or railway Flak units. Thousands of surplus telecommunications operators, maintenance crews and other ground personnel were directed to the front-line troop marshalling centres (*Frontsammelstellen*). In most formations female Luftwaffe auxiliaries took over a substantial share of mainte-nance work. On 31 March II and III/NJG 11 were reduced to 2. and 5.*Staffeln* respectively and subordinated to NJG 2; 1./NJG 11 came under NJG 6. *Kdo Bonow* formed at Oranienburg to continue testing the suitability of the Ar 234 jet bomber for night interception tasks.

April: The Red Army reached the Elbe line and the eastern part of Austria; British troops occupied Lower Saxony; the Americans pushed forward to Thuringia and were preparing for an assault on Southern Germany and the so-called 'Protectorate' (Czecho-slovakia). Germany was split into two parts. In the north – Schleswig-Holstein and Denmark – were jammed together more than 400 night fighters, the remainder of NJG 1, 2, 3, 4, 5, 11 and 102. The Luftflotte Reich had its command post at Missunde, near Schleswig, while the Luftwaffe formations in the northern sector were commanded by *LwKdo Nordost*. *JDiv* 1, 2 and 3 were dis-banded, their tasks taken over by 14 and 15 *Fliegerdivisionen*, which until then had commanded only bomber units. In the south – Bavaria, Austria and the 'Protectorate' – fighter control was taken over by *LwKdo West*. Early in April the *Stab* of IX *Flgkorps(J)* received a directive to transfer to the southern sector but never arrived there, having dispersed somewhere along the way. 7 *JDiv* remained in being until the end of the war, while 8 *JDiv* was probably disbanded. In the southern sector were based the remainder of NJG 6, II/NJG 2, II/NJG 100, 1./NJG 11 and scattered parts of the NJG 101 and NJG 102 training formations. Their total strength amounted to some 200 intact night fighters, but lack of fuel made concentrated operational actions impossible. Most of the Luftwaffe formations in the southern sector fell into enemy hands before the capitulation.

May: Early in the morning of 5 May, in a last desperate attempt to keep its aircraft out of enemy hands, 14 *Flgdiv* ordered those crews who still had enough fuel to fly to Norway or Prague; only a small number obeyed. The truce began at 0800 hrs that day, followed on 7 May by the armistice. In the northern sector night-fighter pilots delivered their machines to the victors, while all of the crews in the areas yet to be occupied blew up their own aircraft. A few pilots fled to Switzerland or landed on Allied-occupied airfields, the German national insignia on their aircraft painted over with a white four-pointed star. The Luftwaffe had ceased to exist.

The next round in the struggle for aerial supremacy at night would be won not by the numbers and quality of the night fighters but by superiority in the high-frequency field. On that point there were no doubts within Luftwaffe command circles, but they drew false conclusions from the events of the early summer of 1944. The successes achieved by the *SN-2*, *Flensburg* and *Naxos*-equipped night fighters only confirmed the view widely held in Luftwaffe command circles, that with these fairly straightforward devices it would be possible to inflict severe damage on the enemy – provided the system could be kept secret and enough of them made available. Possible technical inferiority could always be offset by a high state of training and fighting spent on the part of the crews.

As a result, the industry was instructed to concentrate single-mindedly on production of the FuG 220 *SN-2* series, and development of the second irons in the fire, the FuG 217 and FuG 218, ran into delays. Even worse off was centimetric radar, the development of which came far down the list of priorities.

Yet at the same time all those in responsible positions were fully informed of the flaws of long-wave radar:

- Proneness to jamming by tinfoil strips or transmitters
- Range never more than the altitude of the target
- High-drag aerials
- Limited visual displays[1]

To begin with only the increasing jamming of R/T communications and long-range fighter control were found obstructive. The jamming of the Y- and *Egon* fighter control systems from April onwards was countered by widening the frequency spectrum, while development work on the *Barbara* and *Nachtfee* data-transmission systems began again, although the Luftwaffe command did not reckon on their series production before early 1945.

Reports from the various *Wassermann*, *Mammut* and *Freya* sites on the RAF's increasing jamming activities were still not taken seriously. However, this changed when the new *Jagdschloss* panoramic early-warning radar did not prove as resistant to jamming as expected. On D-Day the British were able to neutralise all German ground control radars so completely in a wide zone around the actual landing area that the Luftwaffe was unable to use a single night fighter.

But worse was still to come. After the Ju 88G of NJG 2 had fallen into British hands one German night fighter control device after another started to become useless. The *SN-2* (with the broad dispersal waveband VII) was occasionally usable until September, but then the RAF found the correct size of *Window* to jam this device too. *Jagdschloss*, in which the Luftwaffe command had such high hopes, proved a complete failure, and by December the air reporting and fighter control services were almost completely blind. Only very experienced personnel were able to distinguish between the echoes caused by jamming and actual aircraft, but that did not prevent even these experts from being withdrawn from the radar sites and sent to the front line near the end of the war.

Ignoring the proven uselessness of the tried and tested ground control radars, the German electronics industry kept on manufacturing them at an ever increasing rate, and in November *SN-2* and *Naxos* output reached its highest level. Meanwhile, the industry was unable at short notice to offer a single combat-ready interference-secure search radar, mainly because fundamental research had been neglected. From October onwards however aircraft flown by the leading night fighter crews were equipped with the *SN-2R* and *Naxos ZR* tail-warning radars, which proved exceptionally useful in the early detection of enemy long-range night fighters. But while *Naxos ZR* was fitted only to the Ju 88G, the He 219 had to make do without even the *SN-2R*, which explains the high losses of this type to RAF Mosquito night fighters.

In December the Luftwaffe command made a final attempt to take the lead in the high-frequency field. The research establishments and industry were exhorted to give their everything, and it was made known that no more restraints would be placed on their inventiveness. As a result, a veritable flood of projects for passive and active night-fighting systems, homers, IFFs and weapon-triggering devices streamed into the RLM during the last few months of the war. Infra-red search also came back into favour again, and even acoustic locating devices were developed and tested. Even if hardly any of these systems were built, let alone brought to operational readiness, it is nevertheless a fact that by the end of the war Germany had once more reached the level of the Allied state of art in this field and had created at least a few devices that were equal if not superior to Anglo-American navigation and location equipment.

Initially, after the setbacks which the night fighter force had to suffer following the loss of the *SN-2*, every effort was made to speed up the development of the FuG 228 *SN-3* (Telefunken) and the FuG 218 *Neptun V/R* (Siemens/FFO). Both were conventional VHF radars with external aerials. The *SN-3*, first called for by the Inspector of Night Fighters late in 1943, differed from the *SN-2* only in having a wider frequency range (1.9 – 2.5 m), a minor advantage. Because the larger part of this frequency range was already being jammed, there was not much point in introducing this radar into service, and production was limited to an experimental series of only 10 sets. *Neptun*, on the other hand, offered better prospects of successful operational use. Despite the fact that the FuG 218 had a shorter range than the *SN-2* and *SN-3*, it had the indisputable advantage of working in an as yet unjammed frequency band (1.6 – 1.9 m). *Neptun* could also be coupled with *Elfe*, which automatically measured the range to the target and fired the guns at a predetermined distance. A few examples of the FuG 218 *V/R* (combined with the tail-warning radar) were fitted to the Bf 110, Ju 88, He 219 and Me 262 and used operationally. Some *Elfe* units are also supposed to have been available but were never used operationally because it was intended to wait for final tests and mass production before suddenly introducing the system into service on a large scale. Only one example of the FuG 218 *G/R* is known to have been built; instead of the usual 2 kW transmitter this system used one of 30 kW, which increased the range at a suitable altitude to 10 km (6.2 mls). The *Neptun G/R* was intended for installation in the Do 335. Another device in the *Neptun* family was *Neptun-Liliput*, which attracted attention on account of its extremely simple construction and very small size. It was tested in a Me 262. For Me 262 night fighters Siemens & Halske developed a 'cockpit ring aerial' for the FuG 218. In this case the aerial dipoles were in the shape of metal strips glued to the wooden fuselage nose, replacing the usual protruding rods.

Work to evolve aerodynamically cleaner aerials for the *SN-2* and *SN-3* had been going on at Telefunken for some time. The result was the *Morgenstern* series of aerials, with dipoles set in a cruciform and attached to a central carrier rod. To achieve even better drag coefficient values the complete aerial could be covered by a conical fabric fairing, with only the dipole ends protruding outside. Only a few Ju 88G-6 night fighters were so equipped because of a decision not to built this device in large quantities. Instead, it was intended to concentrate on development of a centimetric AI radar with internal aerials.

As far as is known, Siemens had not even attempted to develop a *Morgenstern*-type aerial for the *Neptun* radar. Nevertheless, mention is made several times in March 1945 of a FuG 218 combination with an *Obertasse* device that would have been built into the wings. It seems that this device was a parabolic aerial or a rotating dielectric rod radiator, similar to the *Naxos* arrangement.

A rather unusual *SN-2* arrangement seen on a Ju 88G-6 of NJG 5 was probably an experimental modification carried out at the Werneuchen test centre: two aerial holders protruded upwards from the nose section and two downwards, so that the dipole was polarised horizontally. This aerial arrangement was expected to be less sensitive to *Window* jamming, more effective in detecting high-flying bombers, and capable of giving earlier warning of Mosquito night fighters approaching from behind and below. The Ju 88G-6 with this equipment was flown by *Maj* Schoenert only once, on 27 April, but before contact could be established the complete electrical system was knocked out by a short circuit and within a few minutes the aircraft was shot down by a Mosquito.

The FuG 218 would only have been an interim solution anyway, because it was obvious that the future belonged to the centimetric radars. The first German set of this new generation was the FuG 240/1 *Berlin N1A*, evolved from the FuG 224 *Berlin A* ground observation device, a copy of the British H2S. This radar worked on the 9 cm wavelength and the search angle was only 10°, though directional accuracy was extremely good. To compensate for the limited search angle the radar operator could swivel the aerial dish through 60°. The planned start to series production in August 1944 came to nothing because at 150 kg (331 lb) the system weighed three times as much as the *SN-2* (the FuG 218 weighed only 35 kg/77 lb) and the aerial dish was so big that it could not even be fitted into a Ju 88.

While Telefunken was still trying to reduce the size and weight of this system, the company's laboratory staff were already working on new *Berlin* projects that would have given even narrower direction-finding beams combined with far better target definition. Thus the *Berlin N3* AI radar promised a range of 8 km (5 mls), even at low altitudes, and by swivelling the aerial dish it was hoped to achieve a search angle of 90°. With this performance the *Berlin N3* would have been at least equal to the Allied SRC 720 AI radar used on the

Mosquito and P-61 Black Widow night fighters. But while on the enemy side these devices were being produced in large quantities only one *Berlin N3* could be tested on the ground before the end of the war. A total of 24 sets of the improved *Berlin N1A* were completed, 10 of which are supposed to have been fitted to Ju 88 night fighters. The often publicised assertion that these Ju 88s were flown by NJG 1 at Gütersloh in March 1945 just is not true. For one thing, at that time there was not a single NJG 1 aircraft at Gütersloh, and for another, this formation did not have all that many Ju 88s in the first place. It has been established, however, that *Hptm* Krause, CO of I/NJG 4, had test-flown a Ju 88G-6 equipped with a *Berlin* AI set in February 1945. The British acquired an aircraft with this installation at Leck in May 1945 and it was later exhibited at Farnborough. This Ju 88G-6 carried the NJG 4 code, 3C+.

Telefunken had hardly started series manufacture of the *Berlin N1A* late in January when it received an official instruction to produce only a limited quantity because, beginning in April, it would be replaced by the FuG 244 *Bremen 0*. The advantages of this new device were its lower weight (100 kg/220 lb) and a relatively smaller parabolic aerial only 75 cm (29½ in) in diameter, making it suitable for the night fighter versions of the Me 262 and Ar 234 jets. Ground tests had begun in December, flight tests were to start on 15 January, and series production was scheduled to begin in February. In this case also the quantity was limited, to only 100 sets, because the FuG 245 *Bremen* promised even better performance: operating with a 100 kW transmitter, it was hoped to achieve a range of 8–9 km (5–5.6 mls). The FuG 245 *Bremen* was planned to go into production in May, but it never got to that stage. Nor can it be established that *Bremen 0* was flight-tested.

Notes about the discussions taking place during the last few months of the war have an air of unreality about them: seemingly unaffected by the relentlessly advancing enemy forces, which were already on the Rhine and the Oder, the military and the scientists were debating the manufacture of weapons and devices that would only be ready for series production after some three months at the earliest. One of the devices, the first example of which could not be expected before July, was the FuG 247 *Bremerhaven*. It was intended to work on the 3 cm wavelength, had an aerial that could search spirally a 120° conical space, and had a display screen that would show the target, as in an optical gun sight. From another screen the pilot could read off the range, or he could determine it automatically with the *Elfe* weapon triggering system.

The last German electronic device on which some work was done before the capitulation was the FuG 246 *München D* AI radar, which was intended to work on the 1 cm wavelength.

By the end of the war great strides had also been made towards solving the blind firing problem, but none of the *Pauke S* or *SD* devices, which could be coupled with the *Berlin* AI radar, were completed.

Although during the last nine months of the war the RAF bombers switched on their H2S navigational radars only rarely, the FuG 350 *Naxos* remained the only German night fighter device that could indicate the position of a bomber stream with reasonable accuracy. The initial *Naxos Z* served as a basis for several special versions:

Naxos ZR A combined system capable of detecting the British navigation and night fighter radars. Fitted only to the Ju 88G, with the aerial of the tail-warning device built into the tail.

Naxos ZX Evolved to detect 3 cm radar emissions.

Naxos RX Similar to *ZX* but coupled with a tail-warning device.

Naxos ZD Direction-finding device designed to locate 3 cm and 9 cm emissions.

However, as *Naxos* could do no more than give only a rough indication of the position of an enemy navigation radar, there was an obvious need for a precision homer. There existed already a good ground receiver, codenamed *Korfu*, that could accurately locate H2S-carrying aircraft, and attempts were made to produce a modified version suitable for airborne use under the designation FuG 351 *Korfu Z*. This system was built and tested but never reached the operational stage.

Despite the fact that the homing problem had not been solved, the German scientists went a step further and attempted to develop a homing receiver capable of detecting emissions from all centimetric radars. This device was known as *X-Halbe*.

As mentioned above, after *SN-2* had been neutralised determined efforts were made to evolve an effective infra-red search device. A lot of work in this area was done by Zeiss engineers, resulting in the FuG 280 *Kiel Z*, several sets of which were built and tested under operational conditions early in 1945. Incorporating a swivelling parabolic mirror, *Kiel Z* detected the infra-red radiation from exhaust gases and projected it through a photoelectric cell onto a sighting device. However, the drawbacks were similar to those experienced with the earlier *Spanner* devices: although on dark nights it was possible to detect aircraft up to 4 km (2.5 mls) away, on lighter nights *Kiel Z* was also sensitive to starlight, and proved completely useless within the sight of ground fires. Incidentally, the RAF bombers also used infra-red searchlights and receivers for communications between aircraft in flight. On the German side it was intended to detect this radiation by means of an IR telescope codenamed *Falter*, but it is doubtful if this idea was ever fully realised, let alone used operationally.

Another German dream was a completely interference-free and reliable automatic flight control system.

One interesting idea that did become a reality was the *Bernhard/Bernhardine* data-transmission/relay system. This was extremely interference-secure and made the night fighter largely independent of ground-to-air W/T or R/T communications. The ground set *Bernhard* beamed a running commentary on the enemy's movements once every 60 seconds. The *Bernhardine* aircraft set, which had a range of 400 km (248 mls), received and decoded these messages and displayed them by means of a coupled teleprinter. The airborne set could also receive information from its ground counterpart indicating the position and course of the fighter. A typical *Bernhard* transmission looked like this:

  + = Start of message
  27 = Position of the fighter at 270°, i.e. west of the transmitter
  K = Transmitter code, in this case Eggebeck
  60 = Spearhead of the bomber stream at 6,000 m altitude
  QR = Spearhead of the bomber stream in Fighter Map square QR
  18 = Course of the bomber stream 180°, i.e. southwards
  400 = Estimated strength of the bomber formation
  − = End of message

Valuable as these messages were, the night fighter pilots had to look upon such information somewhat sceptically as long as the ground radars of the air reporting service were being jammed by *Window* or transmitters. But here too things were changing for the better following the completion of the prototypes of the *Jagdschloss Z* and *Forsthaus Z* air reporting systems. These units worked on the 9 cm and 3 cm wavelengths and would have been immune to British jamming. Unfortunately, like the latest German AI radars, they came too late to be available for operational service.

The last days of German resistance also saw the end of the long search for a reliable aircraft-to-aircraft identification device. As far as can be ascertained, the FuG 226 *Neuling* was tested by *EKdo Charlotte*, including airborne trials in a Me 262, but apparently was not fitted on any operational aircraft.

But all this concentrated scientific effort of the last few months of the war could no longer have helped the German night fighters, because with a few exceptions none of these systems even reached the testing stage.

182

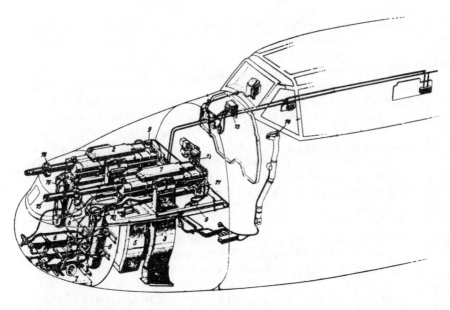

Bf 110G‑2/R3: MK 108 installation in the nose

1. Port weapon
2. Starboard weapon
3. Empty cartridge/link ejection chute
4. Ammunition feed chute
5. Ammunition box
6. Compressed-air bottles with DHAG 5 pressure-reducing attachment
7. External attachment point
8. EPD electro-pneumatic reloading valve
9. EPA electro-pneumatic firing valve
10. Front weapon support
11. Gun-adjusting support
12. Switch box panel
13. SZKK 2 switch, ammunition counter and control box for two weapons
14. Firing button
15. Protective mantle for gun barrel
16. Barrel seal

Developments in the German aircraft industry during the last year of the war show remarkable parallels with those in the high-frequency field. In both instances conventional types were produced in large numbers (in this case the Bf 110 and Ju 88) while the manufacture of advanced models (He 219) was delayed. High-performance aircraft that could have been among the best of their kind in 1944 arrived so late that they had already been overtaken by developments. As a result they were either not put into production at all (Ju 388, Do 335), or production was stopped within a short time (Ta 154). Advanced developments such as the Ar 234 and Me 262 either did not reach the operational units at all, or were available only in insignificant numbers. Also common to both fields was the hectic activity of the development teams which submitted an immense number of projects that could only have reached the test stage by mid-summer 1945 at the earliest.

With the G-4 series the Bf 110 had reached the zenith of its development, although Messerschmitt had made plans for a further variant, the Bf 110H-4, which should have gone into series production in the autumn of 1944. It was at this time that the Emergency Fighter Programme (*Jägernotprogramm*) came into force, under which production was to be concentrated on jet fighters, single-engined fighters and only those twin-engined fighters that could still be classed as modern in mid-1945. The favoured types included the Me 262, Ar 234, Ju 388 and Do 335, possibly the Ju 88G-1 and He 219, but on no account the Bf 110, the production of which soon began to taper off. It fell from 197 in September to 61 in December, and the last 17 Bf 110 night fighters were delivered in February 1945. Formations equipped with the Bf 110 shrank at the same rate: in July 1944 no fewer than 10 complete *Gruppen* were flying Bf 110 night fighters, compared with only six in January 1945.

The final Bf 110G-4 series differed externally from its predecessors mainly in having modified exhaust flame-dampers (straight tubular fairings of larger diameter and diverted under the wings only) and a nose section built to accommodate the *Neptun* aerials. The standard armament of Bf 110 night fighters delivered from June 1944 onwards consisted of 2 × MK 108 in the upper and 2 × MG 151 in the lower nose section, and an oblique armament of 2 × MG FF. On account of the powerful explosive effect of its ammunition – as a rule a burst of only 15 rounds sufficed to bring down a four-engined bomber – the MK 108 cannon was in great demand among the aircrews. By comparison, in 1942 an average of no fewer than 250 rounds of 7.9 mm and over 50 rounds of 20 mm cannon ammunition were needed to achieve the same effect. On the other hand, this heavy cannon also had its drawbacks. Its low muzzle velocity meant that the pilot had to approach the enemy aircraft very closely and accept the risk of damage to his own aircraft from debris from the exploding bomber. For this reason some pilots asked for the MK 108 cannon to be removed from their aircraft and relied instead on the remaining weapons, particularly the oblique guns. The MK 108 was also mounted in this way, but only very seldom, for the above reasons. Another rarely used installation was 2 × MG 151 instead of 2 × MK 108 cannon as the upper pair of fuselage nose guns. In spite of their long flash hiders, the lighter guns produced a blinding effect when fired at night.

Standard Equipment set (*Rüstsatz*) *M1*, two additional MG 151

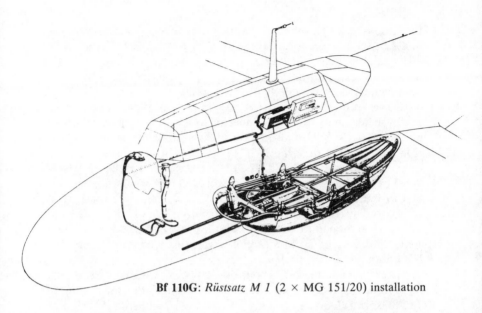

Bf 110G: *Rüstsatz M 1* (2 × MG 151/20) installation

cannon in a ventral tray, was also little used in 1944 because of its detrimental effect on the Bf 110's power/weight ratio and speed.

The Bf 110 may have been classed as obsolete, but in the hands of good pilots this aircraft remained a deadly weapon right up to the end of the war. This is particularly noticeable when the victory claims submitted by I/NJG 1 (He 219) and II/NJG 1 (Bf 110) from June 1944 onwards are compared. Operating at the same time and under the same conditions, the pilots of II *Gruppe* regularly shot down more bombers than the He 219 crews.

As Bf 110 production was tapering off, so Ju 88G output was increasing:

June 1944	285
August	306
October	255
November	339

Even in January 1945 no fewer than 278 Ju 88Gs left the various assembly lines, but then in February the collapse of the communications network and the component manufacturers affected output so much that only 50 aircraft were built. The last available Ju 88G production figures cover March 1945, when just 27 Ju 88G-6 fighters were turned out.

The first Luftwaffe night fighter units to re-equip with the Ju 88G-1 in June 1944 were III/NJG 3, II/NJG 6 and I/NJG 7, and by September the Ju 88C-6 was flown only by NJG 100 and training formations. That month also saw the introduction into service of the first Ju 88G-6 series aircraft, the Ju 88G-6a and G-6b with BMW 801 radial engines. Deliveries of the Ju 88G-6 with Jumo 213A inline engines began in October. All of the Ju 88G-6s carried the same standard armament as the G-1 series.

Powered by the Jumo 213A, the Ju 88G-6 offered exceptional performance and was clearly superior to the Bf 110, particularly at altitude. The Ju 88G-6 also featured far more comprehensive electronic equipment than the Bf 110: all aircraft were fitted with the FuG 350 *Naxos* as standard, and quite a few also had the *Flensburg* and *Korfu* homers. Late in 1944 the Ju 88G night fighters were also first in the queue for *Naxos ZR* and *SN-2R*, and were the first to receive the FuG 218 *V/R*. Early in 1945 all *Staffeln* of NJG 2, 3, 4 and 100 were equipped exclusively with the Ju 88G-1 and G-6, though some mixed Ju 88/Bf 110 *Gruppen* remained on the strength of NJG 5 and 6.

There is some mystery about the Ju 88G-7, a variant frequently mentioned in aviation literature. For instance, the few captured Ju 88Gs with Jumo 213 engines and the FuG 240 *Berlin* AI radar or *Morgenstern* aerials are always described as 'Ju 88G-7' in British publications, thus perpetuating the old and mistaken notion that there was some connection between the electronic equipment and the type designation. An explanation would not be amiss here. During construction of each new type the manufacturer took into consideration the possible use of the latest radio and electronic devices, even though they might not be fitted on the production line. When finally such systems become available and were fitted, this did not lead to any changes in the type designation because the electronic equipment was fitted at a front-line workshop and not at the factory. Likewise, there was no change in the designation of older types when they were retrospectively fitted with new radio sets, guns or other equipment. With the help of Junkers works numbers (*Werknummern*), all of which began with '62,' we can verify that the so-called Ju 88G-7s in fact were part of the Ju 88G-6 series.

The Ju 88G-7 *did* exist, but it was quite a different aircraft. Fitted with more powerful Jumo 213E engines, it also had the pointed wingtips of the Ju 188/388 series, as specifically stated in an RLM aircraft type manual. Only about 10–12 Ju 88G-7s were completed in November 1944, and none were ever delivered to an operational unit. After completing tests at Letzlinger Heide (near Hillersleben) the aircraft were sent back to the works, where some were later flown by the Factory Defence Flight (*Werkschutzstaffel*). Plans for large-scale series production were shelved because the performance of this version did not show any notable improvement over that of the current Ju 88G-6 series.

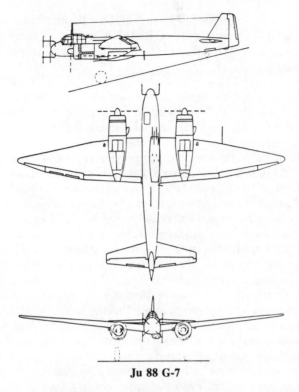

Ju 88 G-7

Compared with the Bf 110 and Ju 88, the He 219 was produced in very modest numbers indeed: on average only 18 aircraft a month left the assembly halls at Rostock and Wiener Neustadt. The record monthly total, 36 aircraft, was achieved in January 1945 when production of this type should have been phased out under the Fighter Emergency Programme. There was of course enough capacity to achieve higher production figures, but for a variety of reasons this never happened. First of all, there was Milch's opposition to what he called a 'one-purpose' type which would have required 30,000 man-hours to build. Heinkel countered this by pointing out that from the 800th aircraft onwards it would require only 10,000 man-hours, while Milch's own favourite, the Ju 88G, would still need 30,000 man-hours after this figure. In answer to the second part of Milch's criticism, Heinkel instructed his design offices to prepare diverse proposals for high-altitude 'destroyer' and reconnaissance variants, a high-speed bomber and a fighter-bomber.

The He 219 situation changed for the better in July 1944 after Milch had resigned as *Generalluftzeugmeister* and his area of responsibility came under the Technical Air Armament office (*Amt Technische Luftrüstung*, TLR). Heinkel was now able to make it plausible to Milch's successor, *Oberst* Diesing, and the Fighter Staff dictators Sauer and Speer that a mass of Bf 110 and Ju 88G night fighters alone could not contest Allied air superiority. It was also necessary to have a superior aircraft, namely the He 219. And it was a fact that in mid-1944 the He 219 was the fastest and most heavily-armed German night fighter, capable of superior high-altitude performance and with unsurpassed take-off and landing characteristics. The He 219 was also the only German aircraft that could, at fully equipped weight and with one engine out, still gain height and, with undercarriage down, go around again on one engine after a landing attempt.

It is of interest to note that excessively close co-operation between the operational units and the manufacturer also had its drawbacks. Whenever requests were voiced by the operational crews, the factory immediately tried to oblige by producing Standard Equipment sets and special modifications. The trouble was, these requests were often contradictory and sometimes led to impractical and time-consuming developments. Thus, for instance, the crews first called for the heaviest possible armament of various 30 mm cannon, only then to voice a preference for lighter 20 mm weapons. Then, following objections voiced by several pilots of II/NJG 1 that the He 219 was only a two-seater, work began on a Standard Equipment set that would accommodate a third crew member, only to be dropped almost immediately in favour of a proper three-seater design. When the He 219's performance advantage over the Mosquito proved insufficient the Heinkel design office evolved a special 'Mosquito hunter' variant; and in anticipation of attacks by future heavy high-altitude bombers, work began on a heavy fighter based on the He 219, the He 419.

Unfortunately, in the course of all this effort at Heinkel no-one noticed that the general shortage of raw materials was causing the time lag between requests from the operational units and their realisation to grow longer and longer. To mention just one example, the first pure He 219 'Mosquito hunter' was delivered only after it had been officially decided that the type would not be used in this role.

Then there was the multitude of Standard Equipment set designations, which changed their meaning when applied to different versions of the He 219. This absurd practice was as confusing to contemporary Luftwaffe technicians and supply personnel as it is to present-day historians. Instead of concentrating on increasing the production of the proven night fighter version, Heinkel continued to work on a large number of projects based on the He 219. In June 1944 two variants were in series production – the He 219A-2 and A-5, differing principally in their engines – while the following developments were under way:

He 219A-6   radically lightened 'Mosquito-hunter' variant
He 219A-7   high-altitude fighter with Jumo 222 engines
He 219B-1   three-seat night fighter with Jumo 222 engines
He 219B-2   high-altitude night fighter powered by DB 603
             engines with exhaust-driven superchargers
He 219C-1   four-seat night fighter with Jumo 222 engines and a
             manned four-gun tail turret
He 219C-2   fighter-bomber with four-gun tail turret
He 419   high-altitude fighter
Hü 211   high-altitude reconnaissance derivative with long-span
             wooden wings, designed by Dr Hütter.

By June 1944 I/NJG 1 had 20 He 219A-0, A-2 and A-5 *Uhus* on
strength. The older A-0 aircraft were retrospectively brought up to

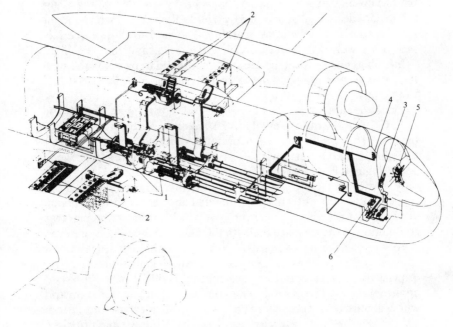

He 219A: Basic armament installation with *Rüstsatz M 1* (total of 6 × MG
151/20)

1. MG 151/20 A
2. Linked ammunition belt containers
3. Firing buttons
4. SZKK 6 electric switch, ammunition counter and control box for all six weapons
5. Reflector sight
6. Dimmer switch

A-2 standard by fitting the more streamlined cabin glazing without the rear gun position, the *SN-2* AI radar, and ejection seats, which were absolutely essential in view of the crew position ahead of the engines. Before the ejection seats became available the crew had to stop both engines and feather the propellers to avoid being mutilated after baling out in an emergency.

The oblique-mounted MK 108 cannon also attracted growing criticism on account of its low muzzle velocity and the pilots asked for this installation to be removed completely or replaced by the well-proven MG FF/M guns. Should the MK 108s be retained as oblique armament, however, the crews made it clear that they had to be fitted at a completely different angle: either flatter, so that the pilot could open fire from a longer range, or almost vertically. Only in this way could the pilot avoid damage to his aircraft from debris blown off the enemy bomber. As a result, the Mauser-Werke evolved a variable mounting for the MK 108, designated the L 188, which allowed the pilot to use the guns at any angle between 45° and 85°. In the event this installation – also demanded by *Oblt* Welter for his Me 262 night fighters – never reached the operational stage. But despite the fact that there were MK 108 delivery bottlenecks, and that the night fighters had no use for it, all He 219s continued to be delivered with this oblique armament, only to be relieved of it at the front-line workshops.

In June a few He 219As were also flown operationally by II/NJG 1, but the pilots – all old Bf 110 hands – were not at ease with the *Uhu*. They found that its performance was not significantly better than that of their usual mounts, felt most uncomfortable sitting ahead of the engines, and most of all bemoaned the fact that the He 219 had only a two-man crew. At their request the front-line workshops replaced the rear entry hatch (intended for access to the oblique guns) with a Plexiglass panel through which a third crew member could observe the airspace beneath the fighter. Some pilots are even supposed to have had a machine gun on a simple lens-type mount fitted in this position for defence against Mosquito attacks. The request for a three-man crew was met by Heinkel with *Rüstsatz 4* applicable to the He 219A-5. This consisted of an additional cockpit with a defensive weapon, fitted on top of the main cabin. The pattern aircraft, He 219V30, was also test-flown by NJGr 10 and criticised because of a 25 km/h (15.5 mph) loss in speed. The 150 hp of extra power available on the He 219A-5 series cancelled this out, but that was all.

After the high-altitude performance of the He 219A-2 and A-5 series had proved inadequate for intercepting Mosquitoes in June and July, Heinkel delivered the A-6 in the following month. Basically a He 219A-5 minus 50 kg (110 lb) of armour plating and with armament reduced to 4 × MG 151 guns, this lightened version was powered by DB 603L engines which incorporated bigger superchargers and were fitted with the GM-1 nitrous oxide injection system. These measures promised a straight and level maximum speed of 615 km/h at 10,000 m (382 mph at 32,810 ft) altitude. In practice, tests soon revealed that the He 219A-6 with its normal 18 m (59 ft 2 in) wingspan was extremely unstable at such altitudes, and had to be banked very carefully in a wide turn to avoid a stall. But it was all in vain in any case: the He 219A-6 was never used as a 'Mosquito hunter', and its armament of 4 × MG 151 guns was rejected by most pilots as too light to combat the heavy bombers. The He 219A-7 and He 219B-series high-altitude interceptors, promised for delivery in summer, were delayed by their Jumo 222 engines, which failed to reach series production. The He 219A-7 with DB 603G engines was also late. Tests with the He 219V25 to V27 prototypes were flown in December, and the first production aircraft were completed only in January. As before, this new version was offered with various armament combinations, but this time the leading operational crews preferred *Rüstsatz 4* comprising 2 × MG 151 in the wing roots and 2 × MG 151 in a ventral tray. The night fighter aces had found this armament quite sufficient for shooting down enemy bombers, as was also proved by other pilots flying the Bf 110 and Ju 88G. Apart from that, heavier armament would have been nothing but a hindrance in the event of an attack by a Mosquito.

The last He 219s built during the war were assembled from spare parts at the pre-operational workshop at Werl and fitted with Jumo 213 engines instead of DB 603s. These machines were designated He 219A-7/R5.

Only one example of the three-seat He 219B-1 was completed and briefly test-flown at Vienna-Schwechat before being damaged in a landing accident and scrapped. More work was done on the He 219B-2 high-altitude interceptor and it is known that at least one B-2 (marked KJ + BB) was test-flown. Basically, this machine was nothing more than an A-5 airframe with extended wings (span increased by 2 m/6 ft 6½ in). A few more B-2s with supercharged DB 603L engines were apparently also completed, but definitely none of the final version with DB 603 engines incorporating exhaust-driven turbo-superchargers were built because Daimler-Benz never managed to master the problems associated with this powerplant. And as only a few Jumo 222 test units were ever delivered the He 219B-3 and He 219C-1 night fighters also remained on paper. Total He 219 production during 1944–45 amounted to 268 operational aircraft, nearly all of which were used by *Stab* and I/NJG 1. Individual He 219As were also flown operationally by II/NJG 1, *NJ-Staffel Finnland* (later *NJ-Staffel Norwegen*), Erg./JG 2 and NJGr 10. The latter *Gruppe* also used some of the 20 He 219 prototypes that had been impressed into operational service.

By contrast, the Ta 154 got hardly anywhere, and two years of effort and preliminary work had to be written off within a few short weeks. Series production had just begun in July when the first two aircraft crashed. The subsequent investigation established that the cold glue bonding the wood had eroded it to such an extent that the wings simply disintegrated in flight. Steps were immediately taken to solve this problem, but when two more Ta 154s crashed during factory test flights in August the Chief of TLR stopped the entire programme. A whole list of other reasons were then found to justify the rejection of this type, which had been promoted by Milch and his office for years. Among other things, there were complaints about an inadequate field of vision for the crew, making the Ta 154 unsuitable for pursuit night fighting. While that was true enough – Kammhuber had already pointed it out after examining the first project drawings – the aircraft had not been intended for that role, having been designed as a Mosquito interceptor, a task for which the view was perfectly satisfactory. Judging by its flight performance and characteristics the Ta 154 would have been undoubtedly the best possible Mosquito interceptor. The trouble was that the problem of how to build a mixed-construction high-performance aircraft was taken too lightly and the engineers had neglected the development of the necessary special manufacturing techniques.

Prof Kurt Tank, the designer of the Ta 154, was absolutely convinced of the superiority of his creation and offered the RLM a variant suitable for interception and pursuit night fighting, the Ta 154C, which featured a bulged cockpit cover and oblique armament. However, the TLR would not entertain another experiment, and in any case the Fighter Emergency Programme had decreed that only two piston-engined night fighters were to be built, the Ju 388J and the Do 335 two-seater.

The Ju 388 was the most conspicuous example of misdirected development. Responding to repeated reports from secret agents that the British would be deploying four-engined high-altitude bombers, Germany's aircraft designers went to work developing special high-altitude night fighters. The only successful design, the Ju 388, could have countered these notional bombers but was practically useless in any other role. It would have been too unwieldy and too slow for Mosquito interception, while its pressure cabin and supercharged BMW 801TJ engines were completely unnecessary in combat with Lancasters and Halifaxes flying no higher than 6,000 m (19,685 ft). The first night fighter prototype of the 388 series, the Ju 388V2 (a modified Ju 188T), began flight tests in January 1944. These trials were concerned mainly with the 'altitude' engines, which for a long time developed less than the expected power and proved somewhat unreliable. For this reason no armament was fitted; instead of the intended 2 × MG 151s plus 2 × MK 108s in a weapon container, the Ju 388V2 was 'armed' with a mock-up. The same applied to its remotely controlled tail gun position and electronic equipment. Another two prototypes joined the test programme during 1944. They were the Ju 388V4 and V5, which were already closely representative of the future production standard. In the meantime, the remotely controlled tail gun installation had been dropped, replaced by 2 × MG 151 oblique weapons. It was also intended to equip the Ju 388J night fighter with the FuG 218 radar and a *Morgenstern* aerial.

Production of the Ju 388J-1 was to start in January 1945, followed two months later by the Ju 388J-2 with a remotely controlled tail gun installation. However, due to various technical problems with the turbo-superchargers, the planned start to series production had to be postponed. Instead, *EKdo 388* under *Hptm* Bonow (formerly of NJG 100) was formed at Rechlin in January to test the aircraft under operational conditions. The results were negative: performance was so disappointing that in February the Ju 388J was dropped once and for all from the development programme.

Basically, this design had been overtaken by developments. As early as September 1944 the General Staff of the Luftwaffe had come to realise that it would not achieve more success with the night fighting methods practised at the time, and that better methods were not possible for lack of suitable aircraft material. The dream solution was to use a long-range night fighter, superior to the Mosquito, to intercept the bomber stream near its bases and then follow it all the way to Germany and back again. This would have been possible with only one aircraft type, the Do 335, but that was still in the experimental stage. And it was impossible to speed up this project – even the sharpest-worded orders and threats of court martial proceedings had no effect: the complicated armament machinery had already been too badly damaged by Allied bombing.

In correct appreciation of this situation *Otl* Knemeyer of TLR proposed to build up a new close-range night fighter force. According to this plan, the role of the less successful single-seat night fighters would be taken over by high-speed jet aircraft provisionally equipped as two-seaters. In Knemeyer's opinion, the aircraft best suited for this task was the Ar 234 – it was as fast as the Me 262, but possessed more docile flight characteristics and had a longer range. Knemeyer was also certain that the radar operator could be accommodated in the space occupied by the automatic aerial camera on the standard Ar 234 reconnaissance version and that armament could be carried in an external weapon container. A man of action, *Otl*

Knemeyer ordered that 30 aircraft from the current Ar 234B-series should immediately be re-equipped as provisional night fighters and fitted with the FuG 218, FuG 120 and FuG 350 as well as 2 × MG 151 in the so-called 'Magirusbombe' weapon container. It could be assumed that, in view of the distressing general situation Germany was in at the time, this project would have been tackled with the greatest possible dispatch, but it was not. Just like in similar cases, the first step was to start with detailed tests with one aircraft, to find out that the whole idea was correct in principle, then order the Arado works to design a special night fighter version – which was turned down by the TLR; then go on to request new, more refined and perfect projects, with the end result that not a single aircraft ever reached operational service.

The Ar 234V-12 (Werk Nr.130 022, PH+ST) began flight tests at Werneuchen in September. In the same month three more should have joined it, followed by another three in October. By early December there should have been 30, which could then have been supplied to an operational unit. In the event, the TLR bureaucrats stepped in before anything could happen, halted any further re-equipment of Ar 234 bombers and authorised only the acquisition of the Ar 234V-19 and V-20 to continue night flying trials at Oranienburg (the runway at Werneuchen had proved too short).

A Special Development Commission for Night and Bad-weather Interception (Entwicklungssonderkommission Nacht- und Schlecht-wetterjagd or ESK) was then appointed under the leadership of Prof Kurt Tank to examine the possibilities offered by the existing projects and prototypes. In November the commission arrived at the same conclusions as had Knemeyer two months earlier: the Ar 234 and Me 262 should be developed as interim solutions. This would lead to special versions and ultimately, in the course of 1945, to completely new types. Prof Tank's idea of the future night fighter was as follows: a swept-wing aircraft with an ordinary piston engine for cruising flight and two BMW 003 turbojets for interception and general performance improvement. But it would also seem that the whole subject was of purely academic interest to Prof Tank: why else should he have requested the defunct Jumo 222 as the cruising engine?

Accepting the commission's verdict on 11 December Göring ordered the immediate preparation of three Ar 234s and three Me 262s for night fighting tasks, and the formation of Test Detachments (EKdos). Of these, EKdo 234 was commanded by Hptm Bisping while EKdo 262 was the one-man show of Oblt Welter, who flew a single-seat Me 262A-1a (Werk Nr. 130 056) equipped with the FuG 218 radar. With this aircraft Welter shot down two four-engined bombers and three Mosquitoes by 24 January 1945. After this *Oblt* Welter became the generally acknowledged expert in turbo-jet night fighters and his rejection of the Ar 234 was accepted without argument. Welter's criticism mainly concerned the clear-view cockpit glazing which produced distracting reflections on take-off and landing, and caused the pilot to be blinded by searchlight beams. When attacking at very close range, the pilot also risked having the glazing smashed by debris from the enemy aircraft. As a result, Arado, which had already proposed definitive night fighter versions with full-view cockpits (the Ar 234C-3 and C-5 *Nachtigall*), was advised to develop a night fighter featuring a conventional cockpit. Project work on this new version started right away and by 10 January the Arado design offices were ready to submit proposals for the Ar 234P-1 to P-5 series. Of these, the Ar 234P-1 to P-3 were to have four BMW 003 turbojets each, while the Ar 234P-4 and P-5 were designed for the more powerful Heinkel HeS 011 units. The first four examples of the P-series were intended to carry an armament of 2 × MG 151 and 2 × MK 108 cannon, augmented on the Ar 234P-5 by 2 × MK 108s in an oblique installation. The electronic equipment was planned to be the same for all five Ar 234P versions: the FuG 244 *Bremen O* centimetric AI radar and the FuG 120 *Bernhardine*, FuG 136 *Nachtfee* and FuG 350 *Zc Naxos* homing and automatic flight control devices. Without doubt, the Ar 234P-5 would have made a first rate night fighter, except that it was not expected to go into series production before June 1945.

The result of all this was that the Ar 234 night fighters stayed on paper, and *EKdo 234* never had more than three aircraft at any one time. It is also true that Welter was right in his criticism of the full-view cockpit: several Ar 234s are known to have crashed on take-off and landing because their pilots were so confused by reflections from the airfield lighting that they stalled their aircraft. For this reason *Hptm* Bonow, who took over as CO of *EKdo 234* on 13 February 1945 after the fatal crash of *Hptm* Bisping, had the side and floor glazing of his cockpit painted black. With this Ar 234 Bonow subsequently flew several operations, though without success.

When it became clear that there would be delays with the Ar 234, work began at Staaken in January 1945 on the conversion of two-seat Me 262 trainers to night fighters, resulting in the Me 262B-1a/U1. This modification carried the standard armament of 4 × MK 108 cannon in the fuselage nose and was equipped with the FuG 218 and FuG 350, with the rotating aerial of the *Naxos* set installed in the cockpit. Aircraft of this type equipped 10./NJG 11 formed under *Oblt* Welter in February. Of course, this variant was only an improvised solution and the Messerschmitt design office – like the other firms – was working flat-out to evolve a whole new family of night fighters based on the Me 262. But time had already run out, and only one example of the purpose-built Me 262B-2a night fighter was completed by April. This version differed from the improvised Me 262 B-1a/U1 in having a more streamlined cockpit and additional oblique armament of 2 × MK 108s. The successor to this first jet night fighter series was intended to have the more powerful HeS 011 turbojets and a centimetric AI radar in the fuselage nose. In response to suggestions from operational pilots Messerschmitt proposed to offer easily exchangeable nose sections with different armament combinations. Another innovation was the planned use of vertically-swivelling oblique armament fitted to one side of the pilot's cockpit. This installation would have been controlled and fired with the *Gnom* sighting device. To increase the type's inadequate endurance Messerschmitt proposed auxiliary fuel tanks which could be either towed in flight or fitted on the wings. An even more advanced project was based on Prof Tank's notion of a swept-wing night fighter. This proposal was to have turbojets in the wing roots, and showed a certain similarity to the later Republic F-84F fighter. Proposals featuring swept-back wings were also submitted by Arado, Focke-Wulf, Gotha and Dornier, but none of them got any further than drawings and performance calculations.

Just like the Ta 154 and Ju 388, the last piston-engined fighter, the Do 335, also met an inglorious end. Although the RLM had selected it as the standard night fighter for 1945 and Dornier had spared no effort and shrank from no propaganda exercise to point out the Do 335's superiority to the jets, the *ESK-Nachtjagd* experts gave it the thumbs-down. The Commission rightly concluded that this aircraft, because of its demanding structure and the impossibility of installing a centimetric AI radar in the fuselage nose, was no longer feasible late in 1944, and that the Ar 234 and Me 262 should have preference. Dornier naturally disagreed, and a clash was inevitable.

The first Dornier projects for a tandem-engined heavy fighter and fighter-bomber were the P.231/1–3, originally submitted in 1942. P.231/3 was envisaged as an advanced piston engine/turbojet combination, but the RLM selected the P.231/2 with two piston engines and allocated the official designation Do 335. The idea of developing the two-seat trainer variant into a night fighter was mooted in 1944, and Dornier received instructions to prepare Do 335V-10 accordingly. Flight tests with this aircraft, equipped with the *SN-2*, began at Diepensee on 24 January 1945. For obvious reasons the *SN-2* aerial was divided, with the vertical dipoles on the port wing and the horizontal on the starboard wing. Do 335V-16, equipped with the FuG 218, was supposed to be delivered to Werneuchen the next day, but this had to be postponed until early February due to delays at Siemens. Other pattern aircraft produced in preparation for production of the planned Do 335A-6 series were Do 335V-15, V-21 and V-22. Dornier had pledged to start series production early in March, but never got that far. It was intended to complete only 30 Do 335A-6s and then to switch over to the Do 335B-6 with DB 603LA engines and featuring more wing area (41 m²/ 441.3 sq.ft). The Dornier design offices were also working on a high-altitude night fighter development parallel to the Ju 338J, the Do 335B-8 with a wing area of 42 m² (452 sq.ft). It was to go into series production in September 1945 but – like the Ju 388 – the project was stopped.

These plans were put forward by Dornier at a meeting of the Special Development Commission for Night and Bad-weather Interception (*ESK-Nachtjagd*) on 24 January 1945, only for the estimated performance figures and delivery dates to be greeted with scepticism. Even more damning were these criticisms from the commission:

1 Excessively high production costs
2 Lack of operational experience with the basic type
3 Climb and maximum speed performance inferior to those of jet types
4 Impossibility of fitting a centimetric AI radar in the nose.

Dornier replied with a flood of calculations and further proposals. A piston-engined fighter would be superior to a jet in endurance, Dornier claimed, and would require less runway for take-off. As for maximum speed, all that was needed was parity with the Mosquito, and that the Do 335 had. In fact, by using a laminar-flow wing the maximum speed could be increased to 750 km/h (465.75 mph). Another boost in speed could be achieved by replacing the rear piston engine with a HeS 011 turbojet, although Dornier encountered general disbelief when he maintained that with this combined powerplant the Do 335 would be able to fly at a continuous speed of 760 km/h (472 mph) for over two hours. As far as the final argument about the centimetric AI radar was concerned, Dornier pointed out that an *Obertasse* device would be built into the wings. If that proved inadequate, there was also the Do 435 'Siamese Twin' with the centimetric AI radar fitted in the wing centre section; this proposal had already been submitted to the RLM.

But the Dornier team failed to persuade the commission of the value of their proposals. Instead, they were given the task of developing a pure jet fighter and, in co-operation with the electronics industry, of evolving and testing low-drag radar aerials. This meant that the Do 335 night fighter was dead and that the available V-series machines would be used only to flight-test the AI radar aerials. Dornier had also prepared a project for a heavy jet-powered night fighter, the P.256, but this did not advance beyond the drawing board.

The single-engined FW 190 and Bf 109 night fighters played only a minor role during 1944–45. Only limited numbers of the FW 190A-8 and A-9 with the FuG 217 or FuG 218 (*Rüstsatz 11*) were used operationally in the autumn of 1944 by NJGr 10, 6. and 10./JG 300, and parts of NJG 11. The Bf 109 could only be fitted with *Yagi* ('spike') aerials on the fuselage for the FuG 218 because its wing leading edge slats prohibited the use of 'Stag antler' (dipole and support) aerials on the wings as on the FW 190. A few Bf 109G-6 fighters equipped with a *Neptun* device were tested at Werneuchen, and possibly also by NJGr 10, but did not become operational. Until January 1945 NJG 11 used the Bf 109G-6, G-10 and G-14 as pursuit and district defence night fighters; afterwards the aircraft were fitted with ETC bomb racks and employed exclusively on night attack operations. A custom-built modification was the Bf 109G-14 flown by *Maj* Müller, which had an MG 151 with a shortened barrel fitted as an oblique weapon.

The Me 410 was used operationally by a special *EKdo* for Mosquito interception until May 1944, but did not prove itself in this role and was replaced by the He 219. A few Me 210s equipped with Hungarian-developed AI radars were flown operationally until the autumn of 1944 by the Hungarian night fighter squadron 5/1.

In early summer of 1944 several FW 189s and FW 58s were modified as provisional night fighters at the Lufthansa workshops at Werneuchen. These aircraft were equipped with the FuG 212 with wide-angle aerials and armed with an oblique MG 151. Both types fully proved themselves with NJG 100 in action against the Soviet night harassment aircraft. If only as a curiosity, we should also mention the Ar 196A floatplanes of the heavy cruiser *Prinz Eugen*, which were occasionally used as night fighters off Courland/Latvia during the winter of 1944–45.

The NJG 101 and 102 training *Geschwader* had had to manage for years with worn-out operational aircraft, but near the end of the war they finally received an excellent trainer, the Siebel Si 204. These machines were regular flying classrooms accommodating up to six radio/radar operators as they learned to use the latest radio and radar devices.

In retrospect it is evident that despite the efforts of the German aircraft industry during the last year of the war only modernised variants of the Bf 110 and Ju 88 reached the operational formations in sizeable numbers and that, apart from the He 219, no purpose-designed night fighter was ever produced. The development of high-performance night fighters such as the Do 335, Ju 388 and Ta 154 either stalled at the beginning or had to be cut short prematurely, while the few jet-powered fighters were only provisional solutions. Their successors were useful only in supplying new ideas to the victorious powers.

Taking into consideration the German inferiority in the high-frequency war, the catastrophic fuel situation, the destruction of the rear-area organisation by American bombing, and other factors that were the result of the slow collapse of the Reich from summer 1944 onwards, it is not surprising that the success rate of the night fighters went down steeply after the invasion and that from then on there were only the occasional spectacular successes to report. Nevertheless, it was at this time that a whole series of young pilots reported most of their kills. For example, *Oblt* Briegleb, a *Staffelkapitän* of NJG 2 and 3, achieved 21 of his confirmed 25 victories after 11 June 1944.

During the night of 5/6 June 1944 the German night fighter force put up 59 aircraft against the thousands of bombers, jamming aircraft and transports flying into German-occupied territory. The results were abysmal: just one victory, reported by *Hptm* Strüning. It was only in the early dawn that *Hptm* Eberspächer of III/KG 51 with his FW 190G-3 managed to shoot down three bombers. During the next weeks crews of II/NJG 4 and III/NJG 5 flew costly night attack operations against the Allied bridgeheads. They were particularly busy early in August, when all the signs pointed to an Allied breakthrough at Avranches.

After a short phase of intensely heavy attacks on targets in the west the USAAF and RAF resumed the air offensive against the Reich. It was mainly the single-engined night fighter *Gruppen* that were thrown against the massed American daytime bombing raids, and during the aerial battles that raged over Germany in late summer 1944 these pilots repeatedly demonstrated their flying skill and unbroken morale. But these valuable attributes were of little help against superior numbers. By August the elite formations had been bled white and had to replenish with inexperienced personnel, a certain recipe for even higher losses.

The RAF night bombing raids in June were aimed mainly at cities housing synthetic oil plants, and during that month the German defences achieved only one sizeable success. During the night of 21/22 June the German electronic countermeasures service managed to interfere successfully with the *Oboe* navigation devices of the PFF Mosquitoes which should have marked Duisburg and Wesseling near Cologne, and the raid disintegrated completely. A total of 37 night fighter crews were operational and shot down 28 bombers, of which I and II/NJG 1 alone accounted for 20.

In July the night fighter success curve went down noticeably: the total of 229 four-engined bombers was 64 less than in the previous month (and equal to only 2.6 per cent of the total sorties), while the night fighters managed to shoot down only 0.35 per cent (according to German estimates) of the more and more frequently used Mosquitoes. In that month the Reich Air Defence achieved only one notable success, during the night of 20 July, when 62 bombers were shot down during RAF raids on Hamburg and Stuttgart.

From July until the end of the war the RAF was satisfied with six to ten highly destructive major raids a month, while swarms of Mosquitoes flew into the Reich territory on an average of more than ten nights a month. Beginning with October these swarms grew into larger formations of 60–80 aircraft, against which the Luftwaffe could do hardly anything. In July three of these 'wonder birds' were destroyed by He 219s of I/NJG 1, of which only one was intercepted near its operational ceiling of 9,000 m (29,530 ft); the other two were shot down at altitudes below 5,000 m (14,400 ft). The transfer of a special Mosquito *Jagdkommando* under *Hptm* Strüning to Jagel did not bring any more success. As a result, and also because of high losses (5.2 per cent of the operational He 219s), the *Uhu* Mosquito hunt was discontinued. From that time onwards the He 219s themselves became victims of the British long-range night fighters. The task of intercepting Mosquitoes was transferred to special single-engined fighter units which had already tried to intercept these fast aircraft. One Mosquito was destroyed on 8 July west of Berlin by Lt Krause flying a FW 190A-8 of 1./NJGr 10.

July saw the last and probably the most successful operation by single-engined night fighters: during the night of 7/8 July I/JG 302 shot down 25 bombers from a formation raiding St Leu d'Esserant.

If the Mosquitoes drove the night fighter command almost to despair – on receiving the signal *Windei* (Windegg, the code word for a Mosquito incursion) all twin-engined night fighters were automatically condemned to inactivity – the timely deployment of forces against major RAF bombing raids was no less difficult. Although the British attack pattern was basically always the same, the RAF had developed many variations to confuse the German defence command. As a rule, a major raid would begin with *Mandrel* jamming aircraft, which put up an interference screen around the Allied-occupied territories or over the sea that could seldom be penetrated by the German ground control radar. On either side of the interference screen the German radar would detect approaching heavy bomber formations and the night fighters would be sent up to intercept them. But these bombers would turn out to be only decoy formations consisting of training units and minelayers that would turn back a safe distance from the coast. However, if a night fighter managed to reach the decoys it enjoyed above-average fighting conditions: no interference from *Window*, no haze and, from the operational point of view, relatively inexperienced opponents. By and large, an attack on a minelaying force usually resulted in plenty of victories.

In the meantime, the real bomber force would break out of the interference screen, always split into two streams and preceded by high-speed formations which would drop variously coloured flares on both the real and decoy targets, marking them according to a system impenetrable to the defences. The bomber streams would be shielded by long-range night fighters and supported by electronic jamming aircraft; they would frequently change course, unite into one formation and then divide again. Finally, the bombers might attack the same target in several waves, or on another occasion raid several objectives in the same night. In short, for the defenders it was always a guessing game with many unknown factors.

The frequent occasions when the night fighters were sent up in error or misdirected that autumn severely damaged the trusting relationship between the flying units and the ground control centres, with the result that the night fighter crews soon ceased to believe a word of their instructions. Nevertheless, they had no choice but to follow directions from the ground because the only airborne radars suitable for long-range detection, *Naxos* and *Flensburg*, became practically useless from late July onwards. The first isolated instances of *SN-2* jamming also appeared in July, and the effectiveness of this AI radar was also much reduced by the British tactic of flying below 3,000 m (9,840 ft) altitude. Under these conditions the radar operators saw so many blips on their screens that it was extremely difficult to identify and follow the target. And when this was accompanied by jamming aircraft flying above the main formation at 5,000–6,000 m (16,400–19,680 ft) and dropping *Window*, it was almost impossible for the night fighters to find the bomber stream in time, particularly as the ground control centres regularly directed the fighters to the jamming aircraft, which were screened by Mosquitoes.

The only way to achieve victories at night was to 'swim' in the middle of the bomber stream, where the electronic interference was relatively limited and the defenders were also to some extent safer from long-range night fighters. Such infiltration was the aim of German night fighter tactics. In theory, interception and infiltration should have been possible but, like most ideals, it turned out to be largely unattainable. To begin with, aircraft from air observer units would fly towards the bombers, continuously transmitting information over the R/T and W/T about the course and altitude of the enemy formation. Once in the air, the night fighters would normally form up around radio beacons to await more definite instructions. After receiving orders from the ground control centre the formation leader would use the *Gruppe* wavelength to inform his crews by W/T and then lead the fighters in close formation towards the enemy. New course information would be passed on by radio or by means of signal flares. In practice, however, the night fighters succeeded in infiltrating the bomber stream in close order for the first time only in February 1945, because the German ground control centres were never quite sure exactly of the location of the enemy formations. To put it another way: by the time they were certain of the course and the target, most of the night fighters were already short of fuel, or were miles away.

Recognising their own helplessness the night fighter command revived the old *Himmelbett* system under a new name: *Gebietsnachtjagd* (regional night fighting). Night after night the night fighters – mainly single-engined aircraft – would cruise around the recognised main penetration lanes. The prerequisite for the successful use of this tactic was reliable communications, in this case 12 kW VHF R/T transmitters, so that the voice of the fighter control officer could penetrate the jamming.

But the ground radar positions also had to struggle with another, until then unknown, difficulty: from summer 1944 onwards they could not distinguish between their own fighters and enemy aircraft on their radar screens because the night fighters no longer switched on their FuG 25a *Erstling* IFF sets. The word had gone around fighter circles that more and more often activation of the IFF set was almost immediately followed by a Mosquito attack. For this reason the radio/radar operators simply switched off their FuG 25 sets, the desire for self-preservation having proved stronger than their strict orders to have the IFF set on. And their suspicions were right: the Mosquitoes had in the meantime been equipped with *Perfectos*, which could activate *Erstling* and then accurately determine the range and position of the German night fighter.

From late summer 1944 onwards the Mosquitoes were everywhere. When the *Jagddivisionen* gave orders to their fighters to take off, the RAF long-range night fighters were already there, lurking near the airfields and radio beacons. The Luftwaffe had no real antidote except to formulate rules designed to minimise its losses. Thus, for instance, it was forbidden to assemble over the airfield, near the main radio beacons or beacon lights; after take-off the night fighter had to fly at maximum speed towards the secondary radio beacon. It was also prohibited to fire recognition flares. These instructions were augmented by reports passed from unit to unit on how best to detect an attacking Mosquito in good time. Among other things, it was asserted that the British radar impulses caused a ticking sound in the FuG 16 radio or aircraft internal R/T communications, or that they activated the indicator lights on the FuBl 2 blind-landing device. So many of these attacks came as a complete surprise that a rumour was born that the Mosquitoes were also armed with oblique guns. The crews who came to this conclusion could at least report about their experiences – but there were more and more who could not. The number of crews fatally hit by RAF night fighters began to rise at an alarming rate. In the end, getting away from a Mosquito became simply a question of luck or daring. Even then, a really tight and fast circle, a quick diving turn, a dive almost to ground level or high-speed flights just above the tree tops did not mean safety from a pursuer who could play the same suicidal game because his AI radar was able to function near the ground. But probably the most dangerous part of night fighter operations was the landing approach, when the pilot always had to assume 'Red Indians along the garden fence' (Luftwaffe aircrew speech code indicating enemy fighters in the vicinity of the home base). Normally, a night fighter pilot would fly to his airfield at the lowest possible altitude, practically hugging the ground, but there were also other tricks that enabled him to reach home. Thus, for instance, *Hptm* Krause of NJG 4 would approach his airfield at 3,000 m (9,840 ft), ask for the airfield lighting to be switched on briefly, and then dive down to level off and land on a darkened runway. Incidentally, these constant low-level flights were the reason for the general equipment of night fighters with the FuG 101 radio altimeter.

It was not only in the air that the night fighters had become the hunted. From July onwards all Luftwaffe bases in the Netherlands, Belgium and West- and South-west Germany were within the range of American fighter-bombers, which made the most of it. The British used different tactics: until August the RAF raided the Dutch-Belgian airfields at night, mainly with Mosquitoes using the 'Boomerang' method, following up in the daytime with raids by large formations of four-engined bombers. As a result, the night fighter units were forced to disperse by day on small, well-camouflaged makeshift landing fields, the rough runways of which were responsible for quite a few bent undercarriages. But these 'blindworm' locations could not remain hidden from the enemy's reconnaissance aircraft for long, and even frequent changes of dispersal fields did not help much, with the fighter-bombers finding their victims everywhere. As these makeshift fields were unsuitable for night landings the fighters had to fly back to their bases in the evenings, when they were often caught by enemy interceptors. In fact, losses caused by damage on the ground and interception in transit topped the list during 1944–45.[2]

Next in the line as targets for the fighter-bombers were the conspicuous ground radar sites. Not even ferro-concrete installations were safe, as shown by the command post of the District Commander

Central Rhine (coded *Dachs*) near Darmstadt, which was temporarily knocked out by a direct bomb hit.

But despite the rapidly worsening fighting conditions, falling success rate and increasing losses, the night fighter crews did not give up. Indeed, their morale was assessed by the Luftwaffe command as higher than that of the day fighter units. During August the night fighters shot down a total of 164 enemy aircraft, equal to 1.6 per cent of the operational force. Luftwaffe losses amounted to 38 aircraft (equal to 2.5 per cent of the operational aircraft), not counting the machines lost on the ground or during check or training flights. Only one more Mosquito was shot down that month, by *Oblt* Finke of I/NJG 1, who was himself killed in this combat.

In September the night fighter force flew a total of 1,301 sorties against more than 6,400 enemy aircraft, of which 76 (1.1 per cent) were shot down. By this time the *SN-2* AI radar was continuously jammed and visual detection was scarcely possible even on the brightest nights as a result of the thick layer of haze that hung over Germany at an altitude of 5,000–6,000 m (16,400–19,680 ft), a product of the exhaust gases and contrails of the thousands of bombers that had flown at that altitude for years. However, that month saw a slight improvement in the performance of the Mosquito hunters: a total of seven were shot down, three of them by *Oblt* Welter[3] of 10./JG 300. By contrast, the *Himmelbett*-controlled single-engined fighters of 4./NJGr 10, which operated from Twente, did not achieve a single victory. At the end of this month II and IV/NJG 1 flew a series of night attack operations against the Allied airborne forces and supply columns in the Arnhem area, but with only scant success.

In October the success rate of the night fighter force sank even lower, and the fuel shortage began to make itself felt. Most formations remained on the ground for more than a week at a time, and when an order came through to take off it was intended for the few leading crews, since enemy radio and radar jamming would have left the younger crews no chance of finding the enemy bombers. The statistics for October speak for themselves: against an estimated 10,000 enemy sorties the Luftwaffe sent up 866 night fighters which shot down 56 enemy aircraft – in other words, less than 0.5 per cent of the total. At the same time the defenders' losses had increased to 6.2 per cent, while the Mosquito hunt cost no less than 12 per cent of the operational interceptors. During that month this specialised high-speed interception effort by parts of NJG 11 was concentrated over the Ruhr and the area around Berlin, and new tactics were tried. To create conditions similar to daytime operations the defenders set up searchlight boxes, forming 'light horizons'. The results were rather meagre, with only two Mosquitoes intercepted and shot down near Berlin.

In November the number of German night fighter sorties rose to 955 and more bombers were shot down (87). But this represented a loss rate of only 0.9 per cent of the total, no more than a pinprick to the RAF. Not even exceptional individual successes – *Ofw* Morlock of I/NJG 1 shot down six bombers in only 12 minutes on the night of 2/3 November – could alter the overall situation.

It is interesting here to compare the successes of I/NJG 1 (He 219) with those of II/NJG 1 (Bf 110): 11 He 219As achieved seven victories (one by *Oblt* Thurner, in addition to Morlock's score), while only nine Bf 110s of II/NJG 1 accounted for 10 enemy bombers (three of which were claimed by *Hptm* Lau). Two nights later the results were similar: 12 He 219As shot down three bombers, while the 10 Bf 110s destroyed four. On the debit side *Ofw* Morlock fell the victim to an RAF long-range night fighter.

On the same night, *Uffz* Gilke, rear gunner of *Ogefr* Ramsauer's crew of II/NJG 1, lived through a ghastly experience. Immediately after Gilke had shouted a Mosquito warning over the intercom Ramsauer swung away and went into a wild dive. In the same moment the intercom failed, the radio/radar operator and gunner assumed that the pilot had been killed, and both men baled out. While the radio man got clean away from the aircraft, Gilke remained hanging from the oblique guns and could not free himself. Finally Ramsauer levelled off and landed smoothly at Hangelar with the half-dead Gilke still on his cockpit roof.

That month NJG 11 gave up the 'Mosquito hunt' over the Ruhr and confined itself to illuminated target defence night fighting, from then on officially designated *Wilde Sau*. As before, these single-engined fighters fully lived up to their old nickname by taking off in weather conditions which kept the twin-engined night fighter force on the ground.

In December the night fighter force reached its lowest ebb against the RAF: its 980 operational aircraft flew 1,070 sorties and achieved a grand total of only 66 victories, or 0.7 per cent of the enemy sorties over Germany. At the same time the defenders' losses were terrible: no less than 114 fighters had been shot down or crashed. On top of that were the rapidly increasing losses caused by destruction on the ground. By December there was hardly an airfield left that was not a target for the fighter-bombers by day and long-range night fighters by night. There were night fighter *Gruppen* that could not risk a single take-off for weeks, since to do so would have been suicide. Thus, for instance, I/NJG 1 was operational on only six nights that month, and the sole victory cost the *Gruppe* six of its own aircraft.

In that month the night fighters destroyed another four Mosquitoes, one of which was inadvertently disposed of by *Hptm* Brewes of II/NJG 1 on the 19th. As he was coming in to land Brewes' Bf 110 was rammed by an intercepting Mosquito. The German pilot managed to land safely less a third of his port wing, but the Mosquito burst into flames and crashed near the airfield boundary.

The month of December was also notable for events that indicated a change from quantity to quality: the Ju 88G-6 with Jumo 213 engines was in full service with the operational units, the first serviceable FuG 218 and *Naxos ZR* were delivered, and the night fighter force tried to win back the initiative by some novel means. Two of these were the use of extremely short strips of tinfoil in an attempt to jam the Mosquito AI radar, and the *Orgelpfeife* method of decoying the enemy's long-range night fighters. The 'Organ pipes' were single night fighters which broadcast simulated R/T traffic in an effort to sound like a whole group of aircraft. A special talent among them was *Ofw* Gildner, a radio operator of 9./NJG 2, who had the knack of imitating the dialects and speech tone of up to a dozen different night fighter crews. Naturally, the frequencies used by these make-believe crews were not needed by other formations, and the course and details of positions in this deceptive radio traffic were completely fictitious. The scheme had two objectives: to keep the tactical frequencies actually used by the operational crews free of interference for as long as possible, and to tempt the enemy towards the supposed area of concentration of the German night fighters. How far this trick proved itself in practice is not known.

December also saw the first successful night interceptions by *Oblt* Welter in his Me 262 jet fighter, and attack operations by night fighters. First formation to take up the ground support role was NJG 6, which was ordered to make night-time low-level attacks on enemy motor transport columns and railways in Lorraine. In the second half of December these raids by the 'night owls' concentrated on the area which the German forces had to reach during the Ardennes offensive. The units taking part were NJG 1, 2, 3 and 6, which flew a total of 390 sorties in their Bf 110 and Ju 88 night fighters equipped with ETC bomb racks but minus their airborne radars. The confusion caused by these raids on the enemy rear areas was not inconsiderable. Moreover, German losses could be kept within reasonable limits because at the time several Mosquito formations had been recalled to Britain for re-equipment with the Mosquito Mk XXX and the American night fighter, Northrop P-61 Black Widow, was not particularly dangerous to the German crews. True enough, their AI radar also worked near ground level, but the German Bf 110 and Ju 88 pilots could easily out-turn the unwieldy American plane and shoot down several in the process.

The night attacks reached their climax between 28 December and New Year's morning. Towards the end of December groups of German night fighters were orbiting, particularly over Bastogne, in expectation of an Allied airborne assault. On 28 December an order requested the formation of special night attack *Staffeln* within the existing NJG, to be made up of crews who had achieved less than five victories. This was countermanded on 2 January and the use of night fighters for night attacks was stopped until further notice on the same day. It is possible that the heavy losses suffered during Operation *Bodenplatte* on 1 January had something to do with it. The gathering of forces for this operation had begun in mid-December, when hundreds of day fighters were withdrawn from North-west Germany and concentrated for a massed surprise blow that was intended to neutralise the Allied air forces on the Belgian and Dutch airfields. The night fighters provided several *Staffeln* to act as pathfinders. The results of this operation are now well known: the Luftwaffe fighters succeeded in destroying 465 enemy aircraft, but themselves lost 400 machines, effectively putting an end to the German fighter force.

In January 1945 the night fighter force flew a total of 1,058 sorties and managed to shoot down 117 enemy aircraft while losing 47 of its own. For the first time parts of NJG 100, the Eastern Front *Geschwader*, also participated in operations against the RAF night bombers. *Oblt* Welter in the meantime was growing even more skilled at night jet interception and succeeded in destroying three more Mosquitoes. Another interesting event took place during a raid on Munich on 28 January, when parts of NJG 6 encountered aircraft from the RAF's 100 Group, a unit composed entirely of jamming aircraft and long-range night fighters. In this action *Ofw* Bahr intercepted and shot down three B-17s and one B-24.

According to reports, crews of night fighters equipped with the FuG 218 were highly satisfied with its resistance to jamming and, thanks to the *Naxos ZR* warning device, Ju 88 losses were much lighter. Generally speaking it had become easier to find the bomber streams because the RAF crews were keeping their navigation radars on much longer than they had a few weeks earlier. As a result, *Naxos* was once again of real practical value.

Although the night fighter force achieved its last major successes in February, the crews also had to face their bitterest defeats. The general situation was clearly taking a turn for the worse, and rapidly dwindling fuel supplies meant that the night fighters could fly only 772 sorties, during which they shot down no fewer than 181 enemy aircraft (equal to 1.2 per cent of the raiding force). German losses remained constant at 47 night fighters. On 13 February 1945 the RAF destoyed the defenceless town of Dresden. The few night fighters that were ordered to take off were fruitlessly whisked from one radio beacon to another until they were forced to land without contacting the enemy. The mass of the Luftwaffe night fighters remained on the ground, allegedly because of unsuitable conditions

RAF Bomber Command major raid on Chemnitz night of 14/15 February 1945

1, 2. RAF jamming aircraft simulate penetration into Northern Germany by an
    intense release of *Window*
3.   *Mandrel* interference screen
4, 5. Diversionary Mosquito raids on the Ruhr and Frankfurt/Main
6.   Assembly area of 2 *JDiv* night fighters to repulse the northerly raid
7.   Assembly area of 3 *JDiv* night fighters to repulse an assumed raid on the Ruhr

1. A major bomber formation thrusts out of the interference screen and then divides near Koblenz
2. The night fighters are ordered south to repulse an expected raid on Frankfurt/Main but
3. the RAF bomber formation continues flying east and
4. unites again over Thuringia
5. Most night fighters are forced to land due to fuel shortage, but a few follow the bombers
6. Single-engined night fighters from the Berlin area fail to reach the bomber stream
7. Diversionary raiders turn back

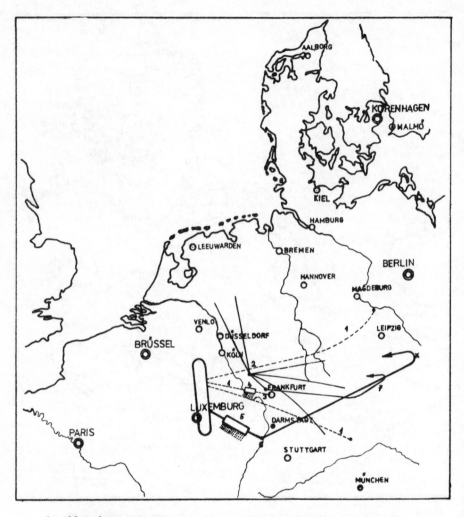

1. Mosquitoes
2. Night fighters assemble near the radio beacon 'Ida' and
3. fly towards Frankfurt/Main to repulse
4. a feint bombing raid while
5. the intensely 'Windowing' main bomber formation thrusts towards Mannheim, only
6. to continue towards Chemnitz
7. The RAF bomber stream can no longer be intercepted by the Luftwaffe night fighters

for interception, and had to look on while the widely spread out enemy bomber formations flew away westwards over their airfields. The second RAF raid on Dresden was also hardly opposed, and once again only a few night fighters were ordered to intercept. The defences operated with more success on the following night, however, when Chemnitz was the chosen victim.

The Allied air offensive codenamed 'Clarion' began on 2 February; its declared aim was the final destruction of the German communications network. For eight days thousands of bombers were flying all over Germany, bombing round the clock. During the first two nights Duisburg, Karlsruhe and Worms, were the targets of 1,000-bomber raids, and with such massed formations in the air the German night fighters just had to shoot down more aircraft. The best scores were those of *Maj* Schnaufer – long since the top-scoring night fighter ace – who destroyed two bombers during the early morning hours of 21 February and another seven in the evening of the same day. During the RAF raid on Duisburg II/NJG 1 achieved 11 victories, of which six were credited to *Hptm* Hager and his crew. But the most successful *Geschwader* in February was unquestionably NJG 6. During the RAF raid on Worms the ground controllers succeeded for the first time in achieving the perfect infiltration of I and IV/NJG 6 into the bomber stream. Once 'in the swim with the heavies' the crews were surprised to notice that there was hardly any interference with their *SN-2* AI radars, and no Mosquitoes appeared. This great opportunity was used to the full, and within 29 minutes eight crews had shot down 21 bombers. The most successful was *Ofw* Bahr with seven confirmed kills, but the best news of all was that not a single German night fighter was lost in this action.

Notable as they were, these were also among the last organised defensive achievements in the night skies of Germany. Some units relinquished their night fighter role in February, and others followed soon afterwards. For instance, the last kill by III/NJG 11 came during the night of 21 February, when *Ofw* Frank with his Bf 109G-14 shot down a Lancaster near Krefeld; the famous I/NJG 1 was operational for the last time during the night of 3/4 April, when the crews of *Hptm* Baake and *Hptm* Rességuir were successful. But for all that, the personal willingness and determination of the few crews still flying had become pointless: no matter how brave their individual efforts, they could no longer stop the destruction of Germany and the killing of civilians.

But the night fighter force did not give up. It was determined to prove to the enemy that it was not yet beaten by implementing Operation *Gisela*, a long-range night fighting action which began in the night of 4 March. The father of this idea was most probably *Maj* Schnaufer, who had found out during some arbitrary pursuits of departing RAF bombers that 'on the other side of the front' he could fly around almost as if it were peacetime because all *Window* and jamming ceased immediately after crossing the line. He then submitted a proposal to his *JDivision*, suggesting that a night fighter force should follow the departing bombers until they had reached the North Sea before attacking the unsuspecting enemy. But the CO of 3 *JDiv*, *GenMaj* Grabmann, wanted to go a step further and attack the bombers only while they were preparing to land on their airfields in Britain.

However, despite the strictest security precautions, the British secret service got to know about this plan, and made this clear to their opponents by conspicuously broadcasting the contemporary hit tune *I dance with Gisela tonight* on their propaganda station *Soldatensender Calais*. The operation was postponed several times but not given up, and then came early March. On the night of the 4th two RAF bomber formations raided the synthetic oil plants at Kamen and Ladbergen with hardly any interference from the German fighter defences. But about 100 Luftwaffe night fighters followed the departing bombers in three waves; the crews were drawn mainly from NJG 2 and 3, but also from NJG 4 and 5, and all were flying the

---

Victories by Luftwaffe night fighters over Britain during Operation *Gisela* on the night of 3/4 March 1945

According to British records the RAF lost a total of 22 aircraft completely destroyed. Of these, the following have been accredited to date:

No.	Pilot, unit	Original claim
1–2	*Hptm* Roth, I/NJG 2	Two four-engined bombers
3–4	*Oblt* Briegleb, 7./NJG 2	One four-engined bomber at 0036 hrs south of Waddington airfield; one four-engined bomber at 0056 hrs 40 km (25 mls) west of Lincoln
5–6	*Lt* Döring, 10./NJG 3	One B-17, one Lancaster
7	*Hptm* Hissbach, II/NJG 2	One four-engined bomber
8–9	*Oblt* Förster, IV/NJG 2	Two four-engined bombers
10	*Fw* Heinz Misch, IV/NJG 3	One four-engined bomber
11	*Fw* Kappe, III/NJG 2	One four-engined bomber
12	*Lt* Wolf, III/NJG 5	One Lancaster north of Humber estuary
13	*Fw* Schmidt, IV/NJG 3	One Lancaster at 0214 hrs over Croft airfield
14	*Hptm* Fladrich, 9./NJG 4	One Lancaster at 0033 hrs north-east of Cambridge
15	*Hptm* Brinkhaus, I/NJG 3	One four-engined bomber

Ju 88G-6. The first wave shot down 22 four-engined bombers, of which eight were doubles scored by the crews of Roth, Förster, Döring[4] and Briegleb. *Oblt* Briegleb pursued a fleeing Lancaster as far as Lincoln in East Anglia before he managed to get into a firing position.

The first burning crashes warned the bomber crews, who flew on towards more westerly airfields so that the second and third waves of German night fighters did not succeed in their interception attempts. Some bombers damaged by the night fighters tried to make emergency landing on darkened airfields, resulting in eight more aircraft being wrecked. On the way back the German night fighters also shot up several communications installations. Then began the most dangerous part of the whole operation: several hundred kilometres of low-level flight across the North Sea, during which the crews had to rely exclusively on astro and dead-reckoning navigation because all German radio-direction beacons were blocked by British jamming.

Of course this operation could do nothing to hold up the RAF aerial offensive, not least because the night fighter force itself had had to suffer heavy losses. For instance, of the 20 serviceable aircraft put up by I/NJG 4, five were wrecked on take-off, and the remainder made crash landings on the German coastline after running short of fuel. A more terrible consequence was the succession of destructive RAF bombing raids on small and medium-sized German towns which had hitherto been spared. Even brave individual performances – such as those of NJG 6, which on 14 March reported 14 victories and two days later, during the RAF raid on Würzburg, 20 victories – could not prevent thousands of tons of high explosive and phosphorus from razing town after town. In any case, by mid-March the night fighter force had already been largely defeated and only a few interceptions were flown. Instead, the fighters turned more and more to night attacks to give some respite to the hard-pressed retreating ground troops. The last long-range interception was flown during the night of 17 March, when 18 leading crews attempted another *Gisela* over Britain, but only one solitary Lancaster was shot down over Hull by *Fw* Hommel of III/NJG 2.

The continuous low-level attacks on their airfields caused the effective strength of the night fighter force to shrink rapidly. The last units to fight on till the end with some success were parts of NJG 3, 5 and 100, and, above all, 10./NJG 11, the single- and two-seat Me 262s of which shot down 43 Mosquitoes from January until the end of the war. In addition, this unit also destroyed five Mosquito and P-38 Lightning high-altitude reconnaissance aircraft by day. This high ratio of 48 kills in 70 sorties clearly shows the superiority of the

Me 262. Next to *Oblt* Welter the most successful pilot of this unit was *Fw* Becker, who achieved eight confirmed kills in 10 sorties.

One of the many tragedies was that the final decline of the night fighter force during the last three months of the war claimed the lives of several highly decorated pilots. It came about because only these men could, had to and still wanted to fly operationally. Among those who fell in combat between February and the end of hostilities were the Knights Cross bearers *Otl* Borchers (NJG 5), *Hptm* Dreher (NJG 3), *Hptm* Friedrich (NJG 6), *Hptm* Hissbach (NJG 2), Maj Leickhardt (NJG 5) and *Maj* Semrau (NJG 2).

The night fighter units on the Eastern Front are, quite undeservedly, hardly mentioned in the literature of the last war. The confirmed victory total of 510 enemy aircraft shot down by NJG 100 in 22 months speaks for itself, and is even more impressive considering the fact that most of the time this unit had fewer than six *Staffeln*. Likewise, the figure of 30 pilots who achieved more than nine kills each while serving with NJG 100 is quite respectable. The Eastern Front night fighter ace was *Oblt* Francsi with 56 confirmed night victories.

True enough, the Eastern Front night fighters did not have to face streams of four-engined bombers escorted by long-range night fighters. Nor did they have to contend with the high frequency jamming suffered by their comrades in the West. Nevertheless, their victories were achieved under very difficult conditions, and they had to master completely different problems, ranging from the development of special tactics to a lack of suitable aircraft. For one thing, in the East the night fighters had to combat an enemy who never gave away his intentions with a high volume of radio traffic. For this reason the *Himmelbett* centres had to be manned at random throughout the night. If an enemy aircraft was detected by the ground sites, the details which they passed on to the night fighters were often very inaccurate because most of the time the Soviet intruders were flying very low. Under these conditions the airborne AI radars did not show anything either.

Odd as it may sound, the shooting down of a Soviet Po-2 biplane night harassment aircraft – which could fly safely at speeds below 100 km/h (62 mph) – called for exceptional flying ability on the part of a Ju 88 pilot. He had to stalk his prey close to the ground with wheels and flaps down, all the while risking a sudden stall that he would have no chance to correct. At these low airspeeds it was also extremely difficult to follow the enemy if he made a quick turn.

But the Eastern Front night fighter units had more to cope with than these small single-engined biplanes. There were also the twin-engined Il-4 and North American B-25 Mitchell, and the four-engined Pe-8, none of them easy opponents. These bombers were fast, manoeuvrable, well armed and could take a lot of combat damage. Apart from that, from summer 1944 onwards all night fighter units stationed in the East also had to fly operations against the RAF raids in the West. Another extra restriction was the directive that the Eastern Front night fighters should operate near the front line only between 2300 and 2400 hrs; at all other times the Flak had permission to fire at anything that moved in the air.

Technical conditions in the East were also much more unfavourable than in the Reich Air Defence area. If the Ju 88 and Bf 110 proved of little use for the interception of the slow-flying harassing aircraft, the Do 217N – regarded by officials in Berlin as the ideal 'short-life' aircraft for the East – turned out to be completely unsuitable. Its principal defects were the undercarriage, which would shear off in rough field landings; and the DB 603 powerplants, for which there were no spare parts at all.

The complete equipment of the Eastern Front night fighters with AI radar came very late, the first *SN-2* arriving only after all units in the Reich Air Defence area had had their fill. It is also beyond question that stockpiling and the supply of replacement parts were incomparably worse than in the Reich. Finally, the repeated redeployment of units had a damaging effect on their combat efficiency, there being long delays before the ground personnel joined the aircraft and crews in the new operational area.

As with all other Luftwaffe formations on the Eastern Front, the operational use of the night fighter force depended on the ground situation, and the requirements of the Army were more or less paramount. Thus in May, because the Army General Staff expected the major enemy effort in the Southern sector and the area of Army Group North Ukraine, the night fighter formations were transferred from the Baltic to the South.

It was intended that the new II/NJG 100 should reinforce III and IV/NJG 6 stationed in Romania, Bulgaria and Hungary, while I/NJG 100 occupied the Biała-Podlaska-Pinsk-Orsha-Minsk-Baranovichi triangle in the Central sector. Stationed further north, over the Western Baltic area, were the operational sections of NJG 102, and even Ar 196A floatplanes from the heavy cruiser *Prinz Eugen* deployed outside Liepaja (Libau) took part in night interceptions. A few crews from IV/NJG 5 at Mainz were also temporarily transferred to Stubendorf in Upper Silesia to intercept Soviet aircraft bringing supplies to the partisans in the Beskide area during the full moon period of June 1944.

Against all expectations, the Soviet summer offensive started on 22 June on the Central sector, and within a month the Red Army had penetrated right up to the borders of East Prussia and the River Vistula. The crews of I/NJG 100 piled up successes as never before –

Oblt Pützkuhl alone shot down 12 enemy aircraft in just three sorties, for instance – but could do nothing to hold up the Soviet offensive in any way. After the front line had stabilised early in August the crews of I *Gruppe* found new bases in East Prussia and the Warsaw area, from which they flew sorties against both Soviet and British night bombers. In this they were joined by parts of NJG 5 also stationed in East Prussia at that time.

Of the night fighter formations deployed in the Southern sector only the units based in Hungary were used more frequently. These comprised III/NJG 6, parts of II/NJG 100, *Einsatzkommando* of NJG 101, and the Hungarian night fighter squadron 5/1. These crews fought with great success against British Wellington bombers dropping mines in the Danube, formations of four-engined bombers penetrating over Czechoslovakia, and Soviet courier aircraft supplying Tito's partisans in Yugoslavia.

On the other hand, IV/NJG 6 and most of II/NJG 100 stationed in Romania were hardly used at night because the Ploeşti oilfields were raided only by American day bomber formations. As a result, the Luftwaffe night fighters had to act as daytime *Zerstörer* and, as over the Reich territory, often suffered heavy losses at the hands of enemy escort fighters. Nevertheless, a few night fighters managed to shoot down a P-38 Lightning now and again.

The Soviet offensive in the Central sector was followed by a breakthrough into Romania, and the Luftwaffe night fighter units were redeployed once more. Their dispersal was complete: IV/NJG 6 was transferred into the Reich, II/NJG 100 moved back via Gross Beckereck and Bašaid (north of Belgrade) and Tapioszentmarton to Malacki (near Bratislava); 4.*Staffel* went to Silesia and was redesignated 3./NJG 100; and the former 3.*Staffel* became 4.*Staffel* and was based near Brno (Brünn). Only these two *Staffeln* remained active in the night fighter role until the end of the war, operating mainly over Silesia against Soviet bombers and courier aircraft, and flying evacuation and supply sorties to help surrounded German troops.

Although 5. and 6.*Staffeln* of NJG 100 received the latest Ju 88G-6 night fighters in November, they were used only for low-level attacks on trains and road transport, while as in nearly all Luftwaffe formations most of the personnel of both units had to fight as infantrymen for the last few months of the war. Some were more fortunate than others: III/NJG 6 and the operational sections of NJG 101, for instance, managed to withdraw back into Germany just in time.

Almost simultaneously with Romania, Finland repudiated its alliance with Germany, and the German forces stationed there were pulled back into northern Norway. *NJ-Staffel Finnland*, formed only

216

a few months earlier, was transferred to Trondheim and later renamed *NJ-Staffel Norwegen*.

In the last few months of hostilities I/NJG 100 and II and IV/NJG 5 were fighting a war on several fronts: by night against British and Soviet bombers, by day against American and, particularly, Soviet spearheads on the ground. At times they were even called on to act as day *Zerstörer* against Soviet raiders.

This period also had its ironic aspects. Thus, during the retreat a flight of NJG 100 somehow found itself in Norway and, as the fortunes of war would have it, was tasked – together with parts of *NJ-Staffel Norwegen*, based at Gardemoen – with flying all the way around South Sweden to Courland in Latvia to evacuate soldiers and civilians before the Soviet occupation.

All night fighter operations against Soviet raiders terminated late in April, and the final moves saw I/NJG 100 transferring to Lübeck while II/NJG 100 collected its forces near Linz and Hörsching. On 4 May this *Gruppe* received orders to fly with 11 aircraft to Prague–Rusyne (Rusin) airfield. A day later came the Czech uprising in that city, and the night fighter crews flew on to Saaz where they destroyed all but one of their aircraft and surrendered to the Americans. This last aircraft of II/NJG 100, with its national insignia painted over with four-pointed stars, landed at Lechfeld on 7 May, to the surprise of the American Air Force personnel on that field.

Notes

1 Unlike modern electronic devices, the WW 2 radar screens had no afterglow effect, so that the target appeared only briefly once every six seconds as a notch on the display screen.

2 For example, between 15 September 1944 and 30 April 1945 the parts of NJG 6 stationed in the Reich territory lost a total of 362 aircraft with more than 20 per cent damage. Of these, 91 were destroyed on the ground, 45 were shot down by long-range night fighters in transit and only nine were lost to the defensive fire of enemy bombers.

3 *Oblt* Welter became the foremost expert in this kind of air combat, with 35 confirmed Mosquito kills by the end of the war.

4 After this operation *Lt* Döring of 10./NJG 3 was recommended for the Knights Cross but never received it. Some 20 years later Herr Hans Ring discovered the award documents, leading to the truly unique situation of a German serviceman being awarded the Knights Cross in 1965.

Epilogue

It is idle to debate whether Germany could have won the war if this or that had happened, because the country's available resources were insufficient for the achievement of Hitler's war aims in any case. But it is also clear that the war would have certainly taken another course and countless people would have lived to see the year 1945 if the importance of home air defence had been recognised in good time.

During the formative stages of the Luftwaffe air defence was neglected in favour of the offensive formations, without however creating a weapon suitable for strategic war. At the same time, the possibility that a strategic air force could penetrate deep into the Reich territory was completely overlooked. The Luftwaffe had difficulty in finding military targets at night, and it was assumed that the enemy would be similarly handicapped. For this reason night fighting experiments were carried out only in a half-hearted manner before the war and then terminated when they ran into difficulties. The successes of the 1939–40 campaigns added to this sense of complacency and home air defence was deemed even more unimportant than before. The approaching danger was not recognised until much later, and when it could no longer be ignored it was pushed to the back of too many official minds.

So it happened that the Allied air forces took the lead and the Luftwaffe command was repeatedly forced to respond to Allied initiative. While it is true that this is characteristic of most defensive actions, a carefully considered and timely response can sooner or later leave the defender favourably placed to regain the initiative – as the RAF had done in the Battle of Britain.

Analysis of the operations of the Reich Air Defence reveals a continuous theme of 'too little and too late'. This began with the formation of a night fighter *Gruppe* only after it had become evident that the Flak on its own could not prevent British night intrusions. In the same way the Command persisted with regional air defence zones, failing to understand that only a centrally controlled defence organisation could counter a centrally controlled attack. Thus, for instance, the *Nachtjagddivision* was subordinated to Luftflotte 2, one of the two higher Luftwaffe command posts in the occupied Western territories. As a result, even the Luftwaffe Commander Centre, who really should have been in command of the entire Reich Air Defence, had no authority over the southern area of the Reich territory. Gen Kammhuber's proposals for the expansion of the night fighter force were acted upon only hesitantly, while his request for a centrally controlled fighter fleet was turned down flat. As if that was not enough, when the air war reached its climax in autumn 1943 XII *Fliegerkorps* – which controlled all night fighter formations – was disbanded and the Reich Air Defence decentralised more than ever.

Germany also lost the technical lead it had held in 1939. The relationship between technology and military success or failure was more distinct in the night fighter arm than in any other part of the Luftwaffe.

A specialised night fighter was needed as early as 1940, yet the demands of the night fighter force were partly met only three years later by special versions of long-established aircraft types, the Bf 110G-4 and the Ju 88C-6. High-performance night fighters such as the He 219 and Ju 88G-6b reached the units either in insufficient quantities or so late that the fuel shortage meant that only insignificant numbers could be used operationally.

But the really decisive advantage was achieved by the British in the high-frequency field. Until 1942 they had nothing comparable with the German *Freya*, *Würzburg* and *Lichtenstein* devices, but the tide had already begun to turn. While the British had started to work intensively on the centimetric wavelength in 1941 – thus creating a basis for the later production of the H2S and first-rate AI radars – it was believed in Germany that it would be possible to achieve the optimum with long-wave radars, and all research in the centimetric field was stopped. As a result, Kammhuber was forced to build up his *Himmelbett* night fighting system with ground radars of very limited range, and to use night fighters fitted with unwieldy and drag-producing aerials. If Kammhuber and his units had been provided with the required high-performance radars and night fighters, the *Himmelbett* zones could have been extended and their number correspondingly reduced, and a small number of fighters could have been used so effectively that the Home Air Defence would have managed with far fewer resources. As things were, Kammhuber was forced to build up an extravagantly expensive organisation that provoked the suspicions of his superiors and, due to various technical difficulties, was also extremely cumbersome to manage.

The decision to choose a common frequency for both the *Würzburg* and *Lichtenstein* systems without making prompt provision for secondary frequencies led to the crisis of summer 1943. Although by changing over from ground-controlled to 'free' interceptions the night fighters managed to gain a temporary breathing space, they never again regained control of the airspace over Reich territory.

At first the 'Wild Boar' method seemed the ideal solution, being inexpensive and quite effective, but it cost the lives of many pilots. With the exception of the Nuremberg raid, the 'Tame Boar' method did not yield the expected results because it lacked the necessary technical prerequisites: panoramic ground radar, interference-secure ground control of the fighter formations, jamming-proof AI radars with high-resolution displays, and a reliable air-to-air identification method.

After Germany had fallen behind in the high-frequency war it was easy for the enemy to ascertain each new German electronic measure and block it with a new device in a very short time. With the collapse of the early-warning organisation in France at the beginning of July 1944 the Reich Air Defence command became completely helpless. From then on Germany was limping along not one but two steps behind the enemy.

Good as they were, the efforts of the *Jägerstab* came too late. The expansion of night fighter formations to their full establishment strength – in some cases three years after their formation – could no longer have a positive effect on the force because the collapse of the ground control system and the fuel shortage forced most otherwise fully intact Luftwaffe formations to stay on the ground. A situation unparalleled in the history of warfare had arisen: at the zenith of its armed strength and combat readiness the night fighter force could no longer be sent into action.

Though during the last few weeks of the war the operational use of the first turbojet night fighters, the *Berlin* AI radar and the *Bernhard* ground/air control system seemed to improve matters, all these measures came too late.

Considering all these omissions, delays and faulty decisions, and the conditions under which the crews had to fight, the achievements of the Luftwaffe night fighter force are truly amazing. They had to face overwhelming numbers from the very beginnning and, although right through the war years they were never capable of protecting the homeland from damage, their several thousand aerial victories prove that the Luftwaffe night fighters had to be taken seriously as a foe right until the end of 1944. Their morale also remained high until the bitter end, as shown by the successes scored during the last few days of hostilities.

In five short years this arm of the Luftwaffe underwent greater technical and tactical change than any other branch of the armed forces. The standard day *Zerstörer*, which had to work in conjunction with batteries of searchlights, had grown into a heavily armed aircraft filled with complex electronics, a fighting machine that could either fly under ground control for hundreds of miles in all weathers to contact enemy aircraft, or detect and intercept them on its own.

The German night fighter force may have gone under in 1945, but its organisation and operational methods continue to influence the air defence of both West and East.

Appendices

1. List of abbreviations with translations (*eq = equivalent to*)

BehBelSt *Behelfsbeleuchterstaffel*   Auxiliary illuminator flight
Bel *Beleuchter*   Illuminator; marker
Bofu *Bordfunker*   Radio (radar) operator
Dunaja *Dunkelnachtjagd*   Dark night fighting (without searchlights)
EiV *Eigenverständigungsanlage*   Intercom
EKdo *Erprobungskommando*   Proving or Test Detachment
E-Stelle *Erprobungstelle*   Proving or Test Centre
ETC *Elektrische Trägervorrichtung für Cylinderbomben*   Electrically operated bomb racks for cylindrical bombs
FFO *Flugfunk Forschungsanstalt*   Aviation Radio Research Establishment
Fhj *Fahnenjunker*   Officer cadet
Fl.Abt *Fliegerabteilung*   Air Detachment; Flying Detachment (WWI)
FlaV *Flammenvernichter*   Exhaust flame damper
Fluko *Flugwachkommando*   Central Observation Post
FM *Fernmelde*   Telecommunications
FuG *Funkgerät*   Radio set; AI radar set
FuMG *Funkmessgerät*   Ground radar set
Fw *Feldwebel*   eq Sergeant (RAF)
Gef.Stand *Gefechtsstand*   Command post
Gen.Lt *Generalleutnant*   eq Major General; Air Vice Marshal (RAF)
Gen.Major *Generalmajor*   eq Brigadier; Air Commodore (RAF)
Gen.Oberst *Generaloberst*   Colonel-General; Air Chief Marshal (RAF)
GFM *Generalfeldmarschall*   General Field Marshal; Marshal of the RAF
Henaja *Helle Nachtjagd*   Illuminated night fighting
Hptm *Hauptmann*   eq Captain; Flt Lt (RAF)
Jafü *Jagdführer*   Area Fighter Leader
Jasta *Jagdstaffel*   Fighter squadron (WW 1)
JDiv *Jagddivision*   Fighter division
JG *Jagdgeschwader*   eq Fighter wing
JKorps *Jagdkorps*   Fighter corps
JLO *Jägerleitoffizier*   Fighter Control Officer
Kdo *Kommando*   Detachment
Kdore *Kommodore*   Commodore of a *Geschwader*
Kdr *Kommandeur*   Commander of a *Gruppe*

222

KG *Kampfgeschwader* eq Bomber wing

Konaja *Kombinierte Nachtjagd* Combined night interception method

LBeoSt *Luftbeobachterstaffel* Air observer flight

LDv *Luftwaffendienstvorschrift* Luftwaffe service manual

Lfl *Luftflotte* Air Fleet

LG *Lehrgeschwader* Tactical development *Geschwader*

Ln *Luftnachrichten* Luftwaffe Signals Service

Lt *Leutnant* eq Pilot Officer (RAF)

Lw *Luftwaffe* German Air Force

Lw.Befh. *Luftwaffenbefehlshaber* Lw commander

Maj *Major* Major; Squadron Leader (RAF)

MG *Maschinengewehr* Machine gun

MK *Maschinenkanone* Automatic cannon

NJ *Nachtjagd* Night fighting; night interception

NJG *Nachtjagdgeschwader* eq Night fighter wing

NJGr *Nachtjagdgruppe* Night fighter *Gruppe*

NNJSchw *Nahnachtjagdschwarm* Close range night fighter section

NO *Nachrichtenoffizier* Signals Officer; also Intelligence Officer

NSGr *Nachtschlachtgruppe* Night attack *Gruppe*

NVA *Nachrichtenmittelversuchsanstalt* Experimental Communications Establishment

NVW *Nachrichten- und Verbindungswesen* Signals and communications system

Ob.d.Lw. *Oberbefehlshaber der Luftwaffe* C-in-C of the Luftwaffe

Obgfr *Obergefreiter* No RAF equivalent

Oblt *Oberleutnant* eq Flying Officer (RAF)

Ofw *Oberfeldwebel* eq Flight Sergeant (RAF)

OKL *Oberkommando der Luftwaffe* Supreme Command of the Luftwaffe

OKW *Oberkommando der Wehrmacht* Supreme Command of the Armed Forces

Otl *Oberstleutnant* eq Wing Commander (RAF)

PK *Propaganda Kompanie* War reporter company

RLM *Reichsluftfahrtministerium* State Air Ministry

RLV *Reichsluftverteidigung* Reich Air Defence

St *Staffel* eq Flight (RAF)

Stfw *Stabsfeldwebel* eq Warrant Officer

TLR *Technische Luftrüstung* Technical Air Armament Office

TO *Technischer Offizier* Technical Officer

TVK *Truppenversuchskommando* Service Experimental Detachment

Uffz *Unteroffizier* eq Corporal (RAF)

VersNJSt *Versuchsnachtjagdstaffel* Experimental night fighting flight

WB *Waffenbehälter* Weapon container

WT *Waffentropfen* Detachable weapon pod

z.b.V. *zur besonderen Verwendung* Special purpose

ZG *Zerstörergeschwader* eq Heavy fighter wing

2. Formation dates of main Luftwaffe night fighter units

NJG 1

I *Gruppe*
22.6.1940 from ZG 1, IV/ZG 26

II *Gruppe*
1st formation 22.6.1940 from IV(N)/JG 2; on 1.7.1940 became III *Gruppe*
2nd formation 1.7.1940 from Z/KG 30; on 7.9.1940 became I/NJG 2
3rd formation 7.9.1940 from I/ZG 26

III *Gruppe*
1.7.1940 from II/NJG 1

IV *Gruppe*
1.10.1942 from II/NJG 2

NJG 2

I *Gruppe*
1.9.1940 from II/NJG 1 and 1./ZG 1

II *Gruppe*
Nov 1940 4.*Staffel* from 1./ZG 2
1.11.1941 activation of *Gruppe* from 4./NJG 2 and transfers from 4. and
  6./NJG 1; on 1.10.1942 became IV/NJG 1. Existing III *Gruppe* became
  new ᵀI *Gruppe*

III *Gruppe*
1st formation Mar 1942; on 1.10.1942 became II *Gruppe*
2nd formation Jul 1943 from V/NJG 6
9.*Staffel* Sep 1944 from *LBeoStaffel* 3
On 30.10.1944 redesignation IV/NJG 3; existing IV/NJG 3 became new III
  Gruppe

IV *Gruppe*
30.10.1944 from I/NJG 7; on 23.2.1944 became NSGr 30

V *Gruppe*
Nov 1944 retraining of III/KG 2; did not reach operational status

NJG 3

I *Gruppe*
1.10.1940 from V(Z)/LG 1

II *Gruppe*
1.9.1941 from II/ZG 2 and Z/*Erg.Gruppe*

III *Gruppe*
1.11.1941 from II/ZG 76 and 4./NJG 1

IV *Gruppe*
Nov 1942 from parts of III/NJG 2; 30.10.1944 exchanged designation with
  III/NJG 2

NJG 4

I *Gruppe*
1st formation spring 1941 from I/ZG 26; Dec 1941 transferred back as I/ZG 26 to Eastern Front
2nd formation Sep 1942 from parts of I/NJG 3 and III/NJG 4

II *Gruppe*
1st formation spring 1941 from II/ZG 26; Dec 1941 redesignated II/ZG 26 (except 5.*Staffel*)
2nd formation Apr 1942 from 5./NJG 4 and new personnel

III *Gruppe*
May 1942 from 1., 4. and 8./NJG 1

IV *Gruppe*
Activation order 1.1.1943; on 1.8.1943 became I/NJG 6

NJG 5

I *Gruppe*
Sep 1942 from II/ZG 2

II *Gruppe*
1st formation Dec 1942; on 10.5.1944 became III/NJG 6
2nd formation from former V/NJG 5

III *Gruppe*
Apr 1943

IV *Gruppe*
1st formation Dec 1942; on 1.8.1943 became I/NJG 100
2nd formation Sep 1943

V *Gruppe*
11.8.1943; on 10.5.1944 became II *Gruppe*

NJG 6

I *Gruppe*
1.8.1943 from IV/NJG 4

II *Gruppe*
15.9.1943

III *Gruppe*
10.5.1944 from II/NJG 5

IV *Gruppe*
May 1943

V *Gruppe*
Jun 1943; in Jul became III/NJG 2

NJG 7

I *Gruppe*
May 1943 from III/KG 3; Jun 1944 became I/NJG 7; Nov 1944 redesignated IV/NJG 2
4.(*Erg.*)/NJG 7; Jun 1944 from 12./NJG 51; Nov 1944 redesignated *Stabs-staffel* NJG 3

NJGr 10

Activated 1.1.1944; on 27.10.1944 1.*Staffel* redesignated 3./NJG 11

NJG 11

I *Gruppe*
1.*Staffel* 28.8.1944 from parts of 6./JG 300; Jan 1945 became 7./NJG 11
2.*Staffel* 28.8.1944 from parts of 1./NJGr 10; Jan 1945 became 1./NJG 11
3.*Staffel* Nov 1944 from rest of 1./NJGr 10; Jan 1945 became 8./NJG 11

II *Gruppe*
4.-6.*Staffel* Nov 1944 from 10./JG 300; Mar 1945 became 5./ NJG 11

III *Gruppe*
Jan 1945 from 1. and 3./NJG 11 and new personnel; Mar 1945 became 2./NJG 11
10./NJG 11 on 28.1.1945 from *Kdo Welter*

3. Commanding Officers of night fighter Geschwader and Gruppen

Sources are War Diaries, which report the date of joining the unit, and paybooks, which give the date the appointment was confirmed. The author has used whichever was available.

NJG 1
Falck	26.6.1940 – 30.6.1943
Streib	1.7.1943 – Mar 1944
Jabs	Mar 1944 – end of war

I/NJG 1
Radusch	1.7.1940 – 6.10.1940
Streib	18.10.1940 – 1.7.1943
Frank	1.7.1943 – 27.9.1943
Meurer	28.9.1943 – 21.1.1944
Förster	Jan 1944 – 1.10.1944
Baake	2.10.1944 – end of war

II/NJG 1

Stillfried	2.10.1940 – 6.10.1940
Ehle	6.10.1940 – 17.11.1943
von Bonin	18.11.1943 – 25.10.1944
Breves	26.10.1944 – end of war

III/NJG 1

von Bothmer	1.7.1940 – 1.11.1940
Schön	1.11.1940 – 1.2.1941
von Graeve	8.2.1941 – 5.6.1942
Thimmig	6.6.1942 – 31.5.1943
Lippe-Weissenfels	1.6.1943 – 20.2.1944
Drewes	1.3.1944 – end of war

IV/NJG 1

Lent	1.10.1942 – 1.8.1943
Jabs	1.8.1943 – 1.3.1944
Schnaufer	1.3.1944 – 26.10.1944
Greiner	1.11.1944 – end of war

NJG 2

Hülshoff	1.11.1941 – 31.11.1943[1]
Sayn-Wittgenstein	1.1.1944 – 21.1.1944
Radusch	4.2.1944 – 11.11.1944
Semrau	12.11.1944 – 8.2.1945
Thimmig	8.2.1945 – end of war

I/NJG 2

Heyse	1.9.1940 – 23.11.1940
Hülshoff	24.11.1940 – 31.10.1941
Jung	1.11.1941 – Dec 1943
Buschmann	Dec 1943 – Jan 1944
Zechlin	20.2.1944 – 12.5.1944
Rath	12.5.1944 – end of war

II/NJG 2

Lent	1.11.1941 – 1.10.1942 (became IV/NJG 1)
Bönsch	2.10.1942 – Dec 1942 (ex-III/NJG 2)
Patuschka	3.12.1942 – 6.3.1943
Sewing	7.3.1943 – Dec 1943
Sayn-Wittgenstein	Dec 1943 – 1.1.1944
Semrau	1.1.1944 – 1.11.1944
Hissbach	1.11.1944 – 14.4.1945
Brinkhaus	15.4.1945 – end of war

III/NJG 2

Bönsch	3.4.1942 – 1.8.1942 (became II/NJG 2)
Semrau	Jul 1943 – 1.1.1944 (new formation, ex-V/NJG 6)
Ney	1.1.1944 – Nov 1944 (became IV/NJG 3)
Ferger	Nov 1944 – 10.4.1945 (ex-IV/NJG 3)
Merker	11.4.1945 – end of war

IV/NJG 2 (ex-I/NJG7)
Bengsch   Aug 1944 – 23.2.1945 (became NSGr 30)

NJG 3
Schalk   29.3.1941 – 1.8.1941
Lent   1.8.1943 – 7.10.1944
Radusch   12.11.1944 – end of war

I/NJG 3
Radusch   7.10.1940 – 2.10.1941
Knoetzsch   3.10.1941 – 30.9.1942
Lippe-Weissenfels   1.10.1942 – 31.5.1943
Peters   1.6.1943 – 14.8.1943
Mylius   15.8.1943 – 13.12.1943
Szameitat   14.12.1943 – 2.1.1944
Husemann   4.1.1944 – end of war

II/NJG 3
Radusch   3.10.1941 – 1.8.1943
Sayn-Wittgenstein   15.8.1943 – end Nov 1943
Szameitat   Dec 1943 – 14.12.1943
Havenstein   15.12.1943 – Sep 1944
Hüschens   Sep 1944 – end of war

III/NJG 3
Nacke   1.11.1941 – 21.4.1943
Mylius   22.4.1943 – 14.3.1943
Sigmund   31.8.1943 – 3.10.1943
Barthe   15.10.1943 – end of war

IV/NJG 3
Simon   1.11.1942 – 7.10.1943
Schulz   8.10.1943 – Jan 1944
Buschmann   Jan 1944 – Jul 1944
Ferger   Jul 1944 – Nov 1944 (became III/NJG 2)
Ney   Nov 1944 – 4.3.1945 (ex-III/NJG 2)
Tober   5.3.1945 – end of war

NJG 4
Stoltenhoff   18.4.1941 – 20.10.1943
Thimmig   20.10.1943 – 14.11.1944
Schnaufer   14.11.1944 – end of war

I/NJG 4
Herget   1.9.1942 – Dec 1944
Krause   Dec 1944 – end of war

III/NJG 4

Holler	1.5.1942 – 22.6.1943
Kamp	23.6.1943 – 6.12.1944
Meister	6.12.1944 – end of war

IV/NJG 4

Wohlers	1.1.1943 – 9.2.1944 (from 1.8.1943 I/NJG 6)

NJG 5

Schaffer	30.9.1942 – 1.8.1943
Radusch	2.8.1943 – 3.2.1944
Lippe-Weissenfels	20.2.1944 – 12.3.1944
Borchers '	15.3.1944 – 5.3.1945
Schoenert	6.3.1945 – end of war

I/NJG 5

Wandam	end Sept 1942 – 4.7.1943
Hoffmann	4.7.1943 – end Apr 1945
Lang	Apr 1945 – end of war

II/NJG 5

Schoenert	1.12.1942 – 5.8.1943
Meurer	5.8.1943 – 27.9.1943
Baer	28.9.1943 – 27.1.1944
Fellerer	Feb 1944 – 10.5.1944 (became III/NJG 6)
Leickhardt	3.5.1944 – 6.3.1945 (ex-V/NJG 5)
Tham	10.3.1945 – end of war
Rapp	5.4.1945 – end of war

III/NJG 5

Borchers	Apr 1943 – 15.3.1944
Zorner	16.3.1944 – 21.10.1944
von Meien	22.10.1944 – 6.2.1945
Engel	6.2.1945 – Apr 1945
Piuk	Apr 1945 – end of war

IV/NJG 5

Sayn-Wittgenstein	end 1942 – 9.8.1943 (became I/NJG 100)
von Niebelschütz	1.9.1943 – 2.1.1944 (new formation)
Altendorf	3.1.1944 – Sep 1944
Höfele	Oct 1944 – 20.4.1945
Bussmann	21.4.1945 – end of war

V/NJG 5

Peters	15.8.1943 – 3.5.1944
Leickhardt	4.5.1944 – 10.5.1944 (became II/NJG 5)

NJG 6

Schaffer	10.8.1943 – 8.2.1944
Wohlers	9.2.1944 – 15.3.1944
von Reeken	16.3.1944 – 14.4.1944
Griese	15.4.1944 – 12.9.1944
Lütje	13.9.1944 – end of war

I/NJG 6

Wohlers	1.8.1944 – 9.2.1944
Reschke	19.2.1944 – 24.4.1944
Hadeball	26.4.1944 – 3.7.1944
Friedrich	12.7.1944 – 16.3.1945
Spoden	19.3.1945 – end of war

II/NJG 6

Leuchs	15.9.1943 – 14.7.1944
Schulte	23.7.1944 – end of war

III/NJG 6

Fellerer	10.5.1944 – Feb 1945 (ex-II/NJG 5)
Johnen	Feb 1945 – 31.3.1945
Floitgraf	1.4.1945 – end of war

IV/NJG 6

Lütje	Jun 1943 – 26.10.1944
Becker	20.10.1944 – end of war

V/NJG 6
on 15.8.1943 redesignated III/NJG 2

I/NJG 7

Bengsch	Jan 1944 – Aug 1944 (became IV/NJG 2)

NJGr 10

Schoenert	1.1.1944 – 6.3.1945
Lüdtke	6.3.1945 – disbanded end Apr 1945

NJG 11
No *Geschwaderstab*

I/NJG 11

Müller	26.8.1944 – end of war

II/NJG 11

Finkeldey ?	(data not confirmed)

III/NJG 11

Krause	12.1.1945 – end of war

NJG 100
No *Geschwaderstab*

I/NJG 100

Sayn-Wittgenstein	1.8.1943 – 5.8.1943
Schoenert	5.8.1943 – 31.12.1943
Lechner	1.1.1944 – 23.2.1944
Bonow	
(acting CO)	23.2.1944 – May 1944
Bellinghausen	May 1944 – 8.7.1944
Fischer	8.7.1944 – end of war

II/NJG 100

von Meien	2.7.1944 – 21.10.1944
Zorner	20.7.1944 – end of war

Nachtjagdschule 1, later NJG 101²

Vollbracht	4.7.1941 – 13.1.1942
Knoetzsch	Jan 1942 – Oct 1942
von Bülow	Oct 1942 – Oct 1943
Specht	Oct 1943 – Dec 1943
Sewing	Dec 1944 – Mar 1945

I/NJG 101

Grommes	? – end 1942
Rossiwall	Jan 1943 – 1943

II/NJG 101

Schwab	Oct 1942 – Mar 1945
Boehm	Mar 1945 – 6.4.1945

III/NJG 101

Peters	autumn 1941 – 1.6.1943
Thimmig	1.6.1943 – 19.10.43 (became I/NJG 102)
new formation	Aug 1944

NJG 102

Blumensaat	Dec 1943 – ?
Ewers	? – 1.6.1944
Hülshoff	1.6.1944 – 25.3.1945

I/NJG 102

von Bonin	Oct 1944 – ?

II/NJG 102

Dorman	? – end of war

1 Before forming their own *Geschwader* staffs the *Gruppen* of NJG 2–4 were subordinated to NJG 1.
2 The few details available have been confirmed by questioning survivors.

4. The night fighter aces

This list does not claim to be anywhere near complete and contains only an estimated 85 per cent of the night fighter pilots who achieved seven or more victories. Due to a shortage or lack of documentary evidence, most of the pilots of the single-engined night fighters of JG 300, 301 and 302 are omitted. The listed victory scores include only those successes achieved while the pilots were members of night fighting formations; daytime victories during that period (marked D) are counted. Aerial victories achieved while the pilots were serving in *Zerstörer* or bomber units are marked with Z or B.

Decorations: Only the highest award known to have been made to each pilot is listed.

Br	= Brilliants to the Knights Cross
S	= Swords and Oakleaves to the Knights Cross
EL	= Oakleaves to the Knights Cross
RK	= Knights Cross
RK(B)	= Knights Cross as bomber pilot
RK(J)	= Knights Cross as day fighter pilot
RK(Z)	= Knights Cross as *Zerstörer* pilot
DK	= German Cross in Gold
EP	= Goblet of Honour
*	= estimated number of victories
†	= only those victories confirmed by documentary evidence are counted

Readers are invited to help complement and improve this list.

Rank	Name	Decoration	Victories	Unit	Date killed during war
Oblt	Adelhütte, Hans	DK	*15–20	?	
Hptm	Altendorff, Rudolf	DK	25, 4Z	NJG 3, 4, 5	
Lt	Altner, Herbert	DK	21	NJG 5	
Hptm	Andres, Ernst	RK(B)	?	NJG 4	11.2.45
Hptm	Augenstein, Hans-Heinz	RK	46	NJG 1	6.12.44
Hptm	Autenrieth, Hans	DK	23	NJG 1, 4	
Hptm	Baake, Werner	RK	41	NJG 1	
Hptm	Baer	?	12	NJG 3, 5	27.1.44
Lt	Bahr, Günther	RK	37	NJG 1, 4, 6	
Maj	Barte, Walter	DK	23	NJG 1, 3	
Hptm	Bauer, Martin		7	NJG 1, 7	
Fw	Becker, Karl-Heinz		7	NJG 11	
Hptm	Becker, Ludwig	EL	44	NJG 1	26.2.43
Hptm	Becker, Martin	EL	58	NJG 3, 4, 6	
Uffz	Behrens	?	*8–12	NJG 100	
Oblt	Beier, Wilhelm	RK	36	NJG 1, 2	
Hptm	Bellinghausen, Theodor	DK	7	NJG 100	

232

Rank	Name	Decoration	Victories	Unit	Date killed during war
Lt	Benning, Anton	RK	10, 18D	JG 301	
Hptm	Bergmann, Helmut	RK	36	NJG 4	6.8.44
Ofw	Berschwinger, Hans	DK	*20	NJG 1	15.2.44
Oblt	Bertram, Günther	DK	35	NJG 100	
Fw	Beyer, Konrad	EP	*10–15	?	
Hptm	Bietmann		7	NJG 1	11.2.42
Oblt	Birkenstock, Hans Jörg		9	NJG 4, 6	19.5.44
Oblt	Bockemeyer, Rolf		7	NJG 1, 5	
Hptm	Boensch, Herbert		10, 1Z	NJG 2	1.8.42
Maj	von Bonin, Eckart-Wilhelm	RK	39	NJG 1	
Hptm	Bonow, Kurt	DK	*10	NJG 5, 100	
Otl	Borchers, Walter	RK	48, 11Z	NJG 3, 5	5.3.45
Oblt	Brandt, Fritz	DK	12	NJG 2, 3	
Oblt	Bretschneider, Klaus	RK	14, 17D	JG 300	24.12.44
Lt	Breukel, Wendelin	EP	14	NJG 2	1944
Hptm	Breves, Adolf	RK	18	NJG 1	
Oblt	Briegleb, Walter	DK	25	NJG 2, 3	
Hptm	Brinkhaus, Franz	DK	25	NJG 2, 3	
Hptm	Brinkmann	DK	*20	NJG 3	
Fw	Brunner		8	NJG 1, 6	
Maj	von Buchholz, Fritz	EP	11	NJG 1	25.3.45
Lt	Bunje, Helmut		12	NJG 6	4.8.44
Hptm	Burggraf, Wilhelm	DK	10	JG 301	
Hptm	Buschmann, Franz		*10	NJG 1, 3	28.6.44
Hptm	Bussmann, Rolf	DK	23	NJG 1, 2, 5	
Ofw	Dahms, Helmut	EP	*24	NJG 100	
Ofw	de Fries, Heinz		10	NJG 100	
Oblt	Delakowitz, Richard		7	NJG 4	
Lt	Denzel		9	NJG 1	26.6.43
Oblt	Dimter, Willi		7	NJG 1	7.9.42
Lt	Döring, Arnold	RK	13, 10B	NJG 2, 3	
Hptm	Dormann, Wilhelm	DK	14	NJG 1	
Hptm	Dreher, Johann	RK(B)	2	NJG 3	4.3.45
Maj	Drewes, Martin	EL	47, 2Z	NJG 1	
Hptm	Drünkler, Ernst	RK	47	NJG 1, 5	
Ofw	Düding, Rudi		*18	NJG 100	
Hptm	Eberspächer, Helmut	RK(B)	3	SKG 10, KG 51	
Oblt	Ebhardt, Rolf		8	NJG 1	
Oblt	Eckhardt, Reinhold	RK	19, 3Z	NJG 1, 3	30.7.42
Maj	Ehle, Walter	RK	35, 3Z	NJG 1	
Ofw	Eickmeier, Bruno		*10	NJG 1	4.9.43
Hptm	Elstermann, Willi		*9	NJG 3	2.2.45
Hptm	Engel, Walter	RK(B)	9	NJG 5	
Oblt	Engel, Wilhelm	DK	20	NJG 1, 4, 6	
Fw	Engling, Egon		12	NJG 2, 3	26.3.45
Oblt	Erhardt, Peter	DK	22	NJG 5	

Rank	Name	Decor-ation	Victories	Unit	Date killed during war
Oberst	Falck, Wolfgang	RK	–, 7Z	NJG 1	
Fw	Fehre		8	JG 300	? 1944
Hptm	Fellerer, Leopold	RK	41	NJG 1, 5, 6	
Oblt	Fengler, Georg	DK	16	NJG 1, 4	
Lt	Fensch, Frithjof	EP	*10–15	NJG 4	
Hptm	Fenske, Walter	EP	12	NJG 1, 2	28.3.44
Hptm	Ferger, Heinz	DK	*30	NJG 2, 3	10.4.45
Oblt	Finster, Lenz		10	NJG 1	24.12.43
Fw	Fintscher, Hugo	EP	13	NJG 2, 3	
Hptm	Fischer, August		12	NJG 1, 5, 100	
Hptm	Fladrich, Kurt	DK	15	NJG 4	
Oblt	Förster, Josef	DK	21	NJG 2, 3	
Maj	Förster, Paul	EP	5, 3Z	NJG 1	1.10.44
Oblt	Francsi, Gustav	RK	56	NJG 100	
Hptm	Frank, Hans-Dieter	EL	55	NJG 1	27.9.43
Lt	Frank, Rudolf	EL	45	NJG 3	26.4.44
Oblt	Franz, Günther		8	NJG 1, 3, 6	
Maj	Friedrich, Gerhard	RK	30	NJG 4, 6	16.3.45
Lt	Fries, Otto	DK	18	NJG 1	
Hptm	Geiger, August	EL	53	NJG 1	29.9.43
Hptm	Geismann, Johannes	RK(B)	–	NJG 1	
Fw	Gerstmayr, Lorenz	DK	15–20	NJG 3	1944
Lt	von Gienanth, Hans		10	NJG 1	
Oblt	Gildner, Paul	EL	44, 2Z	NJG 1	24.2.43
Ofw	Glitz, Willi	DK(B)	*10	NJG 3	1944
Oblt	Graef, Fritz		7	NJG 4	
Oblt	Gref, Hans	DK	20–25	NJG 100	
Hptm	Greiner, Hermann	EL	50	NJG 1	
Maj	Griese, Heinrich	DK	14	NJG 1, 4, 6	
Lt	Grimm, Heinz	RK	27	NJG 1	13.10.43
Oblt	Györy, August	RK(B)	–	NJG 3	1.1.45
Hptm	Hadeball, Karl	RK	33	NJG 1, 4, 6 NJGr 10	
Hptm	Hager, Johannes	RK	48	NJG 1	
Lt	Hahn, Hans	RK	12	NJG 2	11.10.41
Fw	Hartl, Andreas	DK	†12	6./JG 302	8.4.44
Uffz	Hausschild		*10	NJG 100	
Maj	Havenstein, Klaus		*10	NJG 3	23.9.44
Oblt	Heilig, Bruno		12	NJG 2	6.1.45
Ofw	Heiner, Engelbert	RK	11	NNJSchw Lfl 4	1943
Hptm	Heldt, Alfred		9	NJG 3	16.12.44
Hptm	Henning, Horst	RK(B)	6	NJG 3	7.10.44
Oblt	Henseler, Wilhelm		11	NJG 1	
Maj	Herget, Wilhelm	EL	57, 12Z	NJG 3, 4	
Oberst	Hermann, Hajo	S	9	JG 300	
Oblt	Hermann, Kurt	DK	9	NJG 2	

234

Rank	Name	Decoration	Victories	Unit	Date killed during war
Ofw	Herzog		9–12	NJG 1	20.10.43
Ofw	Hillenbrux, Werner	EP	*12	NJG 1	30.1.44
Fw	Hiller, Otto	EP	*10	NJG 5	
Oblt	Hirschfeld, Ernst-Erich	RK	*8, 16D	JG 300	28.7.44
Hptm	Hissbach, Heinz-Horst	RK	34	NJG 2	14.4.45
Maj	Hoffmann, Werner	RK	51, 1Z	NJG 3, 5	
Maj	Holler, Kurt	DK	19	NJG 2, 3, 4	22.6.43
Fw	Holtfreter, Günther		*10	NJG 3	?
Hptm	Hopf, Werner	DK	21	NJG 5	7.10.44
Ofw	Hörwick, Anton	RK(B)	–	NJG 2, 7	19.2.45
Otl	Hülshoff, Karl	DK	11	NJG 2	
Maj	Husemann, Werner	RK	32	NJG 1, 3	
Maj	Ilk, Iro	RK(B)	†4	JG 300	25.9.44
Otl	Jabs, Hans Joachim	EL	31, 19Z	NJG 1	
Hptm	Jank, Wolfgang		11	NJG 5, 100	
Oblt	Jarsch, Lothar		10	NJG 2	
Hptm	Johnen, Wilhelm	RK	34	NJG 1, 5, 6	
Oblt	Jung, Erich	DK	28	NJG 2	
Oblt	Kaiser, Adolf	DK	*20	NJG 1, 100	
Hptm	Kamp, Hans-Karl	DK	23	NJG 4, JG 300	31.12.44
Maj	Karlowski, Hans	DK	*13	NJG 1, 2	
Lt	Kaross, Eberhard		10	NJG 100	
Ofw	Karsten, Kurt		*7	NJG 4, 6	
Lt	Keller, Otto	EP	15	NJG 5	
Ofw	Kiesling, Walter		*7	NJG 3	2.45
Ofw	Klaiber		*10	NJG 5, 100	
Hptm	Klemenz, Otto Karl	DK	29	NJG 1, 5	
Hptm	Knacke, Reinhold	EL	44	NJG 1	3.2.43
Oblt	Köberich, Günther	EP	14	NJG 3	8.3.44
Hptm	Koch, Herbert	DK	23	NJG 3	
Lt	Kociok, Josef	RK	21, 12Z	NJG 200	26.9.43
Stfw	Kollak, Reinhard	RK	49	NJG 1, 4	
Hptm	König, Hans-Heinz	RK(J)	4, 24D	NJG 1 JG 11	24.5.44
Hptm	Konter, Helmut		*15–20	NJG 100	3.45
Fw	Koppe, Heinz		9	NJG 2, 3	
Hptm	Kornblum, Dietrich	RK(B)	†1	NJG 2	27.11.44
Lt	Köster, Alfons	RK	25	NJG 2, 3	7.1.45
Fw	Kraft, Georg	DK	15	NJG 1	18.8.43
Hptm	Kraft, Josef	EL	56	NJG 1,4,5,6	
Hptm	Krahforst, Josef		*10	NJG 4	9.44
Hptm	Krause, Hans	RK	28	NJG 3, 4, 101	
Oblt	Kuthe, Wolfgang		8	NJG 1	14.4.43
Fw	Kutzner, Otto		9	NJG 2, 3	
Hptm	Lau, Fritz	RK	28	NJG 1	

Rank	Name	Decoration	Victories	Unit	Date killed during war
Lt	Laufs, Peter	DK	8, 4Z	NJG 2	27.1.42
Ofw	Launer, Richard	EP	10	NJG 1, 4, 6	
Maj	Lechner, Alois	RK	45	NJG 2, 5, 100	23.2.44
Maj	Leickhardt, Hans	DK	30	NJG 1, 5	5.3.45
Oberst	Lent, Helmut	Br	102, 8Z	NJG 1, 2, 3	7.10.44
Hptm	Leube, Hermann	DK	22	NJG 3	28.12.44
Maj	Leuchs, Rolf		10	NJG 6	
Ofw	Lindinger, Eduard	RK(B)		NJG 1, 5	
Oblt	Linke, Lothar	RK	25, 2Z	NJG 1	14.5.43
Maj	Prince zur Lippe-Weissenfeld, Egmont	EL	51	NJG 1, 5	12.3.44
Hptm	Loos, Kurt	DK	13	NJG 1, 5	
Ofw	Lüddeke, Robert	EP	*10–12	NJG 2	
Otl	Lütje, Herbert	EL	50	NJG 1, 6	
Ofw	Maisch		*26–28	NJG 100	
Ofw	Mangelsdorf, Rudolf		13	NJG 2, 3	
Hptm	Mangold, Egon	EP	*10	NJG 100, 200	
Lt	Matzak, Kurt	DK	15	NJG 1	
Hptm	von Meien, Ulrich	EP	9	NJG 100, 200, 5	
Lt	Meissner, Hans	DK	20	NJG 3	
Hptm	Meister, Ludwig	RK	39	NJG 1, 4	
Hptm	Merker, Hans-Hermann	RK(B)		NJG 7, 2	
Hptm	Meurer, Manfred	EL	65	NJG 1, 5	21.1.44
Fhj-Ofw	Migge, Günther	DK	8	JG 300, NJGr 10, NJG 11	
Maj	Milius, Walter		11	NJG 1, 3	
Ofw	Misch, Heinz		10	NJG 2, 3	
Lt	Möckel, Wolfram	EP	10	NJG 3	
Hptm	Modrow, Ernst-Wilhelm	RK	33	NJG 1	
Ofw	Möller, Klaus	DK	14	NJG 3	
Ofw	Morlock, Willi	DK	16	NJG 1	5.11.44
Maj	Müller, Friedrich-Karl	RK	30	JG 300, NJGr 10, NJG 11	
Oblt	Müller, Hans	DK	*15–20	NJG 3	
Oblt	Nabrich, Josef	DK	18	NJG 1	28.11.44
Oberst	Nacke, Heinz	RK(Z)	-, 12Z	NJG 3, 101	
Maj	Ney, Berthold	DK	19	NJG 2, 3	
Ofw	Ney, Siegfried	EP	12	NJG 1	28.3.42
Hptm	von Niebelschütz, Wolfgang	EP	11	NJG 4, 5	2.1.44
Lt	Niklas, Helmut		8	NJG 1, 3	30.1.44
Fw	Oberheide, Heinz		*10	NJG 3	8.2.45
Oblt	Oloff	DK	10	NJG 1	

A Do 217N of NJG 101
pursuing a US bomber
formation over the Alps
Goldmann

The FuG 2

Only a few
last product
featuring n

Ju 88A-4s of the
illuminator *Gruppe*
III/KG 3 were flown in
the standard RLM 70/71
camouflage until May
1944. This unit's losses at
the hands of friendly Flak
were high (*see below*)
Goldmann

The Allies found abandoned and destroyed Luftwaffe night fighters everywhere

Price, USAF

Oblt W

Bf 110G 9W + B0 of *Einsatzkommando* **NJG 101 was used operationally on the Eastern Front.**
(Creek)

Centre: Ju 88G-6 of *Stab* I/NJG 100 in East Prussia, autumn 1944. Note the black undersurfaces **of**
wings and fuselage
Oberst

Bottom: FW 189A provisional night fighter of NJG 100. It is equipped with the FuG 212 and an
oblique MG 151
Hentz

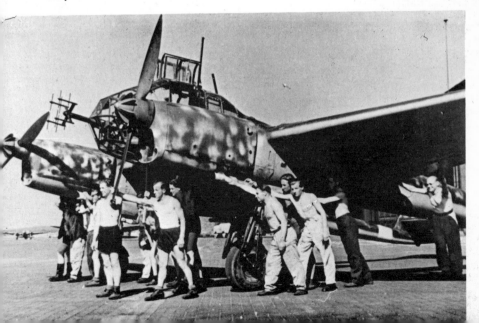

Ju 88G-6 of 7./NJG 5 with underwing bomb racks for night attack operations

AMF Dübendorf

Above: Its national insignia painted over, the last aircraft of II/NJG 100 landed on the American-occupied Lechfeld airfield on 7 May 1945   USAF

Below: B4 + SA of *NJ-Staffel Norwegen*, which escaped from Trondheim to Sweden shortly before the capitulation   Widtfeldt

Rank	Name	Decoration	Victories	Unit	Date killed during war
Hptm	Dr Patuschka, Horst	RK	23	NJG 2	6.3.43
Oblt	Perle, Helmut		12	NJG 2	9.43
Hptm	Peters, Erhard	DK	23	NJG 3, 4	20.2.44
Ofw	Pfeiffer, Karl	EP	11	NJG 1	
Lt	Potthast, Fritz	EP	9, 2Z	NJG 1	22.5.44
Hptm	Prues, Walter		7	NJG 1	4.8.44
Hptm	Puttfarken, Dieter	RK(B)	5	KG 51	23.4.44
Oblt	Pützkuhl, Josef	DK	26	NJG 5, 100	
Oberst	Radusch, Günther	EL	64	NJG 1, 2, 3, 5	
Oblt	Rapp, Werner	DK	18	NJG 1, 5	
Lt	Rasper, Hans		8	NJG 1, 101	
Hptm	Rath, Gerhard	ED	58	NJG 2, 3	
Lt	Rathke, Waldemar	EP	10–15	NJG 100	
Maj	Rauh, Hubert	RK	*31	NJG 1, 4	
Oblt	Raum, Hans	EP	17	NJG 3	
Ofw	Reitmeyer, Ernst	DK	†23	NJG 5	
Maj	Reschke, Heinz		10	NJG 6	24.4.44
Oblt	Reuter, Heinz		12	NJG 2, 3	
Uffz	Rohlfing, Walter	EP	*10-15	NJG 3	
Hptm	Rökker, Heinz	EL	64	NJG 2	
Lt	Rolland, Heinz	EP	15	NJG 1	4.12.44
Otl	Rossiwall, Theodor	RK(Z)	2, 15Z	NJG 1, 4	
Fw	Rupp, Bruno	DK	16	NJG 3	
Ofw	Säwert, Heinz	DK	16	NJG 5, 6	22.8.44
Maj	Prince zu Sayn-Wittgenstein, Heinrich	S	83	NJG 2, 3, 5	21.1.44
Fw	Schadowski, Hans	DK	23	NJG 3	
Oblt	Schäfer, Ernst		9	JG 300, 302	29.7.44
Oblt	Schäfer, Hans		12	NJG 2, 3	
Lt	Schaus, Jakob	DK	23	NJG 4	
Ofw	Scheer, Klaus	DK	24	NJG 100	
Ofw	Schellwat, Fritz	DK	19	NJG 1	
Ofw	Scherfling, Karl-Heinz	RK	33	NJG 1	21.7.44
Ofw	Schmale, Willi		*9-12	NJG 1,3	
Ofw	Schmidt		17	NJG 6	
Hptm	Schmidt, Dietrich	RK	40	NJG 1	
Oblt	Schmied, Hans	DK	13, 15Z	NJG 3, 100	
Maj	Schnaufer, Heinz-Wolfgang	Br	121	NJG 1, 4	
Hptm	Schneeweis, Wolfgang	RK	17	NNJSchw Lfl 6	28.7.43
Fw	Schneider, Gottfried	DK	†20	NJG 2	
Oblt	Schön		9	NJG 1	20.10.43
Maj	Schoenert, Rudolf	EL	64	NJG 1, 2, 5, 100	

Rank	Name	Decoration	Victories	Unit	Date killed during war
Fw	Schratter, Robert		†9	NJG 5	14.6.44
Hptm	Schröder, Eduard	DK	24, 5D	NJG 3	
Hptm	Schulte, Helmuth	RK	25	NJG 5, 6	
Hptm	Schulz, Albert	DK	*12	NJG 2, 3	30.1.44
Oblt	Schüren, Ernst	DK	*15–20		
Maj	Semrau, Paul	EL	46	NJG 2	8.2.45
Lt	Seuss, Wilhelm		8	NJG 4, 5	
Hptm	Sigmund, Rudolf	RK	28	NJG 1, 3	3.10.43
Maj	Simon, Erich	EP	15–17	NJG 3	7.10.43
Fw	Simross, Herbert		*14	NJG 100	
Ofw	Sommer, Hermann	DK	19	NJG 2, 102	11.2.44
Hptm	Söthe, Fritz	DK	*20	NJG 4	?
Oblt	Speidel, Werner		*10	NJG 3	
Hptm	Spoden, Peter	DK	24	NJG 5, 6	
Maj	Stamp, Gerhard	RK(B)	2, 2D	JG 300	
Oblt	Stock, Hermann		8	NJG 3	
Oberst	Streib, Werner	S	65, 1Z	NJG 1	
Ofw	Strohecker, Karl		*24	NJG 100	
Hptm	Strüning, Heinz	EL	56	NJG 1, 2	24.12.44
Hptm	Szameitat, Paul	RK	29	NJG 3	2.1.44
Hptm	Szardenings, Rudolf		12	NJG 3	
Oblt	Teige, Waldemar	RK	9, 2B	NNJSchw Lfl 1	3.10.42
Hptm	Telge, Wilhelm	EP	14	NJG 1	1.9.43
Fw	Ter Steegen, Herbert		10–12	NJG 5	24.5.44
Hptm	Tham, Gustav	EP	14	NJG 5, 10	
Otl	Thimmig, Wolfgang	DK	23	NJG 1, 2, 4	
Oblt	Thun, Rudolf		7	NJG 5, 6	
Oblt	Tischtau		*9	NJG 5	20.4.44
Hptm	Tober, Friedrich		8, 2Z	NJG 3, 4	
Oblt	Tonn, Wolfgang		*10	NJG 1	12.44
Lt	Tschiersch, Martin	EP	*10 –15	NJG 2	1944
Uffz	Villforth		7	NJG 2	
Ofw	Vinke, Heinz	EL	54	NJG 1	26.2.44
Lt	Völker, Heinz		9	NJG 2	22.7.44
Oblt	Wagner, Gerhard	EP	14	NJG 5	
Oblt	Walter, Albert	EP	11	NJG 4, 6	24.2.44
Hptm	Wandam, Siegfried	EP	10	NJG 1, 5	4.7.43
Lt	Weihe, Hermann		*7	NJG 100	19.4.45
Fw	Weinmann		†10	NJG 6	
Otl	Weinreich, Helmut	RK(B)	†1	JG 301	18.11.43
Oblt	Welter, Kurt	EL	56, 5D	JG 300, NJG 11	
Oblt	Werth, Johann	EP	14	NJG 2	
Fw	Werthner, Hans		*8	NJG 2, 3	
Lt	Wirtz, Ludwig	DK	*20	NJG 1, 2	
Ofhr	Wischnewski, Hermann	RK	16, 2D	JG 300	

Rank	Name	Decoration	Victories	Unit	Date killed during war
Maj	Wohlers, Heinrich	RK	29	NJG 1, 4, 6	15.3.44
Lt	Wolf, Robert	DK	21	NJG 5	4.44
Oblt	Woltersdorf, Helmut	DK	16, 8Z	NJG 1	6.6.42
Oblt	Wulff, Ulrich		*8	NJG 5	16.12.43
Hptm	Zechlin, Ernst		10	NJG 2, 5	
Maj	Zorner, Paul	EL	59	NJG 2, 3, 5, 100	

5. German night fighter successes 1940–1945

This survey has been compiled by Hans Ring from more than 5,500 documentary confirmed individual aerial victories and estimates based on other reliable sources.

Year	Reich Air Defence and Western areas		Mediterranean area	South-east	Eastern Front	Total
	Night	Day				
1940	42	–	–	–	–	42
1941	421	1	5	–	–	427
1942	687	4	51	–	38	780
1943	1,820	110	45	–	425	2,400
1944	2,335	100	2	–	545	2,982
1945	528	–	–	–	33	561
Total	5,833	215	103	–	1,041	7,192

German night fighter successes by unit

NJG 1	2,311	night and day victories
NJG 2	c. 800	,,　,,　,,
NJG 3	c. 820	,,　,,　,,
NJG 4	579	,,　,,　,,
NJG 5	c.850	,,　,,　,,
NJG 6	c. 400	,,　,,　,,
NJG 101	c. 200	,,　,,　,,
NJG 102	c. 50	,,　,,　,,
NJG 100, 200 and independent Eastern Front night fighter sections	c. 1,000	,,　,,　,,
JG 300, 301, 302, NJGr 10 and NJG 11	c. 400	,, ('Wild Boar' only)
Total	c. 7,410	night and day victories

6. Most successful German night fighter pilots 1940–1945

Note: The 1941, 1942 and 1943 totals are cumulative, while the figures for 1944/45 represent victories achieved in that period only.
(F = Long-range night fighting. † = killed in action)

Name	Victories	Name	Victories	Name	Victories
1941		18 Herget	14	29 Augenstein	26
1 Streib	22	19 Semrau	14	30 Jabs	26
2 Gildner	21	20 Sommer	14	31 R. Frank	26
3 Lent	20	21 Radusch	13	32 Linke	25 †
4 Prince z. Lippe	15	22 Holler	13	33 Baake	23
5 Beier	14F	23 Griese	13	34 Patuschka	23 †
6 Eckhardt	13	24 Kollak	12	35 Hager	22
7 Griese	13	25 Ney	12 †	36 Meister	22
8 Hahn	12F	26 Geiger	12	37 Kociok	21 †
9 Knacke	11	27 Hahn	12 †	38 Bussmann	20
10 Köster	11F			39 Eckhardt	19 †
11 Schoenert	10			40 Hoffmann	19
12 Sommer	10F	**1943**		41 Zorner	19
13 Fenske	9	1 Lent	76	42 Thimmig	19
14 Strüning	9F	2 Prince Sayn-		43 Holler	19 †
15 Semrau	9F	Wittgenstein	68		
16 Ney	9	3 Streib	63		
17 Herzog	9	4 Meurer	62	**1944/45**	
18 Völker	9 †	5 Schoenert	56	1 Schnaufer	79
19 Hermann	9F	6 H. D. Frank	55 †	2 Rökker	56
20 Kollak	8	7 Geiger	53†	3 Francsi	56
21 L. Becker	8	8 Prince z. Lippe	51	4 M. Becker	52
		9 Herget	47	5 Kraft	49
1942		10 L. Becker	44 †	6 Drünkler	46
1 Lent	49	11 Gildner	44 †	7 Raht	42
2 Knacke	40	12 Knacke	44 †	8 Drewes	40
3 L. Becker	40	13 Radusch	42	9 Zorner	40
4 Gildner	38	14 Schnaufer	42	10 Greiner	38
5 Prince z. Lippe	38	15 Strüning	40	11 Borchers	c. 38
6 Streib	37	16 Vinke	37	12 Hoffmann	33
7 Beier	36	17 Beier	36	13 Modrow	33
8 Prince Sayn-		18 Ehle	35 †	14 Semrau	31
Wittgenstein	24	19 v. Bonin	35	15 D. Schmidt	30
9 Schoenert	23	20 Lechner	35	16 Hissbach	28
10 Strüning	23	21 Kollak	32	17 Jung	27
11 Patuschka	19	22 Lütje	31	18 Johnen	27
12 Eckhardt	19†	23 Szameitat	29	19 Hager	26
13 Ehle	16	24 Hadeball	29	20 Lent	26 †
14 Woltersdorf	16†	25 Sigmund	28 †	21 Briegleb	25
15 H. D. Frank	15	26 Wohlers	28	22 Friedrich	25
16 Köster	15	27 Scherfling	28	23 Krause	25
17 Lütje	15	28 Grimm	27 †	24 Leickhardt	25

7. Series of five or more victories in one night

Date	Rank, name	Unit	Victories
16/17.9.42	Hptm Knacke	I/NJG 1	5
29/30.3.43	Hptm Geiger	III/NJG 1	5
13/14.5.43	Hptm Lütje	III/NJG 1	6
25/26.5.43	Hptm Ehle	II/NJG 1	5
11/12.6.43	Maj Streib	I/NJG 1	5
21/22.6.43	Hptm Frank	I/NJG 1	6
21/22.6.43	Hptm Radusch	II/NJG 3	5
24/25.7.43	Hptm Prince Sayn-Wittgenstein	IV/NJG 5	6 (Eastern Front)
17/18.8.43	Lt Musset	II/NJG 1	5
27/28.10.43	Hptm Lechner	I/NJG 100	7 (Eastern Front)
25/26.11.43	Hptm von Bonin	II/NJG 1	5
3/4.12.43	Hptm Szameitat	II/NJG 3	5
20/21.12.43	Hptm Herget	I/NJG 4	8
1/2.1.44	Maj Prince Sayn-Wittgenstein	NJG 2	6
14/15.1.44	Lt Breukel	II/NJG 2	6
20/21.1.44	Hptm Fellerer	II/NJG 5	5
21/22.1.44	Maj Prince Sayn-Wittgenstein	NJG 2	5
15/16.2.44	Hptm Peters	III/NJG 3	5
19/20.2.44	Fw Frank	II/NJG 3	5
19/20.2.44	Ofw Vinke	IV/NJG 1	5
24/25.2.44	Hptm Zorner	III/NJG 5	5
6/7.3.44	Lt Scheer	I/NJG 100	5 (Eastern Front)
22/23.3.44	Hptm Martin Becker	I/NJG 6	6
30/31.3.44	Hptm Martin Becker	I/NJG 6	7
11/12.4.44	Hptm Bergmann	III/NJG 4	7
3/4.5.44	Hptm Bergmann	III/NJG 4	6
3/4.5.44	Hptm Drewes	III/NJG 1	5
21/22.5.44	Hptm Drewes	III/NJG 1	5
24/25.5.44	Hptm Schnaufer	IV/NJG 1	5
6/7.6.44	Lt Rökker	II/NJG 2	5
7/8.6.44	Hptm Brinkhaus	II/NJG 2	6
21/22.6.44	Hptm Modrow	I/NJG 1	5
5/6.7.44	Oblt Pützkuhl	I/NJG 100	6 (Eastern Front)
18/19.7.44	Fhj-Ofw Altner	III/NJG 5	5
2/3.11.44	Ofw Morlock	I/NJG 1	6
7/8.2.45	Hptm Rath	I/NJG 2	6
21/22.2.45	Lt Bahr	I/NJG 6	7
21/22.2.45	Hptm Hager	II/NJG 1	6

Date	Rank, name	Unit	Victories
21/22.2.45	Lt Rökker	I/NJG 2	6
21/22.2.45	Hptm Schnaufer	NJG 4	7
14/15.3.45	Hptm Becker	I/NJG 6	9 (incl. 3 by radio/radar operator Lt Johannsen)
15/16.3.45	Hptm Rath	I/NJG 2	5
16/17.3.45	Oblt Jung	II/NJG 2	8 (incl. 1 by radio/radar operator Fw Heidenreich)

8. Monthly survey of German night fighter successes over the Reich territory and the occupied areas of Western Europe

Note: Except for figures marked with an asterisk, RAF Bomber Command losses in this survey do not include aircraft shot down while on training, reconnaissance, maritime patrol and minelaying sorties, or on special operations. On the other hand, the listed German night fighter victories do include aircraft belonging to RAF Coastal Command, Fighter Command, 2 TAF and USAAF.

Shot down by night fighters	RAF Bomber Command		
	Sorties	Missing	Written off[1]
1940			
July	8	1,722	40	3
August	4	2,188	52	11
September	9	3,141	65	21
October	12	2,242	27	32
November	4	1,894	50	34
December	5	1,385	37	23
	42	12,572	271	124

1 Aircraft damaged by enemy action that crashed or made crash landings on British territory, or were badly damaged.

Shot down by night fighters		RAF Bomber Command		
		Sorties	Missing	Written off
1941				
January	8	1,030	12	12
February	18	1,617	16	32
March	19	1,728	35	36
April	40	2,249	67*	12
May	41	2,416	42*	14
June	66	3,228	81*	15
July	63	3,243	97*	28
August	67	3,344	128*	45
September	34	2,621	82*	62
October	20	2,501	70*	40
November	32	1,713	94*	21
December	13	1,411	32*	16
	421	27,101	756	333
1942				
January	16	2,216	56	32
February	5	1,162	18	?
March	41	2,224	78	4
April	46	3,725	130	8
May	59	2,702	114	6
June	147	4,801	199	13
July	102	3,914	171	5
August	100	2,454	161*	4
September	86	3,489	190*	6
October	38	2,189	109*	4
November	10	2,067	73	2
December	37	1,758	91*	5
	687	32,701	1,390	89
1943				
January	44	2,556	86	4
February	61	5,030	101	3
March	96	5,174	161	3
April	161	5,571	253	11
May	167	5,130	234	8
June	223	5,816	275	7
July	150	6,170	188	18
August	290	7,807	275	10
September	178	5,513	191	8
October	149	4,638	159	6
November	128	5,208	162	11
December	169	4,123	170	5
	1,816	62,736	2,255	94

Note: During 1943 an additional 158 RAF aircraft were lost on minelaying operations.

Shot down by night fighters	RAF Bomber Command		
	Sorties	Missing	Written off
1944			
January	308	6,278	314	11
February	183	4,263	199	?
March	269	9,032	283	6
April	215	9,873	214	9
May	243	11,353	274	8
June[1]	291	13,592	293	14
July[1]	258	11,500	229	9
August[1]	164	10,013	186	5
September	76	6,428	96	3
October	56	10,193	75	4
November	87	9,589	98	10
December	85	11,239	88	6
	2,235	113,353	2,349	85
1945			
January	117	9,603	121	4
February	185	13,715	164	20
March	194	11,585	168	34
April	33	8,822	51	3
May	–	349	3	?
	529	44,074	507	61

1 Totals for these months include aircraft of RAF Fighter Command, Coastal Command, 2 TAF and USAAF.

9. Confirmed Mosquito kills

According to reliable estimates a total of 50 Mosquito bombers, reconnaissance aircraft and night fighters were shot down by German night fighters. The following provisional list details only those victory claims backed by surviving documentary evidence.

Date	Rank, name	Unit	Type of night fighter
20/21.4.43	Maj Lent	IV/NJG 1	Bf 110G-4
	Oblt Linke	IV/NJG 1	Bf 110
17/18.8.43	Fw Hakenjoos	JG 300	Bf 109G-6
12/13.12.43	Hptm Meurer	I/NJG 1	He 219A-0
13/14.1.44	Oblt Schmidt	8./NJG 1	Bf 110G-4
20/21.4.44	Hptm Zorner	III/NJG 5	Bf 110G-4
6/7.5.44	Oblt Baake	3./NJG 1	He 219A-2
24/25.5.44	Hptm Müller	1./NJGr 10	FW 190A-6
27/28.5.44	Fw Rauer	I/NJG 1	He 219A-2 (2 kills)
10/11.6.44	Hptm Modrow	I/NJG 1	He 219
	Oblt Nabrich	I/NJG 1	He 219
11/12.6.44	Oblt Nabrich	I/NJG 1	He 219
24/25.6.44	Lt Hittler	I/NJG 1	He 219
1/2.7.44	Oblt Finke	I/NJG 1	He 219
7/8.7.44 ,	Oblt Krause	1./NJGr 10	FW 190A-8
10/11.7.44	Maj Karlewski	I/NJG 1	He 219
18/19.7.44	Hptm Strüning	3./NJG 1	He 219
12/13.9.44	Maj Griese	NJG 6	Ju 88G-6
18/19.9.44	Oblt Welter	10./JG 300	FW 190A-8[1]
19/20.9.44	Oblt Welter	10./JG 300	FW 190A-8
27/28.9.44	Oblt Welter	10./JG 300	FW 190A-8
6/7.12.44	Fw Liersch	IV/NJG 6	Ju 88G-6
12/13.12.44	Uffz Scherl	III/NJG 1	Bf 110G-4
17/18.12.44	Oblt Lau	4./NJG 1	Bf 110G-4
18/19.12.44	Hptm Breves	II/NJG 1	Bf 110G-4
22/23.12.44	Lt Möckel	II/NJG 2	Ju 88G-6
2/3.1.45	Oblt Welter	10./NJG 11	Me 262
5/6.1.45	Oblt Welter	10./NJG 11	Me 262
10/11.1.45	Oblt Welter	10./NJG 11	Me 262[2]
2/3.2.45	Ofw Siewert	II/NJG 6	Ju 88G-6
15/16.3.45	Hptm Rökker	I/NJG 2	Ju 88G-6
21/22.3.45	Fw Becker	10./NJG 11	Me 262
23/24.3.45	Fw Becker	10./NJG 11	Me 262[3]
24/25.3.45	Fw Becker	10./NJG 11	Me 262
27/28.3.45	Fw Becker	10./NJG 11	Me 262
30/31.3.45	Fw Becker	10./NJG 11	Me 262
16/17.4.45	Oblt Witzleb	III/NJG 1	Bf 110G-4

1 Welter had seven Mosquito kills credited between 25 July and 4 September while serving with 1./NJGr 10.
2 Welter shot down a total of 35 Mosquitoes.
3 Two kills within three minutes.

10. Major German airborne electronic systems

1. *Communications*

FuG 10P Long and short wave transceiver, used for both R/T and W/T communications. Frequency range 300–600 kHz (1,000–500 m) and 3–6 MHz (100–50 m). Weight 100 kg (220 lb). Fixed braced wire aerial between the fuselage and fin, or retractable trailing wire. The FuG 10P differed from earlier versions in having the standard E 10L long-wave receiver replaced by the EZ6 unit for the G6 direction-finder set. Manufactured by Lorenz.

FuG 16ZY VHF transceiver, used for both R/T and W/T communications, and as fighter control- and homing device in combination with the FuG 10P. Frequency range 38.5–42.3 MHz (7.7–7.1 m). Aerial: loop or oblique wire to the FuG 10P aerial. Remotely controlled, the FuG 16ZY could select frequencies for Y-control, *Gruppenbefehlswelle* (for comunications between individual aircraft in formation), *Nahsicherung und Flugsicherung* (R/T communications between the pilot and the ground), and the *Reichsjägerwelle* ('Fighter Waveband' running commentary). Manufactured by Lorenz.

2. *Guidance*

FuG 120 Bernhardine Ground to air communications. A radio beacon signal receiver combined with the EBl 3 (part of the standard FuBl 2 blind landing receiver) and reacting to transmissions from *Bernhard* ground stations. The received information (bearing of the ground station and running commentary on the air situation) was recorded in code on a strip of paper by the attached teleprinter unit. The device operated in code on a strip of paper by the attached teleprinter unit. The device operated in the 30–33.3 MHz frequency band. Range 400 km (248 mls) at 5,000 m (16,400 ft) altitude. Accuracy of reading: 0.5°. Developed and manufactured by Siemens.

FuG 135 Uhu Data transmission device combined with the FuG 16 and designed to communicate three values – the course, altitude and distance of the enemy bomber formations, for instance – from the ground site to the fighter. These figures were shown simultaneously on a triple visual display. The course data could also be switched into the aircraft's automatic flight control system. Mention of the codeword *Papagei* (Parrot) either enciphered or deciphered the spoken message from the JLO (Fighter Control Officer). Operated in the 38.5–42.3 MHz frequency band. Developed and manufactured by Siemens.

3. *Navigation and Homing*

Peilgerät (PeilG) 6 Ludwig Long and medium wave direction finding set and homing device. Frequency range 150–1,200 kHz. The effectiveness of this set was improved by adding the APZ6 or PPA2 automatic direction finding devices. D/F loop fitted into a dorsal fuselage flush mounting; auxiliary whip aerial built into the FuG 10 radio mast. Manufactured by Telefunken.

FuG 10ZY This radio set featured a fixed R/D loop and a supplementary homing device for navigation to a ground station.

FuG 120 Bernhardine Described in guidance section.

FuG 125 Hermine VHF radio beacon signal receiver for single-engined single-seat night fighters. Frequency range 30–33.3 MHz; range via earphones 200 km (125 mls); weight 10 kg (22 lb). Manufactured in small series by Lorenz (?) in 1945.

Naxburg Ground installation designed to track and give bearings on emissions from H2S navigational radar. Consisted of modified *Würzburg* aerial dish combined with the FuG 350Z *Naxos* homer. Range: 160–256 km (100–159 mls).

4. *Radio altimeters*

FuG 101 Precision radio altimeter for twin-engined aircraft. Frequency 375 MHz; power output 1.5 kW. Measuring range 150–170 m (490–560 ft); measuring accuracy 2 m (6.56 ft); weight 16 kg (35.3 lb). Aerials fitted under wings. Developed and manufactured by Siemens/LGW.

5. *Search*

Spanner I–IV Infra-red search systems. *Spanner I* active, with an IR searchlight, lens and sighting screen; *Spanner II–IV* passive homing devices, with lens and sighting screen. Developed by AEG and built in small series.

FuG 280 Kiel Z Passive IR search device. Comprised a lead sulphide selenium cell with amplifier, indicator and cathode ray screen. Range 4 km (2.5 mls); weight 42 kg (92.6 lb). Developed by Zeiss and built in small numbers for trials.

FuG 202 Lichtenstein BC AI radar. Frequency 490 MHz; output1.5 kW. Range 3,500–200 m (11,480–656 ft); search angle 70°; weight 24 kg (53 lb). Evolved from *Lichtenstein B* coarse high altitude radio altimeter developed in 1939. Operational trials in August 1941; built in series 1942–43. This device had a direct receiver comprising an oscillating autodyne with a six-stage sound bandwidth amplifier. Featured four nose aerials, each consisting of four dipoles with reflectors, acting together through a switching unit for transmission or reception. Three display screens indicating range, azimuth and elevation. Developed and built by Telefunken.

FuG 202 Lichtenstein BC/S AI radar. An experimental system with additional side aerials on the wings to achieve a search angle of 120°.

FuG 214 Lichtenstein BC/R An experimental tail-warning radar; development discontinued in favour of FuG 216.

FuG 212 Lichtenstein C-1 AI radar. Successor to FuG 202 *BC*; same performance as earlier model but redesigned mechanically to reduce weight to only 60 kg (132 lb), incl. aerial. From August 1943 the receiver could be switched to any frequency within the 420–480 MHz range. Display changed to two cathode ray indicators as standard. Aerials as for FuG 202 *BC*. Developed and built by Telefunken; in production June–November 1943.

Lichtenstein C-1 Weitwinkel ('Wide angle') Used in conjunction with FuG 220 *SN-2b* to overcome the latter's poor close range reception. Single pole aerial. Search angle 120°; range 2 km (1.25 mls).

FuG 212/2 Lichtenstein C22   AI radar. An experimental development with minimum range reduced to 150 m (490 ft). Development discontinued in favour of FuG 220 *SN-2*.

Fu220 Lichtenstein SN-2   AI radar, developed from FuG 213 *Lichtenstein S* ASV radar. Frequency range 73/82/91 MHz, later expanded to operate over 37.5–118 MHz, the so-called 'dispersal wave band'. Power output 2.5 kW; range 4 km–300 (500) m (2.5 mls–984 (1,640 ft). Search angle: azimuth 120°, elevation 100°; weight 70 kg (154 lb). Featured superheterodyne receiver; transmitter and receiver connected together to the aerials via a deflector and phasing unit. Two cathode ray indicators. Developed by Telefunken; in large scale production from September 1943.

Variants: FuG 220 *SN-2a*   Wing-mounted aerials. Experimental only

              FuG 220 *SN-2b*   With Lichtenstein C-1 wide-angle central attachment

              FuG 220 *SN-2c*   Without C-1 wide-angle attachment

              FuG 220 *SN-2d*   Dipoles arranged diagonally (45°) to improve performance under *Window* jamming by narrowing the beam width. Combined with additional tail-warning aerial.

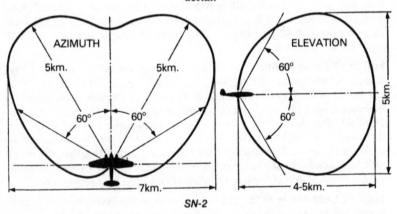

SN-2

FuG 228 Lichtenstein SN-3   Long-range AI radar. Frequency range 115–148 MHz; power output 20 kW. Range 8,000–250 m (5 mls–820 ft). Search angle: azimuth 120°, elevation 100°; weight 95 kg (209 lb). Aerial similar to that of *SN-2c* but with thicker forward dipoles. Later experimentally fitted with *Morgenstern* array with ¼ and ½-wavelength aerials. Developed and manufactured by Telefunken. Total of 10 sets completed and delivered for trials; no details of operational use available.

FuG 216 Neptun   Family of radars developed and manufactured by FFO.

FuG 216 Neptun R-1   Tail-warning set. Frequency 182 MHz; power output 1 kW. Transmitter and receiver each comprised four aerial rods fitted above and below the wings. One cathode ray indicator showing range only.

FuG 216 Neptun V AI radar for single-seat single-engined night fighters. Frequency 125 MHz; power output 1.2 kW. Range 3.5 km–500 m (2.2 mls–1,640 ft); search angle 100° (?). Aerials: rods or 'Stag antlers' (dipoles and supports) on the port and starboard wings of FW 190 fighters only. One display showing elevation, range and azimuth deviation. Experimental only, for proof-of-concept trials.

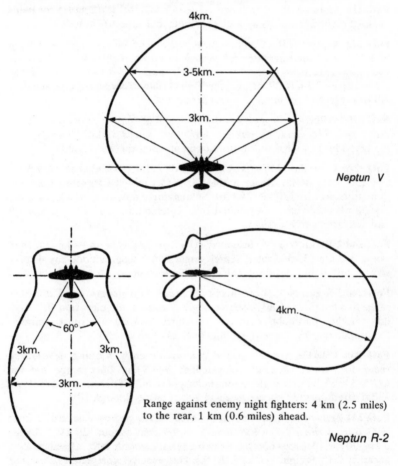

Neptun V

Neptun R-2

Range against enemy night fighters: 4 km (2.5 miles) to the rear, 1 km (0.6 miles) ahead.

FuG 217 Neptun A family of radars developed and manufactured by FFO.

FuG 217 Neptun R-2 Tail-warning set. Weight 27 kg (59.5 lb).

FuG 217 Neptun J-2 AI search device for single-seat single-engined night fighters. Weight 27 kg (59.5 lb).

FuG 217 Neptun V/R Combined AI and tail-warning set for twin-engined night fighters. Two click-stop frequencies of 158 and 187 MHz. Search angle 120°; weight 35 kg (77 lb); range 4 km–400 m (2.5 mls–1,310 ft). Rod or 'Stag antler' aerials.

249

FuG 218 Neptun   A family of radars developed jointly by Siemens/FFO and manufactured by Siemens.

FuG 218 Neptun R-3   Tail-warning set; rod aerials.

FuG 218 Neptun J-3   AI search device for single-seat single-engined night fighters. Rod aerials.

FuG 218 Neptun V/R   Combined AI search and tail-warning set for twin-engined night fighters. 'Stag antler' (dipole and support) aerials.

FuG 218 Neptun G/R   Combined AI search and tail-warning set with a 30 kW transmitter, later intended to have an output of 100 kW. Choice of six click-stop frequencies in the 158–187 MHz range. Search angle 120°; range 5 km–120 m (3.1 mls–394 ft); weight 50 kg (110 lb). 'Stag antler' type aerials. All of these systems entered series production.

FuG 219 Weilheim   Progressive development of *Neptun* series. Frequency range 172–188 MHz; output 100 kW. Max range 15 km (9.4 mls) (?). Designed by Siemens; still in development when the war ended.

FuG 240/1 Berlin N-1a   Centimetric AI radar. Wavelength 9–9.3 cm (=3,250–3,330 MHz). Range 5 km–300 m (3.1 mls–984 ft) without altitude limitation; weight 180 kg (397 lb). Search angle 55°; two circular cathode ray display screens. Developed by Telefunken; 10 sets completed and delivered early in 1945.

FuG 240/2 Berlin N-2   Centimetric AI radar. Wavelength 9–9.3 cm. Max range 6–8 km (3.75–5 mls); search angle 55°. Single cathode ray display screen. Still under development when the war ended.

FuG 240/3 Berlin N-3   Centimetric AI radar. Wavelength 9–9.3 cm. Max range 6–8 km (3.75–5 mls). Search angles: azimuth 90°, elevation 20°. Aerial: rotating parabolic reflector searching forward air space spirally. Panoramic display. Developed into FuG 244.

FuG 240/4 Berlin N-4   Projected centimetric early warning/surveillance radar for contact aircraft. Wavelength 9–9.3 cm. Max range 6–8 km (3.75–5 mls). Search angle: upper hemisphere only. Dielectric rod radiator aerial fitted dorsally on the fuselage and rotating through 180°.

FuG 244 Bremen 0   Centrimetric AI radar developed by Telefunken from FuG 240 *Berlin N-3*. Wavelength 9–9.3 cm; output 20 kW. Range 5 km–200 m (3.1 mls–656 ft). Search angles: azimuth 100°, elevation 20°; accuracy ±1°. Weight 100 kg (220 lb). One example completed before the end of the war.

FuG 245 Bremen   Centimetric AI radar developed by Telefunken; planned successor to FuG 244. One laboratory set completed and tested before the end of the war.

6. *Blind firing and weapon triggering systems*

FuG? Lichtenstein 0   Designed to fire *Schräge Musik* night fighter guns. Frequency 490 MHz (?). Aerials as *Lichtenstein BC*, fitted parallel to the oblique guns above the fuselage. One example tested in 1943.

FuG 215 Pauke A   Could be used on six click-stop frequencies in the 410–490 MHz range. Aerials: initially similar to those of the *Lichtenstein C-1* wide-angle device, but with thicker broad band dipoles; later a 70 cm (27.5 in) diameter parabolic reflector under a plywood covering in the fuselage nose. Developed by Telefunken; ten sets built for proof-of-concept trials. All *Pauke* sets offered automatic range control and featured a display screen and an electric sight.

FuG 222 Pauke S   Automatic gun ranging and blind firing device. Wavelength 9–9.3 cm; range 10 km–300 m (6.25 mls–984 ft); search angle: azimuth 100°, elevation 20°; accuracy ±1°; weight 220 kg (485 lb). Display: as PPI (plan position indicator) for azimuth and elevation, and gun sighting display with target selection. Developed by Telefunken; three sets built for proof-of-concept trials.

FuG 247 Bremerhaven (ex-**Pauke SD**)   Automatic gun ranging and blind firing device. Wavelength 3 cm; max range 10 km (6.25 mls); search angle 120°; accuracy ±2°; weight 120 kg (264.5 lb). Rotating parabolic reflector that searched through a 120° cone-shaped field ahead of the aircraft. Quasi-optical display on a cathode ray tube screen, plus a range finder. Projected, probably under development at Telefunken.

EG 3 Elfe 3   Automatic weapon firing device intended for use in combination with the FuG 216–219 and FuG 248 (q.v.). Developed and manufactured by FFO. Designed to hold the echo of the transmitted impulse at the 3 km mark on the display screen. When the target echo reached this impulse the contact was transferred via a tracking circuit to a second, preset mark (at 500 m for example) and the guns were fired automatically. Developed and manufactured by FFO.

FuG 248 Eule   Blind firing device. Frequency 10,000 MHz; range 2 km (1.25 mls). Provided automatic range measurement via *Elfe* in the EZ 42 gyro gunsight. Used funnel-shaped aerials built into the wings. Developed and manufactured by Telefunken.

7. *Airborne passive homers*

FuG 221 Freya-Halbe   Designed to detect and home onto emissions from *Freya*-jamming aircraft. Reception in the 115–135 MHz band; range 100 km (62.1 mls). Aerials: rod-shaded dipoles above and below the wings. Developed by Siemens and built in small series.

FuG 221a Rosendaal-Halbe   Detection of and homing onto emissions from aircraft equipped with ASV radar, and *Monica*, *Rosendaal* and *Magic Box* tail-warning radars. Reception in the 190–230 MHz band; range 100 km (62.1 mls). Developed by Siemens and built in experimental series only.

FuG 227 Flensburg   Detection of and homing onto emissions of *Monica* tail warning radar (version 1) or various jamming transmitters (versions 2 and 3). Reception in the 80–230 MHz band; range 100 km (62.1 mls). Wing-mounted dipole aerials with supports. Developed by Siemens; total of 250 sets built.

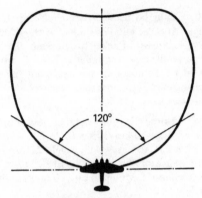

FuG 227 *Flensburg*

FuG 350 Naxos Z Detection of and homing onto emissions from aircraft carrying the H2S target-approach and navigation radar. Reception in the 2,500–3,750 MHz band; range 50 km (31 mls). Rotating and dielectric rod aerial fitted dorsally on the fuselage or in nose radome on *Berlin* and *Morgenstern* equipped aircraft. Provided azimuth measurement only. Evolved by Telefunken and developed into 25 different variants, of which the following deserve special mention:

Naxos Zc	Provided intensified blip on the display screen
Naxos Zr	Combined with tail-warning device (on Ju 88 only); aerial in the fuselage tail
Naxos ZX	Expanded reception band to detect emissions in the 9 cm and 3 cm ranges
Naxos RX	As *ZX* but coupled with tail-warning device
Naxos ZD	Combination of Z and *ZX*; test sets only.

A total of some 700 *Naxos Z* and *ZR* sets were used operationally.

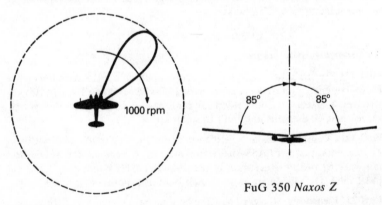

FuG 350 *Naxos Z*

FuG 351 Korfu Z Detection of and homing onto emissions from 9 cm and 3 cm radars. Significantly more sensitive than *Naxos* series. Max range 300 km (186 mls). A number of experimental sets saw operational service.

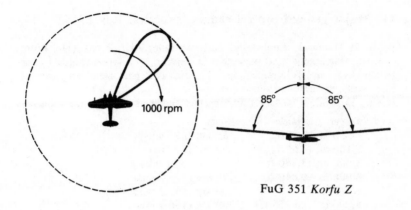

FuG 351 *Korfu Z*

8. IFF (Identification Friend/Foe)

FuG 25a Erstling Reception frequency 125 ±1.8 MHz (output 8 kW); transmitting frequency 160 MHz (output 1.5 kW). Responded to *Freya*, *Würzburg* and *Gemse* ground control radars by transmitting identifying impulses. Range 100 km (62 mls). Built in large quantities by GEMA, Brinkler and other firms.

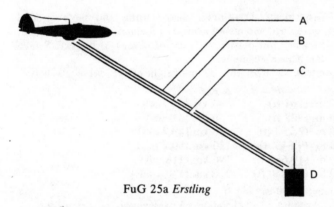

FuG 25a *Erstling*

A   Ground radar position indicator wavelength
B   IFF interrogation wavelength *(Kuh-Welle)*
C   Response wavelength *(Gemse-Welle)*
D   Ground radar device with *Kuh/Gemse* or *Kuckuck* facilities

FuG 226 Neuling Ground-to-air and air-to-air IFF, and flight control. Triggered by standard ground control radars. Developed and manufactured by Lorenz. Large-scale production started but only a few prototype sets were used operationally.

11. Major ground control radars (situation July 1944)

FuMo 51 Mammut Long-range early warning radar. Fixed installation; controls, instruments and personnel in bunker. Developed jointly by *Ln VersuchsKdo* and Telefunken. Search radius 100° (the signal was scanned electrically, the antenna remaining fixed).

Range: Dependent on target altitude and height of site, average values:

Target	altitude	Range
50 m	(164 ft)	35 km (21.7 mls)
100 m	(328 ft)	50 km (31 mls)
1,000 m	(3,280 ft)	100 km (62.1 mls)
3,000 m	(9,840 ft)	170 km (105.6 mls)
6,000 m	(19,685 ft)	250 km (155.2 mls)
8,000 m	(26,250 ft)	300 km (186.3 mls)

Range accuracy: ±300 m (984 ft)
D/F accuracy: Azimuth ±0.5°; no elevation
Weight: 25,000 kg (55,115 lb)
Dimensions: Height 10 m (32 ft 9½ in); width 30 m (98 ft 5 in)
Anti-jamming provisions: Broad variable wavelengths ('dispersal wavebands') only; no provision for alternate frequencies
IFF capabilities: None
Remarks: Development of *Freya*. Purely naval radar first evolved for ship observation. Later used against aircraft.

FuMG 402 Wassermann Long-range early warning and fighter ground control radar, developed and manufactured by Siemens. Fixed installation; controls, instruments and personnel (crew of seven) in bunker. Search radius: 360°, mechanical scanning.

Range: Dependent on target altitude and height of site, average values:

Target	altitude	Range
50 m	(164 ft)	35 km (21.7 mls)
100 m	(328 ft)	50 km (31 mls)
1,000 m	(3,280 ft)	80 km (49.7 mls)
3,000 m	(9,840 ft)	130 km (80.7 mls)
6,000 m	(19,685 ft)	190 km (118 mls)
8,000 m	(26,250 ft)	210 km (130.4 mls)

Range accuracy: ±300 m (984 ft)
D/F accuracy: Azimuth ±¼°; elevation ±¾° (elevation measurement possible only within a 3°–18° arc above the horizon)
Acquisition altitude: Probably up to 12,000 m (39,370 ft)[1]
Weight: 30,000–60,000 kg (66,140–132,280 lb) depending on aerial arrangement
Dimensions: Height of aerial mast 37–57 m (121 ft 4 in–186 ft 11½ in); width of mast 6–12.4 m (19 ft 8¼ in–40 ft 8¼ in), depending on aerial arrangement
Anti-jamming provisions: Continuous frequency changes within 1.9–2.5 m, 1.2–1.9 m and 2.4–4.0 m ranges
IFF capability: Responded to FuG 25a *Erstling*.

FuMG 80 Freya Mobile and motorised air search and fighter ground control radar manufactured by GEMA.

Search radius: 360°, mechanical scanning.
Range: Dependent on target altitude and height of site, average values:

Target altitude		Range
50 m	(164 ft)	20 km (12.4 mls)
100 m	(328 ft)	30 km (18.6 mls)
1,000 m	(3,280 ft)	60 km (37.3 mls)
3,000 m	(9,840 ft)	100 km (62.1 mls)
8,000 m	(26,250 ft)	120 km (74.5 mls)[2]

Range accuracy: ±150 m (490 ft)
D/F accuracy: Azimuth ± 0.5°; no elevation
Weight: 6,200–6,500 kg (13,700–14,330 lb)
Dimensions: Height 8–10 m (26 ft 3 in–32 ft 9½ in), depending on aerial used; width 6 m (19 ft 8¼ in)
Anti-jamming provisions: Broad variable wavelength in the 1.80–4.80 m range (the so-called *Köthenwellen*)[3] and 1.50–1.80 m range (D-band), and the A, B and C-bands with limited alternate wavelengths: A-band 2.32–2.48 m; B-band 2.08–2.24 m and C-band 3.00–3.30 m. Full *Wismar*[4] wavebands: I   1.9–2.5 m production/service
                      II   1.2–1.9 m in preparation
                      III   2.5–4.0 m in preparation
Resistance to *Window*: Fitted with *Freya-Laus* device
IFF capability: All later models responded to FuG 25a *Erstling*; some older sets were retrospectively modified.

FuMG 401 Freya Fahrstuhl Air search and height finding radar developed jointly by GEMA and *Ln Versuchs Rgt*. Fixed installation. Search radius: 360°, mechanical scanning.
Range: Dependent on target altitude and height of site, average values:

Target altitude		Range
2,000 m	(6,560 ft)	65 km (40.4 mls)
6,000 m	(19,685 ft)	160 km (99.4 mls)
8,000 m	(26,250 ft	185 km (114.9 mls)
10,000 m	(32,810 ft)	230 km (142.8 mls)

Range accuracy: ±200 m (656 ft)
D/F accuracy: Azimuth 1.5–2°; elevation between ±50 m and ±1,000 m (164 ft–3,280 ft), depending on target altitude and distance
Weight: 17,000 kg (37,480 lb)
Anti-jamming provisions: Two broad variable wavelengths (1.80 m and 2.80 m).
IFF capacity: None.

FuMG 404 Jagdschloss Panoramic early warning radar manufactured jointly by GEMA, Siemens and Lorenz. Fixed installation. Search radius: 360°; automatic rotation of aerial at 10 rpm.
Range: Dependent on target altitude and height of site, average values:

Target altitude	Range
100 m (328 ft)	15 km (9.3 mls)
1,000 m (3,280 ft)	50 km (31 mls)
3,000 m (9,840 ft)	80 km (49.7 mls)
6,000 m (19,685 ft)	120 km (74.5 mls)
8,000 m (26,250 ft)	120 km (74.5 mls)[5]

Weight: 25,000–30,000 kg (55,115–66,140 lb)
Dimensions: Width of aerial 24 m (78 ft 8½ in); height of aerial 5 m (16 ft 5 in); total height of installation 12 m (39 ft 4¼ in)
Anti-jamming provisions: Continuous alternate wavelengths in 1.9–2.2 m and 1.2–1.9 m bands
IFF capability: Intended, but not yet available (July 1944 Tr.).

FuG 65 Würzburg-Riese Fighter ground control radar and height-finding system for air warning radars. Fixed installation and rail-mounted. Developed by Telefunken.
Search capabilities: Azimuth 360°, elevation from −5° to +95°; mechanical scanning.
Range: 80 km (49.7 mls) in search mode; 50–60 km (31–37.3 mls) in direction-finding mode.
Range accuracy: ±100 m (328 ft); D/F accuracy: Azimuth ±0.2°, elevation ±4–16°.
Weight: 15,000 kg (33,070 lb)
Dimensions: Height 7.9 m (25 ft 11 in); width 7.5 m (24 ft 7 in)
Anti-jamming provisions: As on *Würzburg D*
IFF capability: None.

---

[1] Was still under test in July 1944 when this report was prepared.
[2] Provided only incomplete acquisition of targets above 5,000 m (16,400 ft) altitude.
[3] Named after Köthen in Thuringia, garrison town of the Experimental Signals Rgt. The set transmitted and received simultaneously on several wavebands, receiving on both jammed and clear frequencies, the crew switching over to the best waveband.
[4] An anti-*Window* device. The appliances then under preparation were intended to completely eliminate *Window* jamming on selected wavebands.
[5] Provided only incomplete acquisition of targets above 5,000 m (16,400 ft) altitude.

12. Luftwaffe night fighters: technical data

Aircraft types used operationally or projected for this role.

Notes: The engine power listed is take-off power without flame dampers at sea level. The permissible continuous power at operational altitude was on average about 20 per cent lower. The maximum speed – unless marked with an asterisk – is that quoted by the manufacturer. In such cases it applies to aircraft flying at 75 per cent of their permissible equipped weight, without flame dampers, external loads, radar aerials and oblique armament, and with engines at their permissible combat and emergency power for a maximum of 1–2 mins. The drag caused by typical night fighter equipment would reduce maximum speed by at least 10 per cent, while the continuous speed actually achieved was about 78–80 per cent of the manufacturer's figure. Long bursts of fire from heavy automatic weapons could reduce the speed briefly by about 70 km/h (43.5 mph). Speed data marked with an asterisk relate to performances achieved by these night fighters when flown at the Rechlin Test Centre or by operational units. F/E stands for flight endurance.

This table does not cover the He 219, Ju 88C-6 and Bf 110 when fitted with various *Rüstsätze* (Standard Equipment sets) because the operational aircraft differed quite appreciably from the factory standard. The following are two such aircraft that do not fit into any of the published type lists:

He 219A-0 coded G9 + LP of 6./NJG 1, flown by *Oblt* Hager, June 1944 Crew: 3; armament: 4 × MG 151 in ventral tray, 2 × MG 151 in wing roots, 2 × MG FF/M in oblique installation. FuG 220 *SN-2* AI radar.

Bf 110G-4 coded C9 + EN of II/NJG 5, flown by *Oblt* Johnen, April 1944 Crew 3; armament: 2 × MG 151 in fuselage nose, 2 × MG FF/M in oblique installation; no defensive machine gun. FuG 220 *SN-2* plus FuG 212 'Wide-angle' AI radars; no FuG 350 *Naxos*. Two long-range fuel tanks; no GM-1 installation.

Likewise, this table does not contain information on detail differences within a production series. The letter/figure designations – Bf 110C-1 to C-4, for instance – indicate differences not noticeable on photographs, such as instrumentation changes, strengthened undercarriage, or modified or new radio equipment.

Type	Service unit(s), period	Engine, power	Attack armament	Max speed at altitude	Time to altitude	Range	Ceiling	Remarks
Arado Ar 68E	10./JG 53 autumn 1939	1 × 640 hp Jumo 210D	2 × MG 17	335 km/h at 2,650 m (208 mph at 9,695 ft)	–	414 km (257 mls)	8,100 m (26,575 ft)	
Ar 234B-2	Kdo Bonow Mar-Apr 1945	2 × 900 kg (1,980 lb) Jumo 004B	2 × MG 151 in weapon containers	760 km/h at 6,000 m (472 mph at 19,685 ft)	7,800 m (25,590 ft) 20 min	1,900 km (1,181 mls)	11,500 m (37,730 ft)	2 crew; FuG 218
Ar 234C-3N *Nachtigall*	E-Stelle Oranienburg	4 × 800 kg (1,764 lb) BMW 003A	2 × MG 151 2 × MK 108	880 km/h at 6,000 m (546 mph at 19,685 ft)	1,000 m (3,280 ft) 16.7 min	1,215 km (755 mls)	11,000 m (36,090 ft)	2 crew
Ar 234C-7	Project	2 × 1,300 kg (2,866 lb) HeS 011	1 × MG 151 2 × MK 108 + R4M rockets	–	–	–	–	2 crew
Ar 234P-1, -2	Projects	4 × 800 kg (1,764 lb) BMW 003A	1 × MG 151 2 × MK 108	850 km/h at 6,000 m (528 mph at 19,685 ft)	–	–	–	2 crew
Ar 234P-3	Project	2 × 1,300 kg (2,866 lb) HeS 011	as above	820 km/h at 6,000 m (510 mph at 19,685 ft)	–	–	–	2 crew
Ar 234P-4	Project	2 × 900 kg (1,980 lb) Jumo 004B	2 × MG 151 2 × MK 108	710 km/h at 6,000 m (441 mph at 19,685 ft)	–	–	–	2 crew

Type	Status/Unit	Engine	Armament	Speed	Climb	Range	Ceiling	Remarks
Ar 234P-5	Project	4 × 800 kg (1,764 lb) BMW 003A	2 × MG 151 + 2 × MK 108 oblique	–	–	–	–	2 crew
Ar NJ-I	Project	2 × 1,300 kg (2,870 lb) HeS 011	4 × MG 213 (2 rearwards) + 2 × MK 108 oblique; 1,000 kg (2,205 lb) bombs optional	810 km/h at 9,000 m (503 mph at 29,530 ft)	–	–	12,660 m (41,300 ft)	Delta wings; centimetric AI radar; 3-man crew in pressurised cockpit
Ar NJ-II	Project	as above	as above	775 km/h at 7,000 m (480 mph at 22,960 ft)	–	–	11,450 m (37,400 ft)	Swept-back wings; other details as above
Dornier Do 17P-1	NNJSchw.Lfl 1 Jan 1943	2 × 865 hp BMW 132N	3 × MG 151	400 km/h at 4,000 m (248 mph at 13,123 ft)	–	–	–	One only, presumably with additional armament
Do 17Z-2	NNJSchwärme autumn–winter 1942–43	2 × 1,000 hp Bramo 323P	4 × MG 15	410 km/h (255 mph)	1,000 m (3,280 ft) 3.3 min	2,000 km (1,243 mls)	–	Presumably with additional armament
Do 17Z-7 *Kauz I*	II/NJG 1 and I/NJG 1 summer 1940–winter 1941	as above	1 × MG FF 3 × MG 17	420 km/h at 4,000 m (261 mph at 13,123 ft)	–	2,000 km (1,243 mls)	8,000 m (26,246 ft)	Believed only 2 built, one with searchlight, one with *Spanner* IR installation in the fuselage nose
Do 17Z-10 *Kauz 2*	II/NJG 1, I and II/Erg./ NJG 2, NJG 101, TVK Werneuchen, 1940–43	as above	4 × MG 17 2 × MG 151	420 km/h at 5,900 m (261 mph at 19,357 ft); 350 km/h (218 mph) continuous	–	2,000 km (1,243 mls)	8,000 m (26,246 ft)	9 built, some with *Spanner* IR installation, others with FuG 202

Type	Service unit(s), period	Engine, power	Attack armament	Max speed at altitude	Time to altitude	Range	Ceiling	Remarks
Do 215B-5 *Kauz 3*	I, IV/NJG 1, II/NJG 2 Jan 1941– May 1944	2 × 1,175 hp DB 601Aa	1 × MG FF 4 × MG 17 later: 3 × MG FF 3 × MG 17	500 km/h at 4,800 m (311 mph at 15,748 ft)	–	1,800 km (1,118 mls)	9,000 m (29,527 ft)	First night fighter to be fitted with FuG 202
Do 217J-1	II/NJG 1, II, III, Erg./NJG 2, I, II, IV/NJG 3, I/NJG4. II, IV/NJG 5, NJG 100, 101, 102, TVK Werneuchen	2 × 1,600 hp BMW 801A	4 × MG FF 4 × MG 17 later 2 × MG FF oblique + 8 × 50 kg (110 lb) bombs	455 km/h at 4,200 m (283 mph at 13,780 ft)	1,000 m (3,280 ft) 3.5 min	2,050 km (1,274 mls)	7,200 m (23,620 ft)	Re-equipped to J-2 standard from 1943
Do 217J-2	as J-1	as J-1	as J-1 MG FF later replaced by MG 151; no bombs	as J-1	as J-1	2,100 km (1,305 mls)	7,400 m (24,280 ft)	FuG 202
Do 217N-1	as J-1 Jan 1943– Sept 1944	2 × 1,750 hp DB 603A	4 × MG FF or 4 × MG 17 + 4 × MG FF/M oblique	486 km/h at 6,000 m (302 mph at 19,685 ft)	5,000 m (16,405 ft) 22 min	2,050 m (1,274 mls)	9,000 m (29,530 ft)	FuG 202 or 212
Do 217N-1/U1	as above	as above	MG 151 instead of MG FF; ventral gun position deleted	500 km/h at 6,400 m (311 mph at 21,000 ft)	as above	as above	9,500 m (31,170 ft)	*Rüstsatz* with wooden fairing for better aerodynamics

Do 217N-2	as above from May 1943	as above	as above	as above	6,000 m (19,685 ft) 13 min	2,100 km (1,305 mls)	9,600 m (31,500 ft)	Series production of N-1/U1
Do 335A-6 (V-10)	E-Stelle Deepensee, I/NJG 3	2 × 1,750 hp DB 603A-2	1 × MK 103, 2 × MG 151	688 km/h at 5,500 m (428 mph at 18,045 ft)	–	2,065 km (1,283 mls)	10,100 m (33,140 ft)	
Do 335B-6	Project	2 × 2,000 hp DB 603LA	3 × MK 103	750 km/h (466 mph)	–	–	–	High altitude operations
Do P 256	Project	2 × 1,300 kg (2,866 lb) HeS 011	1 × MK 103, 2 × MG 151	830 km/h (516 mph)	–	1,000 km (621 mls)	–	
Focke-Wulf FW 58C-1,-2	10./ZG 1 winter 1942–43 I/NJG 100 from Jan 1945	2 × 240 hp As 10c	1 × MG 17, 1 × MG 151 oblique	240 km/h (149 mph) at sea level	–	690 km (429 mls)	5,400 m (17,716 ft)	1945 with 'Wide angle' FuG 212
FW 189A-1	I, II/NJG 100, IV/NJG 5 from May 1944	2 × 465 hp As 410A-1	1 × MG 151 oblique	350 km/h at 2,500 m (218 mph at 8,200 ft)	–	940 km (584 mls)	7,000 m (22,970 ft)	'Wide angle' FuG 212
FW 190A-5, -6, -8 FW 190G	III/NJG 1, IV/NJG 3, NNJSchwärme, II/NJG 200, JG 300–302, NJGr 10, NJG 11, TVK Werneuchen, NJKdo FW 190, SKG 10	A-8: 1 × 1,800 hp BMW 801D	2 × MG 131, 4 × MG 151	643 km/h at 8,500 m (400 mph at 27,890 ft)	3,000 m (9,843 ft) 4.5 min	1,520 km (945 mls)	10,300 m (33,790 ft)	*Rüstsatz 11:* FuG 216 or 217 or 218 *Neptun*

Type	Service unit(s) period	Engine, power	Attack armament	Max speed at altitude	Time to altitude	Range	Ceiling	Remarks
Ta 154A-1 *Moskito*	NJGr 10, Stab/NJG 3, Ekdo Ta 154, Erg/JG 2	2 × 1,750 hp Jumo 213A	2 × MK 108 2 × MG 151 + 2 × MK 108 oblique	650 km/h at 9,500 m (404 mph at 31,170 ft)	9,500 m (26,250 ft) 14.5 min	1,370 km (851 mls)	11,000 m (36,090 ft)	
J.P.000.222 004	Project	2 × 2,000 hp Jumo 222+ 2 × 800 kg (1,764 lb) BMW 003	–	–	–	–	–	Swept-back wings; forward-swept tailplane
NJ 1 (FW 272 ?)	Project	1 × 2,000 hp Jumo 222 with pusher propeller + 2 × 800 kg (1,764 lb) BMW 003	4 × MK 108	880 km/h (547 mph)	–	F/E 5 hrs	14,000 m (45,930 ft)	Swept-back wings
Heinkel He 111F, P He 111H-5, -6	NNJSchw Ost winter 1942–43	H-6: 2 × 1,340 hp Jumo 211F	Max 4 × MG FF 2 × WB 81Z	410 km/h at 4,000 m (255 mph at 13,123 ft)	–	1,800 km (1,119 mls)	7,400 m (24,280 ft)	
He 111H-20	NJGr 10, NJG 101, Beh.Bel.St. late 1943	as above	Probably none	–	–	–	–	Training aircraft. Equipped with *SN-2* and *Naxos*. Also used as contact aircraft and illuminators

Type	Units	Engine	Armament	Max speed	Climb	Range	Ceiling	Remarks
He 219A-0, A-2 *Uhu*	I, II/NJG 1, NJSt Finnland/Norwegen, Erg./JG 2	2 × 1,750 hp DB 603A	Basic: 2 × MK 108 4 × MG 151	560 km/h at 5,700 m (348 mph at 18,700 ft)	6,000 m (19,685 ft) 11.5 min	2,100 km (1,305 mls)	9,300 m (30,510 ft)	Armament varied according to *Rüstsatz:* 1) 6 × MG 151 2) 4 × MK 103 + 2 × MG 151 3) 4 × MK 108 + 2 × MG 151 4) 4 × MG 151 + 2 × MK 108 oblique
He 219A-5	I/NJG 1, NJGr 10	2 × 1,800 hp DB 603E	6 × MG 151	585 km/h at 7,400 m* (364 mph at 24,280 ft)	–	2,850 km (1,771 mls)	9,400 m (30,840 ft)	More streamlined, flatter cabin glazing
He 219A-6	as above	2 × 1,750 hp DB 603L	4 × MG 151	615 km/h at 11,000 m (382 mph at 36,090 ft)	–	–	11,400 m (37,400 ft)	Mosquito interceptor
He 219A-7	I/NJG 1	2 × 1,900 hp DB 603G	2 × MK 103+ 2 × MG 151 or 2 × MK 108+ 4 × MG 151	669 km/h at 7,000 m (416 mph at 22,970 ft)	–	2,000 km (1,243 mls)	12,700 m (41,670 ft)	High altitude interceptor Only one in service
He 219B-2	as above	2 × DB 603L with exhaust-driven superchargers	4 × MG 151	640 km/h at 13,000 m (398 mph at 42,650 ft)	–	1,400 km (870 mls)	13,400 m (43,960 ft)	High altitude interceptor with 26.50 m (86 ft 3½ in) wingspan. Only one in service
He 219C-1	Project	2 × 2,500 hp Jumo 222 A/B	4 × MK 108+ 2 × MG 151 oblique	675 km/h at 11,600 m (419 mph at 38,060 ft)	–	1,550 km (963 mls)	12,000 m (39,370 ft)	3-seat interceptor with 4-gun tail turret

Type	Service unit(s). period	Engine, power	Attack armament	Max speed at altitude	Time to altitude	Range	Ceiling	Remarks
He 219D-1	Project	2 × Jumo 213A with MW 50 power boost	4 × MG 151/20+ 2 × MK 108 oblique	660 km/h at 9,450 m (410 mph at 31,000 ft) with MW 50	–	–	–	
He 419V-1	One completed	2 × 1,900 hp DB 603G	2 × MK 108+ 2 × MG 151	679 km/h (422 mph)	–	F/E 2.15 hrs	–	Evolved from A-5. Single fin/rudder assembly, 26.50 m (86 ft 3½ in) wingspan
Junkers Ju 87D-5	I/NJG 100 Aug–Dec 1943	1 × 1,300 hp Jumo 211	2 × MG 151+ 1 × MG 151 oblique	400 km/h at 4,000 m (248.5 mph at 13,123 ft)	–	1,970 km (1,224 mls)	7,500 m (24,610 ft)	Only one in service
Ju 88A-4	NNJSchwarm Lfl 6, I/NJG 7, III/NJG 1, Beh.Bel.St. 1 and 2 winter 1942–43 winter 1943– July 1944	2 × 1,410 hp Jumo 211J	1 × MG 131 1 × MG 81+ (2 × WB 81Z)	472 km/h at 5,300 m (293 mph at 17,390 ft)	5,400 m (17,720 ft) 23 min	2,730 km (1,696 mls)	8,235 m (27,020 ft)	In NNJSchw. service also armed with 1 × MG FF in ventral position
Ju 88C-0, C-1	NJG 2 1940–41	2 × 1,200 hp Jumo 211B/G	2 × MG/FF 2 × MG 17	–	–	–	–	Only a few pattern aircraft (rebuilt Ju 88A-1s)

Type	Units/Service	Engines	Armament	Speed	Climb	Range	Ceiling	Remarks
Ju 88C-2	as above, until 1942	as above	1 × MG FF 3 × MG 17+ 500 kg (1,102 lb) bombs	495 km/h (308 mph)	–	–	–	Total of 62 aircraft (modified Ju 88A-5s); some with dive brakes
Ju 88C-4	NJG 2 1941 to Sep 1944	as above	1 × MG FF 5 × MG 17	as above	–	–	–	Small series built in 1941
Ju 88C-5	NJG 2 until 1944	2 × 1,560 hp BMW 801A	1 × MG FF 3 × MG 17+ 2 × MG 17 in detachable weapon pod	570 km/h (354 mph)	–	–	–	Only a few aircraft completed and entered service
Ju 88C-6	IV/NJG 1, NJG 2, II–IV/NJG 3, I/NJG 4, IV/NJG 6, NJG 100, 101, 102, NJGr 10, TVK Werneuchen, LBeoStaffeln	2 × 1,420 hp Jumo 211J	3 × MG FF 1 × MG 151+ 2 × MG FF 3 × MG 17	455 km/h at 4,500 m (283 mph at 14,765 ft)* Continuous speed with SN-2 + 'Wide angle' + oblique armament	325 m/min (1,070 ft/min)	3,150 km (1,957 mls)	9,000 m (29,530 ft)	First large series, First large series, evolved from A-4. Armament also 4 × MG 151 + 2 × MG 151 oblique
Ju 88R-2	Individual aircraft with C-6 formations autumn 1942 – October 1944, TVK Werneuchen, LBeoStaffeln 1–7	2 × 1,700 hp BMW 801D	as C-6	500 km/h at 6,000 m (311 mph at 19,685 ft)*	–	2,000 km (1,243 mls)	–	Cockpit glazing as C-2 to C-5

Type	Service unit(s), period	Engine, power	Attack armament	Max speed at altitude	Time to altitude	Range	Ceiling	Remarks
Ju 88G-1	III/NJG 1, NJG 2–7, NJGr 10, NJG 100–102, NJ Staffel Norwegen, TVK Werneuchen Jan 1944–May 1945	2 × 1,700 hp BMW 801D	4 × MG 151+ 2 × MG 151 oblique	520 km/h at 6,000 m (323 mph at 19,685 ft)*	–	–	–	Prototype Ju 88V-58 GI + BW first flown June 1943
Ju 88G-6a G-6b	as Ju 88G-1 July 1944 – May 1945	as above	as above	as above	–	Max F/E 5.19 hrs	–	Improved electronic equipment. Built at Dessau; all *Werk Nr* began with 71
Ju 88G-6c	as Ju 88G-1 (except NJG 1), LBeoStaffeln, NJSt Norwegen) from Nov 1944	2 × 1,750 hp Jumo 213	as G-1; on some aircraft oblique guns immediately behind cockpit	540 km/h at 6,000 m (336 mph at 19,685 ft)*	–	F/E 4.48 hrs	10,500 m (34,450 ft)	Built at Bernburg; all *Werk Nr* began with 62
Ju 88G-7	Unknown; presumably only at E-Stellen	2 × 1,750 hp Jumo 213E	–	584 km/h at 9,000 m (363 mph at 29,530 ft)	–	2,220, km (1,380 mls)	9,800 m (32,150 ft)	Only 12, completed in Nov 1944. Pointed wing-tips as on Ju 188/388
Ju 88G-10	Did not reach operational service as interceptor	2 × BMW 801	6 × MG 151	–	–	–	–	Designed as long-range night fighter; used as *Mistel* bomber

				Max speed	Climb	Range	Ceiling	Remarks
Ju 88P-2	TVK Werneuchen, NJGr 10 late 1943	2 × 1,420 hp Jumo 211J	2 × MK 103	–	–	–	–	–
Ju 188R	Project 1943/44	2 × 1,700 hp BMW 801G-2	4 × MG 151 or 2 × MK 103	–	–	–	–	Two mock-ups completed
Ju 388J-1	Only Ju 388V-2 at E-Stelle Rechlin, EKdo 388	2 × 1,890 hp BMW 801TJ	2 × MK 103 2 × MG 151	580 km/h at 12,000 m (360 mph at 39,370 ft)	8,000 m (26,250 ft) 21 min	2,000 km (1,243 mls)	13,000 m (42,650 ft)	4 × MG 131 in tail position
Ju 388J-2	Only Ju 388V-4	as above	as above	as above	–	as above	as above	
Ju 388J-3	Only Ju 388V-5	as above	as above + 2 × MG 151 oblique	as above	–	as above	as above	Without tailgun position
Messerschmitt								
Bf 109E-1	IV(N)/JG 2 autumn–winter 1939–40	1 × 1,100 hp DB 601A	4 × MG 17	570 km/h (354 mph)	–	660 km (410 mls)	10,500 m (34,450 ft)	–
Bf 109E-3	10./NJG 1, Vers. NJ-Staffel Köln, NNJSchwärme Ost late 1940– Feb 1943	1 × 1,100 hp DB 601Aa	1 × MG FF 4 × MG 17	580 km/h (360 mph)	–	–	–	
Bf 109G-5	JG 300, 301, 302 Aug 1943 – early 1944	1 × 1,475 hp DB 605A-1	2 × MG 131 1 × MG 151+ 2 × MG 151 underwing	622 km/h at 6,900 m (386.5 mph 22,640 ft)	5,700 m (18,700 ft) 6 min	984 km (611 mls)	11,550 m (37,890 ft)	

Type	Service unit(s), period	Engine, power	Attack armament	Max speed at altitude	Time to altitude	Range	Ceiling	Remarks
Bf 109G-6	JG 300–302, NJGr 10, NJG 11, III/NJG 4, TVK Werneuchen Aug 1943 – May 1945	1 × 1,800 hp DB 605ASD	as above	640 km/h at 7,100 m (398 mph at 23,290 ft)	6,000 m (19,685 ft) 6 min	990 km (615 mls)	12,100 m (39,700 ft)	
Bf 109G-10	NJGr 10, NJG 11, Aug 1944 – May 1945	1 × 1,800 hp DB 605AS	1 × MK 108 2 × MG 131	688 km/h at 7,300 m (428 mph at 23,950 ft)	9,800 m (32,150 ft) 6.7 min	560 km (348 mls) without aux. fuel tanks	–	
Bf 109G-14	NJG 11 late 1944 – May 1945	as above	as above	640 km/h (398 mph)	–	–	–	
Bf 110C-1, C-2, -4, -6	NJG 1, 3, 4, 101, 102 July 1940 – summer 1943	2 × 1,100 hp DB 601A-1	2 × MG FF 4 × MG 17 from C-5: MG FF/M	540 km/h at 6,890 m (336 mph at 22,605 ft)	–	985 km (612 mls)	9,600 m (31,500 ft)	
Bf 110D-0	NJG 1 summer 1940 – summer 1941	as above	as above	530 km/h (329 mph)	–	–	–	Featured 'Dackelbauch' ('Dachshund belly') ventral fuel tank; strengthened undercarriage
Bf 110D-1, -3	NJG 1, 3–5, 101, 102, NNJSchwärme Ost summer 1940 – April 1943	as above	as above	as above	–	–	–	Rüstsatz U1: Spanner IR device. Underwing aux. fuel tanks

Variant	Units	Engines	Armament	Speed	Climb	Range	Ceiling	Remarks
Bf 110E-1 E-2, E-4	NJG 1-5, 101, 102 NNJSchwärme Ost 1941 – summer 1943	2 × 1,175 hp DB 601Aa or DB 601N	as above	540 km/h (336 mph)	–	–	–	Automatic flight control. Hot water cabin heating
Bf 110F-2	NJG 1-6 summer 1942 – late 1943	2 × 1,300 hp DB 601F	as above	560 km/h (348 mph)	–	1,400 km (870 mls)	–	
Bf 110F-4	NJG 1-6, 101, 102, 200 summer 1942 – spring 1944	as above	2 × MG FF/M or 2 × MG 151 4 × MG 17 *Rüstsätze*: 2 × MK 108 ventrally or oblique	500 km/h at 5,800 m (311 mph at 19,030 ft)*	–	1,600 km (994 mls)	–	First Bf 110-type night fighter built in series. FlaV, FuG 202, FuG 212; 1944 retrofitted with FuG 220 *SN-2*; also operated with 3-man crew
Bf 110G-2	Small numbers with NJG 1, 3-6, 100, 200 from summer 1943	2 × 1,475 hp DB 605A-1	2 × MG FF 2 × MG 151 4 × MG 17+ additional *Rüstsätze*	540 km/h at 8,000 m (336 mph at 26,250 ft)	–	2,000 km (1,243 mls)	–	No night fighting equipment; used on day operations in Western Europe
Bf 110G-4	NJG 1-6, 200, 101, 102, LBeoStaffeln, from summer 1943	2 × 1,475 hp DB 605B-1	2 × MG 151 4 × MG 17 *Rüstsätze*: 2 × MK 108 in ventral tray, 2 × MK 108 2 × MG 151+ 2 × MG 151 in ventral tray; 2 × MK 108 or 2 × MG FF oblique	525 km/h at 7,000 m (326 mph at 22,960 ft; with *R-Sätze* approx 485 km/h (301 mph))	5,400 m (17,720 ft) 7.9 min	2,000 km (1,243 mls)	8,000 m (26,246 ft)	3-man crew; FuG 202, 212, 218, 220 *SN-2*

Type	Service unit(s), period	Engine, power	Attack armament	Max speed at altitude	Time to altitude	Range	Ceiling	Remarks
Me 210	I/NJG 1, Stab 3 JDiv, - LBeoStaffel 1, Hungarian 5/1 Squadron	2 × 1,395 hp DB 601F	2 × MG 151 2 × MG 17	616 km/h (383 mph)	–	2,300 km (1,429 mls)	–	In Reich Air Defence used only as day contact aircraft
Me 410A-1, B-2	LBeoStaffeln 1,7, III/NJG 1, I/NJG 5, EKdo 410, I/KG 51	2 × 1,750 hp DB 603A	Me 410A-1: 4 × MG 151 2 × MG 17 Me 410B-2 6 × MG 151 2 × MG 131	624 km/h at 6,500 m (388 mph at 21,325 ft)	6,500 m (21,325 ft) 10.7 min	–	9,840 m (32,280 ft)	No AI radar fitted
Me 262A-1	One machine with Kdo Welter	2 × 900 kg (1,984 lb) Jumo 004B	4 × MK 108	870 km/h at 6,000 m (541 mph at 19,685 ft)	9,000 m (29,530 ft) 13.2 min	–	–	FuG 218. Single-seater
Me 262B-1a/U1	10./NJG 11	as above	as above	810 km/h at 6,000 m (503 mph at 19,685 ft)	–	–	–	Two-seater. FuG 218, FuG 350
Me 262B-2	One machine with 10./NJG 11	2 × 1,300 kg (2,870 lb) HeS 011	4 × MK 108+ 2 × MK 108 oblique	860 km/h at 6,000 m (534 mph at 19,685 ft)	–	–	–	as above

13. Major powerplants: technical data

Bayerische Motorenwerke AG

BMW 801D	14-cyl air-cooled twin-row radial engine. Capacity 41.8 litres, compression ratio 7.2 : 1. Take-off power 1,700 hp at 2,700 rpm; continuous power 1,440 hp
BMW 003A	Axial-flow turbojet engine. Static thrust 800 kg (1,764 lb) at 9,500 rpm

Daimler Benz AG

DB 601Aa	12-cyl liquid-cooled inverted-vee engine. Capacity 33.9 litres, compression ratio 6.9 : 1. Take-off and emergency power (for 1 min only) 1,175 hp at 2,400 rpm; continuous power at 6,100 m (20,010 ft) altitude 810 hp at 2,200 rpm
DB 601F	Compression ratio 7.2 : 1. Take-off power 1,350 hp at 2,700 rpm; optimum altitude 4,800 m (15,770 ft)
DB 601N	Compression ratio 8.2 : 1. Emergency power at 5,500 m (18,040 ft) altitude 1,190 hp at 2,600 rpm; continuous power at 6,100 m (20,010 ft) altitude 970 hp at 2,400 rpm
DB 603A	12-cyl liquid-cooled inverted-vee engine. Capacity 44.5 litres, compression ratio 7.5 : 1. Take-off and emergency power 1,750 hp at 2,700 rpm; continuous power 1,620 hp at 2,500 rpm
DB 605A	12-cyl liquid-cooled inverted-vee engine. Capacity 35.7 litres, compression ratio 7.5 : 1. Take-off and emergency power 1,475 hp at 2,800 rpm; continuous power 1,355 hp at 2,600 rpm

Junkers Flugmotorenwerke

Jumo 211B	12-cyl liquid-cooled inverted-vee engine. Capacity 34.97 litres, compression ratio 6.5 : 1. Take-off and emergency power 1,200 hp at 2,400 rpm; continuous power at 4,500 m (14,760 ft) altitude 800 hp at 2,100 rpm
Jumo 211J	Take-off and emergency power 1,420 hp at 2,600 rpm; continuous power at 5,000 m (16,400 ft) altitude 960 hp at 2,250 rpm
Jumo 213A	12-cyl liquid-cooled inverted-vee engine. Capacity 34.97 litres, compression ratio 7.2 : 1. Take-off and emergency power 1,740 hp at 3,000 rpm; continuous power at 7,000 m (22,960 ft) altitude 1,200 hp at 2,400 rpm
Jumo 004B	Axial-flow turbojet engine. Static thrust 900 kg (1,980 lb) at 9,000 rpm
Jumo 004E	Static thrust with afterburner 1,300 kg (2,870 kg)

Heinkel-Hirth

HeS 011	Axial-flow turbojet engine. Static thrust 1,300 kg (2,866 lb) at 11,000 rpm

14. Night fighter guns: technical data

Designation	Calibre (mm)	Manufacturer	Length (mm)	Weight (kg/lb)	Rate of fire (rpm)	Muzzle velocity (m-ft/sec)	Weight of shell (g/ozs)	Remarks
MG 17	7.92	Rheinmetall	1,078	10.2 (22.5)	1,180	950 (3,116)	12.8 (0.45)	Fixed weapon
MG 81	7.92	Mauser	890	6.35 (14.0)	1,600	885 (2,903)	–	Flexible defensive weapon; also coupled as MG 81Z
MG FF	20	Oerlikon	1,338	26.3 (58.0)	540	700 (2,296)	134 (4.75)	Already obsolete in 1940 but remained in service as an oblique weapon until 1945
MG 131	13	Rheinmetall	1,168	20.5 (45.2)	930	750 (2,460)	34 (1.2)	Flexible defensive weapon in Do 217, Ju 88, He 219 and Me 410
MG 151/20	20	Mauser	1,710	42.5 (93.7)	800	790 (2,590)	115 (4.09)	Fixed weapon in Bf 110, Ju 88, Do 217 and Me 410
MK 103	30	Rheinmetall	2,318	146 (322)	440	860 (2,820)	530 (18.85)	
MK 108	30	Rheinmetall	1,057	58 (128)	660	520 (1,706)	330 (11.75)	Rate of fire later increased to 850 rpm

15. German night fighter production 1941–1945

Year/Month	Jan	Feb	Mar	Apr	May	June	July	Aug	Sep	Oct	Nov	Dec	Total new constructions	Rebuilds	Total
1941															
Ju 88 incl. *Zerstörer*	12	27	15	3	–	–	–	–	–	–	–	–	66	13	79
Bf 110 incl. *Zerstörer*	50	123	119	83	53	73	29	22	15	15	11	1	594	280	874
1942															
Ju 88 incl. *Zerstörer*	7	12	15	23	26	19	20	16	16	22	35	46	257		
Do 217J	–	–	8	13	35	27	21	12	13	14	4	10	157		
Bf 110 incl. *Zerstörer*	–	4	50	61	35	28	43	63	66	53	73	25	501		
1943															
Ju 88	45	48	49	43	40	43	57	73	66	87	79	76	706		
Do 217J, N	23	30	17	21	20	23	28	20	25	–	–	–	207		
Bf 110	34	27	52	44	46	91	47	28	91	124	114	88	789		
He 219	–	–	–	–	4	–	–	–	7	–	–	–	11		
1944															
Ju 88	30	89	77	165	229	285	276	306	305	255	339	164	2,518		
Bf 110	85	4	67	190	179	116	148	141	187	108	101	61	1,397		
He 219	11	5	11	25	14	16	18	5	27	19	19	25	195		
Ta 154	–	–	–	–	–	4	4	–	–	–	–	–	8		
1945															
Ju 88	278	50	27										355		
Bf 110	37	17	–										54		
He 219	36	9	17										62		
Do 335	1	3	–										4		

16. Inventory of operational night fighters January – September 1944

Type	31 Jan	29 Feb	31 Mar	31 May	31 July	30 Sep
Bf 110G	592	630	576	580	558	574
Do 217J	2	1	–	2	1	–
Do 217N	35	31	34	34	55	54
Ta 154	–	–	–	–	1	1
He 219	12	13	16	54	48	32
Ju 88C-2, -4, -5	4	2	2	2	1	1
Ju 88C-6	323	289	263	229	171	91
Ju 88R-2	16	36	54	79	57	29
Ju 88G-1	3	3	4	176	419	534
Ju 88G-6	–	–	–	–	2	84

17. Radio code words and expressions used by Luftwaffe night fighter crews

Note: These terms were not intended or used for security purposes but rather to avoid misunderstandings. As a result of practical experience some of the words were changed during the course of the war.

German	English	Meaning
Abfahren	Depart	To take off
Abzahlen	Count down	Count down for radio tuning
Anstrahlen, ich bin angestrahlt	Beamed on	My aircraft is damaged by enemy fire
Anton-Nordpol		Interception according to AN-method
Äquator	Equator	In cloud
Alles beim Alten	Everything as before	Weather unchanged
Antreten	Line up/form up to start	Take the shortest course direction (followed by indication)
Autobahn	Motorway	Bearing to the nearest airfield
Autos	Motor vehicles	Twin-engined enemy aircraft
— dicke Autos	Fat motor vehicles	Four-engined enemy aircraft
Bahnhof	Railway station	Base airfield
Bahnsteig	Railway platform	Take-off runway

German	English	Meaning
Berühren	Touch; be in contact with	To be within visual and firing range
Birne	Light bulb	Identification lights
Birseschluss	Stock market closure	Cessation of radio communications
Bürgermeister	Mayor	Barometric pressure over airfield
Büro (gehen Sie ins–)	Go into the office	Go to the radar measurement and reception altitude
Caruso		Course
Christbaum	Christmas tree	Airfield lighting
Christbaum drücken	Depress the Christmas tree	Switch on airfield lighting
Dora-Toni		Bearing to ground radar site
Durst (ich habe –)	I am thirsty	I am short of fuel
Eile	Haste	Own speed
Eisbär	Polar bear	External temperature
Eisenbahn (fahren Sie –)	Go by train	Change over to R/T communications
Emil-Emil		Airborne radar
Endgültig Krähe	Final crow	No enemy aircraft expected, stand down
Ente	Duck	Distance to the target
Es-o-es	SOS ('Save our souls')	I am in distress; emergency
Express		Urgent
Falschmünzer	Counterfeiter;	Enemy decoy transmitter
(achten Sie auf –)	Look out for counterfeiter	Enemy transmitting conflicting orders on Luftwaffe wavelength
Fasan	Pheasant	Expect enemy aircraft
Feierabend	End of workday; start of leisure time	I am abandoning operations and flying home
Feuerzauber	Fire magic	Enemy bomb drop
Fragezeichen	Question mark	Unidentified aircraft
Freude, grosse –	Great joy	Radar information available
Frieda		Lose altitude
(1 × Frieda = 100 m etc.)		
Gardine	Curtain	Fog/mist forming
Gartenzaun	Garden fence	Base airfield
Halten	Hold; stop	Slow down; reduce your airspeed
Hanni	abbr of Hannelore	Altitude (general term)
Haus	House	Dispersal airfield
Heiser (Sie sind –)	You are hoarse	Your tuning/modulation is bad
Indianer	Redskins	Enemy fighters
Kapelle	Chapel	Altitude of target

German	English	Meaning
Karussel	Roundabout, merry-go-round	Fly a circle
„ *Rolf (Lisa)*		Fly a circle to starboard (port)
– *grosses Karussel (Rolf, Lisa)*	Big roundabout	Fly blind-flying circle (starboard, port)
Kino (schön, langweilig)	Picture show (nice, boring)	Visibility (good, bad)
Kirchturm	Church steeple	Own flying altitude
– *gleicher Kirchturm*	Same steeple	At same altitude as the target
Kreis schliessen	Close the circle	Turn into reciprocal course
Kreuzung (erbitte-)	Request intersection	I am in distress; please radio-locate me on the tactical frequency
Küche (gross, klein)	Kitchen (big, small)	Haze (strong, weak)
Kurier	Courier	Target (aircraft)
„ *auf Stube*	Courier in room	Enemy aircraft within ground radar range
Laterne	Lantern	Light beacon
Lisa	abbr of Liselotte	Correct course 10° to port
– *Lisa-Lisa*		Correct course 20° to port
– *Lisa-Lisa-Lisa*		Correct course 30° to port
Lucie-Anton		Landing
Ludwig		Blind curve to port
Marie		Own course
Maskerade	Masquerade	Thunderstorm
Nordpol	North Pole	Above clouds
Orkan	Hurricane	Speed of enemy aircraft
Otto-Otto		Identified target (until about 1941; afterwards *Kurier*)
Pauke-Pauke	Beating the kettledrum	Attack; Tally-Ho!
Paula		Position lights
Pause	Break, intermission	Flight time
Pferd	Horse	Engine
„ *lähmt*	The horse is lame	Engine damage
Postkutsche	Mail coach	Course to target
Quelle	Source; fountain	Position
Rakete	Rocket	Take-off; start
„ *machen*	To rocket	To take-off
Reise, Reise	Travel, travel	Break off operations and fly towards base
Ricardus		Not understood, please repeat
Richard		Blind curve to starboard

German	English	Meaning
Rolf		Correct course 10° to starboard
– Rolf-Rolf		Correct course 20° to starboard
– Rolf-Rolf-Rolf		Correct course 30° to starboard
Rollbahn	Runway, tarmac	Course; bearing
Rübezahl	Turnip count	Transfer from one Y-station to another
Rutsch (kleiner –)	(Small) slide or slip	Belly landing
Salto (Lisa, Rolf)	Somersault	Fly a snap 360° turn (to port, starboard)
Schraube (gross, klein)	Screw (large, small)	Radio beacon (main, secondary)
Seitensprung Lisa (Rolf) 30	Side-jump Lisa (or Rolf) 30	Shift your track to port (starboard) by changing course 10° to port (starboard), flying straight for 10 sec, and then correcting 10° to starboard (port)
Siegheil	Hurray!	Victory (until 1944; thereafter *Horrido*); generally also relating to identified enemy target eg *Siegheil berühren* (touch *Siegheil*) = to be in firing range; *Siegheil machen* (make *Siegheil*) = shoot down an enemy aircraft
Siegfried (3 × *Siegfried* = 300 m etc.)		Climb
Stacheldraht	Barbed wire	Defensive patrol
Stafette	Relay race	Relief aircraft
Stange	Stake, pole	Searchlight
„ *setzen*	Set stake	Switch on searchlight
Stern leuchtet	Star is shining	FuG 25a IFF switched on
Stube	Room, chamber	Standby area, zone
„ *abschliessen*	Lock up the room	Fly towards the standby area (or zone)
Südpol	South Pole	Beneath cloud
tampen	To set sail	To fly direction . . .
taub	Deaf	No reception
Termin	Term, deadline	Fuel supply
tiefe Trauer	Deep sorrow	No radar information
Tuba	Tuba	Request for direction signal for homing flight
untreu werden	Become unfaithful	Go on to air traffic control
Viktor		Understood; 'Roger'

German	English	Meaning
Vorhang	Curtain	Lower and upper cloud ceilings eg *Vorhang 20–30* = Lower cloud ceiling 2,000 m, upper 2,300 m
Vorzimmer	Antechamber, waiting room	Standby zone before landing at base
Welle (aktiv, passiv)	Wave (active, passive)	Radio/radar set (operational, inoperational)
Winter in . . .	Winter at . . .	Icing danger at given altitude
Zigeuner	Gipsy	Low-level attack aircraft; also enemy night fighter
Zucker	Sugar	Aircraft icing

18. German night fighter camouflage and markings

Contrary to the usual view that German night fighters were initially sprayed black only and later light grey, these aircraft displayed an amazing variety of camouflage patterns. In fact from mid-1943 onwards no restrictions seem to have been placed on the inventiveness of operational preparation centre and frontline workshop artists.

Autumn 1939 – spring 1943

1. As the day fighters and *Zerstörer*. Examples are the Bf 109 of IV (N)/JG 2; Bf 110 and Ju 88 of NJG 1 and NJG 2 during the formative period up to autumn 1940.
   Improvised and auxiliary night fighters on the Eastern Front: under-surfaces RLM 65 or 76, upper surfaces RLM 70/71; occasionally uniform RLM 74.
2. Washable night camouflage (black) on the undersurfaces and rear fuselage sides of Ju 88s and Do 17s of NJG 2; also Bf 110s of NJG 1.
3. Dark grey camouflage on the nationality insignia of aircraft used by IV/NJG 5 in Western France early in 1943.
4. Permanent all-over night camouflage; applied in 'cloudy' patterns over the basic colouring of Do 217s. On some Ju 88s of NJG 2 in the Mediterranean area the under parts of engine cowlings and undercarriage doors remained light blue.
5. Late in 1942 some Ju 88s were flown with black undersurfaces and RLM 70/71 segment camouflage on the upper surfaces, with the fuselage sides and engine cowlings sprayed mottled light grey/dark grey.
6. Dispersal/parking area camouflage: washable white winter camouflage on improvised night fighters on the Eastern Front; RLM 79/80 tropical camouflage on some Ju 88s operated by NJG 2.

Markings: The *Geschwader* escutcheon of NJG 1, a diving falcon (based on *Maj* Falck's family coat of arms) was adopted by all NJG. Personal symbols were rare, as shown by the available illustrations. Aircraft used by *NJ-Division* carried a modified variant of the NJG emblem, with lightning streaks replaced by three searchlight beams.

For Operation *Donnerkeil* (Thunderbolt), the Channel dash by the German battleships in 1942, the night fighters were temporarily camouflaged light blue on their undersurfaces and sea green (RLM 72/73) on their upper surfaces, with yellow rear fuselage bands.

The test aircraft flown by TVK Werneuchen had yellow engine undersurfaces and wing tips. Provisional night fighters on the Eastern Front displayed yellow rear fuselage bands, while white rear fuselage bands (applied to the fuselage top and sides only) were carried by aircraft of 1./NJG 3 and NJG 2 in the Mediterranean area.

Spring 1943 – end of the war
1. Camouflage similar to that of the day *Zerstörer* was used on individual aircraft in all Reich Air Defence formations, and widely on provisional night fighters on the Eastern Front, by NJG 100 and NJG 200, and TVK Werneuchen; on Bf 109 and Fw 190 *Wilde Sau* fighters during the early days of JG 300; and on aircraft flown by 1./NJGr 10.
2. Do 217N: undersurfaces RLM 76, upper surfaces RLM 70/71, fuselage sides oversprayed in foggy patterns with RLM 02, 74, 75 and 76.
3. Undersurfaces RLM 76, fuselage sides and upper surfaces with various dots, spots, irregular large patches, and mirror wave patterns in RLM 02, 74 and 75 on RLM 76. The spraying on of various dark grey shades made the basic RLM 76 colouring several shades darker. This camouflage scheme was also used on some single-engined 'Mosquito hunters' of NJGr 10.
4. Undersurfaces and fuselage sides in RLM 76, upper surfaces in RLM 74/75 segment camouflage. This scheme was used predominantly on Bf 110s.
5. White grey on all surfaces was used by *Beh.Beleuchter* (auxiliary illuminators) and Ju 88s of NJG 100.
6. Cadre aircraft of JG 300 and 302, NJG 11: undersurfaces black, upper surfaces and fuselage sides partly uniform RLM 74, partly 'clouded' with RLM 02, 74 and 75.
7. Dispersal area winter camouflage was used by NJG 100 and parts of NJG 101, 102 and NJG 5 based in East Prussia and Silesia.
8. During spring–autumn 1944 a few aircraft had their starboard wing and engine nacelles (except for wing leading edge and tip) painted black. This measure was intended to identify these aircraft for friendly searchlights and Flak.
9. From late 1944 all night fighters earmarked for night attack operations had black fuselage- and wing undersurfaces. Yellow rear fuselage bands were carried by all aircraft operational in the areas controlled by Luftflotten 1, 4, 5 and 6, *Jafü Ungarn* (Fighter Leader Hungary), *Jafü Ostpreussen* Fighter Leader East Prussia) and 8 *J Division* (II and IV/NJG 5, III and IV/NJG 6, NJG 100, 101, 102 and 200; *NJ-Staffel Finnland*).

Yellow markings under the wings and engine cowlings were displayed by test aircraft flown by NJGr 10 and TVK Werneuchen.

279

19. Code markings of night fighter Geschwader, Gruppen and independent Staffeln

B4 +   *NJ-Staffel Finnland;* later *NJ-Staffel Norwegen*
C9 +   NJG 5; also 10. and 12./ZG 1 immediately after formation
      as II/NJG 100
D5 +   NJG 5
D9 +   I/KG 7 and I/NJG 7; occasionally also on some aircraft of
      IV/NJG 2
G9 +   NJG 1; EKdo 410
L1 +   1./NJG 3 until December 1941
R4 +   NJG 2
W7 +   NJG 100
1L +   2./NJGr 10
2Z +   NJG 6
3C +   NJG 4 (from 1 Jan to 3 July 1943 also NJG 5)
4R +   NJG 2
5K +   III (Bel)/KG 3
6V +   NJG 200
7J +   NJG 102
8V +   *NNJSchw Lw Kdo Ost*
9K +   KG 51
9W +   NJG 101

Units using radio callsigns (four-letter combinations) were:
  NNJ-Schwärme of Luftflotten 1, 4 and 6 (close-range night fighter
  sections)
  Luftwaffenkommando Don
  Luftbeobachterstaffeln 1–7 (air observer flights)
  Behelfsbeleuchterstaffeln 1 and 2 (auxiliary illuminator flights)
  Truppenversuchskommando of *E-Stelle* Werneuchen
  2. and 3./NJGr 10

Ordinary fighter identification (numbers) were carried by:
  JG 300, 301 and 302
  1./NJGr 10
  NJG 11

20. Identification markings

The identification markings carried by twin-engined night fighters were generally similar to those used on other multi-engined aircraft: a two-letter combination behind the fuselage cross insignia. The first letter indicated the order of sequence of the individual aircraft within the *Schwarm* or *Staffel*; 'A' was usually reserved for COs of formations (*Commodore*, *Kommandeure* and *Staffelkapitäne*). These letters were different in colour from their background camouflage, or black with coloured edging.

The second letter identified the *Schwarm* or *Staffel* within a *Geschwader*. Although to avoid confusion the letters I, J, O and Q were not used, there were at least three exceptions to this rule: in 1943 the letter 'O' identified 6./NJG 5, and the same letter was also carried by the operational sections (*Einsatzschwärme*) of NJG 101 and 102.

The *Stabsschwärme* and *Staffeln* were identified by the following letters:

A	*Geschwaderstab*	(preceded by a green letter)
B	*Stab* I *Gruppe*	(preceded by a blue letter)
C	*Stab* II *Gruppe*	(preceded by a blue letter)
D	*Stab* III *Gruppe*	(preceded by a blue letter)
E	*Stab* IV *Gruppe*	(preceded by a blue letter)
G	*Stab* V *Gruppe*	(only NJG 5; preceded by a blue letter)

The *Staffeln* within a *Gruppe* were identified by white, red and yellow letters:

I *Gruppe*		II *Gruppe*		III *Gruppe*	
H	1.*Staffel*	M	4.*Staffel*	R	7.*Staffel*
K	2.*Staffel*	N	5.*Staffel*	S	8.*Staffel*
L	3.*Staffel*	P(O)	6.*Staffel*	T	9.*Staffel*

IV *Gruppe*		V *Gruppe*	
U	10.*Staffel*	X	13.*Staffel*
V	11.*Staffel*	Y	14.*Staffel*
W	12.*Staffel*	Z	15.*Staffel*

21. Deployment of Luftwaffe night fighter formations on the Eastern Front

January 1943
Lfl 1/Army Group North: NNJSchw (Siverskaya). LwKdo Ost & LwKdo Don/AG Centre; 12./ZG 1, NNJSchw (Orel, Bryansk); NNJSchw (Poltava). Lfl 4/AG South: 10./ZG 1. No night fighters in Finland (Lfl 5) or under LwKdo Südost.

May 1943
Lfl 1/AG North: No change: No night fighters in Finland (Lfl 5). LwKdo Ost/LwKdo Don: subordinated to Lfl 6; rest of both NNJSchw combined into one. Lfl 4/AG South: One NNJSchw. LwKdo Südost (Romania, Bulgaria, Hungary, Yugoslavia): IV/NJG 6.

July 1943
Lfl 1/AG North: NNJSchw moved to Dno. No night fighters in Finland. Lfl 6/AG Centre: 12./NJG 5 (Bryansk, Orsha, Smolensk, Shatalovka, Sestchinskaya, Orel). Lfl 4/AG South: NNJSchw and 10./NJG 5 (Zilistea, Poltava, Stalino, Dniepropetrovsk). LwKdo Südost: No change.

August 1943
Lfl 1/AG North: NNJSchw reformed as 1./NJG 200 (Dno). No night fighters in Finland. Lfl 6/AG Centre: NNJSchw reformed as 4./NJG 200; 12./NJG 5 as 1./NJG 100. Lfl 4/AG South: NNJSchw and 10./NJG 5 reformed as 5./NJG 200 and 2./NJG 100; new formation 8./NJG 200. LwKdo Südost: No change.

December 1943
Lfl 1/AG North: 1./NJG 200 (Jekabpils/Latvia). No night fighters in Finland. Lfl 6/AG Centre: 3. and 4./NJG 100 (ex-8./NJG 200) (Orsha, Bobruisk, Baranowiczi, St Bykhov). Lfl 4/AG South: 5./NJG 200 (Odessa, Nikolaiev). LwKdo Südost: 2./NJG 100 from Lfl 6 (Bucharest, Buzau, Focsani, Otopeni, Telis, Zilistea).

May–July 1944
Lfl 5/Finland: Det. of I/JG 302; transf. back into Reich. New formation NJ-Staffel Finnland (Helsinki); detachment of 4./NJG 100. Lfl 1/AG North: 4./NJG 100 (Riga); became 2./NJG 100. Op. det. of NJG 102 (Riga, Klaipeda). Lfl 6/AG Centre: 1. and 3./NJG 100 (Bobruisk, Baranwiczi, Pinsk, Bielec). Lfl 4/AG South: 5./NJG 200 disbanded. LwKdo Südost: IV/NJG 6, 4./NJG 100 (ex-2./NJG 100), 5./NJG 100 (ex-1./NJG 200), 6./NJG 100 (ex-4./NJG 200); op. det. NJG 101 (Freihegy, Parndorf); III/NJG 6 from Reich Air Defence.

September–November 1944
Lfl 5/Finland: NJ-St.Finnland transf. to Norway and renamed NJ-St.Norwegen. Lfl 1 and Lfl 6: 1., 2. and 3./NJG 100 (ex-4./NJG 100) (Prowehren, Powunden, Hohensalz, Gr. Schiemanen, Stubendorf, Krakow, Breslau, Oels); op. det. of NJG 102 (Stubendorf, Schönfeld, Oels); IV/NJG 5 (Powunden, Krakau). LwKdo Südost: IV/NJG 6 (transf. into Reich); 4./NJG 100 (ex-3./NJG 100), 5. and 6./NJG 100 (Steinamanger, Novy Sad, Beckerek, Basaid, Tapioszentmarton, Malacki, Novy Dvor, Wiener Neustadt); III/NJG 6; op. detachment of NJG 101.

References

Archival sources

Bundesarchiv/Militärarchiv; Freiburg

RL 7/585, 7/579, 7/580, 8/4–10, 8/11–20, 8/88, 8/97, 8/177, 10/539, 10/540,
10/541, 10/542, 10/558
LW 103/12, 103/26, 103/27, 103/57, 103/58, 103/64
Lw 106/17, 106/30, 106/39, 106/40, 107/93, 107/94, 126/1, 126/2, 149/118
III L 408, III L 410/2, III 412/2, Ro 26/3, O.S.107, O.S.117, L 90–1/13, 2
III/212, IL 41/23

Militärgeschichtliches Forschungsamt, Freiburg
RL 1/11 Quartermaster-General Reports: Strength and Operational Availability (Blue books)

Bibliography

Bekker, C. *Angriffshöhe 4000* Hamburg, 1964
(English edition: *Luftwaffe War Diaries*, Macdonald & Jane's, 1967)
Constable, T./Toliver, R. *Das waren die deutschen Jagdfliegerasse
1939–1945* Stuttgart, 1972
(English edition: *Horrido* London, 1968)
Feuchter, G. W. *Der Luftkrieg* Frankfurt/Bonn 1964
Fischer, A. *Bis der Wind umsprang* Balve, 1961
Green, W. *Warplanes of the Third Reich* Macdonald & Jane's, 1970
Hadeball, H. M. *Nachtjagd* München, 1968
Hahn, F. *Deutsche Geheimwaffen, Band 1: Flugzeugbewaff-
nungen* Heidenheim, 1963
Harris, A. *Bomber Offensive* London, 1947
Hoffmann, K. O. *Geschichte der Luftnachrichtentruppen, Band 2,
Teil 1* Neckargemünd, 1968
Idatte, *La Chasse Obscure* (*La Piège*, 1974)
Irving, D. *Die Tragödie der deutschen Luftwaffe* Berlin, 1970
Johnen, W. *Duell unter den Sternen* Düsseldorf, 1965
(English edition: *Duel under the stars* London, 1968)
Lange, B. *Das Buch der deutschen Luftfahrttechnik* Mainz, 1970
Langevin, *Les prémises de la chasse en France* (*Forces Aériennes*, 1930,
No. 9)
Middlebrook, M. *Die Nacht in der die Bomber starben* Berlin, 1975
(English edition: *Nuremberg Raid* London, 1973)
Nowarra, K. H. *Die deutschen Flugzeuge 1933–1945* München, 1972

Plocher, H. *The German Air Force versus Russia* USAF Historical Studies No. 153–155 New York, 1967/68
Price, A. *Instruments of Darkness* (Revised edition) Macdonald & Jane's, 1977
Price, A. *Luftschlacht über Deutschland* Stuttgart, 1975 (English edition: *Battle over the Reich* London, 1973)
Reuter, F. *Funkmess* Opladen, 1971
Ries, K. *Dora Kurfürst und rote Dreizehn* (Vols. 1–4) Mainz, 1964–69
Ries, K. *Luftwaffenstory 1935–1939* Mainz, 1974
Ries, K. *Markierungen und Tarnanstriche der deutschen Luftwaffe* (Vols. 1–4) Mainz, 1963–72
Ries, K./Obermaier, E. *Bilanz am Seitenleitwerk* Mainz, 1970
Ring, H./Shores, C. *Luftkampf zwischen Sand und Sonne* Stuttgart (English edition: *Fighters over the Desert* London, 1969)
Rossiwall, Th. *Fliegerlegende* Neckargemünd, 1964
Rumpf, H. *Das war der Bombenkrieg* Oldenburg, 1961
Stiller, G. *Verrat am Himmel* (*Bild am Sonntag*, 1974)
Trenkle, F. *Deutsche Ortungsgeräte (Land/See) 1939–45* Düsseldorf o.J.
Völker, K. H. *Die deutsche Heimatluftverteidigung im Zweiten Weltkrieg (Wehrwissenschaftliche Rundschau*, Nos. 2, 3; 1966)
Völker, K. H. *Die deutsche Luftwaffe 1932–39* Stuttgart, 1967
Webster, Ch./Frankland, N. *The Strategic Air Offensive against Germany 1939–45* London, 1961

Acknowledgements
I am also most grateful to the following for answering my many questions and helping with material from their own private archives:

Heinz Bärwolf
Gottfried *Frhr.* v. Banfield
Richard Bateson
Theodor Bellinghausen
Dr Gustav Bock
Kurt Bonow
Dr Walter Briegleb
Rolf Bussmann
Eddie Creek
Oberst a.D. Gustav Ewald
Horst Diener
Arnold Döring
Oberst a.D. Wolfgang Falck
Prof Dr O. H. Fries
Günther F. Heise
General a.D. August Henz
Dieter Herwig
Oberstleutnant W. Jank
Wilhelm Johnen

General a.D. Kammhuber
Fritz E. Krause
Hans Krause
Dr Herbert Kümmritz
Oskar Lambertz
Bruno Lange
Paul Mahle
Beppo Marchetti
Günter Migge
H. J. Nowarra
Patrick S. Brown
Alfred Price
Josef Pützkuhl
Oberst a.D. Günter Radusch
Hans Ring
Rudolf Schoenert
Hanfried Schliephacke
Oberst Gerhard Stamp
Fritz Trenkle